The
Art Student's Guide
to the
Proportions of the
Human Form

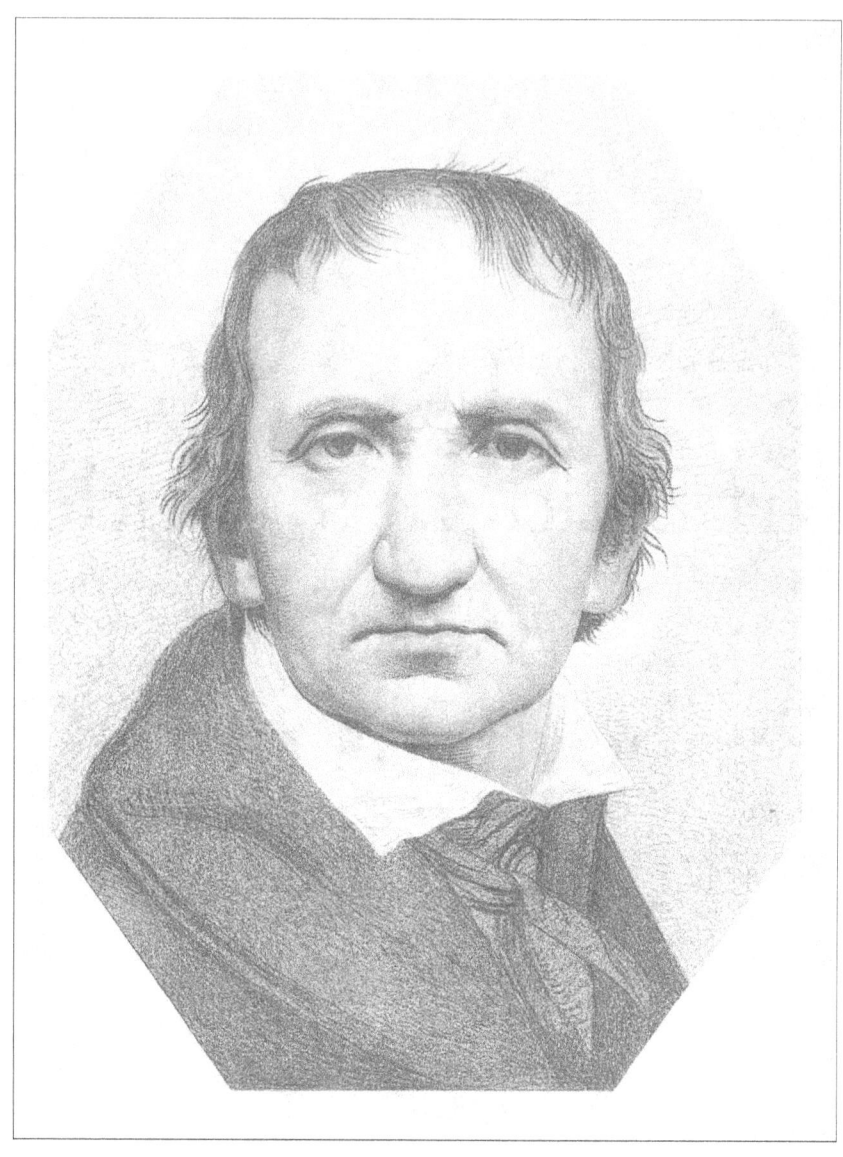

Johann Gottfried Schadow,
Self Portrait, pencil.

The Art Student's Guide to the Proportions of the Human Form

Plates by John Sutcliffe
Translated by James J. Wright
Based of the original treatise entitled
POLYCLETUS
by Dr. Johann Gottfried Schadow

Designed and Edited by Tom Richardson

Published by Tom Richardson
ISBN 978-0-9821678-0-9

CONTENTS

INTRODUCTION

Johann Gottfried Schadow was born in Berlin in 1764. His first teacher was the sculptor Tassaert, who served the court of Frederick the Great. He was offered his master's daughter in marriage but eloped with a girl to Vienna. His new father-in-law furnished the couple money to visit and study in Italy. After three years of study in Rome Schadow returned to Berlin in 1788 and succeeded Tassaert as the sculptor to the court. The years in Rome influenced his style and formed the basis for this work on the proportion of the human form.

This book is an English translation of *Atlas Zu Polyclet Oder von den Maassen des Menschen nach dem Geschlecte Und Alter*. The original book is an oversized 12½ by 19¾ inches. For this version I photographed the double wide pages (each 19¾ by 25 inches) and reduced the photographs to produce a full page view. In addition, individual elements of the pages are reproduced as big as possible to fit onto the 8½ by 11 inch size. After formatting this book I discovered a reduced size version of the original German *Atlas Zu Polyclet* which had evidently been produced by photo-lithograhy on which the original German plates were reduced to 8½ by 11 inches. Those scans form the appendix to this book.

He published other similar books including *Lehre Von den Knochen Und Muskeln den Verhaeltnissen des Menschlichen Koerpers Und von den Verkuerzungen* (The Bones and Muscles of the Human Body), *Ueber einige, in den Propläen Abgedruckten Sätze* which appears to be an article about the studies of the proportion of the head of classical statuary, and *National Physiognomieen oder*

Beobachtungen über den Unterschied der Gesichtszüge (National Physiognomy or Observations about the Difference of Faces).

He produced over two hundred works of sculpture during his half century of work. His fame rests both on his classical sculptures and on the more than one hundred busts he produced. His studies of classical statuary led him to a naturalistic style that emphasized the human being.

Polycletus (Polykleitos) was a Greek sculptor in the fifth and fourth century B.C. He is considered one of the most influenctial sculptors of Greek antiquity. Although none of his own works survive there are numerous Roman copies. The best known is propably the Doryphoros or spear carrier. His great contribution to the naturalistic style was both his sense of proportion and his accurate depiction of the posture of the human body characterized by his use of contrapposto. This is defined as the natural twist of the body from shoulders to hips and a shifted balance of weight to one leg.

His contribution to the knowledge of human proportions and its use in art is his *Kanon* (Treatise) in which he described his aesthetic theories. He also carved a male nude also referred to as Kanon which exemplified his theories of proportion. Some have argued that Doryphoros and Kanon are one and the same. See the Appendix. This is the work that Schadow built on in these plates.

John Sutcliffe was an artist and engraver in London in the nineteenth century.

I am an artist and a scenic artist. These books are my avocation.

-Tom Richardson, 2008

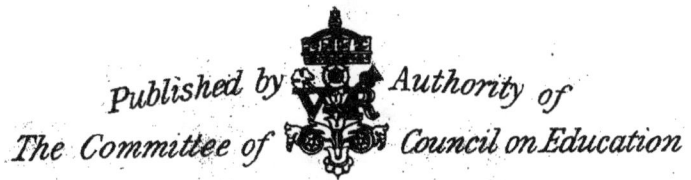

Published by Authority of
The Committee of Council on Education

THE SCULPTOR
AND
ART STUDENTS' GUIDE

TO THE

PROPORTIONS OF THE HUMAN FORM

WITH MEASUREMENTS IN FEET & INCHES
OF FULL-GROWN FIGURES
OF BOTH SEXES & OF VARIOUS AGES.

THE PLATES REPRODUCED BY

JOHN SUTCLIFFE,

FROM THE ORIGINAL TREATISE ENTITLED

POLYCLETUS

BY

DR. GOTTFRIED SCHADOW,

LATE SCULPTOR AT THE COURT OF H.M. THE KING OF PRUSSIA; DIRECTOR OF THE ROYAL ACADEMY OF ARTS IN BERLIN; KNIGHT OF THE ORDER OF MERIT; MEMBER OF THE ACADEMIES OF STOCKHOLM, DRESDEN, COPENHAGEN, ROME, MUNICH, AND VIENNA; CORRESPONDING MEMBER OF THE ACADEMIES OF PARIS AND BRUSSELS; ETC., ETC.

THE TEXT TRANSLATED FROM THE GERMAN BY

JAMES J. WRIGHT.

CHAPMAN AND HALL, LIMITED,

11, HENRIETTA STREET, COVENT GARDEN, LONDON.

1883.

To

The Lords of the Committee of Council on Education.

My Lords and Gentlemen,

As my humble tribute to the assiduous zeal and care you have given to the Art Education of the Country, I beg, with your kind permission to dedicate this Treatise in its English form to you.

I am, My Lords and Gentlemen, Your most obedient, humble Servant,

John Sutcliffe.

TRANSLATORS PREFACE.

The Polycletus of Dr. Schadow, in its English form, will, I venture to hope, enable Art students to pursue the study of the proportions of the human form with the aid of a more complete system of measurement than can be found in the other works on this subject which are at present in use.

In his treatise, Dr. Schadow has adopted a standard of division for the figure of so simple and practical a nature that it cannot fail to interest the student, whose memory will not be unduly taxed in mastering its details.

The style of the original German being somewhat diffuse, I have not hesitated, in some instances, to sacrifice exactness of translation, in order to make the text and references to the Plates as clear as possible to English readers.

The highest aim of the Art student should be to draw and model the human figure correctly, and the best evidence that the Polycletus will have, in some degree assisted students to attain this aim will be the careful noting and collating on their part of the.facts which they learn in- the course of their work. In so doing they will add to the existing knowledge of the proportions of the figure, and advance a science which Dr. Schadow has so ably treated, although, with the characteristic modesty of his erudite countrymen, he claims only to have extended the researches of others, and trusts that his readers will strive for the same object.

JAMES J. WRIGHT.

PREFACE TO THE FIRST EDITION.

(Published at Berlin in 1824.)

Some remarks on the art of delineation in general will not be out of place as an introduction to a work on the laws of proportion of the human figure. In the arts of painting and sculpture, what rules can be given, the application of which shall lead to an exact result, in the mathematical sense? The answer hereto is, only those which cannot be defined by words, lines being used instead for the purpose of making these rules clear and easily understood.

Amongst known laws we have:
>1. The law of distribution of columns.
>2. Of shading construction.
>3. Of perspective.
>4. Of osteology and myology.
>5. Of the proportions of different ages and sexes.

Lines have been applied to express likewise the laws of
>Equilibrium or ponderation.
>Expression of the passions.
>Affections and gestures.
>Costume or drapery.

Many books and treatises have been written on beauty, grace, genius, imagination, originality, style, noble simplicity, calm grandeur, taste, colouring, and composition. A careful study, however, of these works would scarcely lead to any precise knowledge; a fundamental. principle (such as the mathematician's) applicable to painting and sculpture must therefore be sought. There are objects, for instance, with which beauty, grace, or the ideal can have no connection, and the application of these attributes leads only to a spurious affectation. A mania for the misapplication of elegance is seen in the numberless mannered and counterfeit works of art, which even artists of ability have produced.

The two methods of representing forms are, the mathematician's and the artist's. In the drawing of a triangle and a Cupid, the geometrician, as well as the painter, put together certain lines to form a whole, but the former works by fixed rules; the latter, for the most part, according to feeling.

Artists trust to the eye alone, doubtless in the belief that the mathematician's method would fetter them and destroy the charm which freedom, dexterity, and unrestraint lend to their work. The sculptor, however, whose aft is not of an abstract nature, can make use of the mathematical method almost without limit, and the truth gained thereby for this branch of art accounts for the fact that it is subject to fewer anomalies and degradations than painting.

The writings of the ancients show the value they attached to the science of measurement; and, if it can be proved that a definite knowledge of the dimensions of the. human figure can be obtained by means of a scale and a pair of compasses, the knowledge thus acquired must become both necessary and valuable to the painter as well as the sculptor. By means of accuracy and freedom of drawing, an artist can attain perfection, while, on the other hand, the imaginative faculty, when hampered by uncertainty, can never achieve any great work.

THE AUTHOR.

NOTE.

In reproducing the illustrations to this work on Proportion care has been taken to have the measurements as accurate as possible, and, at the same time, while the character of the original lithographs has been very closely given, attention is called to the fact of their being, essentially, diagrams only, to explain the text.

This work has been undertaken with hopes that its publication may assist the great cause of Art Education in this country, and is intended more for the advanced art student and draftsman, than for those who have not attained a certain proficiency in drawing the figure.

JOHN SUTCLIFFE, LITHOGRAPHER.
London, 1883
9, Johnson's Court, Fleet Street.

HISTORY OF THE SCIENCE OF PROPORTION.

A STUDY of the historical records bearing upon this science gives ample proof that the Old Masters recognized the necessity of imparting some knowledge of the proportions of the human body, so that the pupils might acquire an accurate and certain method of working.

In the works of Egyptian historians mention is made of the ability with which the men of talent amongst this people applied the art of measurement in the construction of buildings and sculpture, and in perfecting a knowledge of the earth and the heavenly bodies The Egyptian sculptures bear evidence of the truth of these assertions, and, although they lack the artistic feeling to be found in the works of the ancient Greeks, attention has evidently been given to the proportions of the figures, both as regards height and breadth. This is, perhaps, the only merit in work which may justly be termed mechanical, for the Egyptian sculptors avoided the oblique view of a figure, and in their lowly relieved sculpture the forms are represented either in front view or entirely in profile, and at times the shoulders and torso are in front view, whilst the head and feet of the same figure are in profile.

In the oldest Greek works which are known to us there is an approach to what may be termed the picturesque representation of the human form, or one which was not trammelled by being taken from one point of view only.

It is probable that in the workshops of the oldest Greek sculptors a canon or rule existed with reference to the dimensions of the human body. In proof of this surmise, we may cite "The Group of the Aeginetans," now in Munich. The proportions of the wrestlers are the same, and the features are all alike, so much so, in fact, that the female figure (a Minerva) has the same cast of face.

At a later period the art masters recognized that there should be a difference in the proportions of figures, and the writings of Pliny, Philostratus, and Vitruvius show that some rules had been laid down which bore on this subject. Only a very few lined from the above-named authors have been used by modern artists in connection with a law of proportion.

Parrhasius is said to have been one of the first who taught anything about symmetry, the name by which the science of proportion was known to the, Greeks. After him came Asciepiodor, Miron, Lisippus, Eufranor, and others. Polycletus wrote a commentary on the laws laid down, and, as an illustration be made a statue, which was exclusively known by the title of "Canon." As it is probable that the commentary of Polycletus was written for the same purpose as the present treatise, this name has been chosen for the title of this work.

A period of inaction now followed, until in Italy a revival of the arts and sciences occurred. Giotto, who was born in 1276 and died in 1336, is said to have written about the proportions of the human body. His reputation as a painter procured him many pupils, and, being an artist of high attainments, there is no doubt that hIs attention had been drawn to' this science. Ghiberti, Pietro della Francesca, and Ghirlandajo, are likewise said to have studied this subject, but, owing to want of care, the writings of these men have been lost.

Leon Battista Alberti (born 1398, died 1492), architect and painter, wrote ten books, which were printed in Latin and published in 1481, In these works the proportions of the human body are touched upon, and mention is made of the proportions given by Vitruvius, who had probably copied them from some old Greek author.

Bramante (born 1444, died 1514) wrote about the quadrature of bodies, and applied the principle to the proportions of the human body. There is no proof to be obtained of the existence of his writings.

In Giuseppe Bossi's treatise on Leonardo da Vinci's "Last Supper" (Milan 1810), the following passage appears :

"Luca Congiasio appears to have formed the human body from cubes and triangles, and from these to have determined the proportions."

Vincenzo Foppa then took up the subject, and it was from his works, according. to Lomazso, that Albrecht Duerer studied symmetry. Foppa flourished in 1410, and wrote on the subject of perspective. Congiaslo, a Genoese painter, died in1585. He was a clever artist and had a good many pupils.

Leonardo da Vinci (born 1445, died 1520). Of Da Vinci's scattered treatises, the first which appeared in print was "A Treatise on Painting," published by Langlais, in Paris, 1651, in the Italian and French languages. The manuscript came into the hands of Dufresne, who received from Nicholas Poussin the drawings of the figures, which had been intended to illustrate the works Dufresne then took in hand the publication, and soon after the work appeared in most European languages. A new French edition was published by Deterville, Paris, in 1796. The figures serve to explain the text, which treats principally of ponderation or equilibrio and motion; some remarks on the dimensions of the limbs are, however, interspersed. Giuseppe Bossi, in his work on "The Last Supper," has devoted a chapter to proportion, and in the copper, plate engravings, after Da Vinci, the figure of a man is shown, contained in a square as well as in a circular framing, and in two other plates the left and right profile view is given. In the latter it is shown how the head can be drawn by the aid of measuring instruments.

The text explains how the dimensions of length can be determined, but not those of thickness and breadth, owing to the infinite variety of nature (immensa misteriosa natura), and as a proof of the extreme accuracy of Leonardo da Vinci, Bossi cites a passage in "The History of Painting," which states that Leonardo had divided the head into 248,882 parts. The author does not, however, inform this readers whether this extreme accuracy was intended to illustrate the multiplicity to be found in nature, or as a satire on the laws of proportion.

In Leonardo da Vinci's treatise reference is frequently made to a standard of measurement, but the painter himself never seems to have, been satisfied with it. Da Vinci was, however, the first who separated the head for drawing purposes into two parts, viz., the face and the skull or upper part. Special attention should be paid to this point, as those of his contemporaries and successors, who treated the subject of proportion, took the,face as a standard, meaning thereby the space from the chin to the hair.

This measurement is, however, of an uncertain length, for this reason the word "FACE" in the present treatise is intended 'to mean the distance from the chin to the upper edge of the Cavities of the Eyes.

In the edition of Vitruvius, by Johann de Laet, of Antwerp, mention is made in the appendix of the data given by Pomponius in his work on sculpture. These data prescribe nine times the length of the face as the right height for the male figure. In this edition of Vitruvius reference is also made to the works of Philander, Salmasius, Baldo, Milichio, also to that of a physician, and to another book entitled" The Dimensions of Sculpture," in which ten times the length of the face is taken for the height. These dimensions would, however, far exceed the actual height of a man of medium size, if the forehead and nose are taken to be of equal length.

Paolo Pino, painter and scholar, in his "Dialogue on Painting," published in 1548, has likewise given some proportions of the human figure.

Jean Battista Paggi (born 1554, died 1629), a Genoese painter, and pupil of Luca Combiaso, published in 1601 a table of proportions, which he entitled, "Acus nautica" (The Magnet-needle). This table has become very scarce. Testelin tables are considered to have been copied from this. Amongst the successors of Paggi the most notable, as regards their writings, are Maria Equicola, Nicolo Franco, and Bertano the expounder of Vitruvius.

The celebrated Cardanus in the eleventh book of the "Subtilitate" divided the body into 180 parts. The length of the head, and 7 times. this length, contained 24 such parts, was taken as the height of the figure.

Girolamo Ruscelli (born 1540), architect, and later on a priest, also wrote on the subject of symmetry, but his work is replete with errors.

Francesco Mazzuoli, called Parmeggiano (born 1504), left a plate of proportions, which was engraved by Benigno Bossi. The proportions are too slight.

Michael Angelo is likewise said to have left a single sheet on which the proportions of the male figure were noted, although his assertion always was that the eye of the artist must serve him as measuring instrument.

Johann Paul Lomazzo (born 1588, died 1598), a Milanese painter, who became blind in his 81st year, gave some rules for painters and sculptors in his works, entitled, "Idea del Tempio della Pittura," and "Groteschi Poetici." The proportions therein given appear to have been copied from those of Albrecht Duerer.

Giovanni Battista Armenini, of Faenza, is said to have worked under Rafael, but he is better known by his writings, which were published in Ravenna in 1587 under the title "Veri Precetti della Pittura" (The True Precepts of Painting), and contain the proportions of the human body. Cavaliere Bisagno, in his "Trattato di Pittura" (Treatise on Painting), has recorded all Armenini's faults.

Daniel Barbaro, a Venetian, who was afterwards a patriarch of Aquileja, wrote about Vitruvius and published in 1559 the "Practica della Perspectiva." He maintained that his proportions of the human body held a place between those of Albrecht Duerer and of Vitruvius; the former, according to his views, being too minute, and the latter too general. Barbaro made use of the inch scale. He died in 1561.

Vincenzo Macolano, called Firenzuola (born 1578, died 1667), has also treated of the subject of proportion in his writings. In the earlier portion of his career he was engaged in building construction, afterwards he became a cardinal.

Pietro Antonio Barca, an engineer of Milan, wrote a treatise on painting, and published in 1620 a separate sheet containing the proportions of a Jupiter, a Hercules, Minerva, and Venus. This sheet has been cited as a perfect specimen of typography and calcography. It has become very rare.

Marco di Pino, known by the name of Marco di Siena in Naples, where he painted a great deal, wrote a diffuse work on painting He died in 1587.

Johan Battista Trotti, called Molosso, flourished at Parma in the year 1600. He was a good painter, and his proportions may be regarded as emanating from the school of the Caracci, although he was a pupil of Campi of Cremona, who also wrote a book on painting and sculpture.

Enea Sulmeggia, of Bergamo, one of the best of the painters, who lived at the commencement of the Seventeenth Century, published in 1607 a book of proportions, which has been highly praised. The plates, however, are missing.

Johann Battista Volpato, born at Bassano in 1638, was a self-taught painter. He wrote a book called "La Verita Pittoresca." In 1685, his "Vagante Corriero" was published in Viceuza; in this work tables of proportions are given. His so-called truths cannot be relied upon.

In a small book, entitled "II Disegno del Doni," a profile is given of Baccio Bandineffi, which is, however, considered to be of no use.

Giuseppe Longhi (died 1881), the celebrated engraver, gives in his "Calcography," published in Milan in 1880, a sheet on which there are twenty-seven profiles in three rows, and three heads in front view. His description of a female figure, whose charms, although not equal to the Greek ideal, would be called beautiful by German artists, is remarkable and at the same time fascinating.

THE SPANIARDS.

Sansovino, in his "Varie Lezione," praises a Spanish sculptor, Philippo Borgogna, who had given some proportions, and had reckoned the height of the man as nine times and a third the length of the face.

Johann Arpho do Villafanno, a sculptor of Seville, published, in 1589, a book on anatomy and symmetry, which has been favourably noticed.

Chrisostome Martinez lived at Paris in the year 1660, and studied anatomy. He led a retired and temperate life, and enjoyed the friendship of the celebrated Audran.

Martinez has left two large plates; the one contains the proportions of a man whose skin has been removed. The height of this figure is given as eight times the length of the head. The other plate shows several skeletons in a standing and sitting posture. Those which are in a sitting position are unparalleled and may be taken as standard examples. They were, in fact, regarded as such by the celebrated English anatomist Winslow. These two plates, the figures on which were drawn and engraved by Martinez himself, became the property of the Royal Academy of Arts in Paris, as explained in a statement printed by order of the Royal Academy of Painting in 1740.

Alonso Berrugueto (born at Parades de Nova, died in 1545 or 1561) took up as a special subject of research the proportions of the human body.

THE DUTCH

Samuel van Hoogstraeten, born at Dordrecht in 1627, was a good painter and poet. The second book of his "Limner's Art," published in Rotterdam in 1678, was called "Polymnia" It contains a skeleton and a figure showing the muscles of the body. In order to illustrate the proportions, there are in the same work three plates. Tile first shows two men in front view, back view, and profile; one of these figures is divided into fifteen parts, and the other into sixteen parts or palms, as he terms them. The head is two palms high, so that the total height of one figure is 7½ times, and the height of the second 8 times that of the head. The second plate gives five views of a woman, all being of the same size, and divided into fifteen parts, viz.: seven from the ground line to the privities, and seven from this point to the line of the eyes. By this division the legs came out shorter than the upper part of the body. Both plates have tables giving the dimensions of breadth.

The arms and hands of both the man and woman have been drawn too short, and, when stretched out, do not measure the entire height of the figure. In other respects these proportions may be regarded as the most intelligible which had till then appeared. On a third plate were two proportions of children of different ages, the height of one being taken as four times, and that of the other as five times the length of the head.

Owing to the introduction of light and shade in the figures, clearness has been sacrificed, and the head, hands, and feet have not been carefully treated.

Gerard de Lairesse was born at Liege, in 1640, and died in 1711. At 50 years of age he became blind, but, with the aid of his son and his pupils, he published his great work on. painting. The rules given by his predecessors, and in particular those of Leonardo da Vinci, appear in this work amplified and enriched by the observations of Lairesse. It contains likewise two plates of proportions, viz., those of a man and woman.. They are not, however, of very great value, and are far inferior to those of Hoogstraeten. On the other hand, the paintings of Lairesse are superior, and, amongst Dutch painters, he possessed a nobler style than his compatriots.

Jacob de Witt's "Teekenbock der Proportion" was published at Amsterdam in 1747, with a French translation. De Witt is celebrated for his striking imitations of bas- reliefs.

FRENCH ARTISTS.

Prominent among French artists stands Jean Cousin, of Souci sur Sens. D'Argénville says that Cousin lived in 1589, and Fuseli states that he died in 1590, at the age of 88. Cousin's fame extended through the reigns of four French kings; he first worked at painting on glass, then at oil painting, and he likewise became a sculptor of note.

Although France at that time possessed some clever portrait painters, there were few good historical painters. Cousin was, however, an exception, and he may be regarded as the first man of his time in this branch of art.

The fame of Primaticcio was just then making a stir in Italy, but a long time elapsed before Cousin's countrymen acknowledged his superiority. It is only of late years that careful sketches have been made from those of his works which are still extant.

It is evident from some of the writings of Cousin that he endeavoured to apply geometry to the representation of the living form. In addition to a book on the drawing and proportions of the human body, he described a method of foreshortening the same in all positions, according to rules of perspective. As a means of effecting this he proposed to enclose the separate parts of the limbs in squares, and the head, neck, torso, and lower limbs in oblong framings. A work of this laborious nature undertaken by a talented artist is a direct proof of his conviction that a thorough knowledge of art principles is only to be attained by some such means.

Nicholas Poussin (born 1594, died 1665). In Belloris biography, it is stated that Poussin had the intention of publishing the writings which had been left by Leonardo da Vinci. The observations and definitions of Poussin himself then follow, and some measurements taken from the statue of Antinous, now called the Meleager, are given in conclusion. There are no drawings included in this work.

Dupuis du Grez (born 1640, died 1720) founded a school of drawing in Toulouse, and published a treatise on painting in 1699, in which there are some proportions.

Henri Testelin (born 1616 died 1695) wrote a work entitled "Conferences de l'Académie avec lea Sentimens des plus babiles Peintures." The dimensions of the human body are included in this work.

André Bardou, painter, founded a school of drawing in Marseilles. About the year 1765 he published several writings on painting and sculpture. Amongst them are also references to the proportions of the human body, which differ little from those given in Testelin's tables; the length of the face still being, taken as a standard. There are also two plates; one of a man, the other of a woman and children of three, four, five, and six years of age.

Hilaire Pader, the painter, published in 1649 a French translation of Paul Lomazzo's writings with the title:— "Traité del a Proportion Naturelle et Artificielle des Choses."

In this work exact copies are given: of Albrecht Duerer's plates, but his name is not mentioned except in the preface, where Pader writes of him as a great geometrician. The author's opinion of proportions is that it is a wonderful science, but he counsels his readers not to be influenced too completely by its charms.

Claude Audran. There are as many as nine artists of this name, but the one referred-to here was a painter and assistant of the celebrated Lebrun. His, measurements of the antique statues, published in Paris in 1688, by Girard Audran (engraver to the king), under the title, "Les proportions du corps humain," are more exact and complete than anything that had previously appeared on this subject. Although neither system nor science is connected with these measurements, it is easy to construct one therefrom, as the dimensions which have been actually taken from the marble by means of the compasses and calipers are far more reliable than any which could be taken by the eye alone.

Audran's measurements have, in fact, been employed in the workshops of most sculptors, and they have been copied in nearly all countries and the text translated. These measurements are as varied as are the nature and character of the gods and goddesses, which they represent.

Audran himself remarks that no praise is due to him for his work, but rather to those great masters who first applied to their works the principles which he has been the means of bringing to light.

Watelet, a rich amateur, who did a good many etchings, wrote a poem called "L'Art de Peindre," which was published in 1760. In his reflections, accompanying the poem, is a chapter on proportions. The dimensions given appear to have been copied from Audran, whose name is, however, not mentioned. Two plates of outline drawings of the Antinous and Venus, with some dimensions of length, are also given, but they are superficially and lightly treated.

Bouchardon, a celebrated sculptor (born in 1698, died 1762), published some excellent drawings, which were engraved by Demarteau, and served as models for a considerable time in all schools of drawing. He also published a work on anatomy for artists and proportions of the male figure, which do not, however, include more than previously given by Watelet.

Charles Antoine Jombert wrote a work called "Méthode pour apprendre le Dessin," it was published in Paris in 1755, in quarto, and contained a good many copper engravings, showing parts of the human body and some academical drawings. In the fourth chapter, there are the antique statues, which had been measured by the painter Corneille, but in much smaller size than those given by Audran. The measurements appear to have been noted with exactitude.

Jombert has adopted the nose as a standard, and, in order to obtain the separate parts, he had divided this feature into six minutes.

Jean Baptiste Corneille (born 1646, died 1684), must, according to the above date, he takes his measurements a considerable time before they were published in Jombert's works. Corneille's style of work is earliest and thorough, and forms a great contrast to the light and superficial manner of Cochin. In the second chapter of his work Jombert gives an historical review of the science of proportions as adopted by Polycletus, Vitruvius, Albrecht Duerer and others. In addition to this, all the tricks of painting are described, and in this respect it is one of the most complete text-books to be found.

Horace Vernet, the celebrated painter and director of the French Academy, has published two large sheets. The one, which contains the text, is entitled "Tableau du Squelette de l'homme pour le cour de Zoonomie, considéré dans sea Rapports avec les Arts." The other, a lithographed sheet, shows a back view of the male skeleton, a front view of the female skeleton, and a child of five years in profile. Vernet is the first artist who adopted a standard based on an exact stale, instead of taking a part of the human body, for instance, the head or the foot, as standard.

As in works of art the figures are seldom made life size, it was considered better to determine the proportions of the respective parts by means of the length of the foot or head. This method was found to be convenient for the purpose of roughly sketching on paper on a small scale the first idea. The separate studies for the entire work, made from nature or from lay figures, are also drawn on paper, and are consequently always to a smaller scale than in nature.

The cartoons for large fresco paintings were transferred to the size required by means of scale-paper. It may therefore be concluded that most of the artists of that day never became acquainted with the true dimensions of the different parts of the human body. It is very probable that this want of knowledge is at the root of the faults to be observed in so many. figures, such as too small a mouth, and extreme shortness of hands and feet. Such errors as these were never committed by the Greek sculptors.

In one of Horace Vernet's descriptive plates, the bones are explained, and likewise the functions of the cartilage, ligaments, and sinews. The entire height and the proportions of the separate parts of children of five, ten and fourteen years of age, as well as the proportions of the man and woman, are given in two columns of figures. These small sheets contain, in fact, a wealth of scientific knowledge, and the method of arranging the data is very convenient for artists, as the sheets can be hung against the wall of the studio, and thus be always at hand. This review of the works of those French artists who have written on the subject of proportions is not complete, and in order to make it so, information would have to be collected in France.

ENGLISH ARTISTS.

John Chamberlain published in London, in 1796, freehand drawings by Leonardo da Vinci. Amongst them are skeletons with explanatory text and proportions. The writing of the text being reversed must be read by means of a looking-glass.

The proportions which Leonardo da Vinci gives in the above mentioned treatise on painting have been taken from the living form. In the present work this method of measurement has also been employed. For the purpose of the artist a too minute analysis of the formation and size of such parts of the body as sutures and bony ridges, which are hidden beneath the skin, would, in fact, prove a waste of time. In Chamberlain's writings there is a great deal of interesting matter concerning Leonardo da Vinci, which cannot be found elsewhere.

Amongst English artists a certain Cozens has been referred to by Italians, as having published some proportions of the human head. This work has been severely criticized.

Flaxman, who is known principally by his outline drawings for the Iliad, Dante, etc., referred, in his lectures to pupils, to action of the human limbs, the proportion of the body, and a method of enclosing figures in squares and circles. The latter part of the subject was illustrated by drawings.

See "Lectures on Sculpture," by John Flaxman, Esq., R.A., Professor of Sculpture in the Royal Academy,

—London, John Murray, 1829.

GERMAN ARTISTS.

Albrecht Duerer (born 1470, died 1528) possessed a poetic nature, and a strong inclination for exact knowledge. His mathematical acquirements were applied to building construction, to his work in connection with fortifications, and to the art of perspective, which he well understood. Duerer was the first artist who endeavoured to employ mathematics in the representation of the human body, His measurements for the separate parts of the figure have been found inconvenient in practice. In his work on the subject, only one of the male figures is natural, and this appears to have been drawn from life. The other figures seem to have been formed by enclosing the parts in squares of given dimensions, and afterwards extending the same parts into oblongs of the same superficial area. An exaggerated slimness has resulted from this method. There are no figures of children or of young persons in the book.

Michael Angelo's criticism on this work is said to have been conveyed in the following phrase :

— "Poca e debole cosa questo libro."
"A work of a poor and weak character."

Leonardo da Vinci's opinion, however, of Michael Angelo's own work was still more severe. After seeing his paintings of children Da Vinci remarked that the muscles of the children were the same in number, and equally as strong as those in his figures of adults.

Fiorillo, in the second volume of his work (page 860), states that Duerer's paintings and writings were spread all over Europe, and created great excitement even in the most remote lands. At that time, Berrugante's laws of proportion of the human body were used in Spain. This artist had studied in Italy, and was held in high esteem.

There was, however, an opinion amongst some artists that it would be better to adopt the system of Pomponio Gaurico, than of Fiippo de Borgogna, or even the teaching of Duerer, whose book on symmetry had in the year 1599 been translated from Italian into Portuguese. It is said that Ferando Gallegos of Salamanca even travelled to Germany to see Albrecht Duerer, but this. assertion was denied by Bermudez. Louis da Costa, born in Lisbon in 1599, is reputed to have translated Duerer's work, under the title "Quattro Livros de Simetria dos Corpos Humanos Compostos por Alberto Dureiro." (Four books on the symmetry of the human body, compiled by Albrecht Duerer) This translation was dedicated to Saint Lucas.

Joachim Sandrart, born in 1688, published a large work on German painters, sculptors, and architects. It contains a great many rules and instructions. Sandrart chose, however, for the proportions of the human body Audran's work, and copied his measurements of antique statues.

George Bergmueller, born in 1688, at Duerkheim, in Bavaria, was a good oil painter, and his frescoes were well executed. He was director of the academy in Augsburg, and a work of his called "Anthropometria" was printed in 1723. In the preface he mentions that men of eminence, and notably the celebrated Albrecht Duerer, had striven to impart to art-students a knowledge of proportions by means of drawings and printed descriptions, but Duerer's laws had only been illustrated by forms of grown persons.

The plates in Bergmueller's work contain figures of different ages, from birth upwards, and of both sexes; the female figures are, however, of equal proportions with those of the male sex. He asserts that deep study and careful observation of nature enabled him to produce the work, and enlighten those who were struggling to overcome the difficulties of their art. A glance at his plates and a close scrutiny of his rules prove, however, that this "Anthropometria" was based rather on a system created by the author himself than on the laws of nature.

George Lichtensteger, copper-plate engraver, in Nuremberg, published in 1746 his "Arithmetical and Geometrical Treatise on the Proportions of the Body." The writing is an imitation of that of an adept; he gives as examples the dimensions of Noah's Ark, of the Tabernacles, the Temple of Solomon and the New Jerusalem. St. Augustin is mentioned, and praise is bestowed on the mathematician Adelbulner, of Altorf, from whom Lichtensteger avers he learned the rules by which the figures of harmonic proportion in music can be applied to the proportions appertaining to art. In the figures accompanying the work, straight lines are frequently employed, and the rules for drawing the human form are perfectly incomprehensible.

Daniel Preisler (born 1666, died 1787) was director of the academy of painting in Nuremberg. He published a book on drawing entitled "Die Durch Theorie Erfundene Practik" (Through Theory to Practice), which was for a long time almost exclusively used in all schools of drawing in Germany.

Justin Preisler, his son (born in 1698), added to the above mentioned work a fourth part, containing the proportions of the human body. The first plate gives those of a child, whose height is taken as four times the length of the head; the head is also drawn separately in front view, and in profile. The proportions of the female are given in three views on the second plate, the height of the figure being equal to eight times the length of the head. The third plate contains seven male figures, of different ages, from the child to the full grown man. There are three principal lines in all these figures, touching, respectively; the skull, navel and ground. The dimensions of width are not given, and the figures are all shown in front view.

Joseph Mattersberger, a sculptor (born in Breslau, in 1827), published eleven plates of proportions, showing a child of three years, one of seven, and one of twelve years, and figures of eighteen and twenty-four years; also figures of a man, a Hercules, a slim and a stout woman. The last are in the style of Albrecht Duerer. The appearance of the plates is not very promising; there is no text, but written dimensions are given. A close examination, however, of the plates reveals a good deal of useful matter.

Rafael Mengs published a method of representing geometrically a well proportioned head, but no confidence should be placed in this method, as it appears to have no truthful basis.

J. H. Meil published in Berlin, in 1789, a course of instruction in drawing for children. The subject of proportion is adverted to in some judicious remarks, which are illustrated by one or two small outline drawings.

An unknown hand printed at Kosnigsberg, in 1799, a book on the art of drawing, giving some proportions and outline drawings of the weakest description.

Pflugfelder, a painter of Hanover, brought out in 1805 a book on drawing, containing five plates of proportions, also of a very poor kind.

The following proportions have been taken from an old book written in Sanscrit, and called "Silpi Sastri," that is, "Of the fine arts";

A line is divided into 480 parts.
Top part of the head -------------- 15
Face -------------------------------- 55
Neck -------------------------------- 25
Chest -------------------------------- 55
To the navel ----------------------- 55
The stomach ----------------------- 53
To the knee ----------------------- 90
Knee -------------------------------- 80
The leg --------------------------- 102
_____
480

This division does not quite give a height equal to 7 times the length of the head, The measurements appear to have been taken from the figure of a well formed man.

In all probability, a great many more works appeared both in Germany and France on the subject of proportions, especially for use in the numerous drawing schools which existed in those two countries.

Giuseppe Bossi in his "Clenacolo" mentions that the ancients wrote about this science in the following works :

"Simmetria," by the elder Pliny.
"Analogia," by the younger Phiostratus.
"Comedita" and "Equita di Membra," by Suetoziius.
"Equalita" and "Congruenza," by the younger Pliny.
"Commisuramento," by Vitruvius.
"Convenienza de Parti" and "Atta Composizione di Membra," by Cicero.
"Reciproca competenza di Membra," by Aulus Gellius.

The author adds that the above writers defined the science as being the mutual and harmonious relations between the various parts of the body.

Many artists, men of learning, physicians, etc., have published writings of a fragmentary character on the subject of proportions. Some of these writings are mere plagiarisms. Questions relating to the effects of growth, the difference of features in the two sexes, in youth and in old age, the form of the new-born child were not treated as a science, and therefore received no attention. Artists confined themselves to working from the best models they could procure, when representing the living form. Patrons and lovers of art, who were mostly ignorant of the proportions of the nude figure, were not disposed to criticize too severely.

The paintings of Dominichino in Grotta Ferrata, and those of Albano, are especially valuable, however, on account of the fine examples of the human figure which they contain. Genius may indeed dispense with school rules, and the eye of a Rafael may be equal in accuracy to any measuring instrument. The figures in his paintings are, in fact, harmonious throughout, and the hands and feet are never drawn too small. The varied character of Rafael's figures is less apparent in those of his pupil Julio Romano, and despite the acknowledged greatness of Michael Angelo, the repetition of one form is frequently, observed in his works.

Ghirlandajo, Masolino and others introduced between their large figures boys and girls, as well as full grown persons of small stature.

In the time of Pietro Cortona, Ciroferri and Luca Giordano, artists represented the same man, woman, and child in hundreds of examples, and their talent was principally shown in the wonderful ease and dexterity with which they executed works of great size.

The progress that has been made in all sciences has of necessity led to a more truthful rendering of artistic subjects, and much of the conventionality of the schools has ceased to exist. The researches, which have been made in the animal and vegetable worlds have been attended with such successful results, principally on account of the science of analysis, but the dissection of the human body has done very little towards the development, either of a knowledge of its outer form, or of a science embodying rules by means of which its proportions of length, breadth, and depth might be learned. This want was soon detected by artists gifted with powers of careful observation, and in excuse for the slow growth of a science of proportion, it must be observed that in many respects it formed an entirely new branch of education, and many years necessarily elapsed before accurate data could be collected.

PLATES

Printing Notes from the Original Book:

TYPOGRAPHY: FLEET PRINTING WORKS, 14, WHITEFRIARS STREET, E.C.

LITHOGRAPHY: 9, JOHNSON'S COURT, FLEET STREET, E.C.   RELIEF ENGRAVING: JOHN SWAIN, 58, FARRINODON STREET, E.C.

BOOKBINDERS: DIPROSE BROTHERS, WHITE HART YARD, CATHERINE STREET, STRAND.

This version set in Garamond.

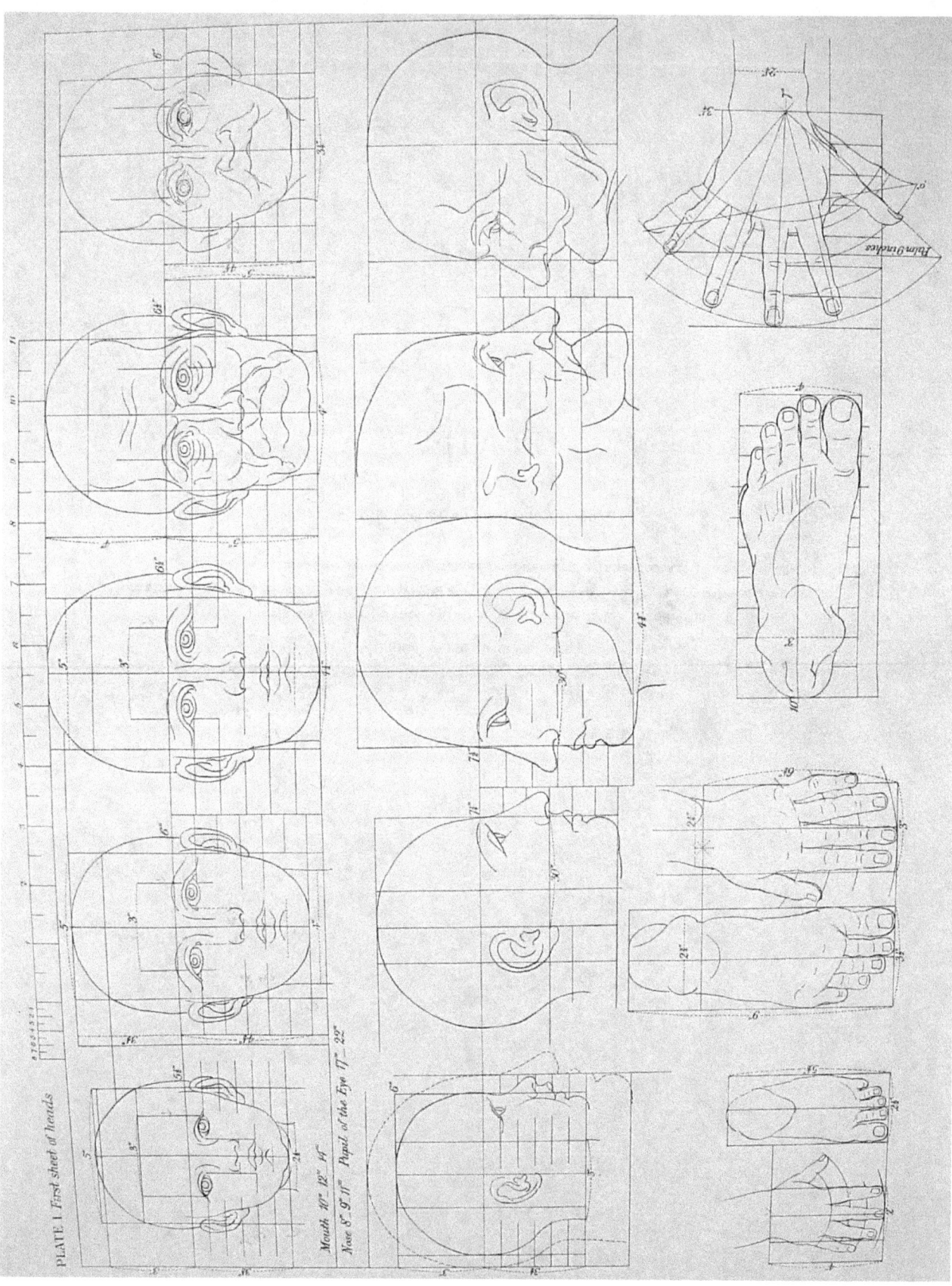

PLATE I. *First sheet of heads*.

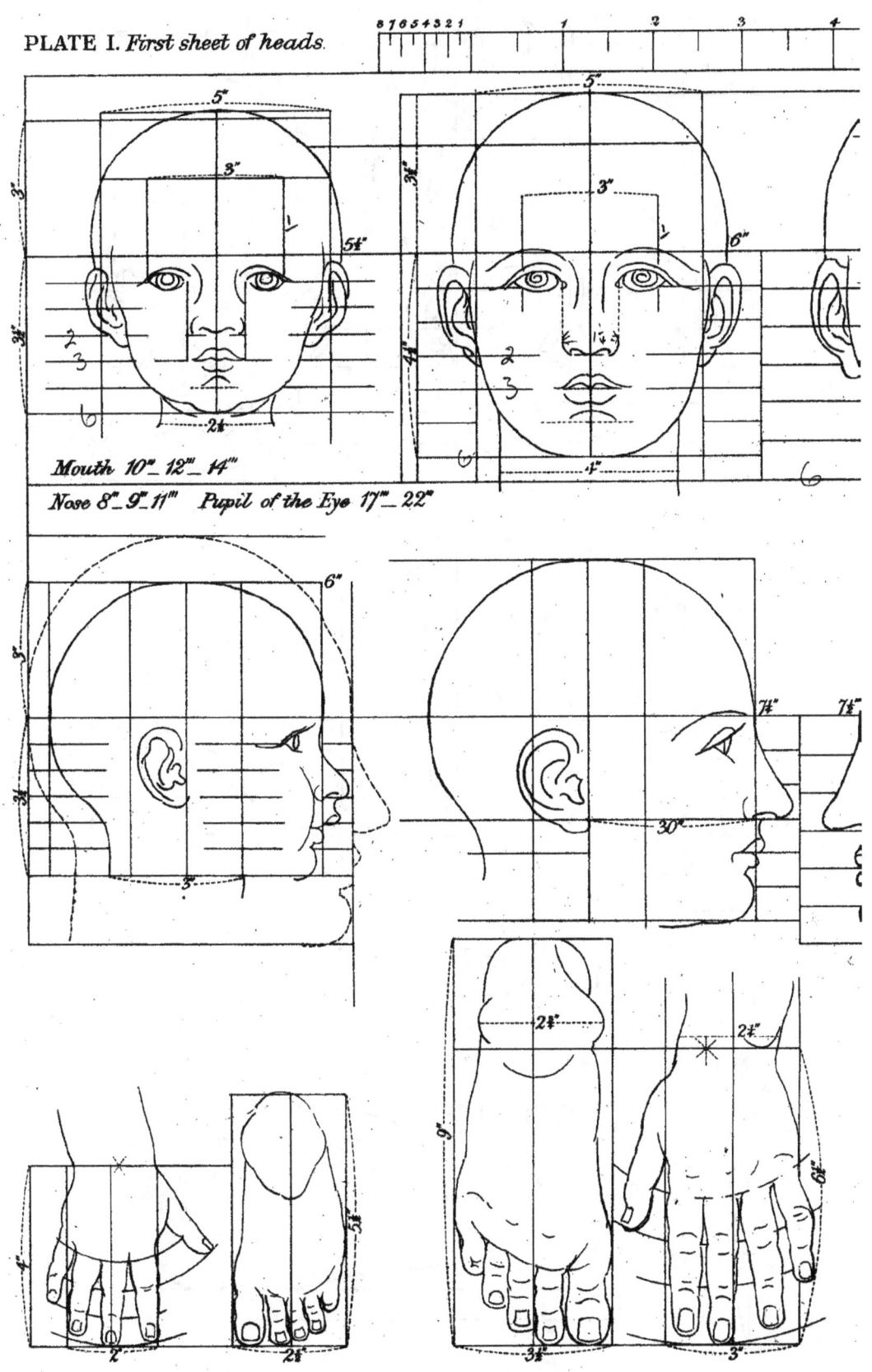

Mouth 10″_ 12‴_ 14‴

Nose 8″_ 9″_ 11‴   Pupil of the Eye 17‴_ 22″

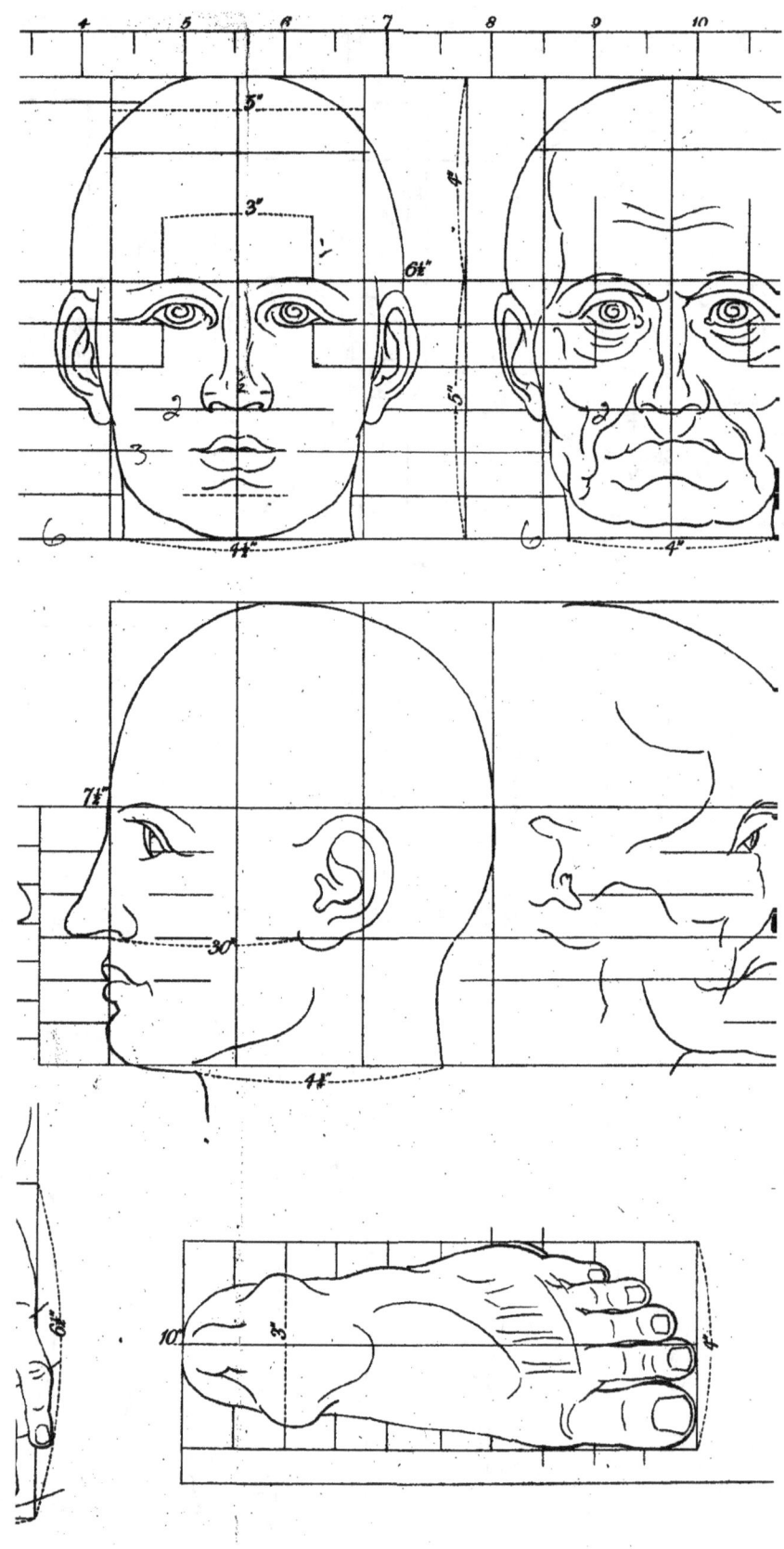

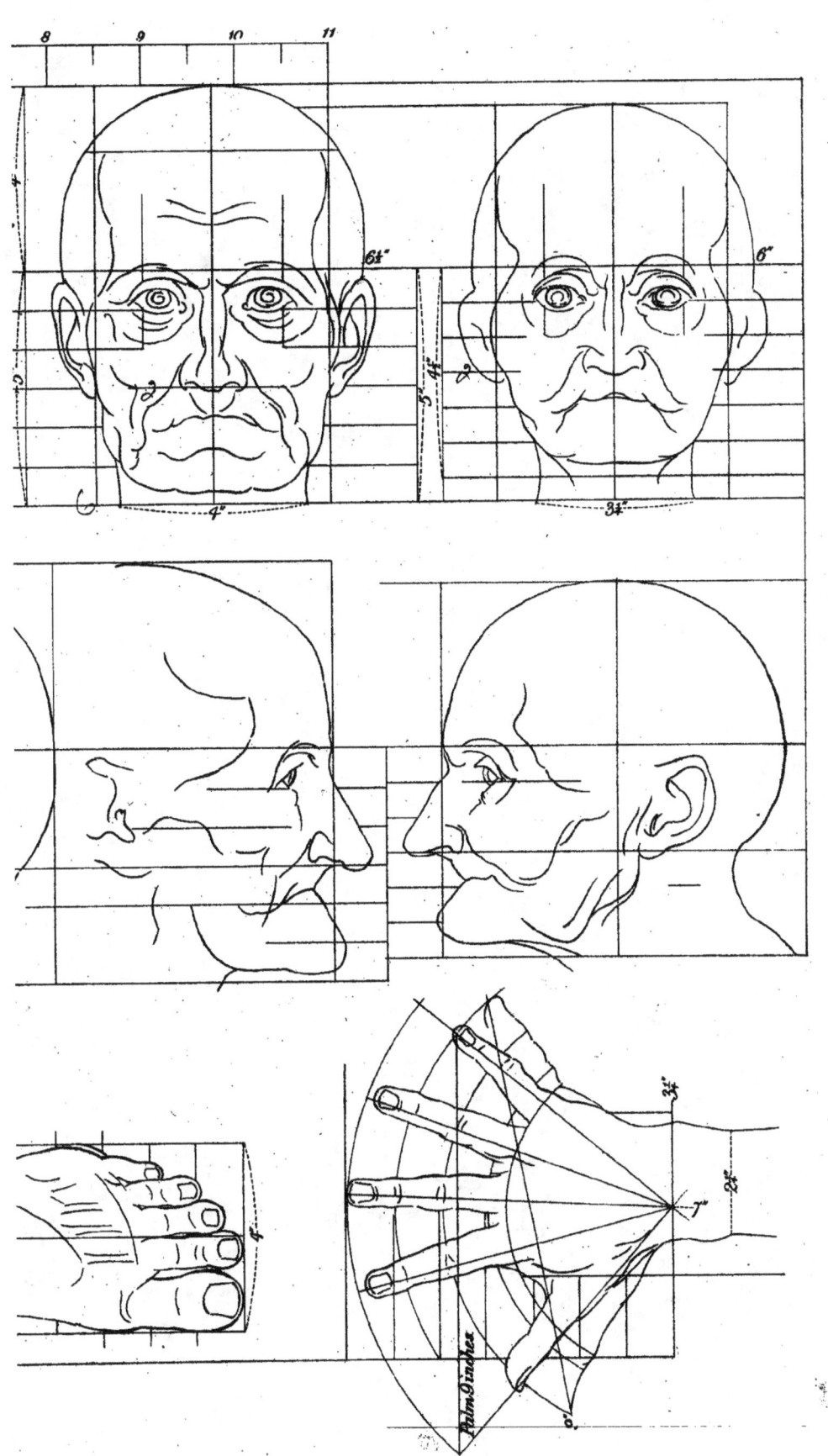

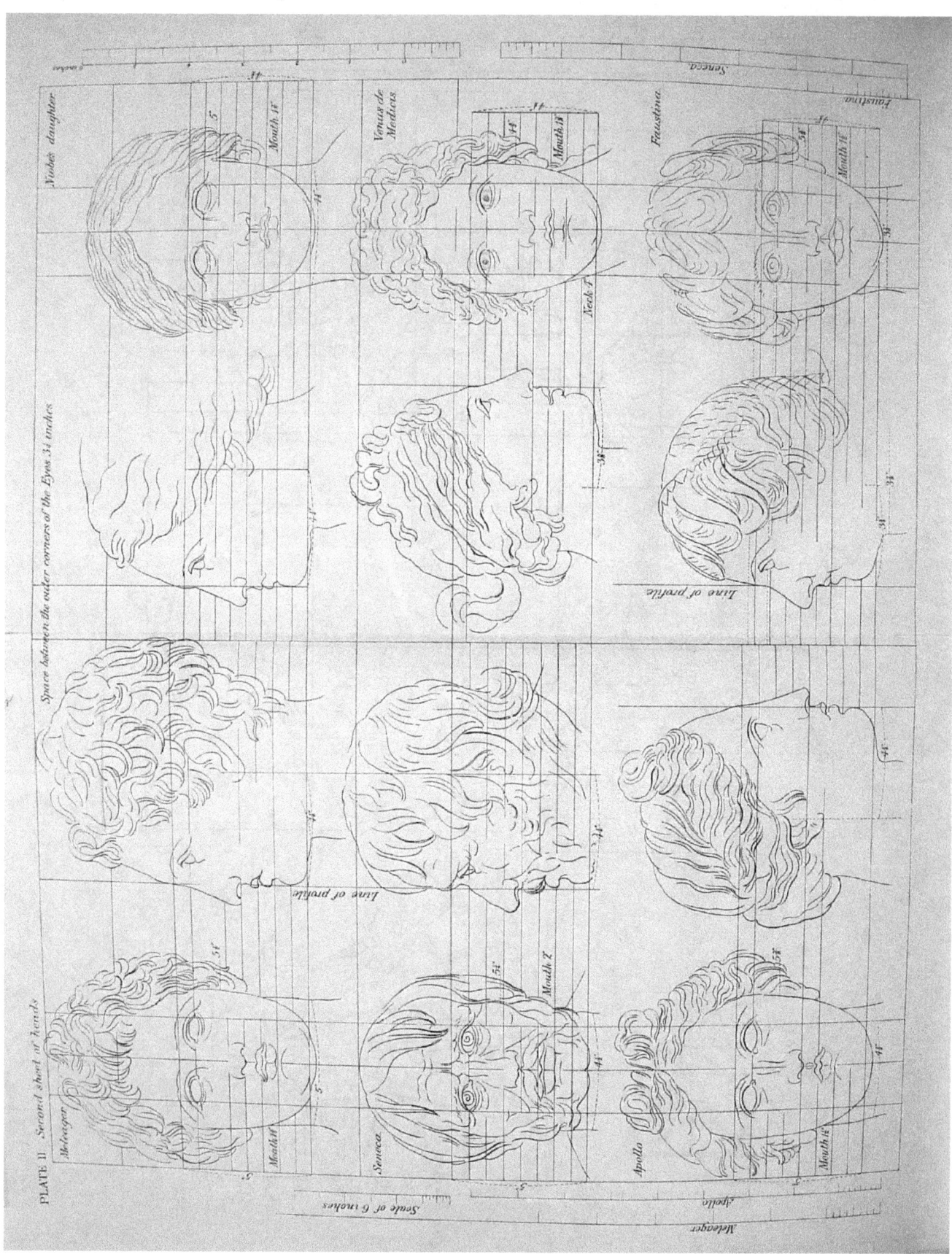

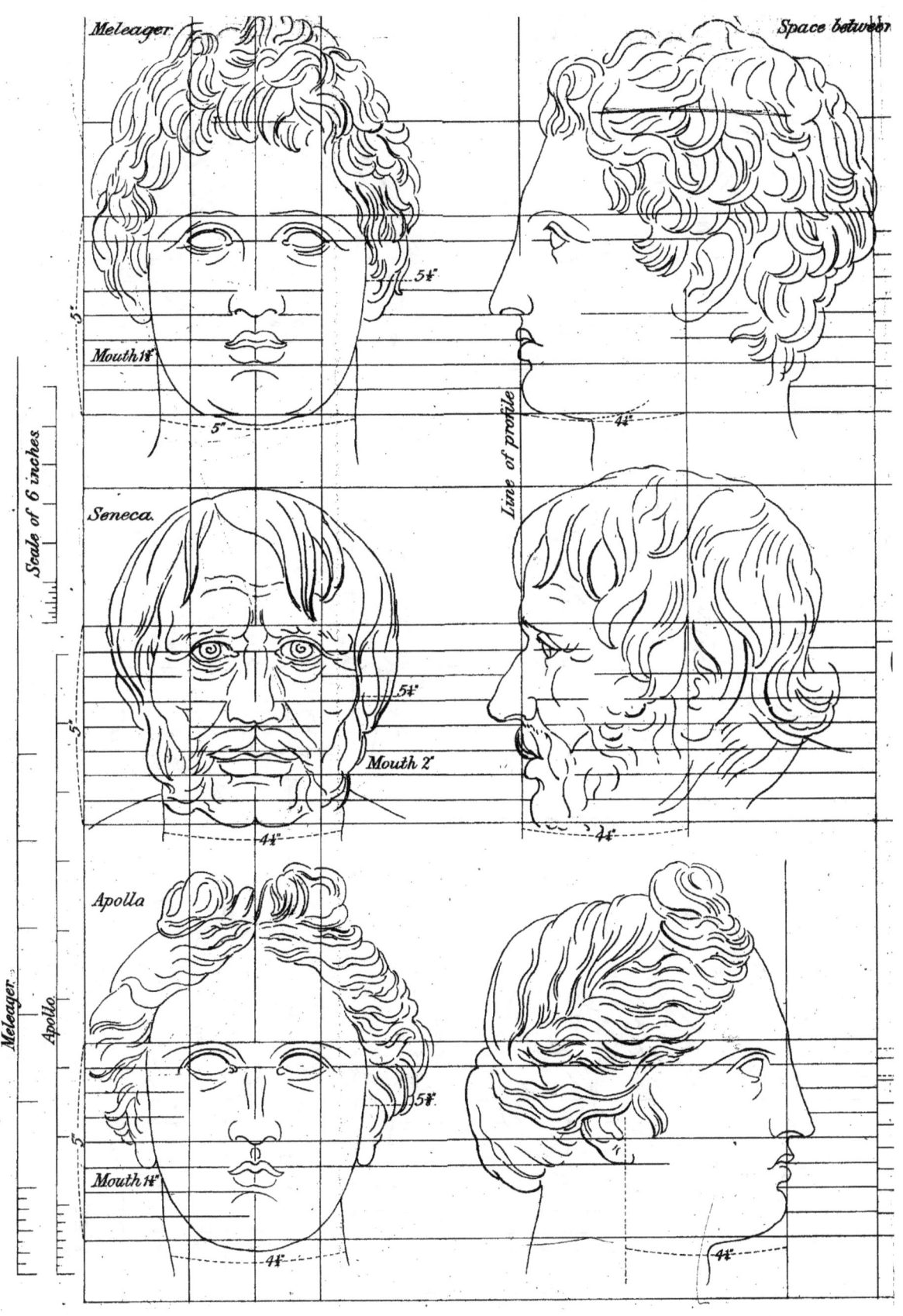

Meleager

Space between

5¼"

Mouth 1⅜"

5"

Line of profile

4¼"

Scale of 6 inches

Seneca

5¼"

Mouth 2"

4¼"

4¼"

Meleager

Apollo

Apolla

5⅜"

Mouth 1⅜"

4¼"

4¼"

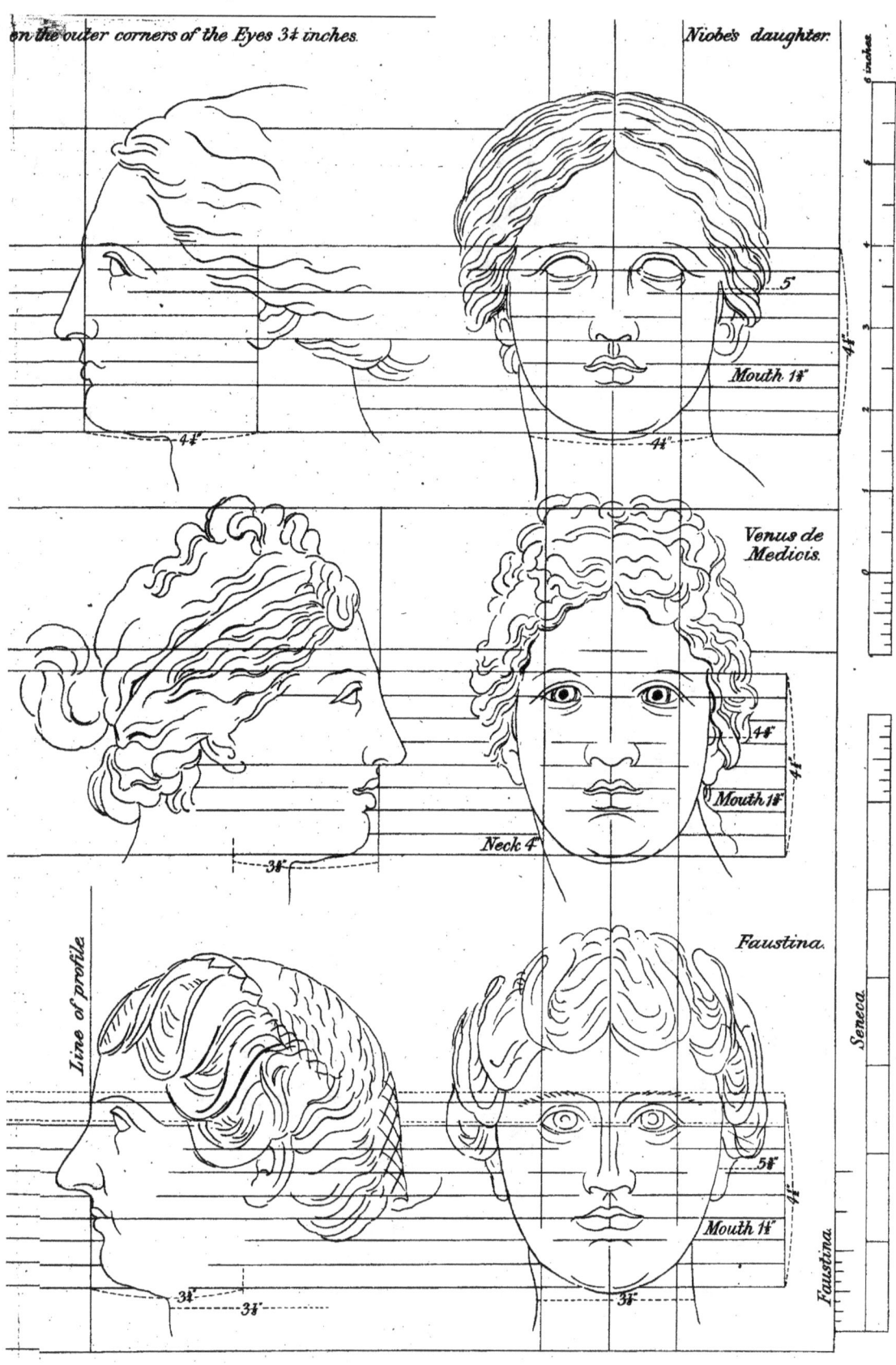

on the outer corners of the Eyes 3¼ inches.

Niobe's daughter.

6 inches

5

Mouth 1⅜"

4¼"

4¼"

Venus de Medicis.

4¼"

4¼"

Mouth 1⅜"

Neck 4"

3⅜"

Line of profile

Faustina.

Seneca

5⅜"

4¼"

Mouth 1⅜"

Faustina.

3⅜"

3⅜"

3⅜"

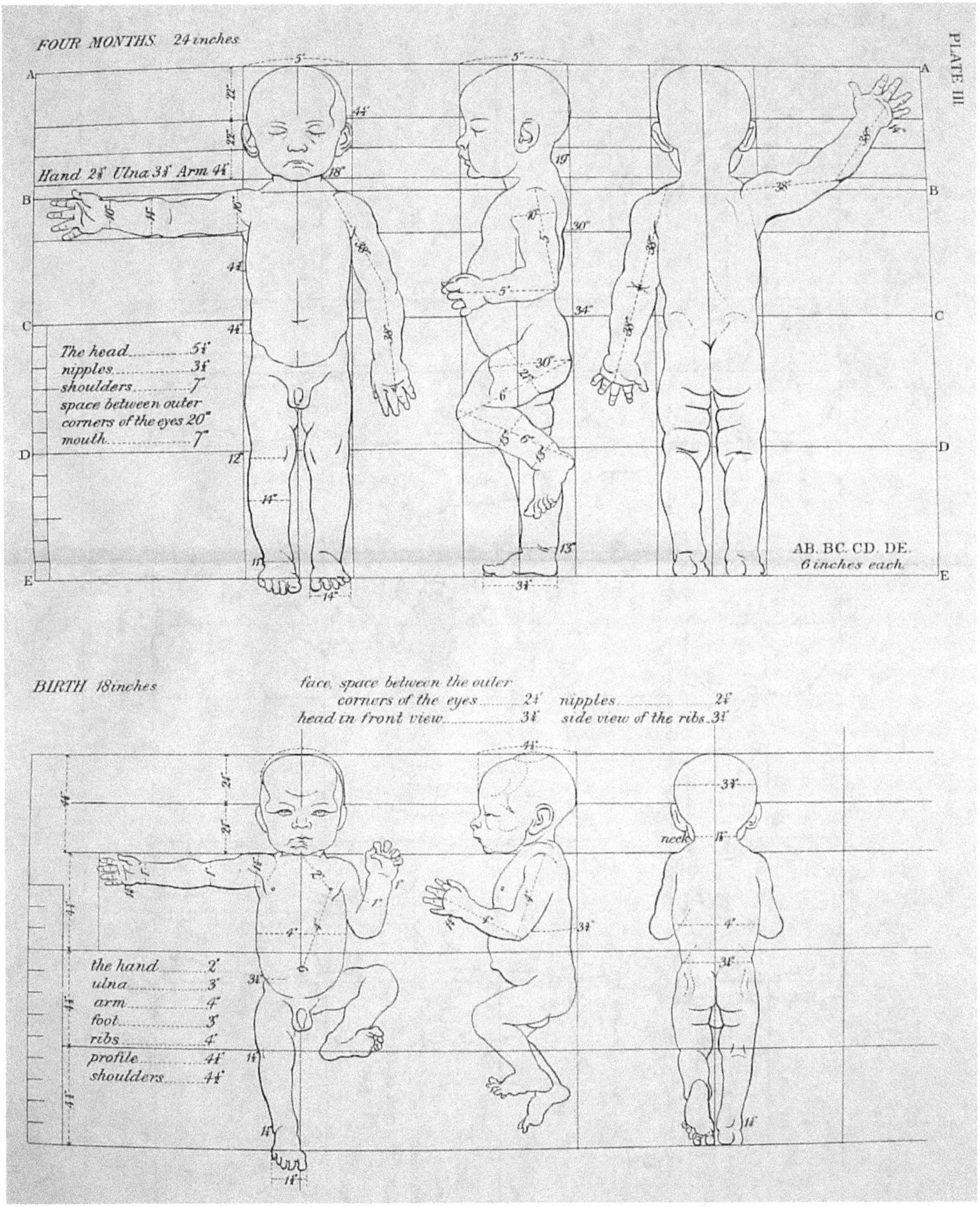
PLATE III
FOUR MONTHS. 24 inches
Hand 2¾ Ulna 3¼ Arm 4¼
The head.........5¼
nipples.........3¼
shoulders.........7
space between outer corners of the eyes 20"
mouth.........7
AB. BC. CD. DE. 6 inches each.
BIRTH. 18 inches
face, space between the outer corners of the eyes.........2¼ nipples.........2¼
head in front view.........3¼ side view of the ribs 3¼
neck
the hand.........2
ulna.........3
arm.........4
foot.........3
ribs.........4
profile.........4¼
shoulders.........4¼

PLATE III.

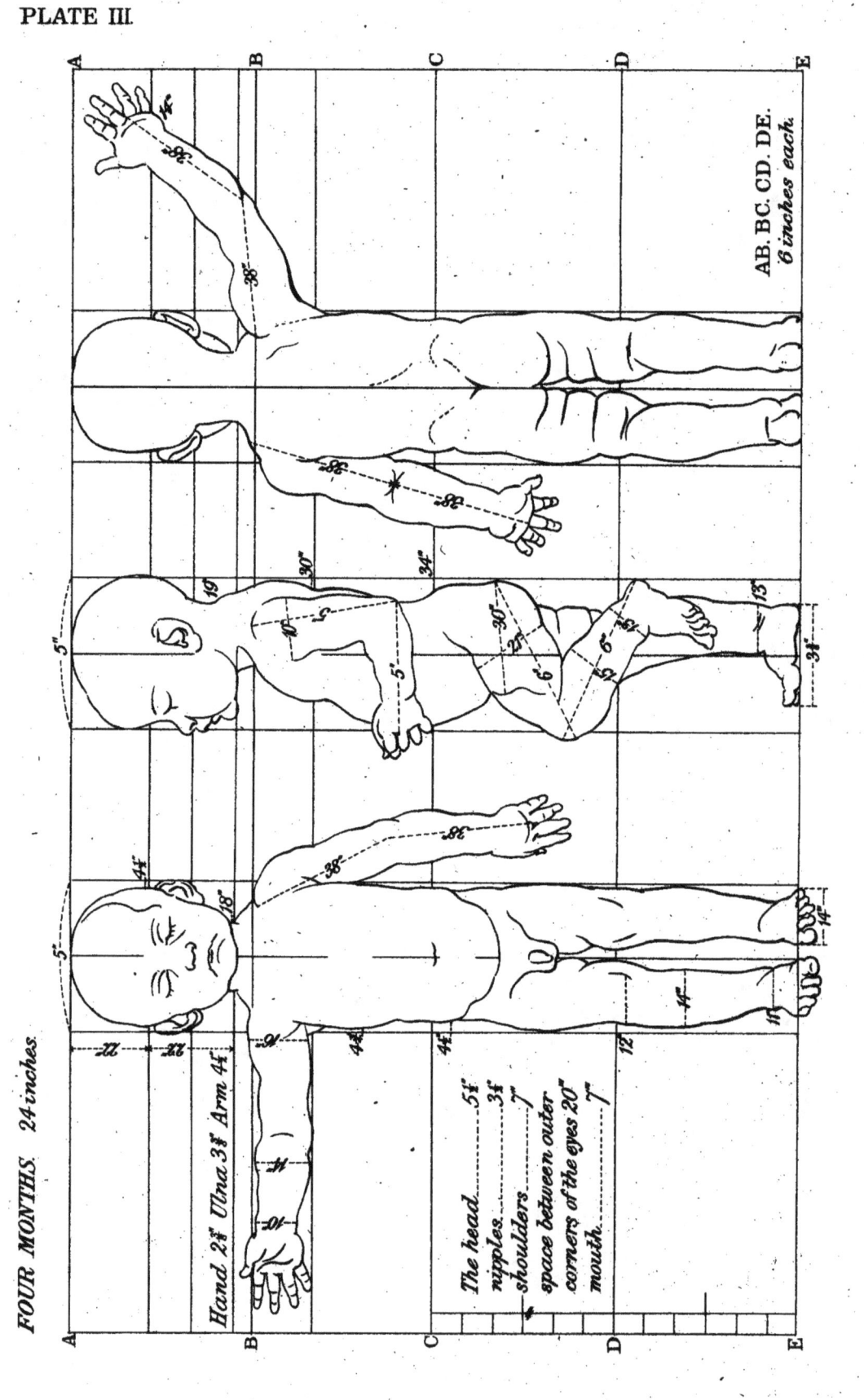

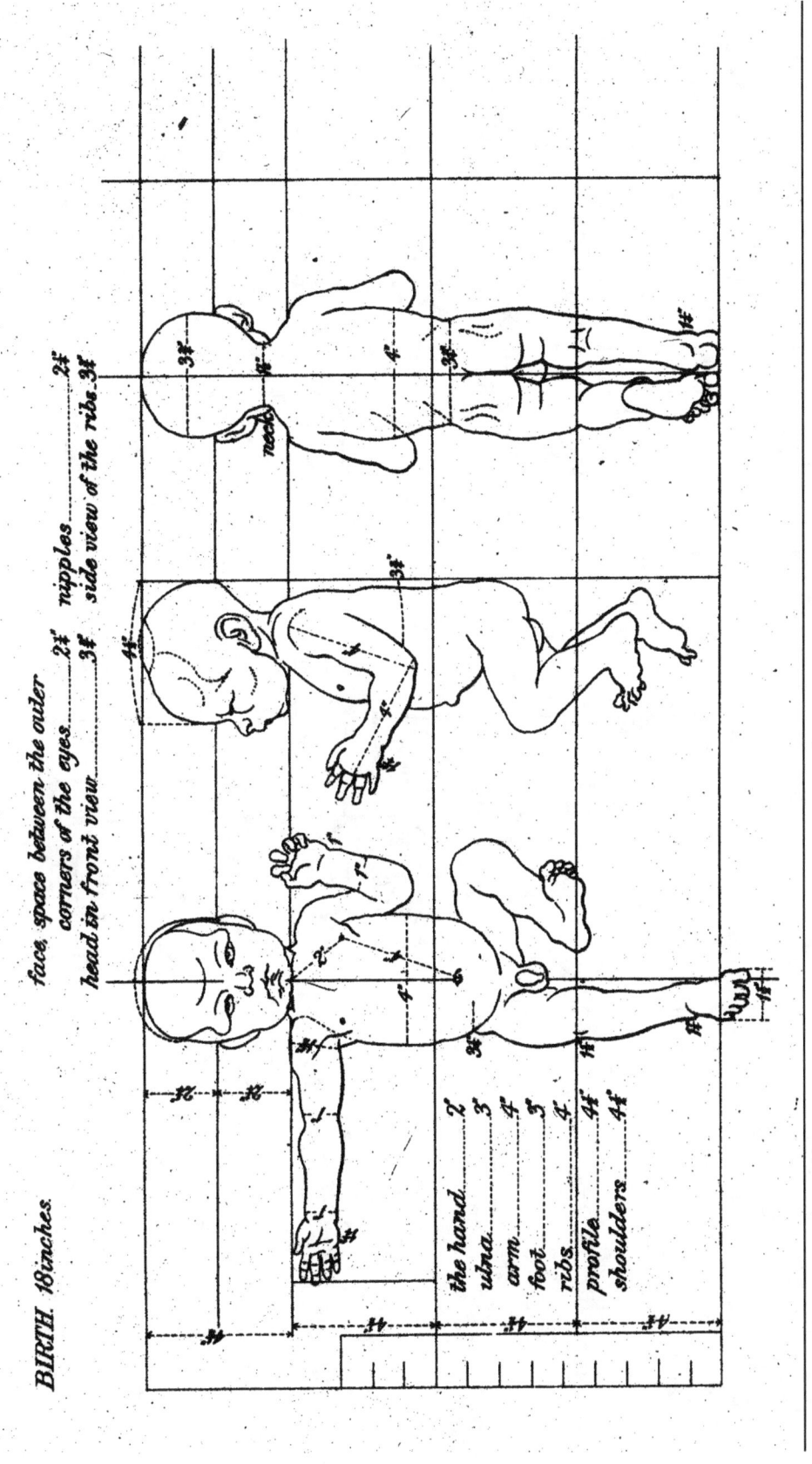

BIRTH. 18inches.

face, space between the outer
corners of the eyes .... 2¾"   nipples .... 2¾"
head in front view .... 3¾"   side view of the ribs. 3¾"

the hand .... 2"
ulna .... 3"
arm .... 4"
foot .... 5"
ribs .... 4"
profile .... 4¾"
shoulders .... 4¾"

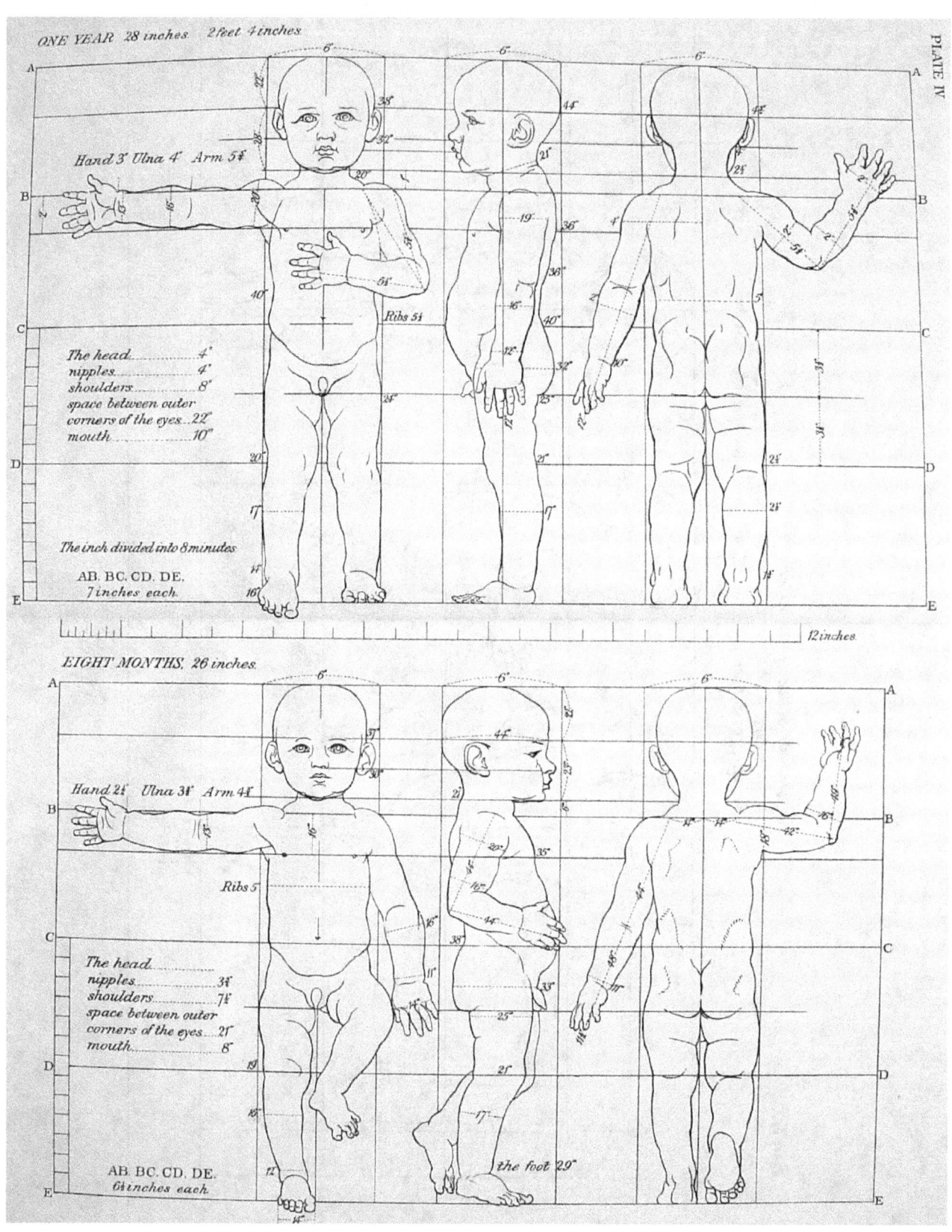

PLATE IV.

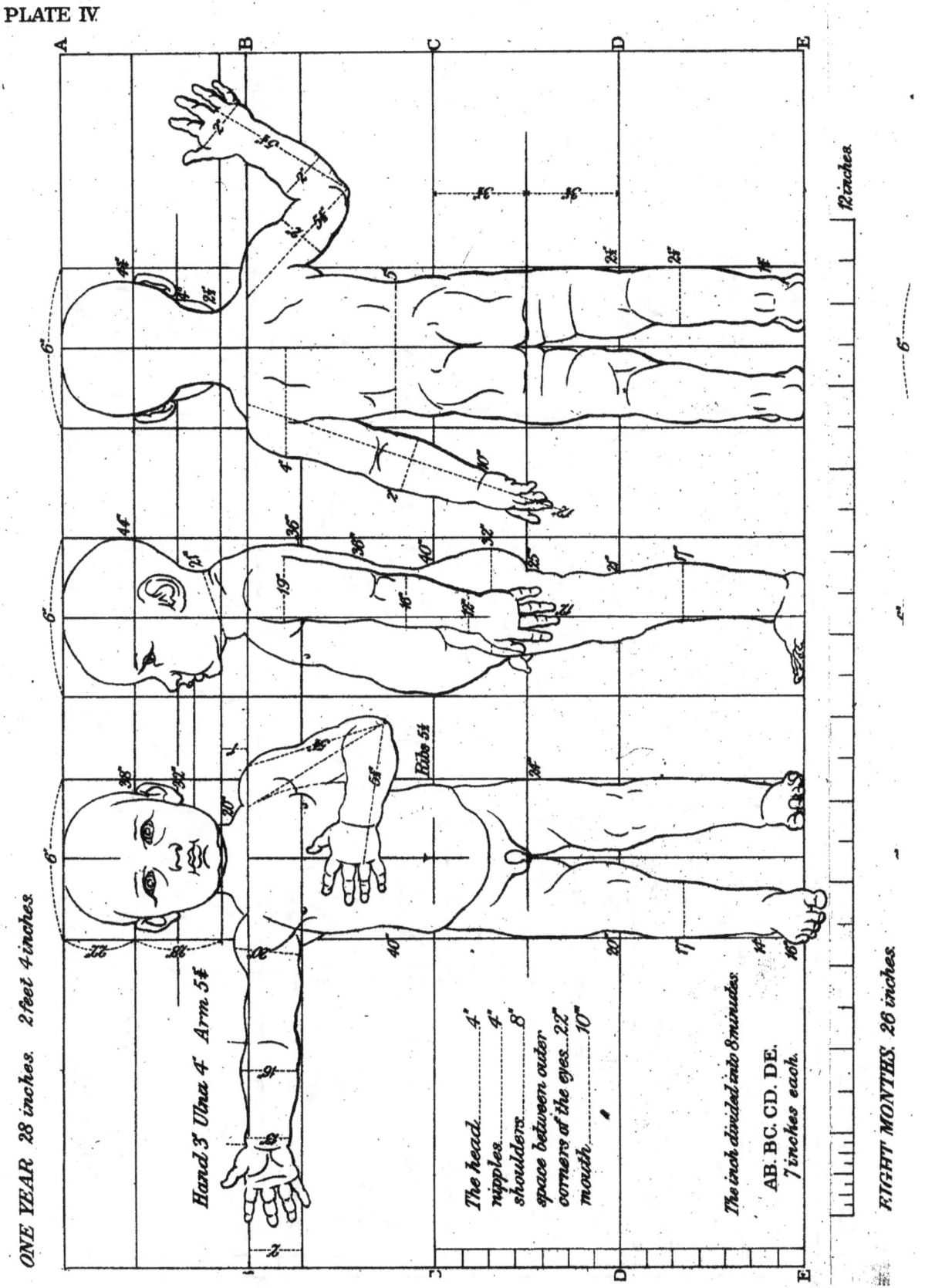

ONE YEAR. 28 inches.   2 feet 4 inches.

Hand 3" Ulna 4" Arm 5¾

The head............. 4"
nipples.............. 4"
shoulders............ 8"
space between outer
corners of the eyes..2⅖"
mouth............... 10"'

The inch divided into 8 minutes.

AB. BC. CD. DE.
7 inches each.

EIGHT MONTHS. 26 inches.

12 inches.

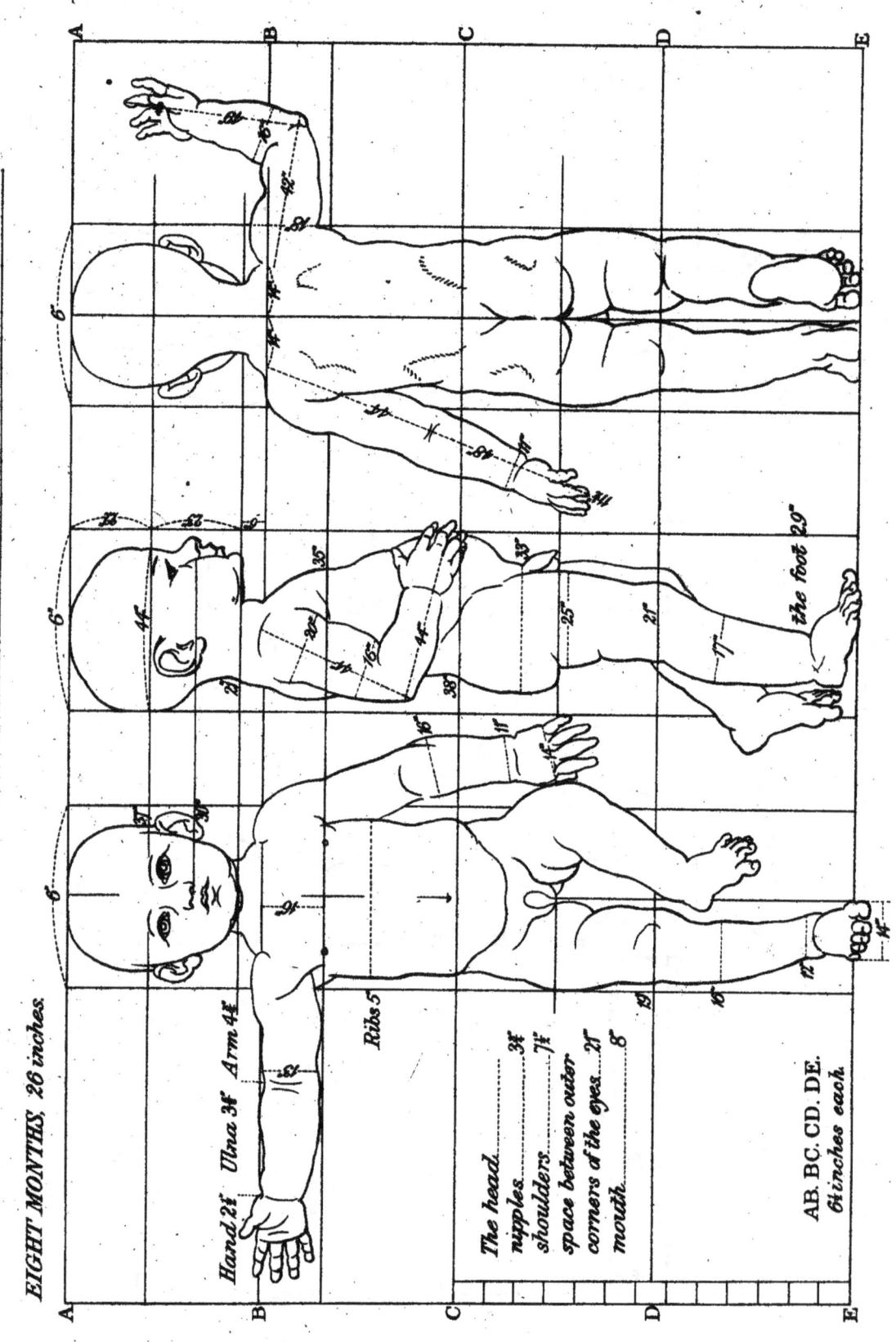

EIGHT MONTHS, 26 inches.

Hand 2⅜ Ulna 3⅞ Arm 4⅞

Ribs 5

The head........
nipples........ 3⅜
shoulders........ 7⅜
space between outer
corners of the eyes.. 2⅞
mouth........ ⅞

AB. BC. CD. DE.
6¼ inches each.

the foot 2.9"

44

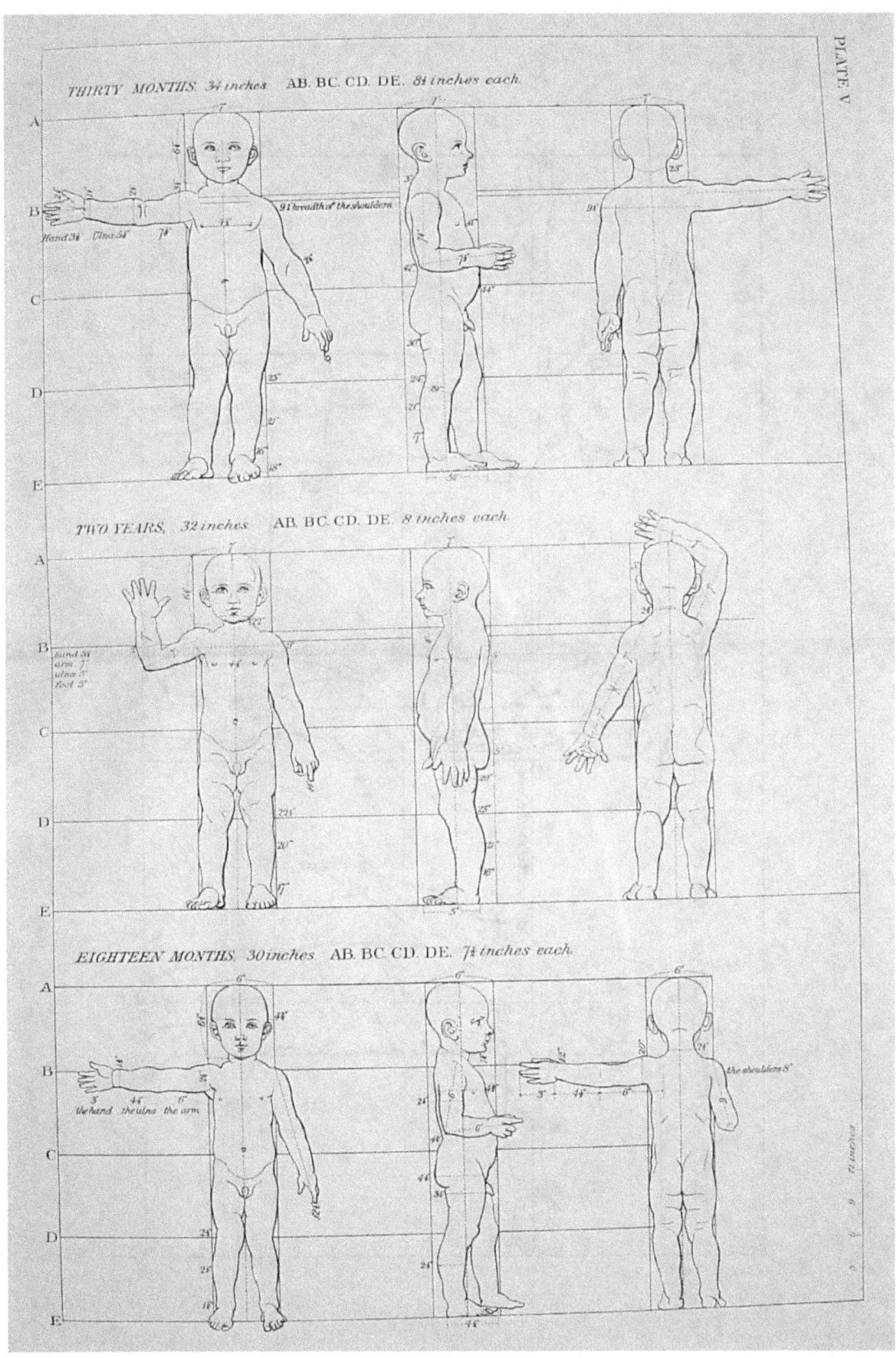

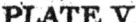

PLATE V.

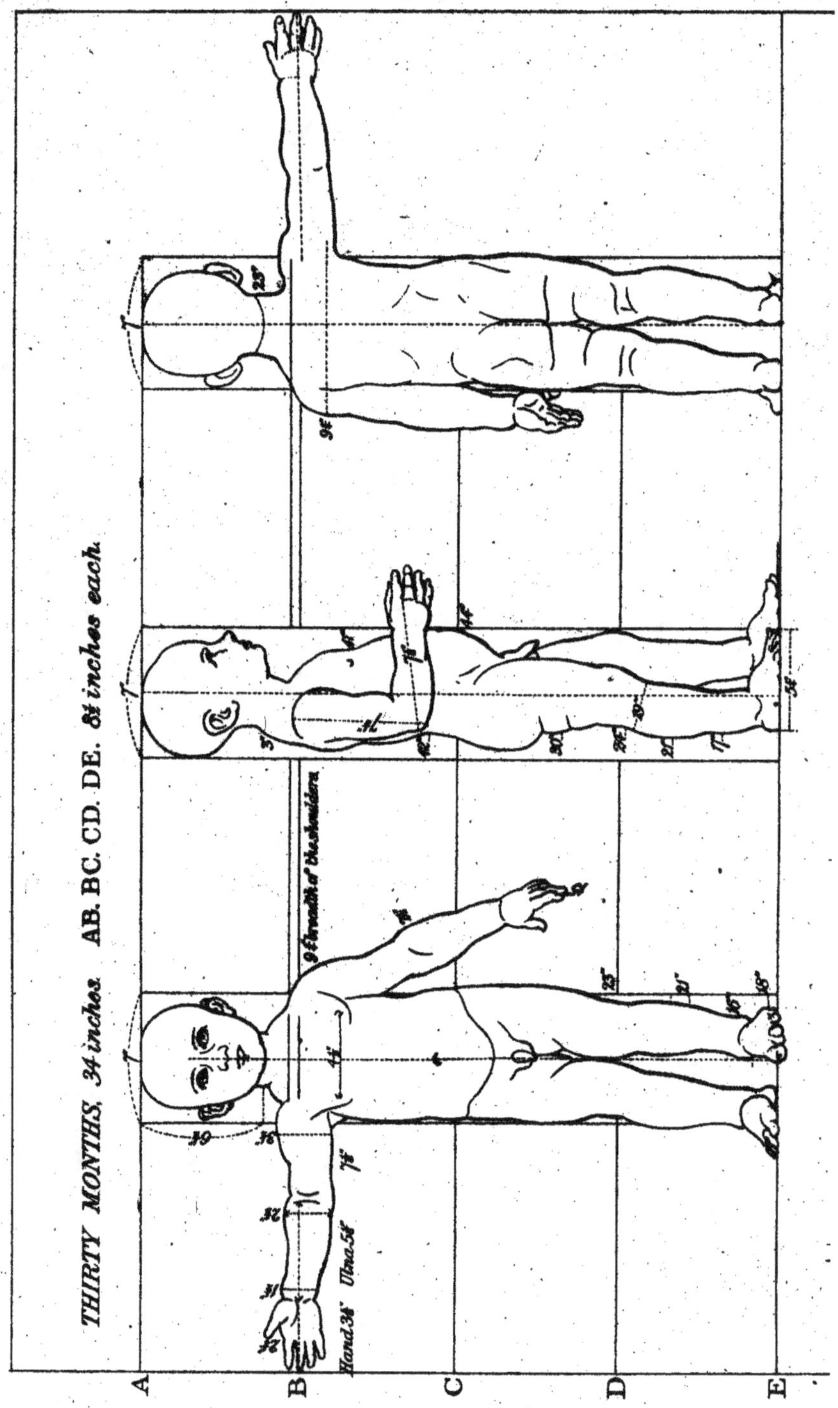

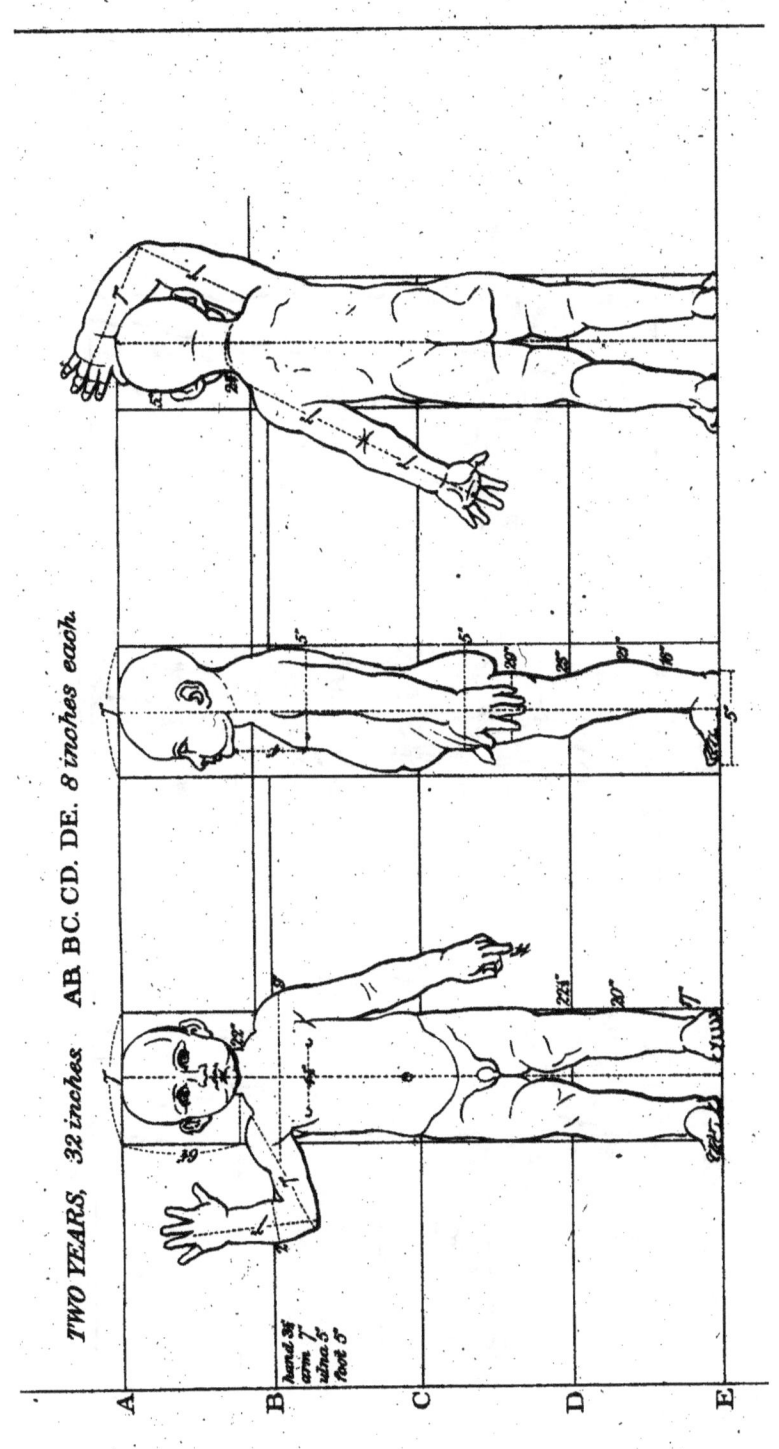

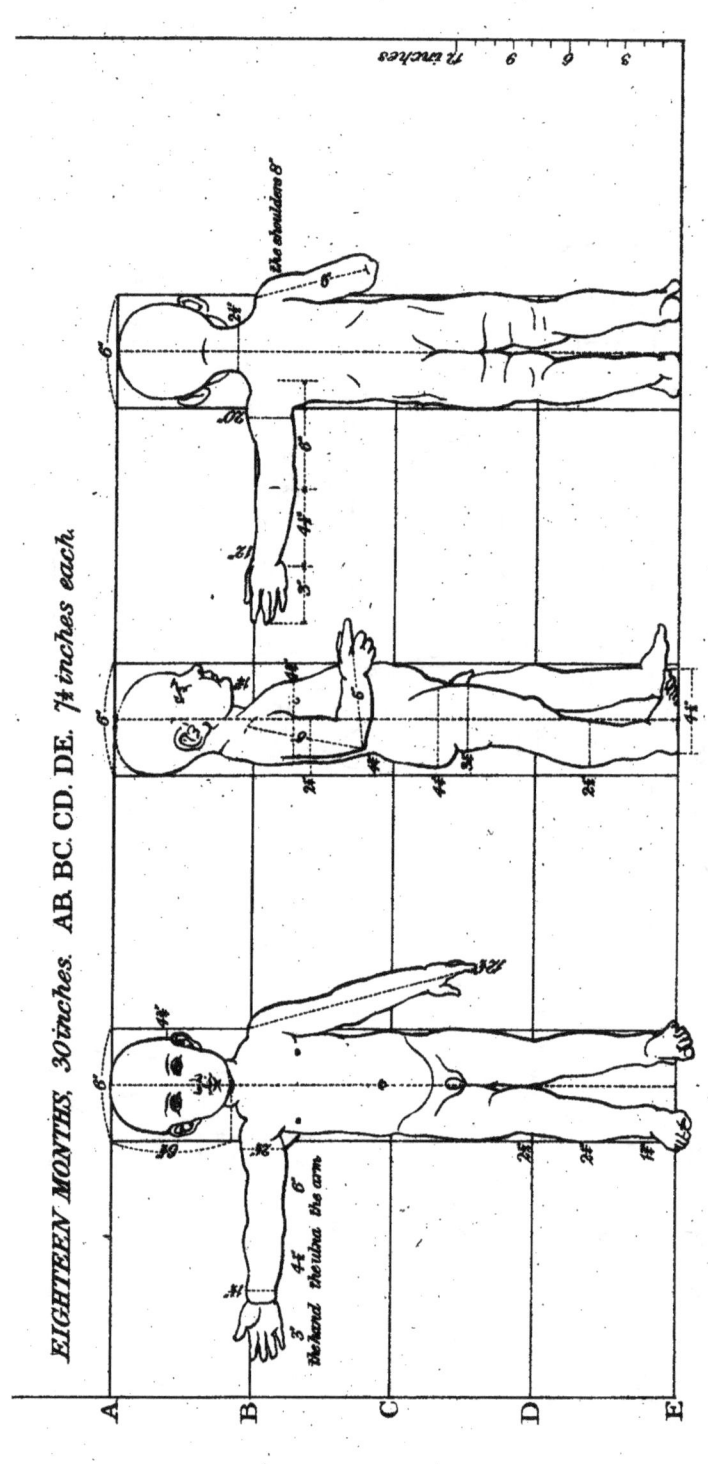

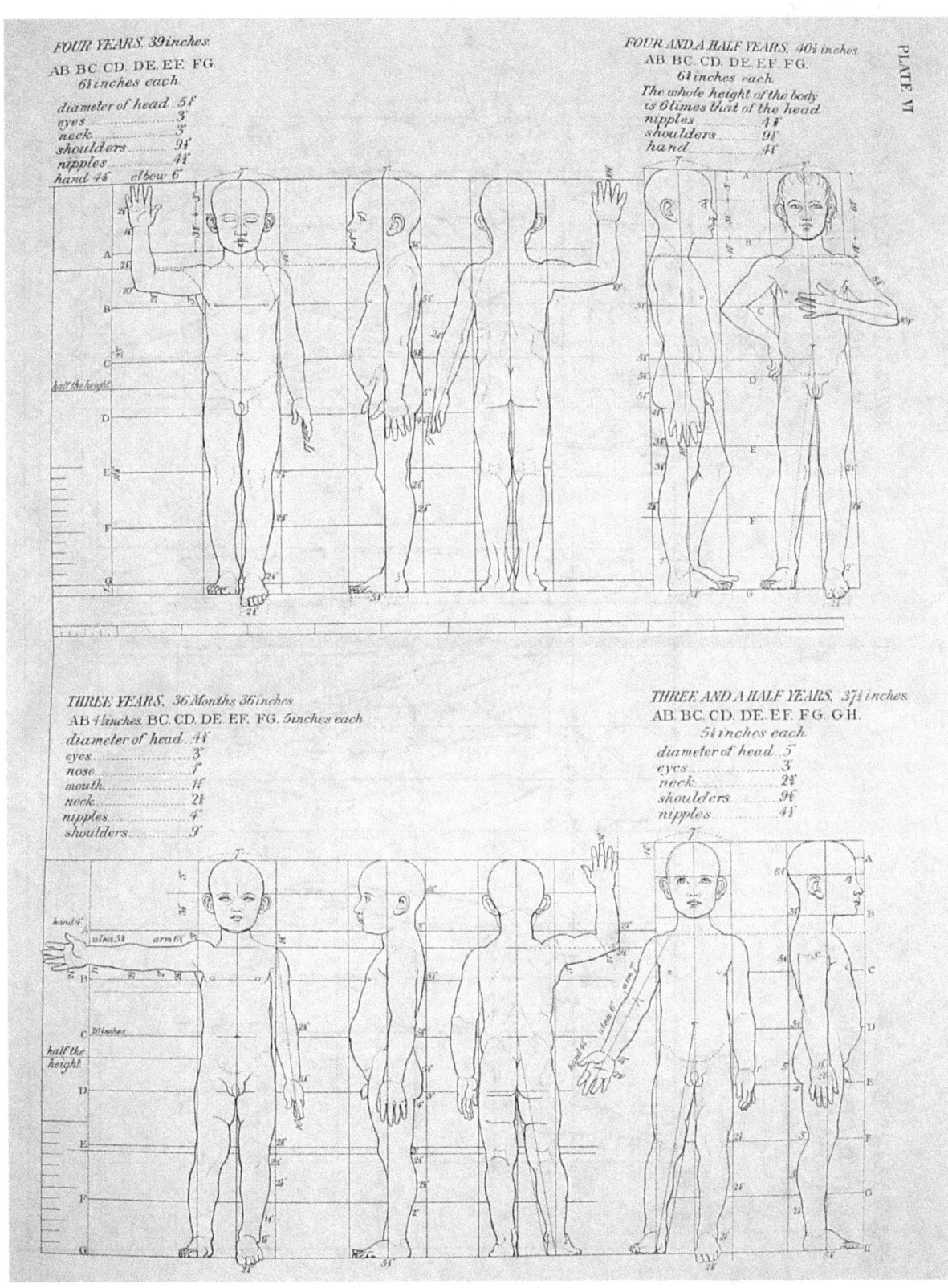

PLATE VI

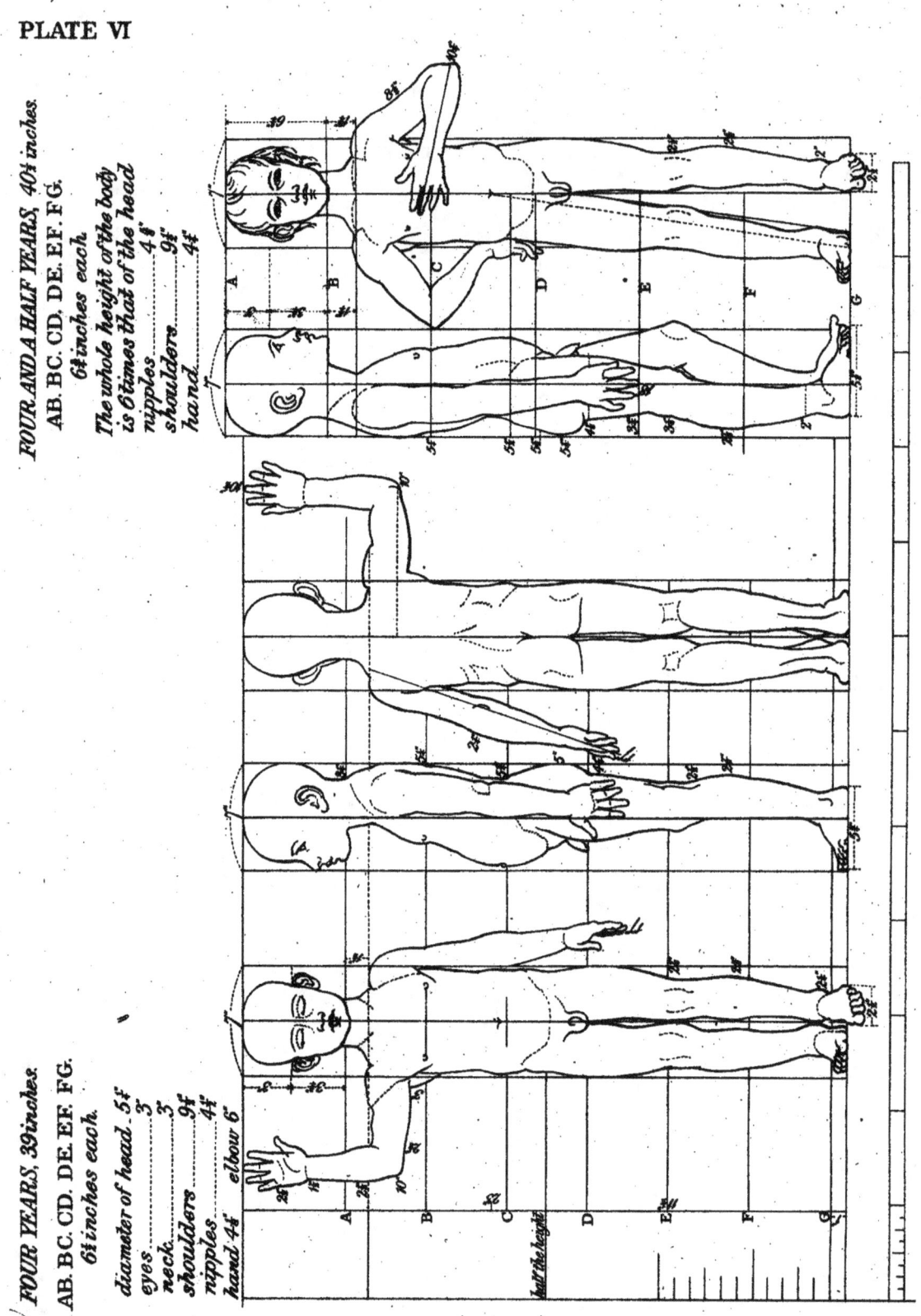

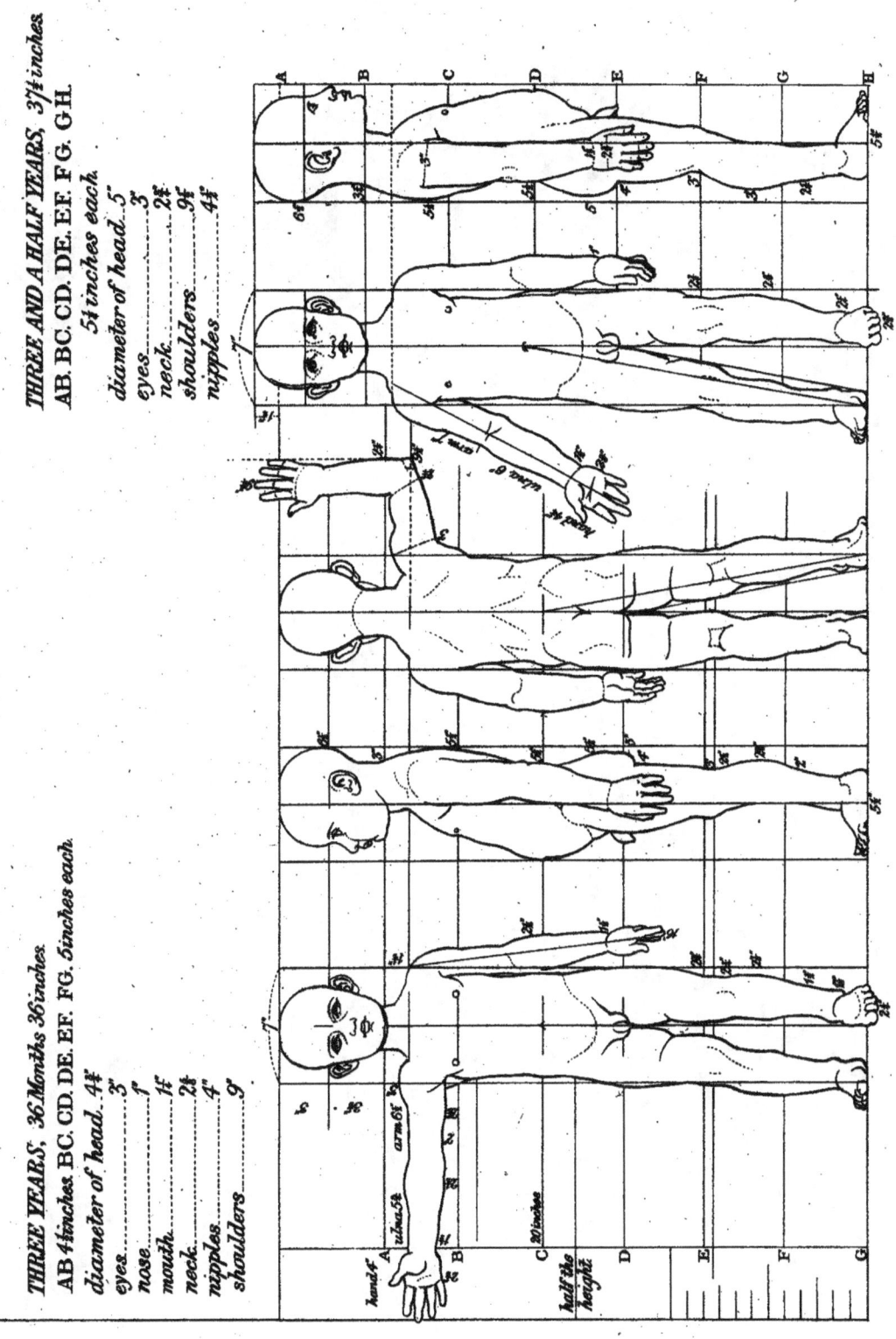

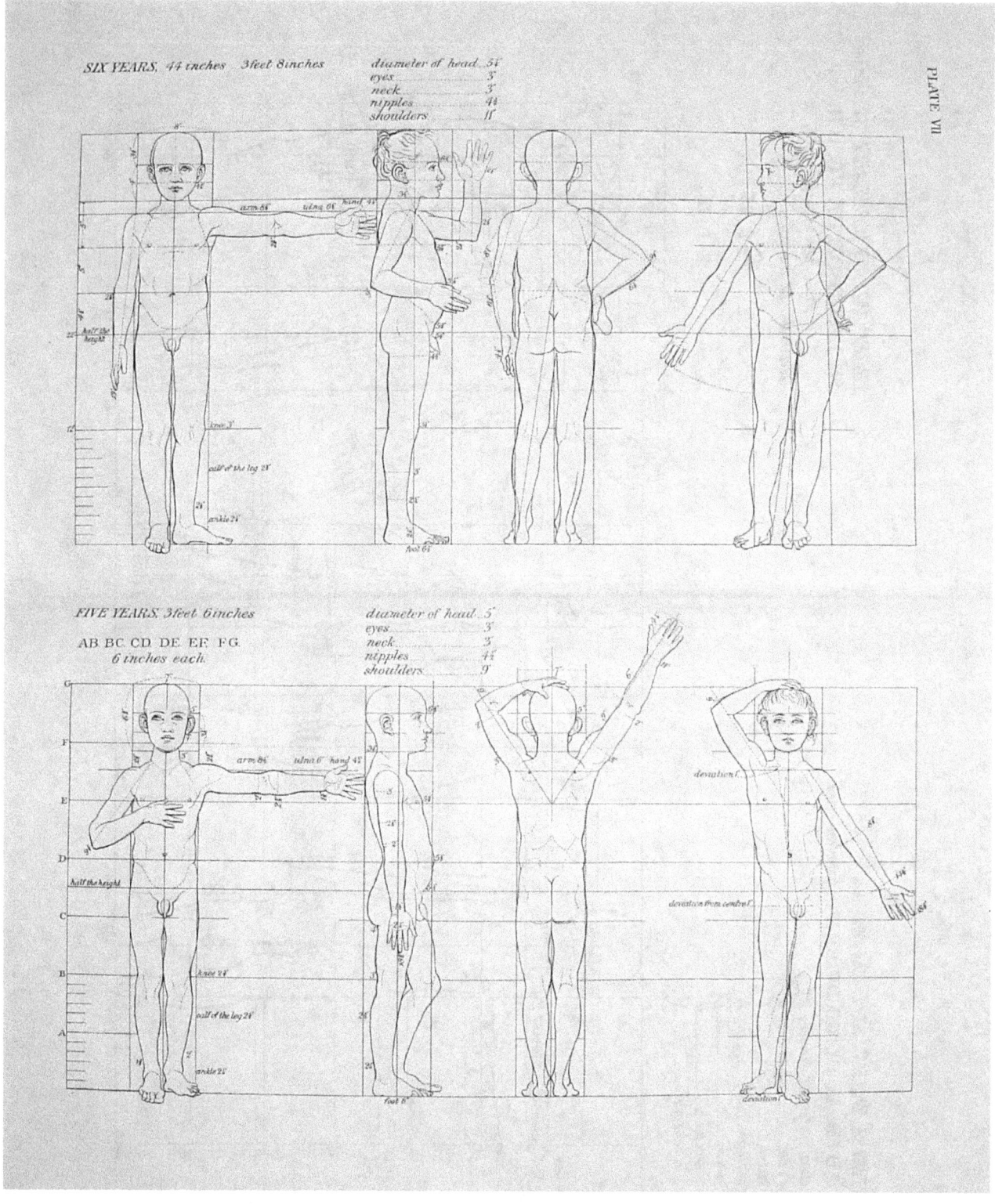

PLATE VII.

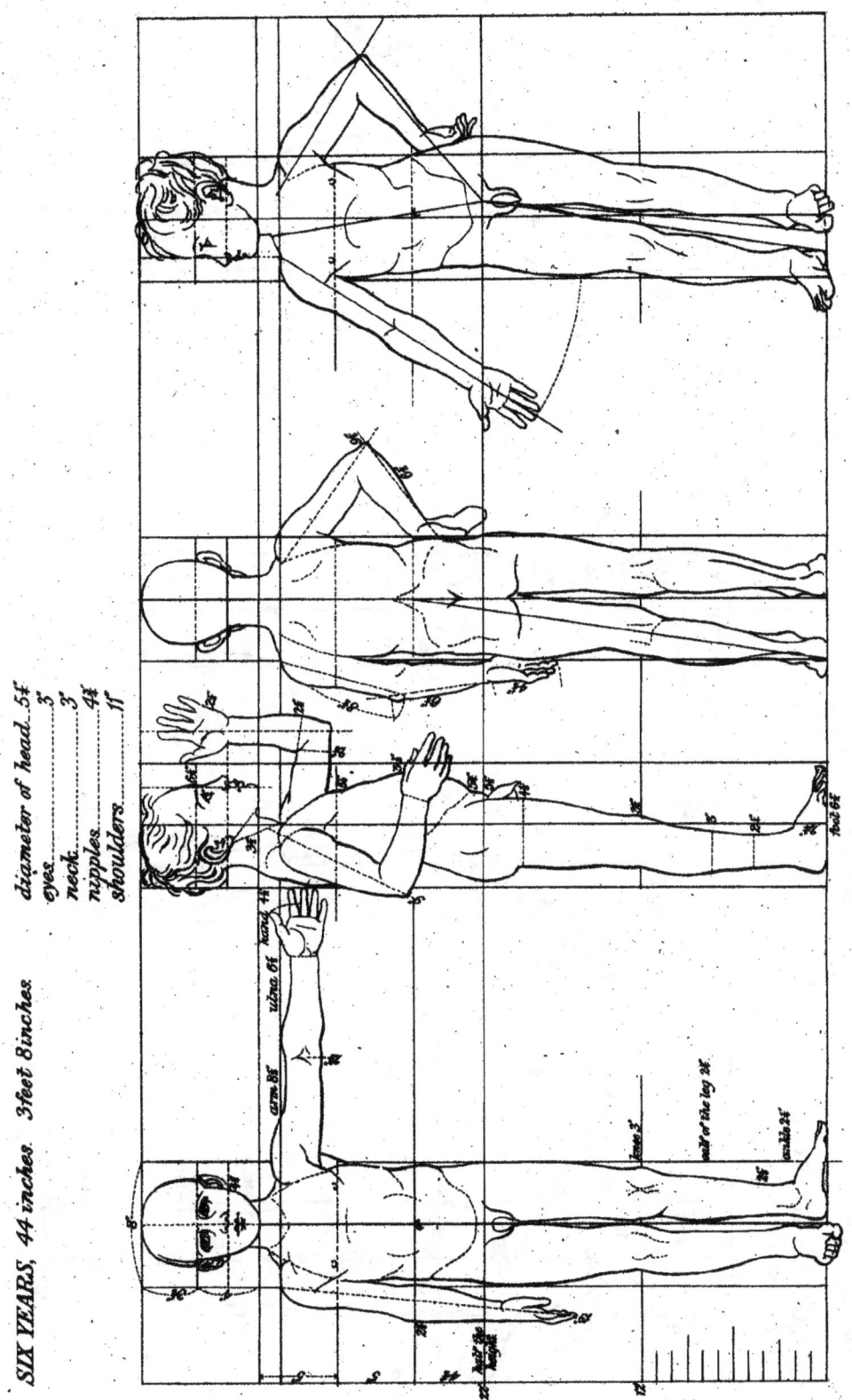

SIX YEARS. 44 inches. 3 feet 8 inches.

diameter of head..5¼
eyes............3
neck............3
nipples.........4¼
shoulders.......11

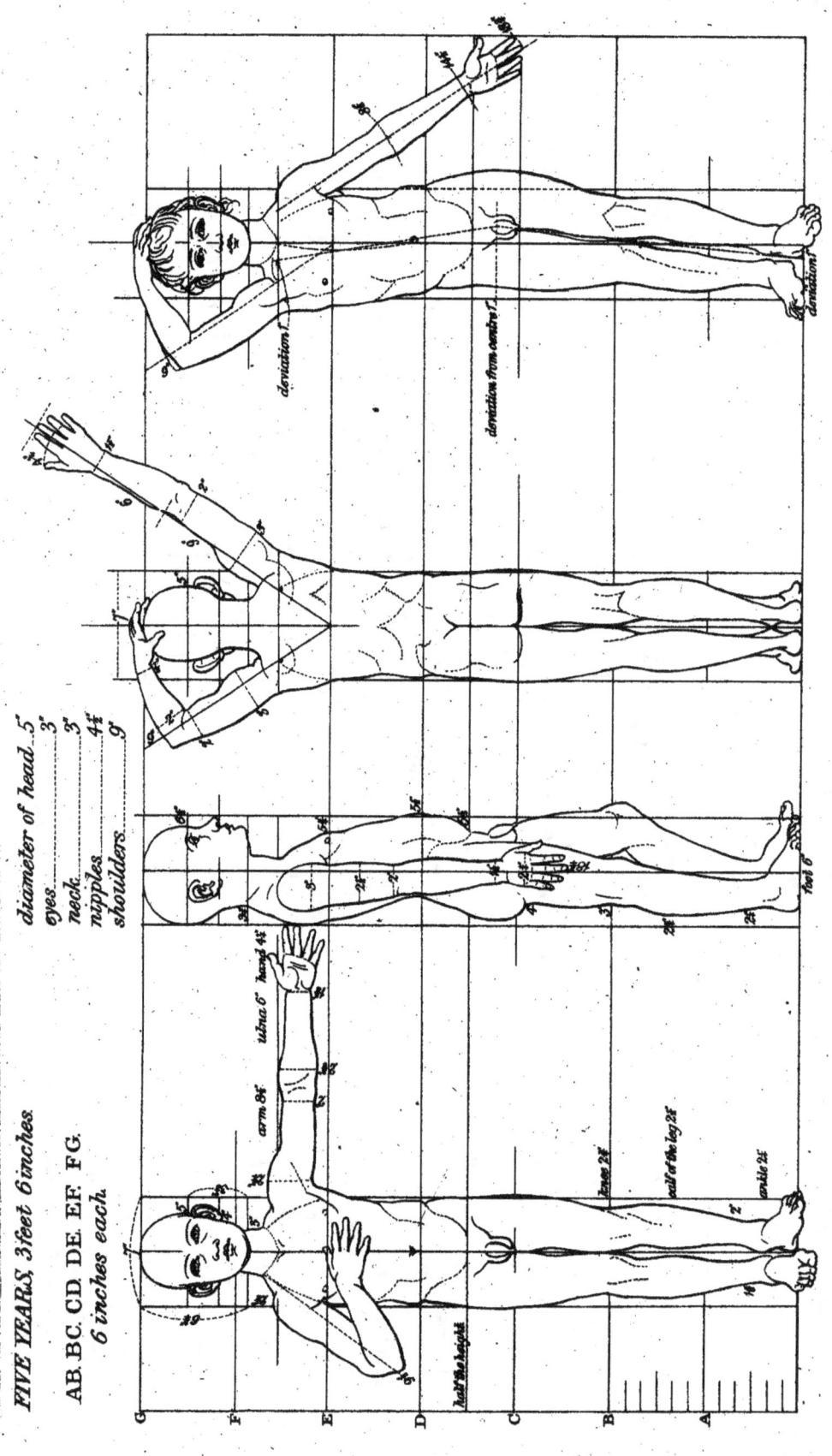

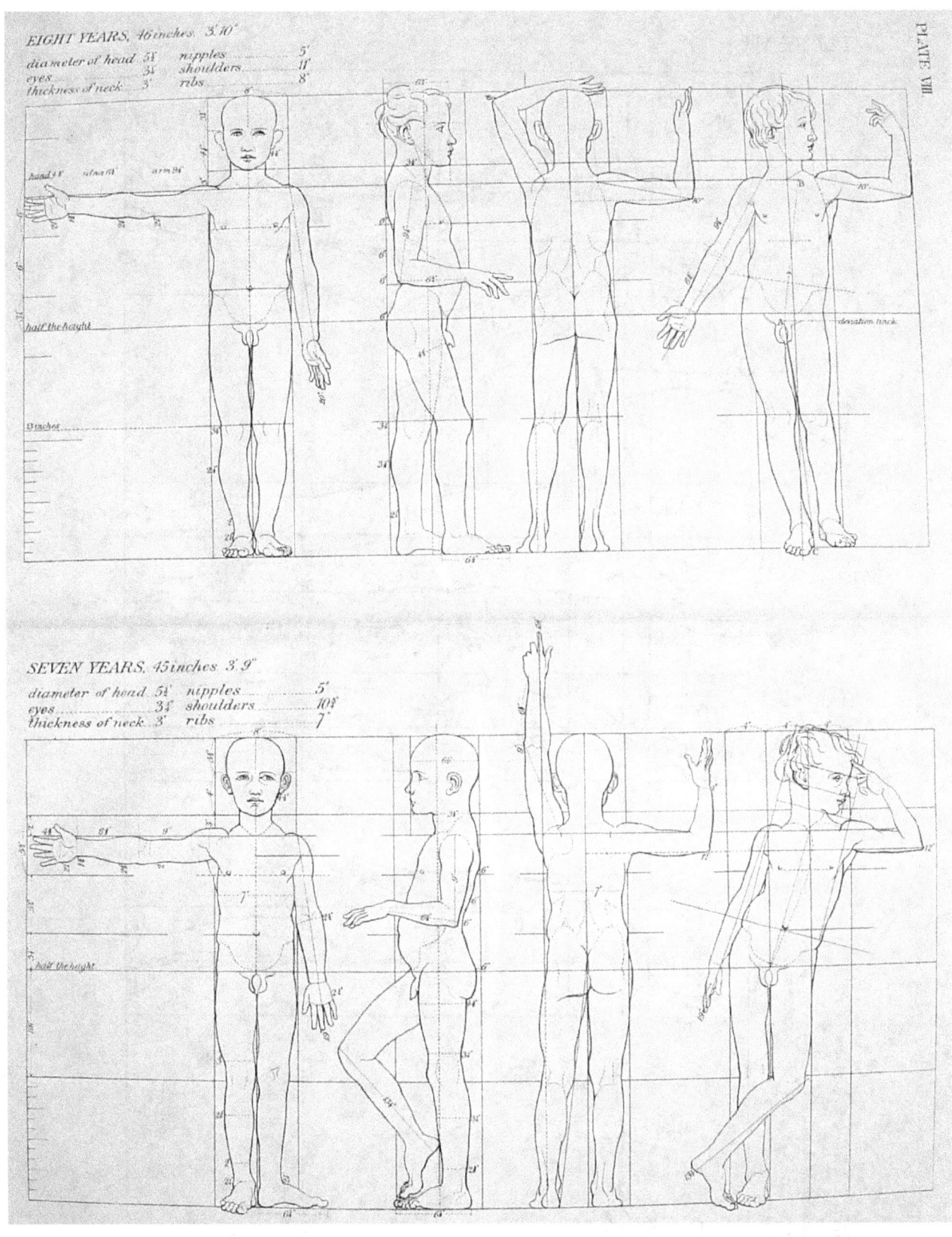

PLATE VIII

EIGHT YEARS, 46 inches. 3' 10"

diameter of head	5¼	nipples	5'
eyes	3¼	shoulders	11"
thickness of neck	3'	ribs	8"

SEVEN YEARS, 45 inches. 3' 9"

diameter of head	5¼	nipples	5'
eyes	3¼	shoulders	10¾
thickness of neck	3'	ribs	7'

PLATE VIII.

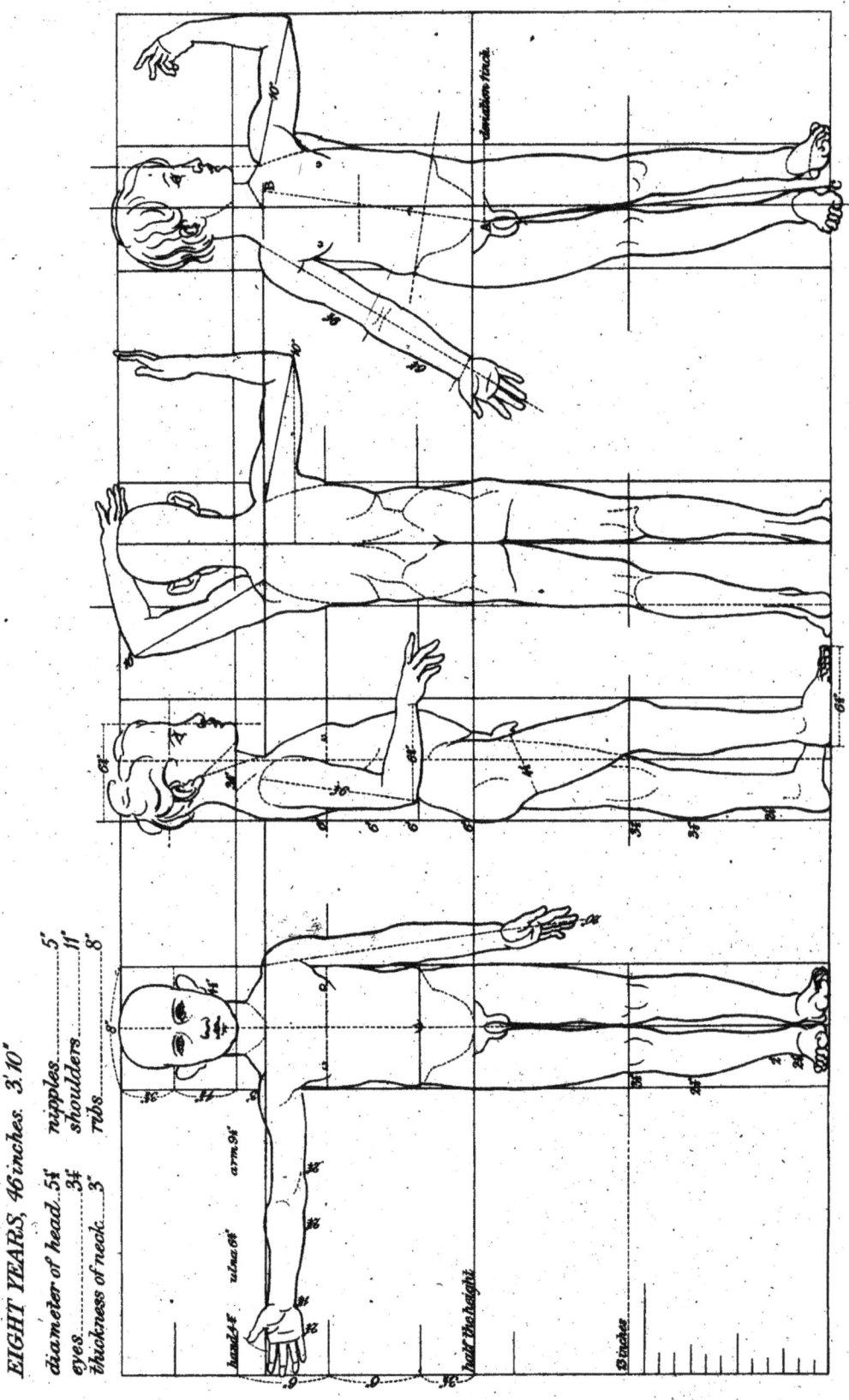

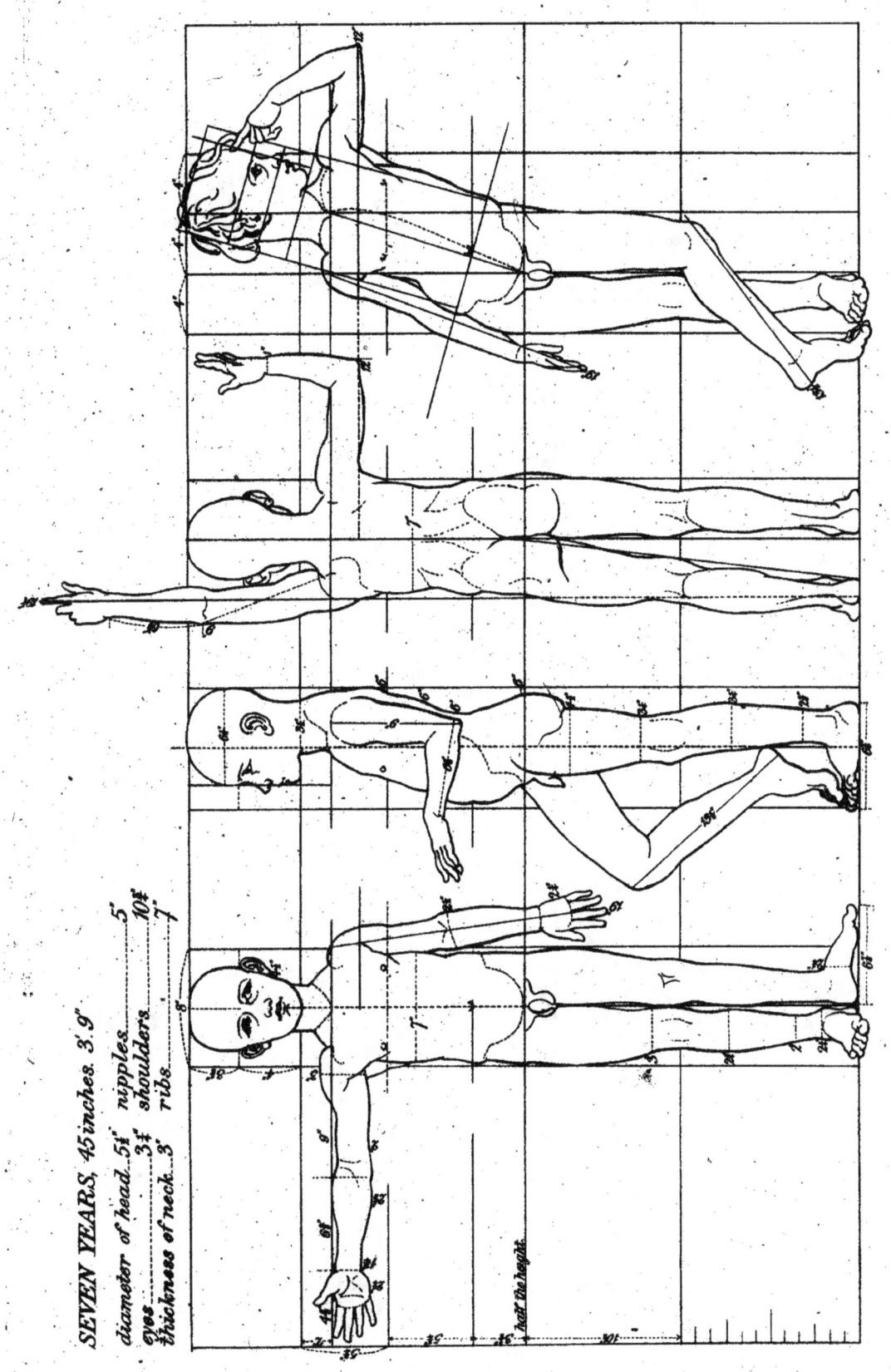

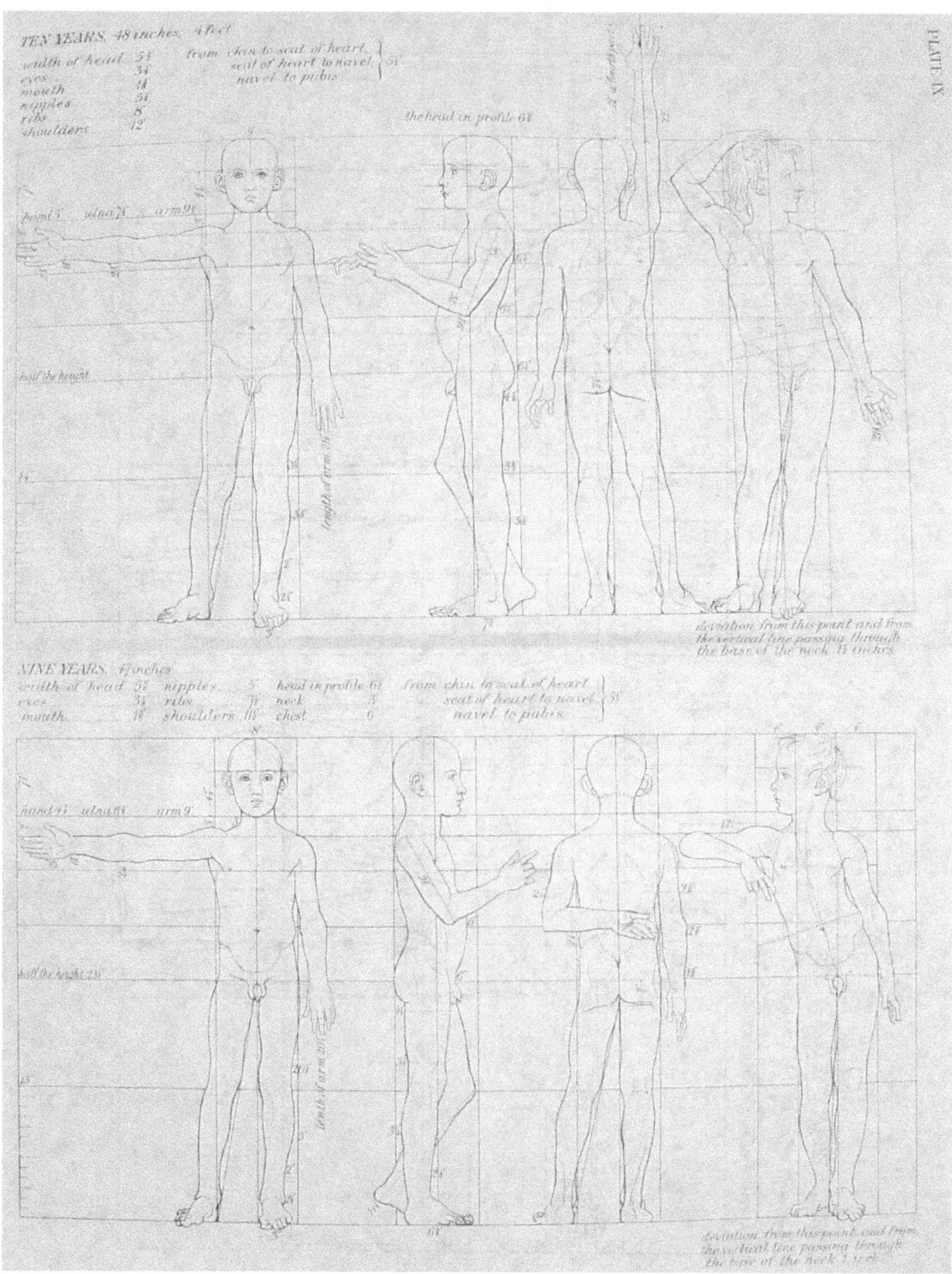

PLATE IX.

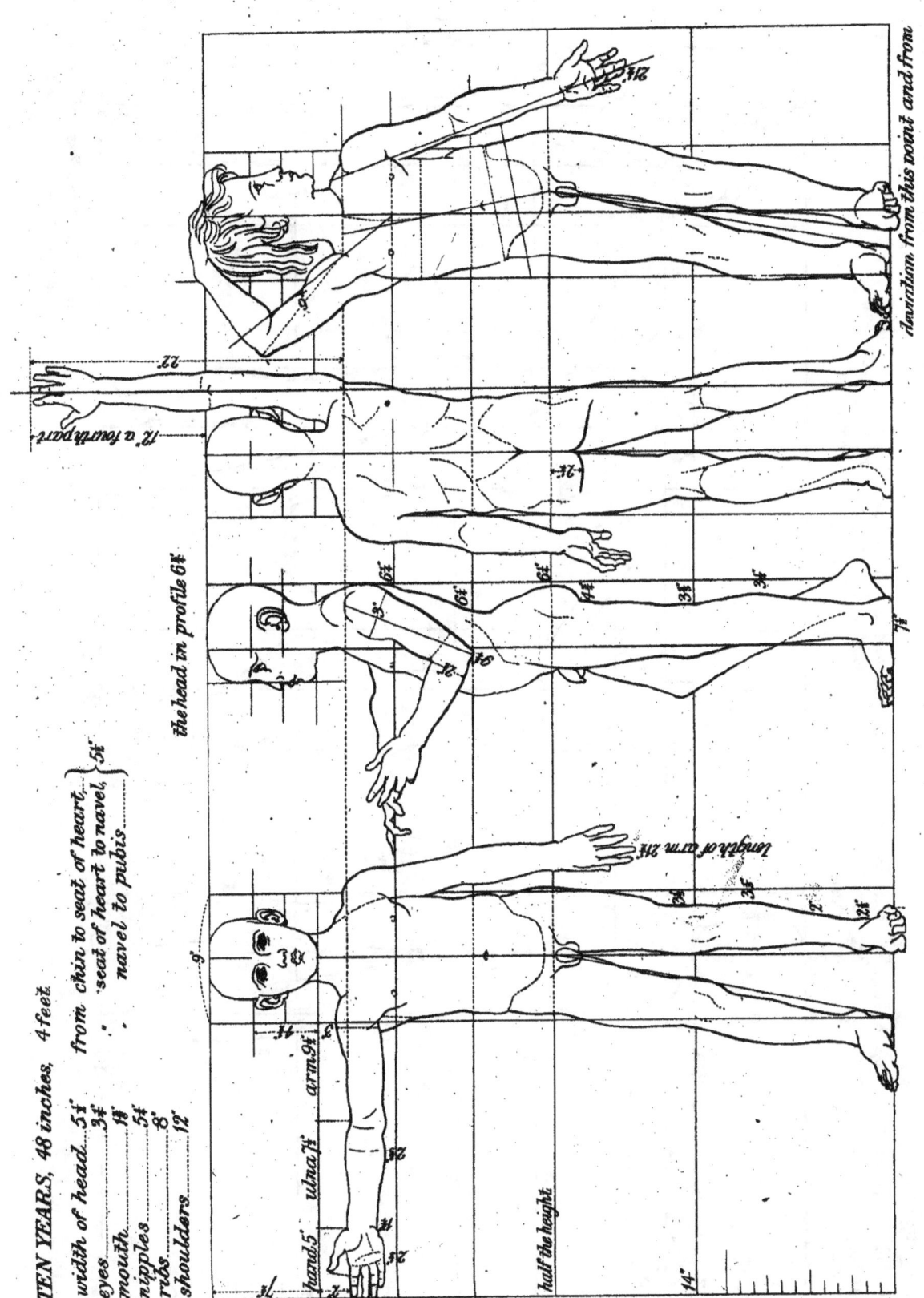

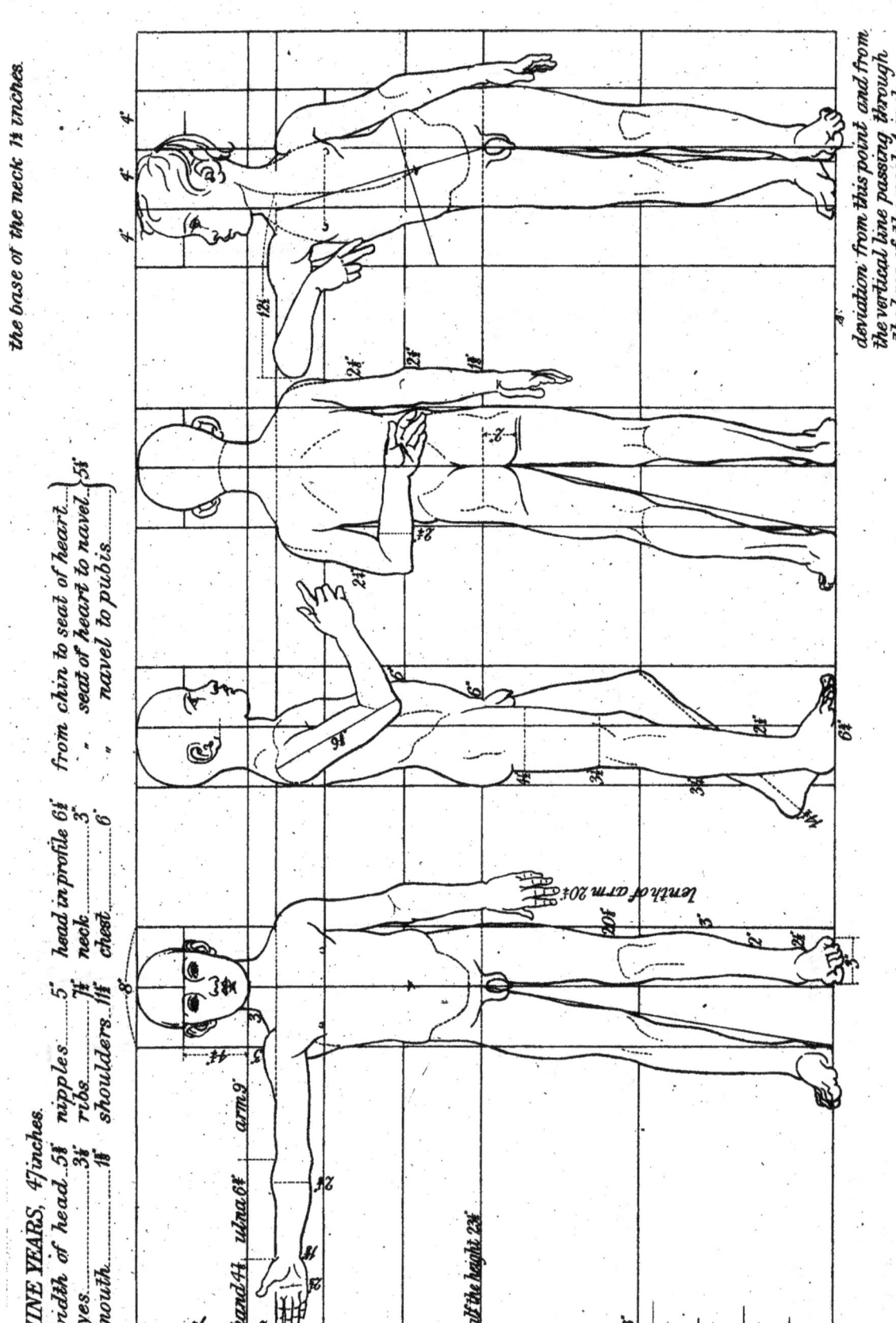

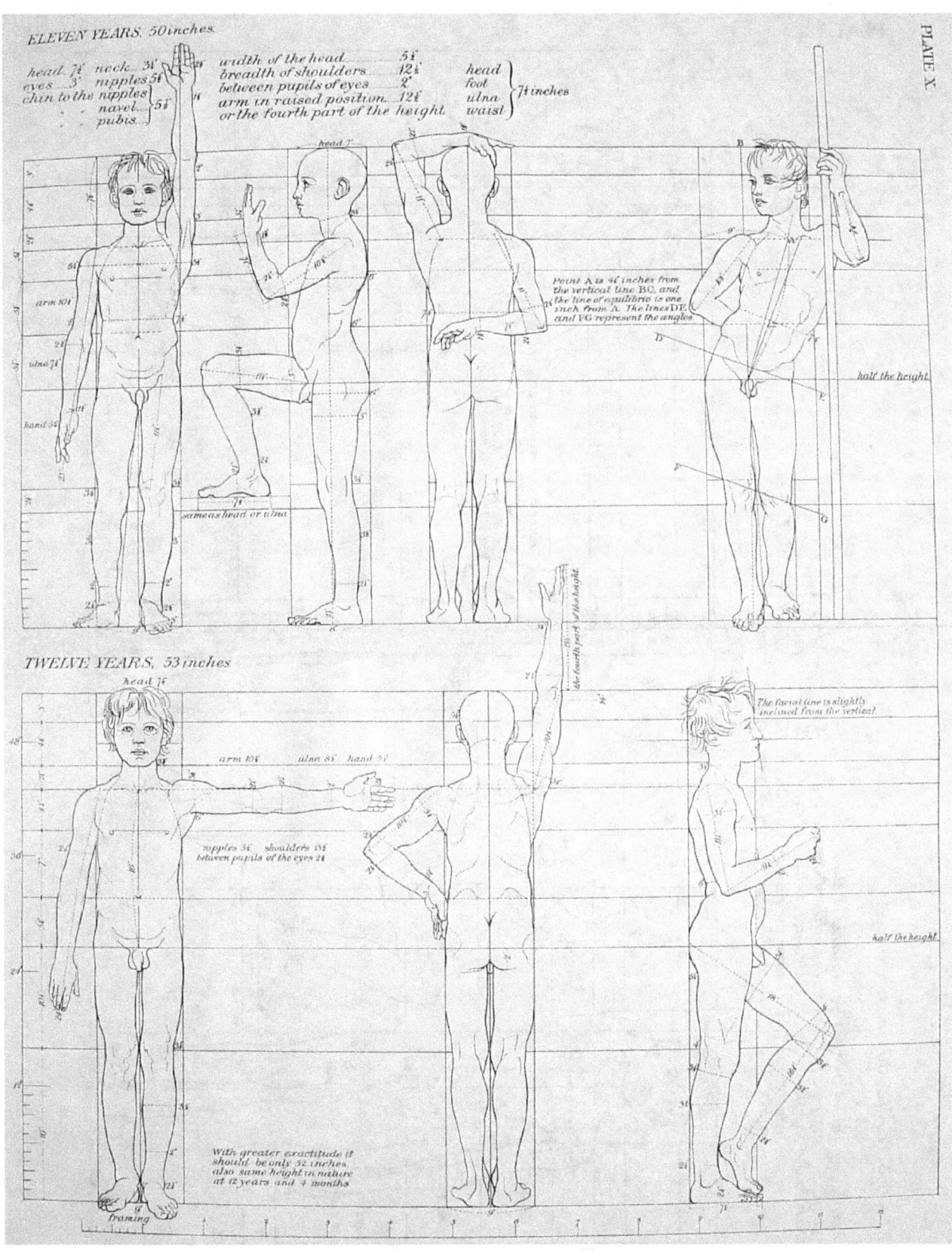

PLATE X.

ELEVEN YEARS, 50 inches.

head...7¼° neck...3¼°
eyes...3° nipples 5¼°
chin to the nipples
  ,, ,, navel...5¼°
  ,, ,, pubis...

width of the head......5¼°
breadth of shoulders......12¼°
between pupils of eyes...2°
arm in raised position...12¼°
or the fourth part of the height

head
foot
ulna   } 7¼ inches
waist

Point A is 4¼ inches from the vertical line BC, and the line of equilibrio is one inch from A. The lines DE and FG represent the angles.

half the height

¼ of the height

same as head or ulna

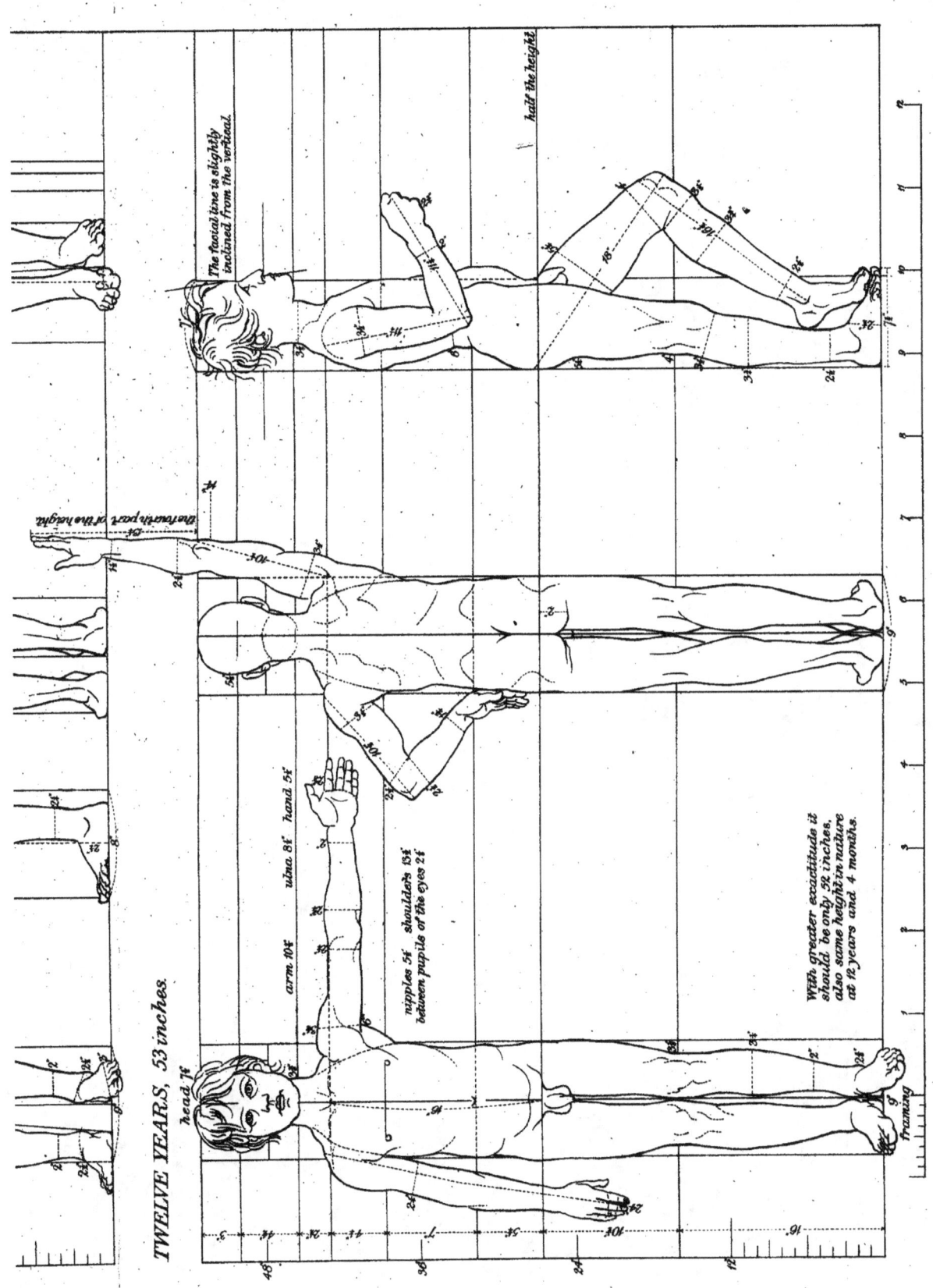

TWELVE YEARS, 53 inches.

head 7¼

arm 10¾   ulna. 8¼   hand. 5¼

nipples 5¼   shoulders 13¾
between pupils of the eyes 2⅝

With greater exactitude it
should be only 52 inches,
also same height in nature
at 12 years and 4 months.

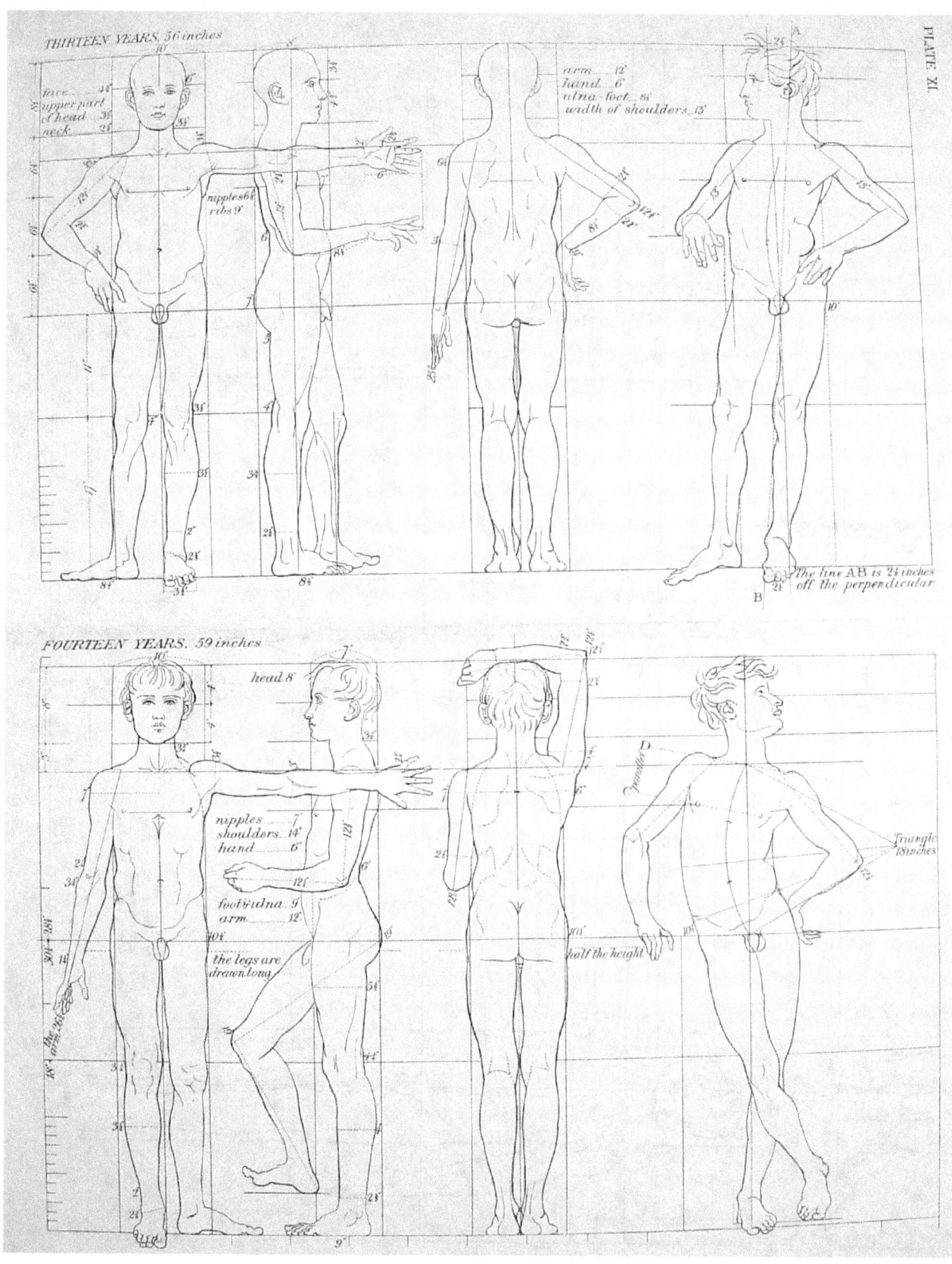

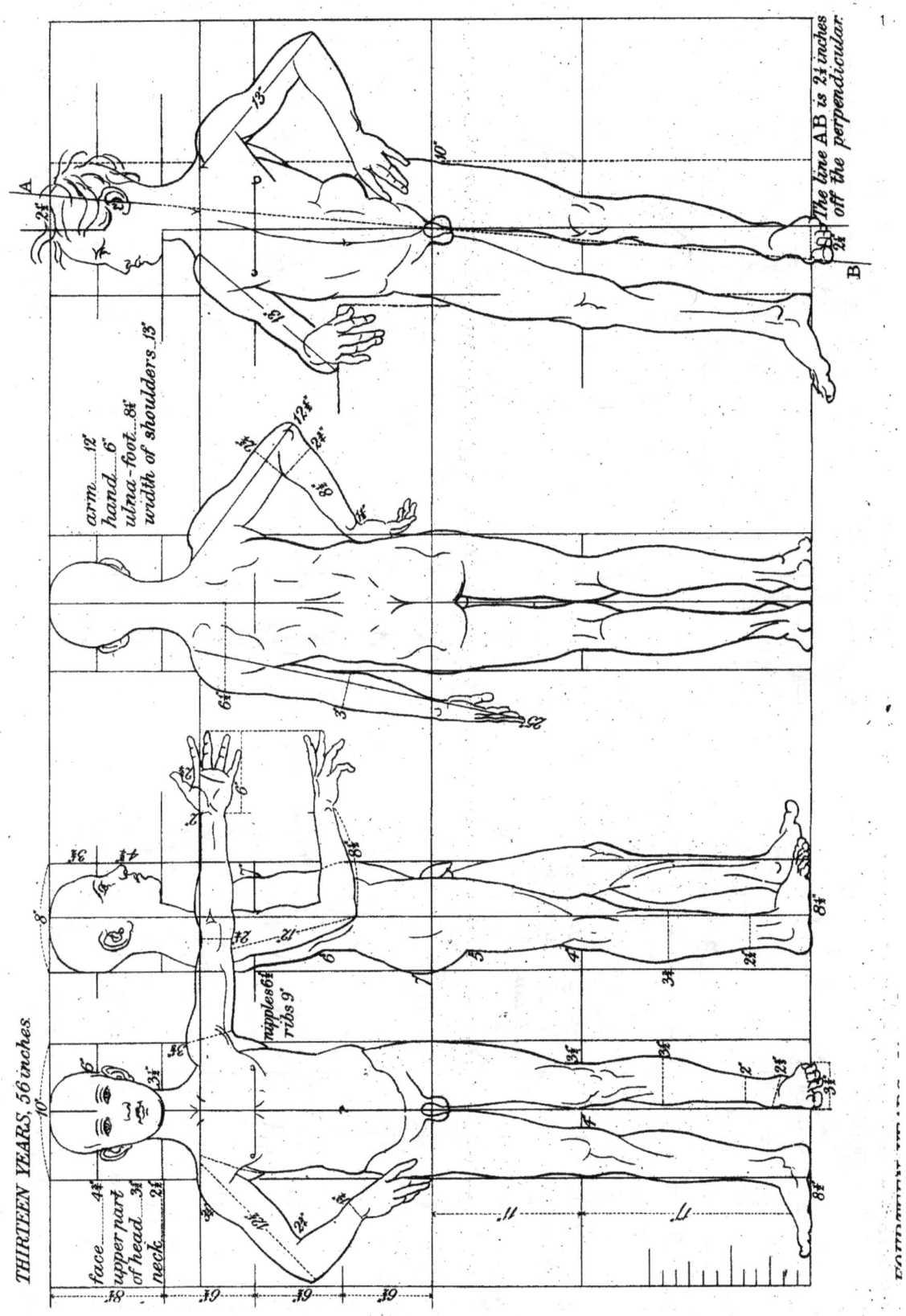

THIRTEEN YEARS, 56 inches.

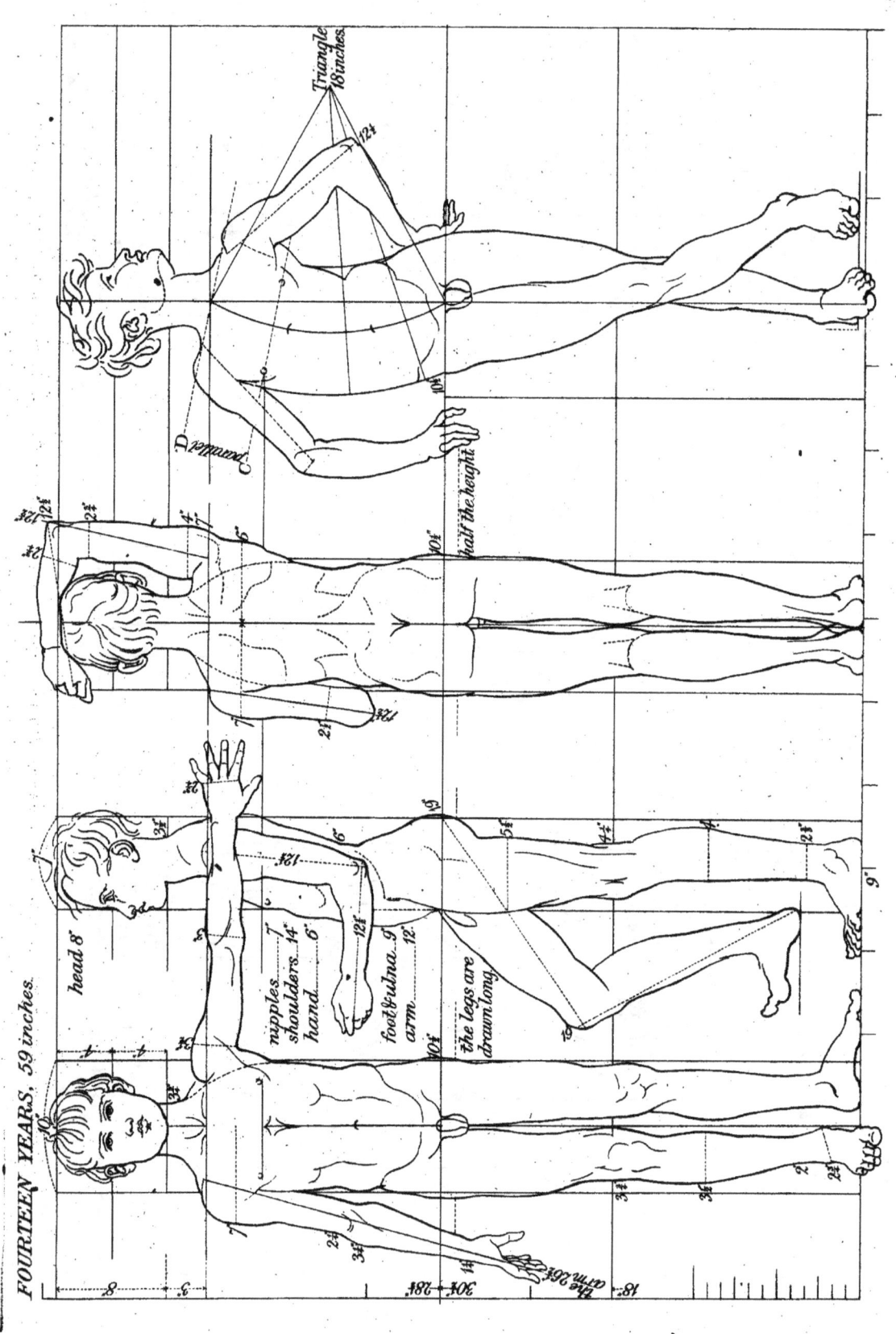

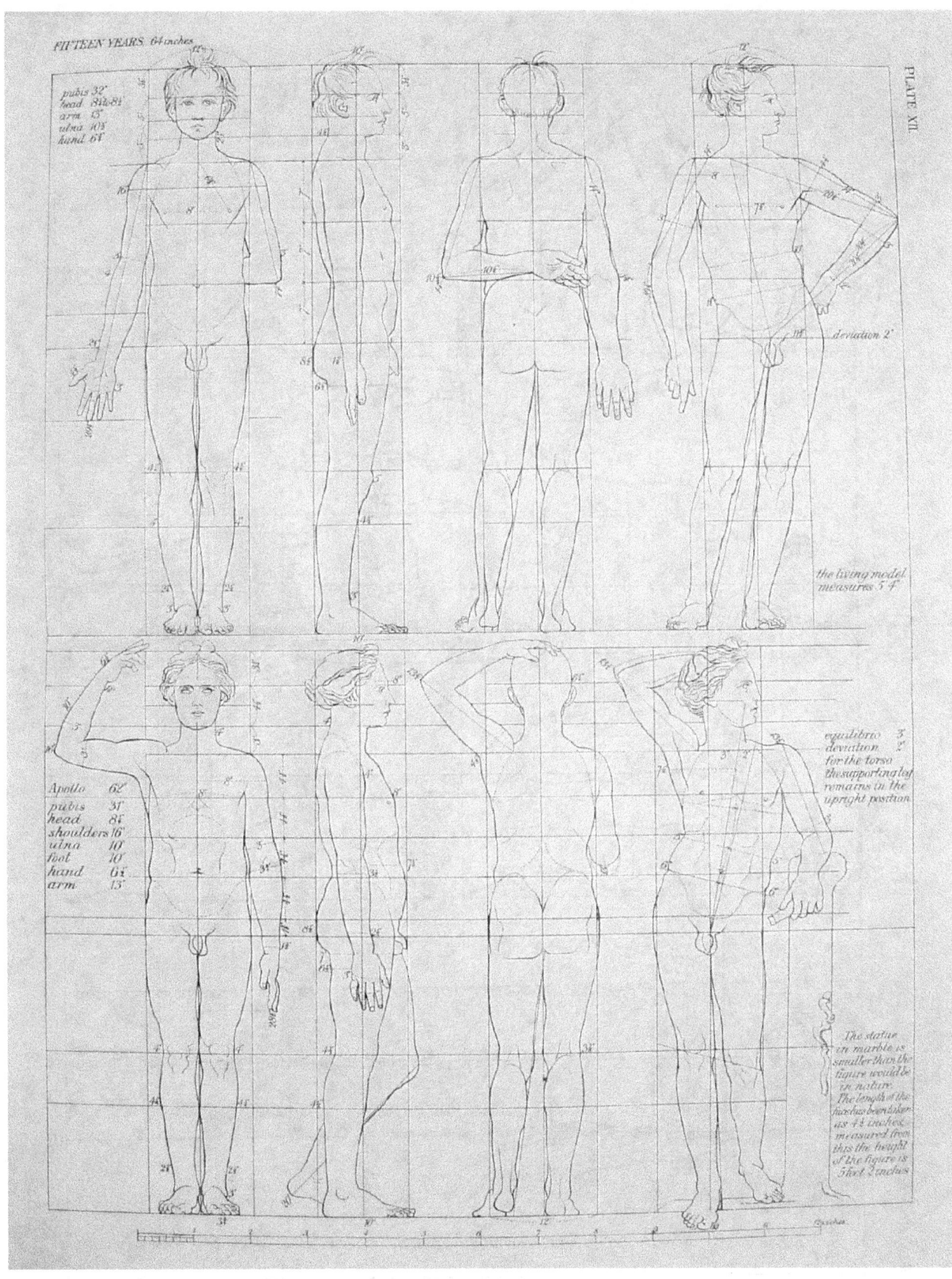

PLATE XII.

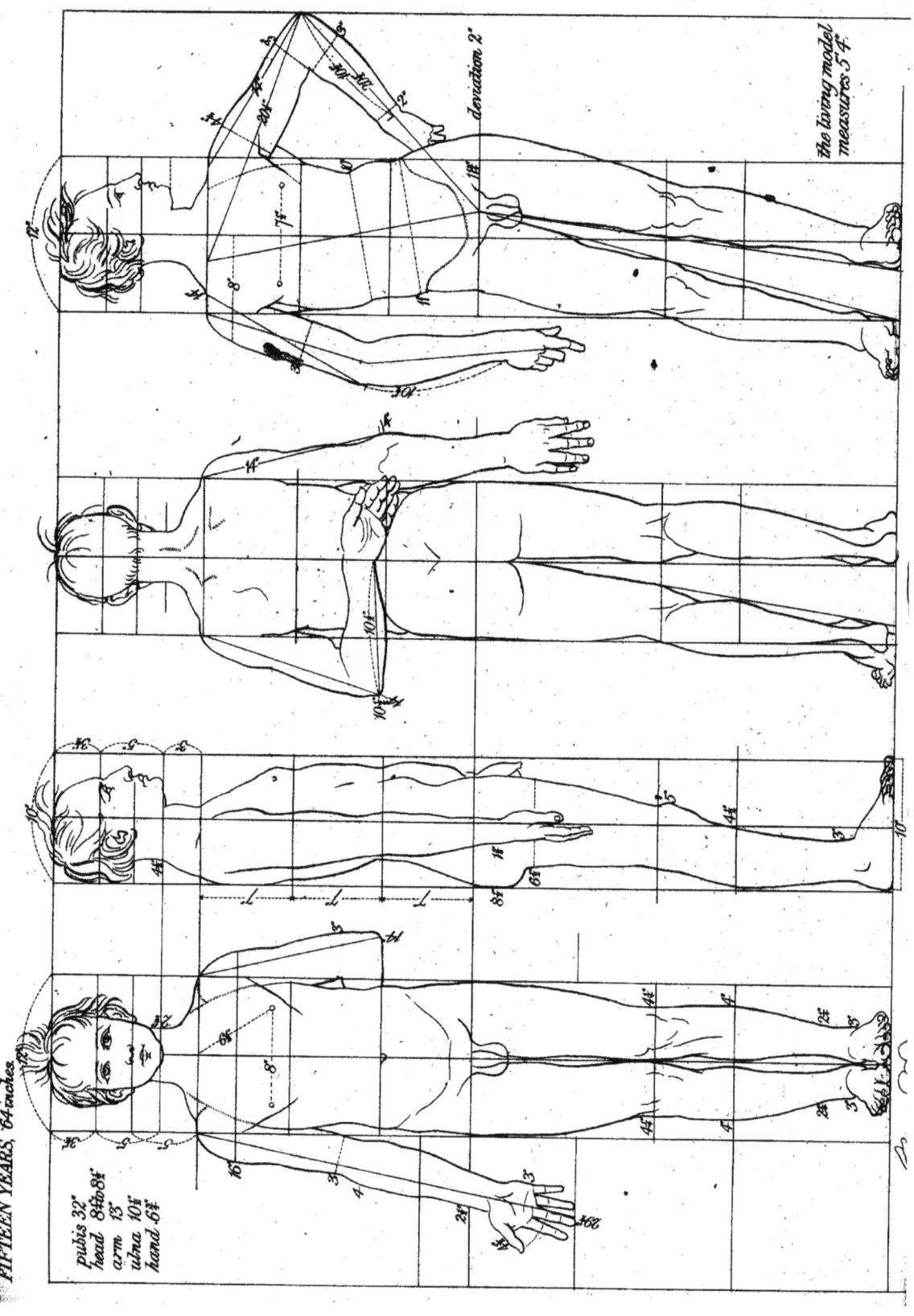

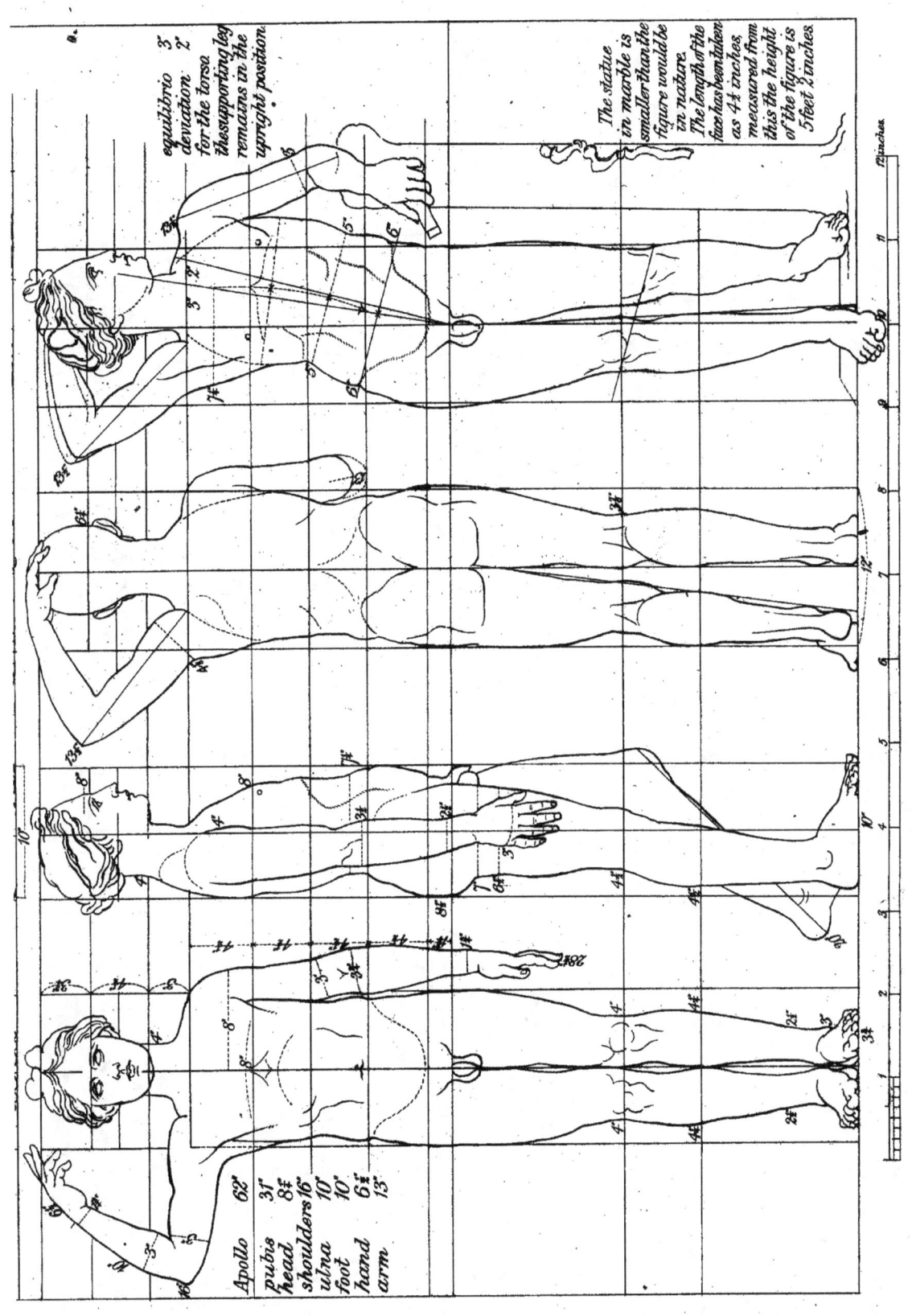

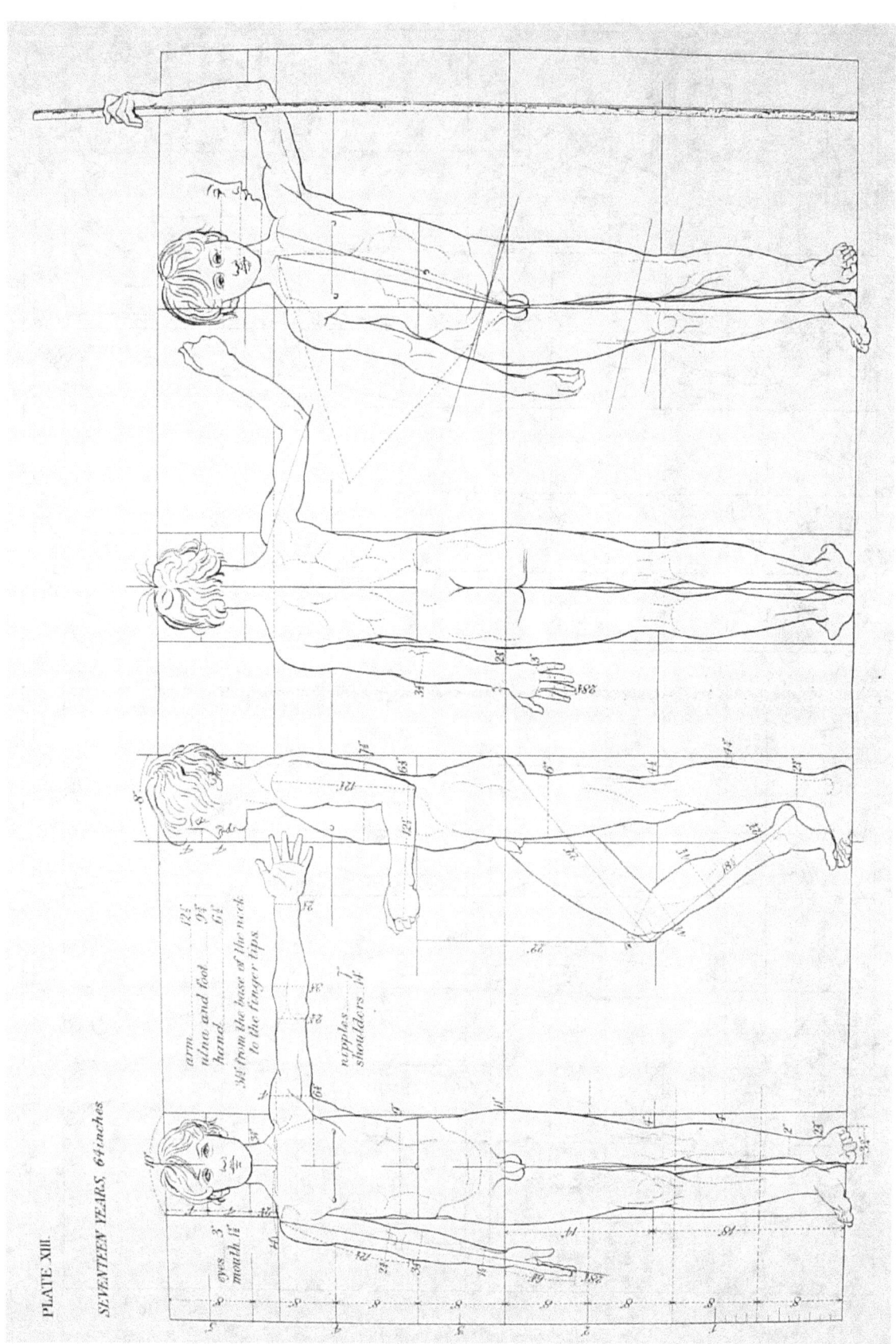

PLATE XIII.

SEVENTEEN YEARS, 64 inches.

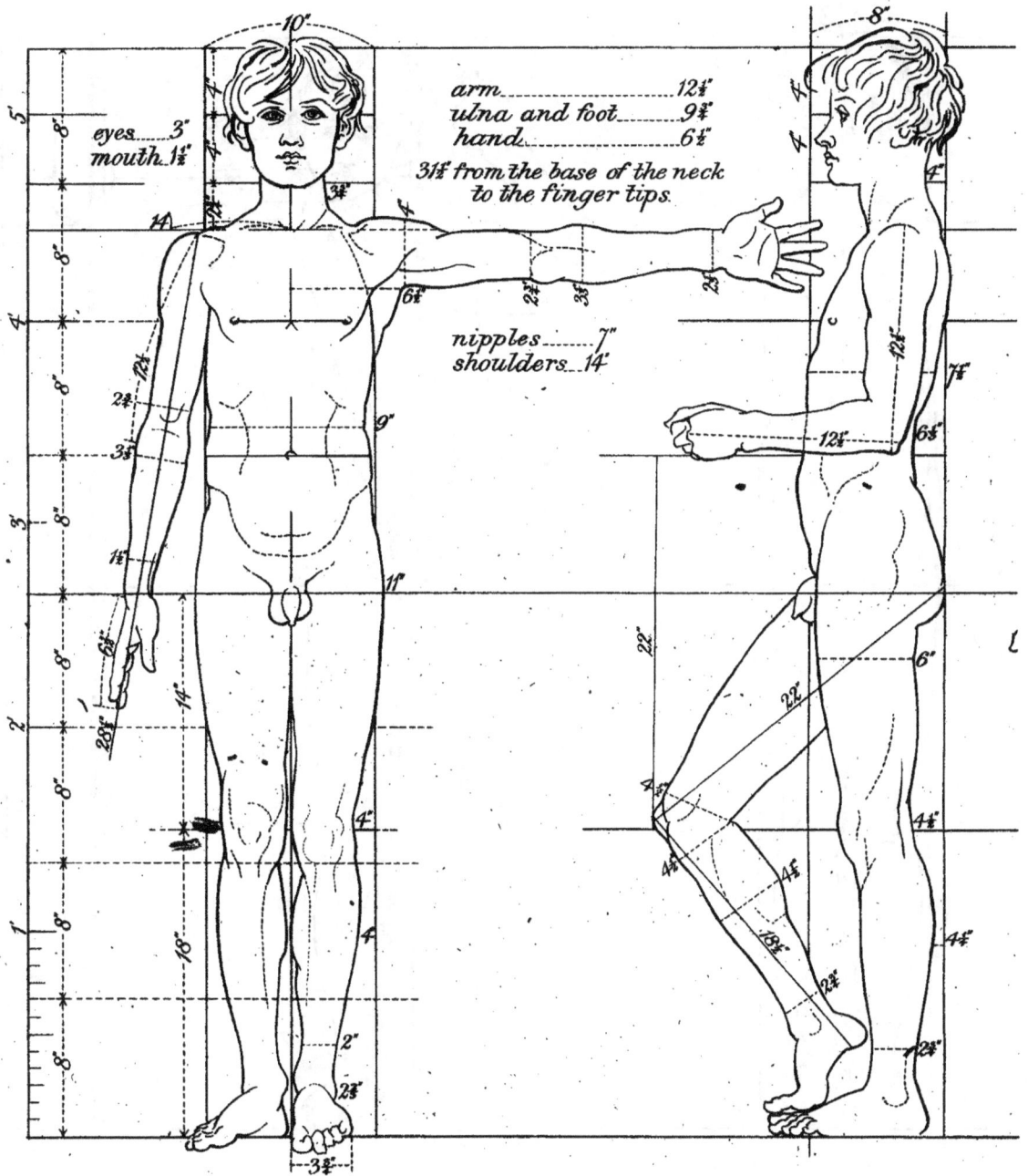

eyes .... 3"
mouth .. 1¾

arm .... 12¼"
ulna and foot .... 9¾"
hand .... 6¼"

31¾ from the base of the neck
to the finger tips.

nipples .... 7"
shoulders .. 14"

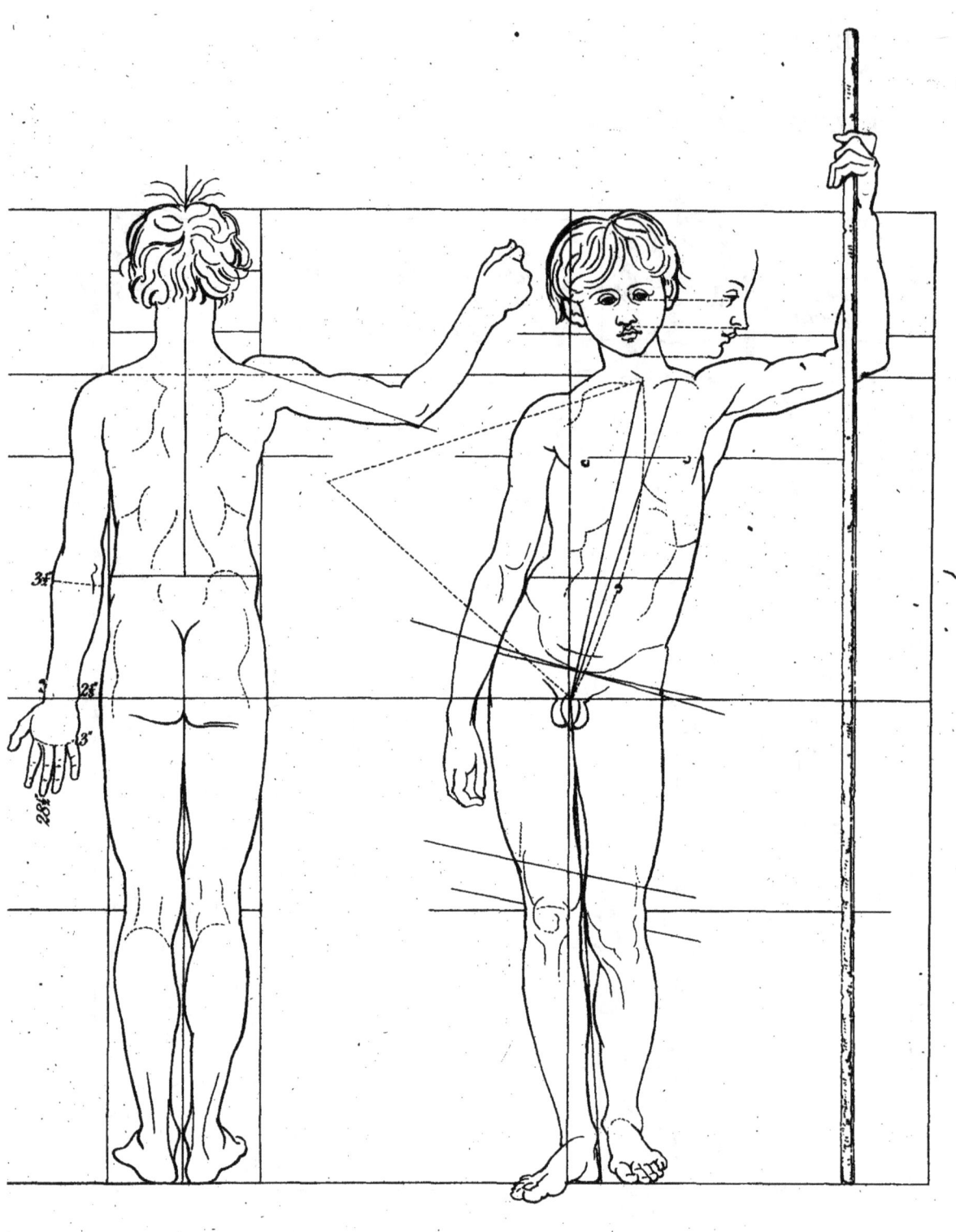

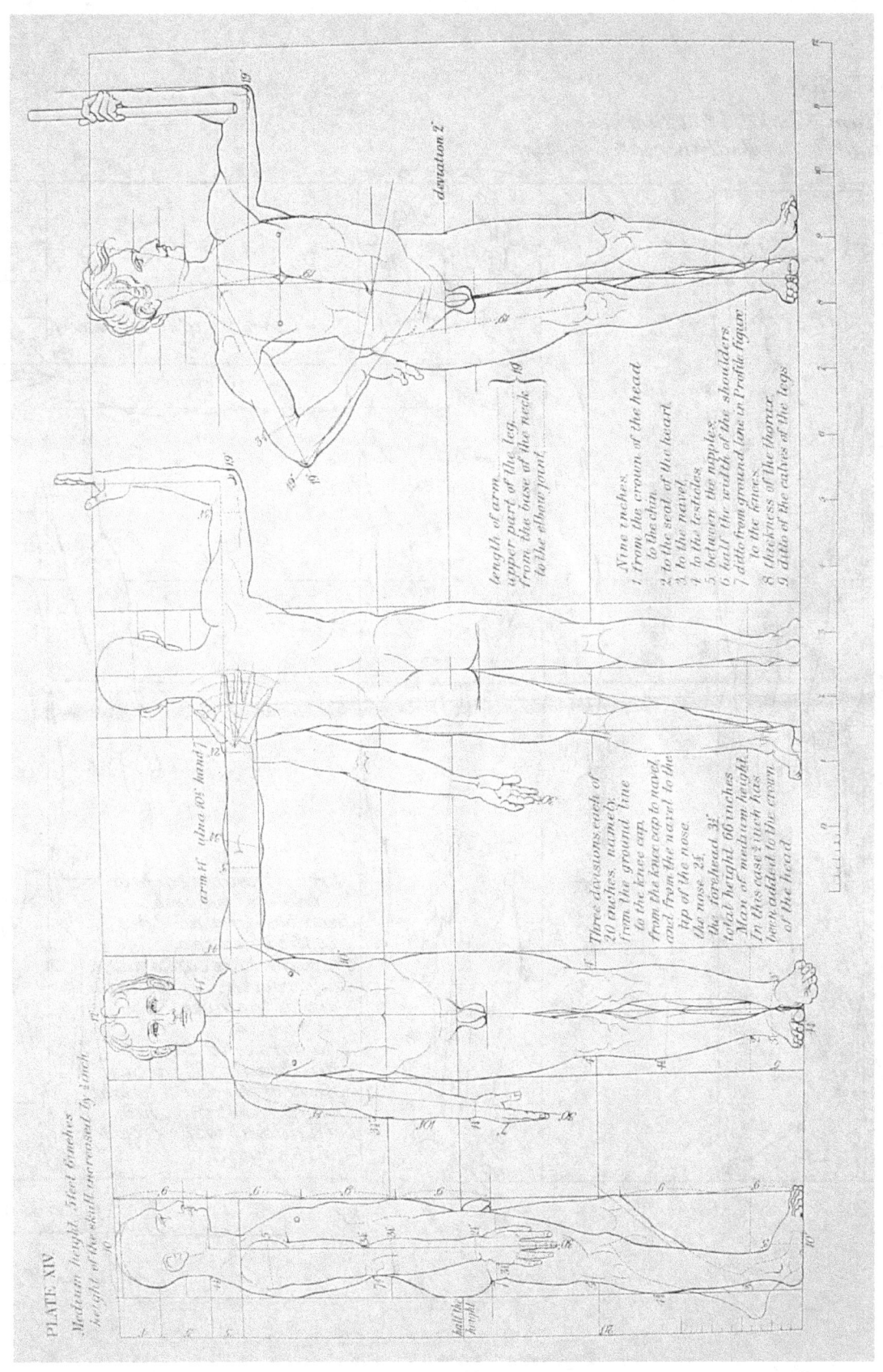

PLATE XIV

Medium height, 5 feet 6 inches

height of the skull increased by 1 inch

length of arm,
upper part of the leg,
from the base of the neck
to the elbow joint.

deviation 2"

Nine inches.
1. From the crown of the head
   to the chin.
2. to the seat of the heart
3. to the navel.
4. to the testicles
5. between the nipples;
6. half the width of the shoulders
7. ditto from ground line in Profile figure
   to the knees.
8. thickness of the thorax
9. ditto of the calves of the legs

Three divisions each of
20 inches, named;
from the ground line
to the knee cap.
from the knee cap to navel.
and from the navel to the
top of the nose.
the nose 2½,
the forehead 3½.
total height 66 inches.
Man of medium height.
In this case ¾ inch has
been added to the crown
of the head.

arm 31"   ulna 10" hand 1"

PLATE XIV.

Medium height, 5 feet 6 inches.
  height of the skull increased by ½ inch.

arm 14″ ulna 10½″ hand 7″

half the
height

Three divisions, each of
20 inches, namely,
from the ground line
  to the knee cap,
from the knee cap to navel,
and from the navel to the
  tip of the nose:
the nose 2½,
  the forehead 3½,
total height 66 inches.
  Man of medium height.
In this case ½ inch has
been added to the crown
  of the head.

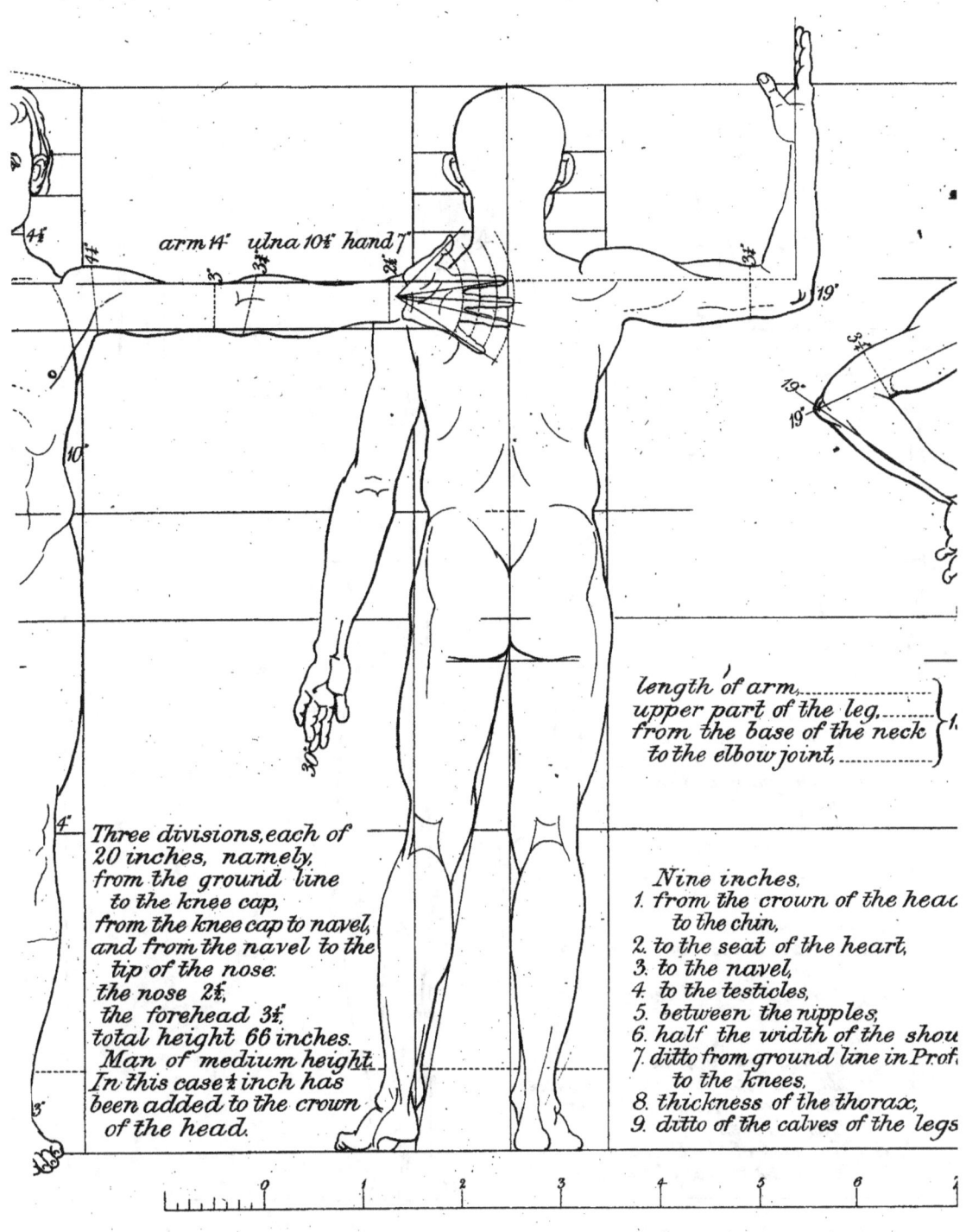

arm 14" ulna 10½" hand 7"

length of arm
upper part of the leg,
from the base of the neck
to the elbow joint,

Three divisions, each of
20 inches, namely,
from the ground line
to the knee cap,
from the knee cap to navel,
and from the navel to the
tip of the nose:
the nose 2½,
the forehead 3½,
total height 66 inches.
Man of medium height.
In this case ½ inch has
been added to the crown
of the head.

Nine inches.
1. from the crown of the head
to the chin,
2. to the seat of the heart,
3. to the navel,
4. to the testicles,
5. between the nipples,
6. half the width of the shou
7. ditto from ground line in Prof.
to the knees,
8. thickness of the thorax,
9. ditto of the calves of the legs

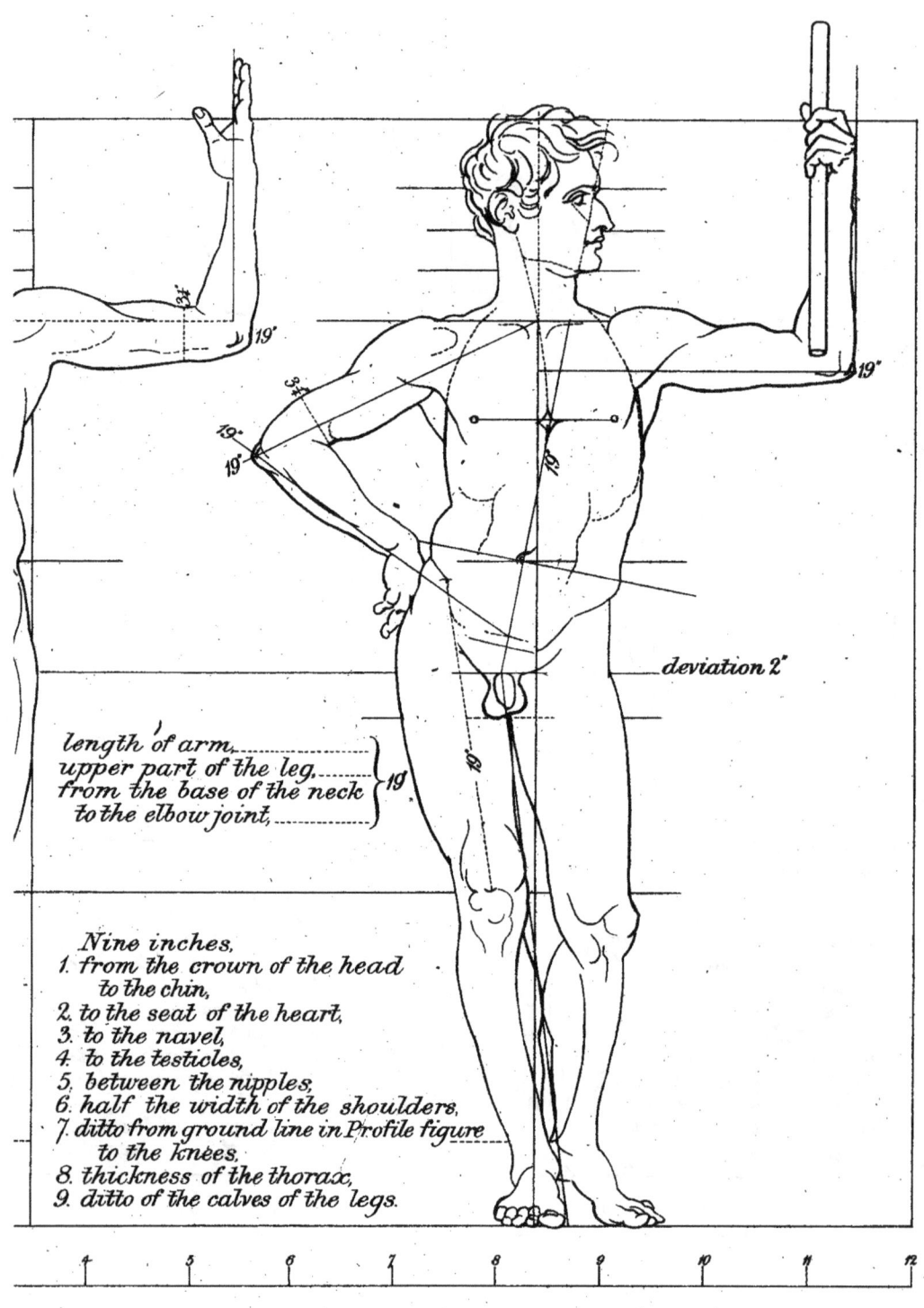

length of arm,
upper part of the leg,
from the base of the neck
to the elbow joint,
} 19

deviation 2"

19°

Nine inches,
1. from the crown of the head
    to the chin,
2. to the seat of the heart,
3. to the navel,
4. to the testicles,
5. between the nipples,
6. half the width of the shoulders,
7. ditto from ground line in Profile figure
    to the knees,
8. thickness of the thorax,
9. ditto of the calves of the legs.

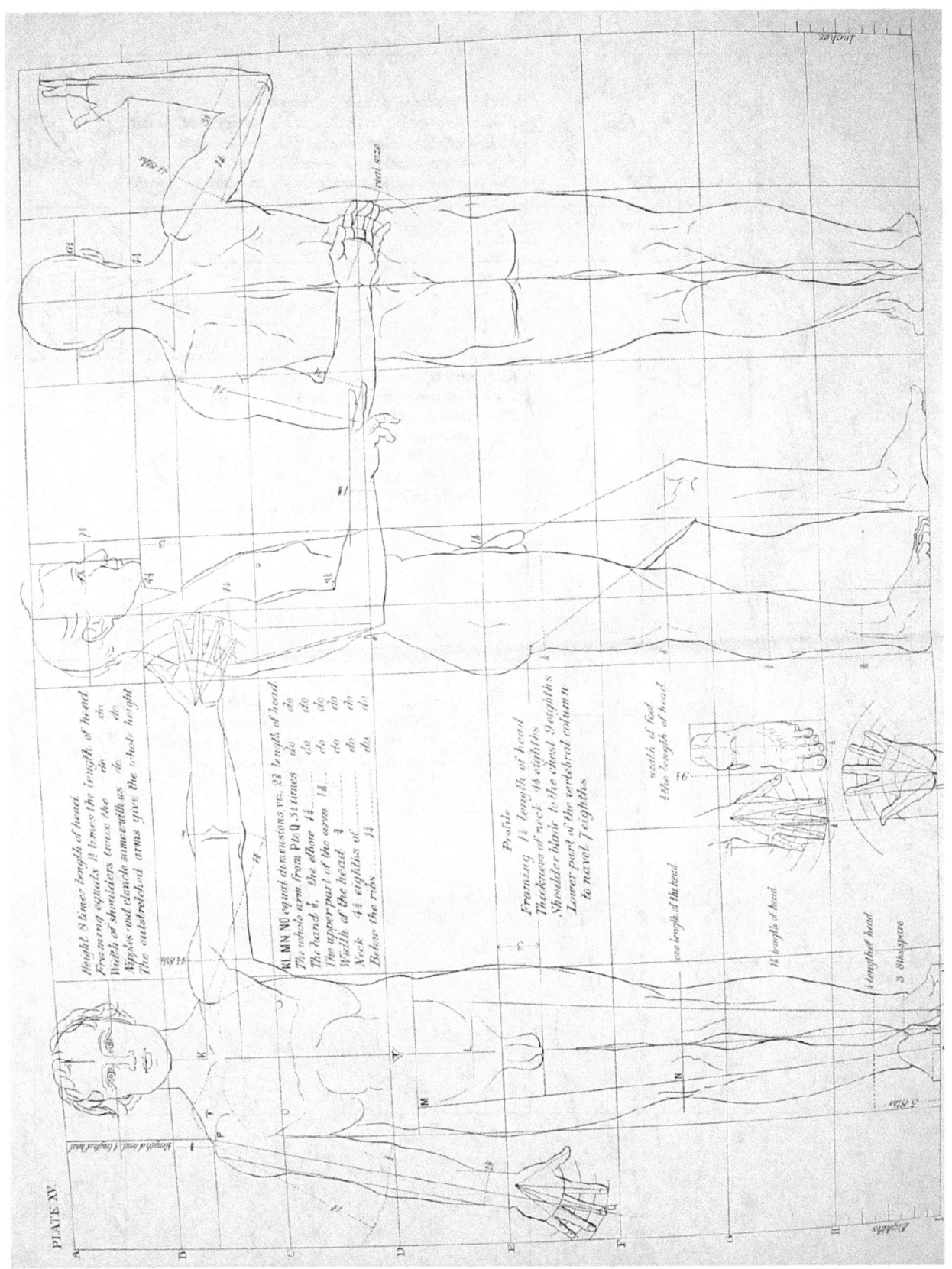

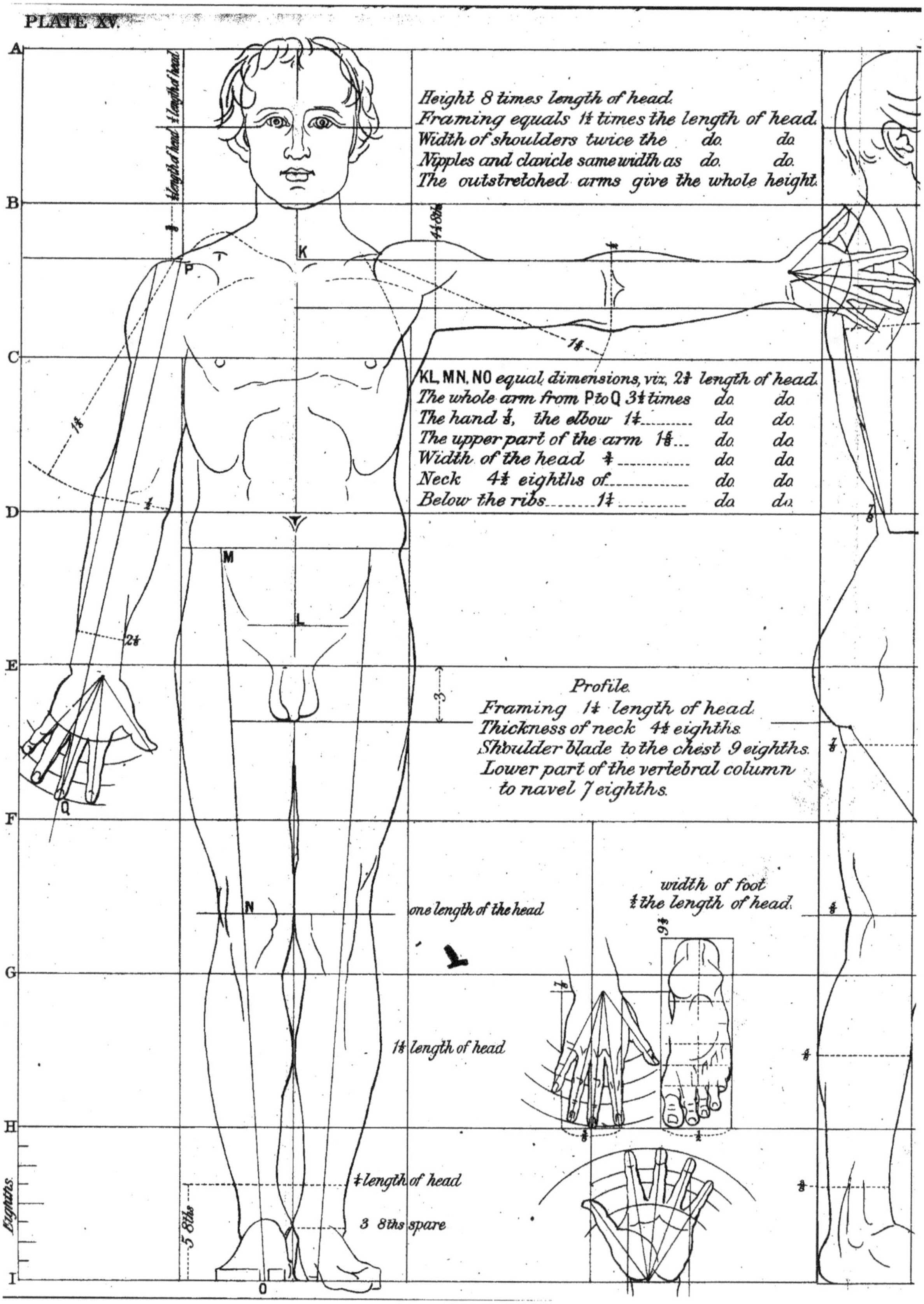
PLATE XV.
Height 8 times length of head.
Framing equals 1¼ times the length of head.
Width of shoulders twice the do. do.
Nipples and clavicle same width as do. do.
The outstretched arms give the whole height.
KL, MN, NO equal dimensions, viz. 2¼ length of head.
The whole arm from P to Q 3¼ times do. do.
The hand ⅞, the elbow 1¼ do. do.
The upper part of the arm 1⅝ do. do.
Width of the head ¾ do. do.
Neck 4½ eighths of do. do.
Below the ribs 1¼ do. do.
Profile.
Framing 1¼ length of head.
Thickness of neck 4½ eighths.
Shoulder blade to the chest 9 eighths.
Lower part of the vertebral column to navel 7 eighths.
one length of the head
width of foot ⅜ the length of head.
1⅛ length of head
⅛ length of head
3 8ths spare
5 8ths
Eighths.
A
B
C
D
E
F
G
H
I
K
L
M
N
O
P
Q
T

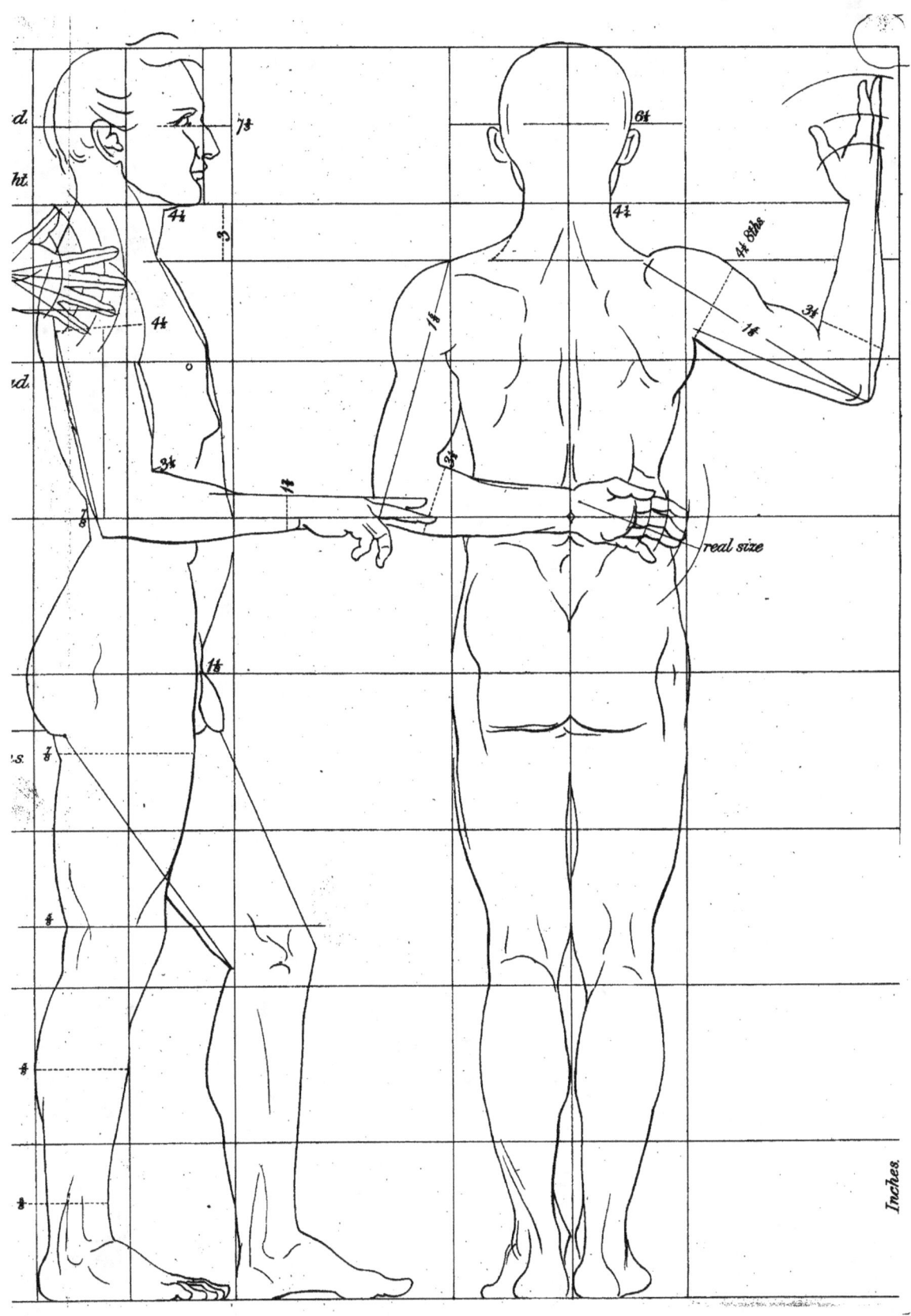

79

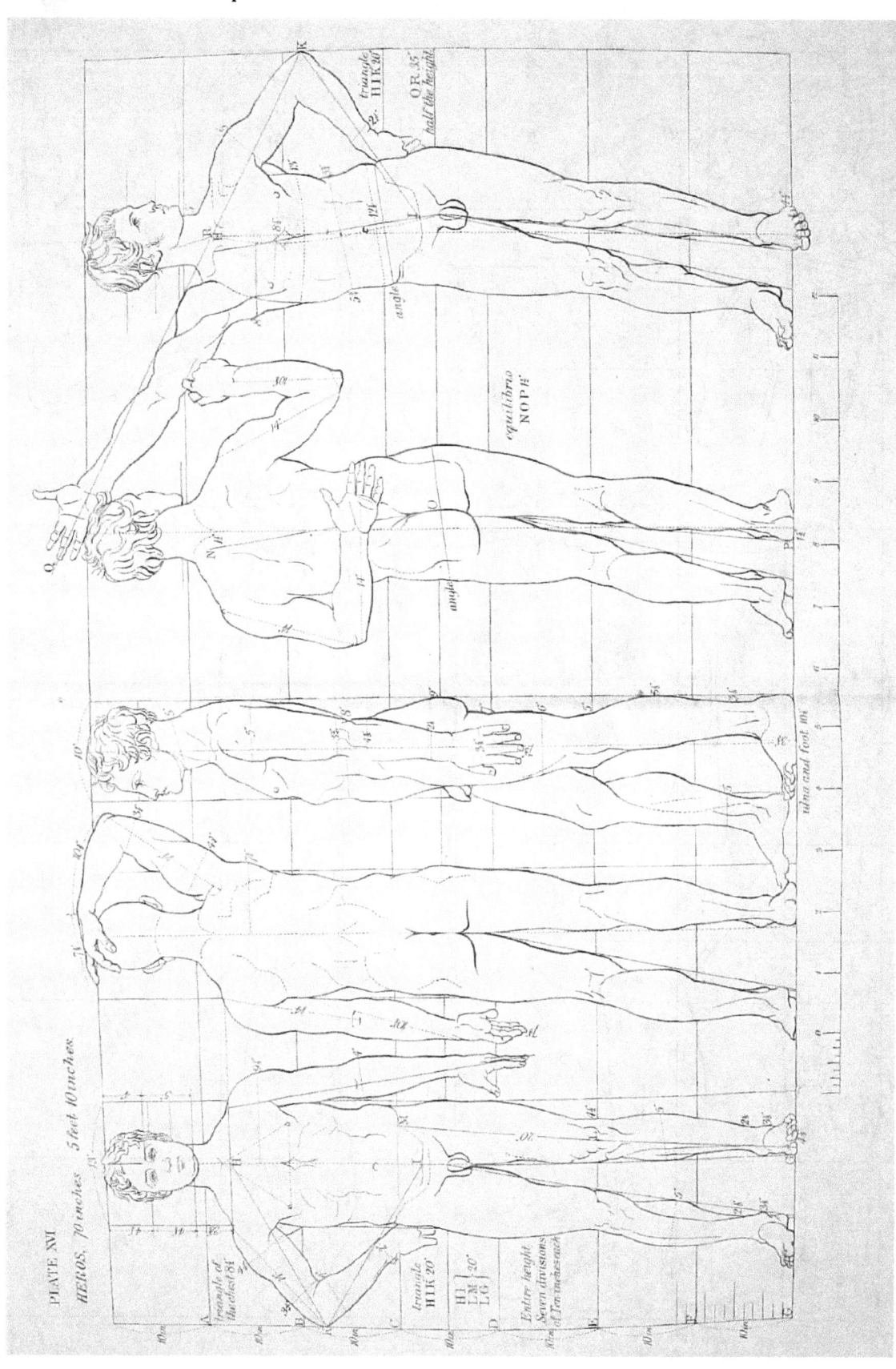

PLATE XVI.

HEROS, 70 inches. 5 feet 10 inches.

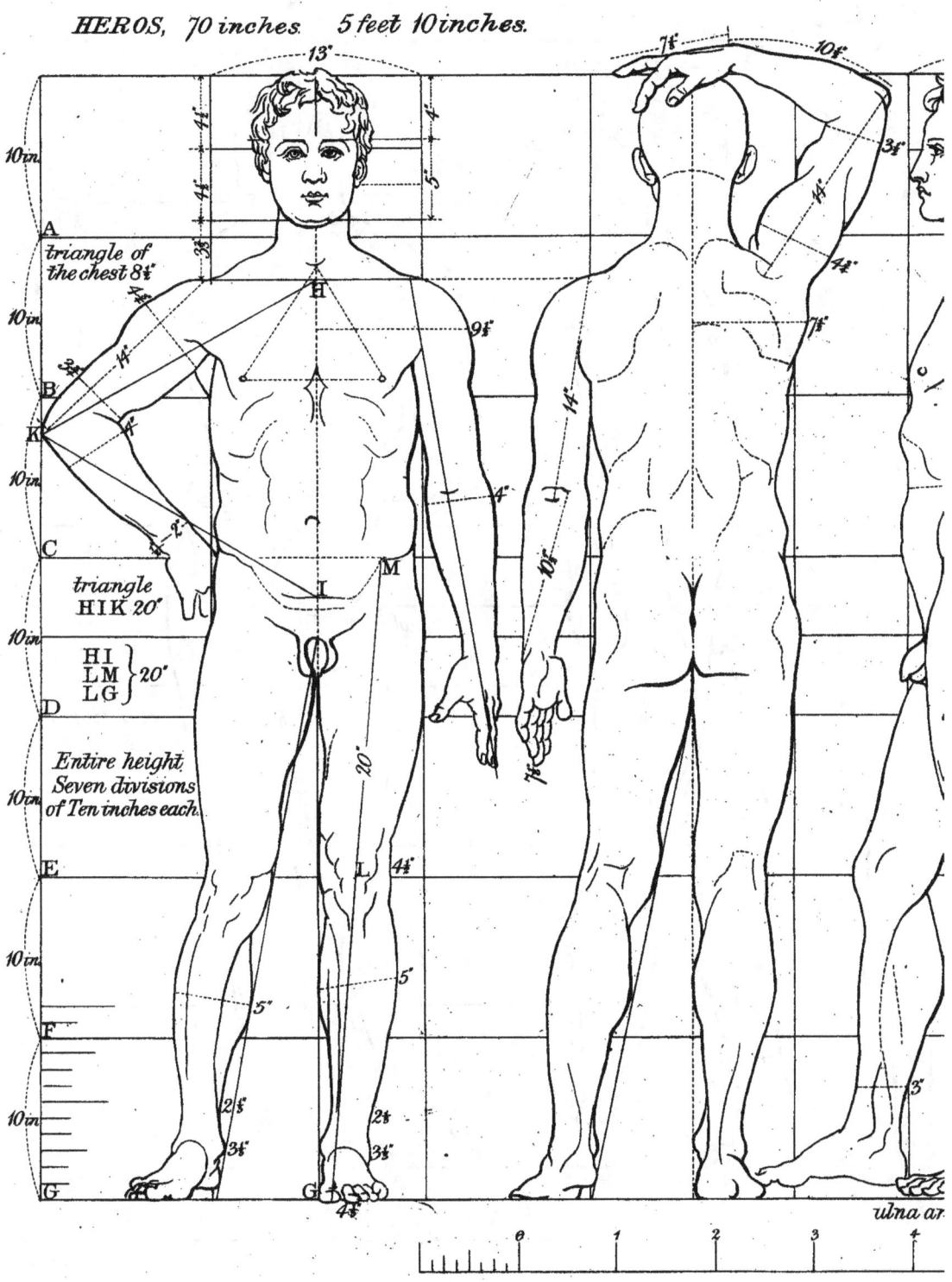

81

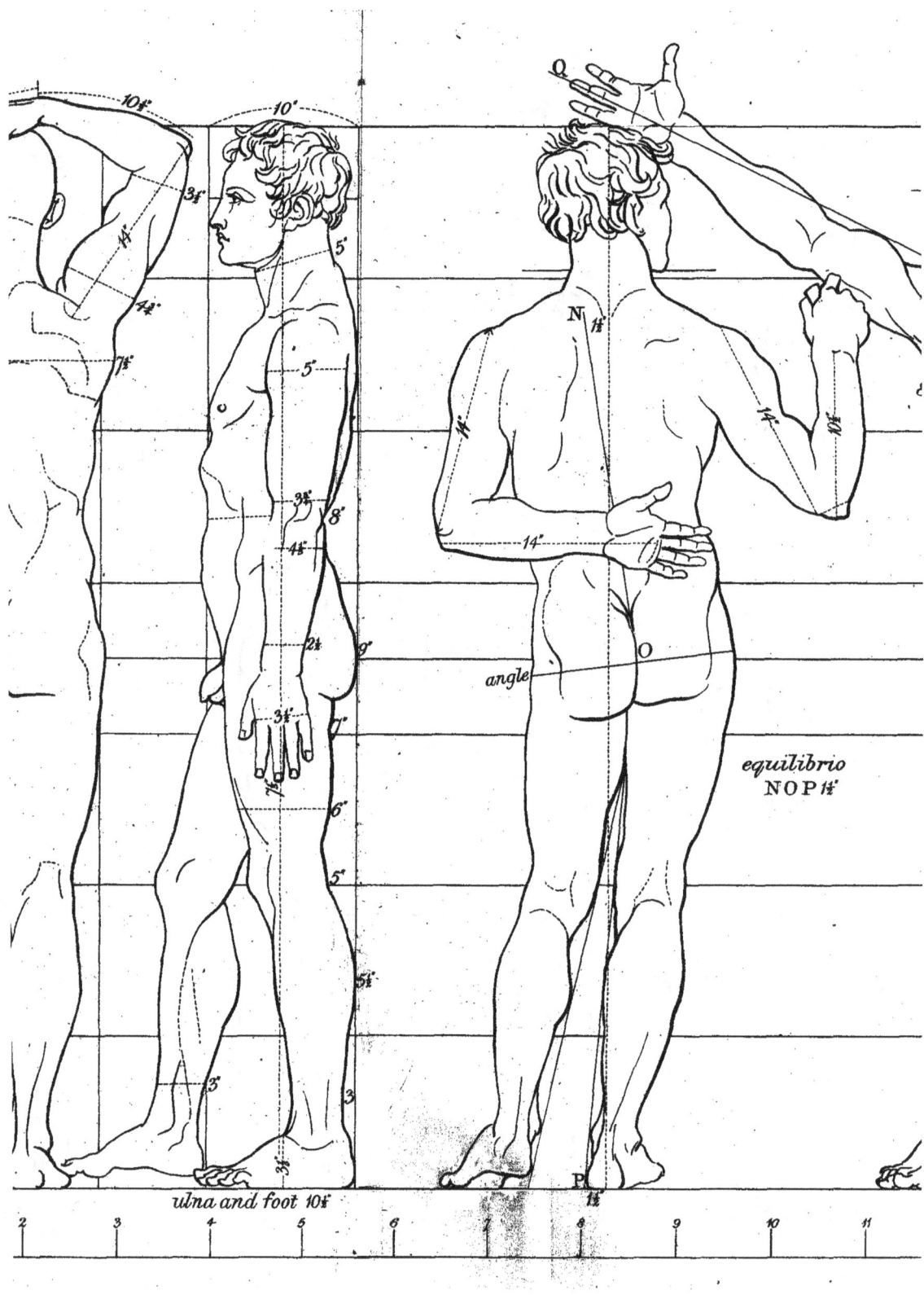

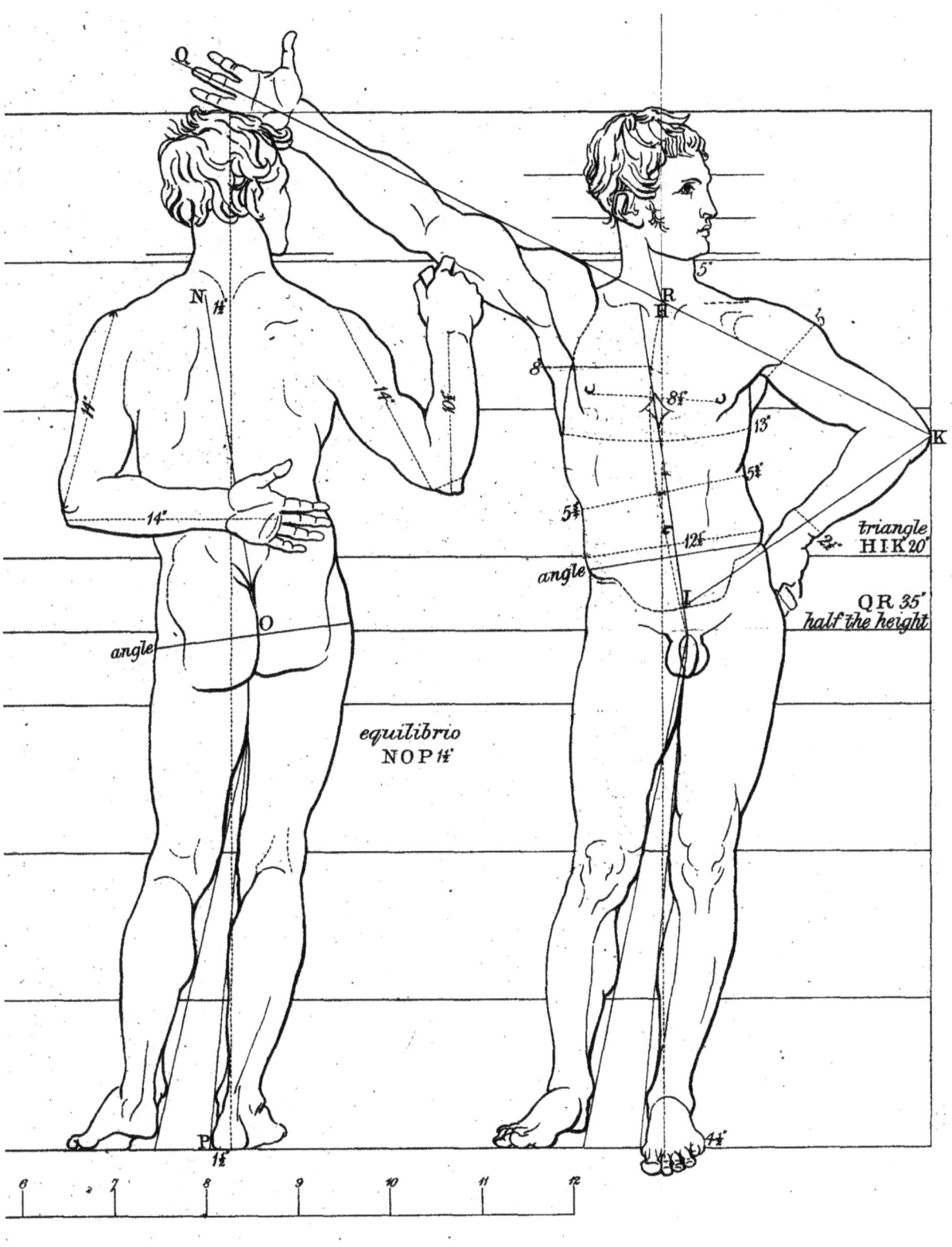

triangle
H I K 20"

Q R 35"
half the height

equilibrio
N O P 1½"

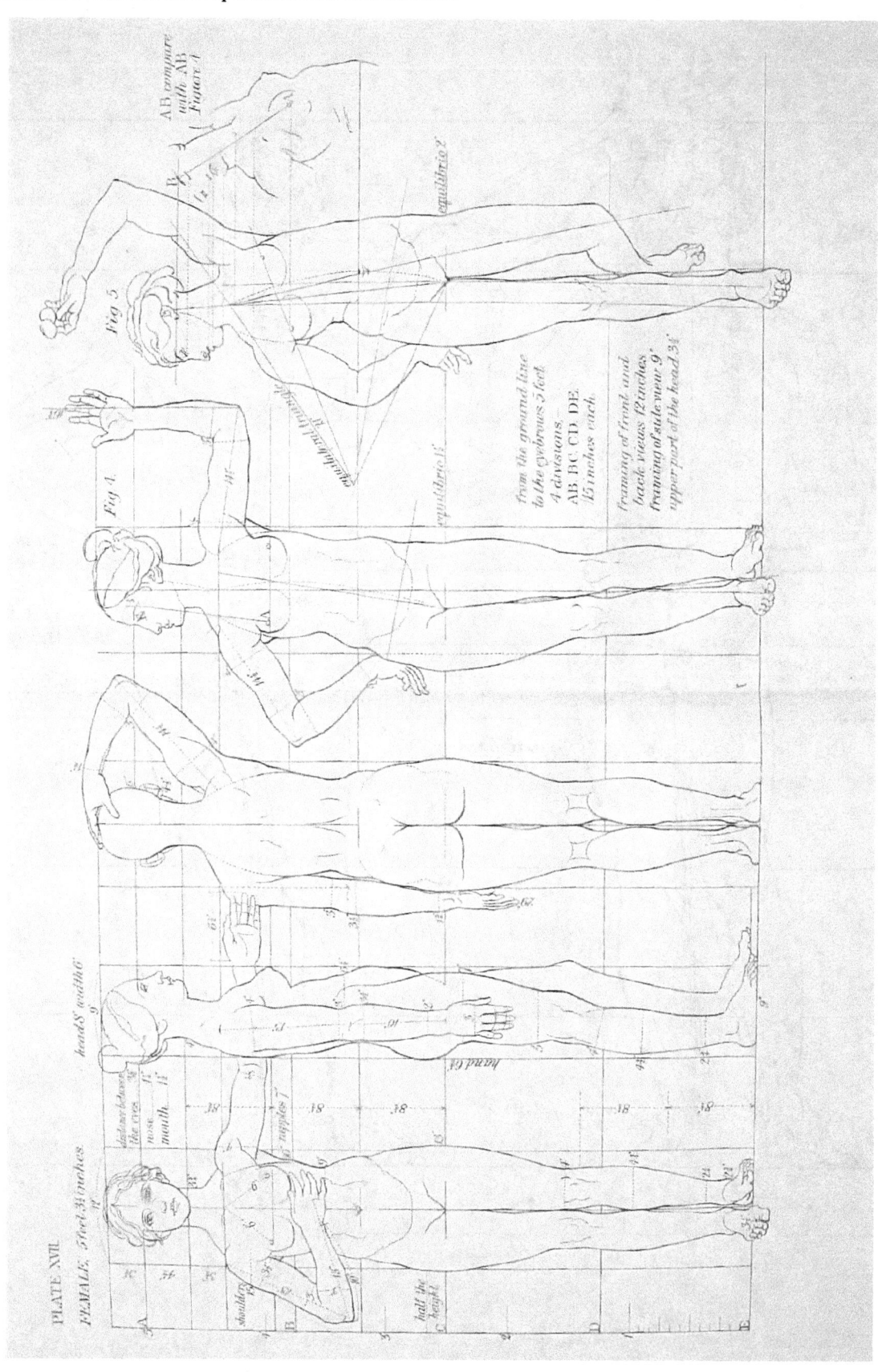

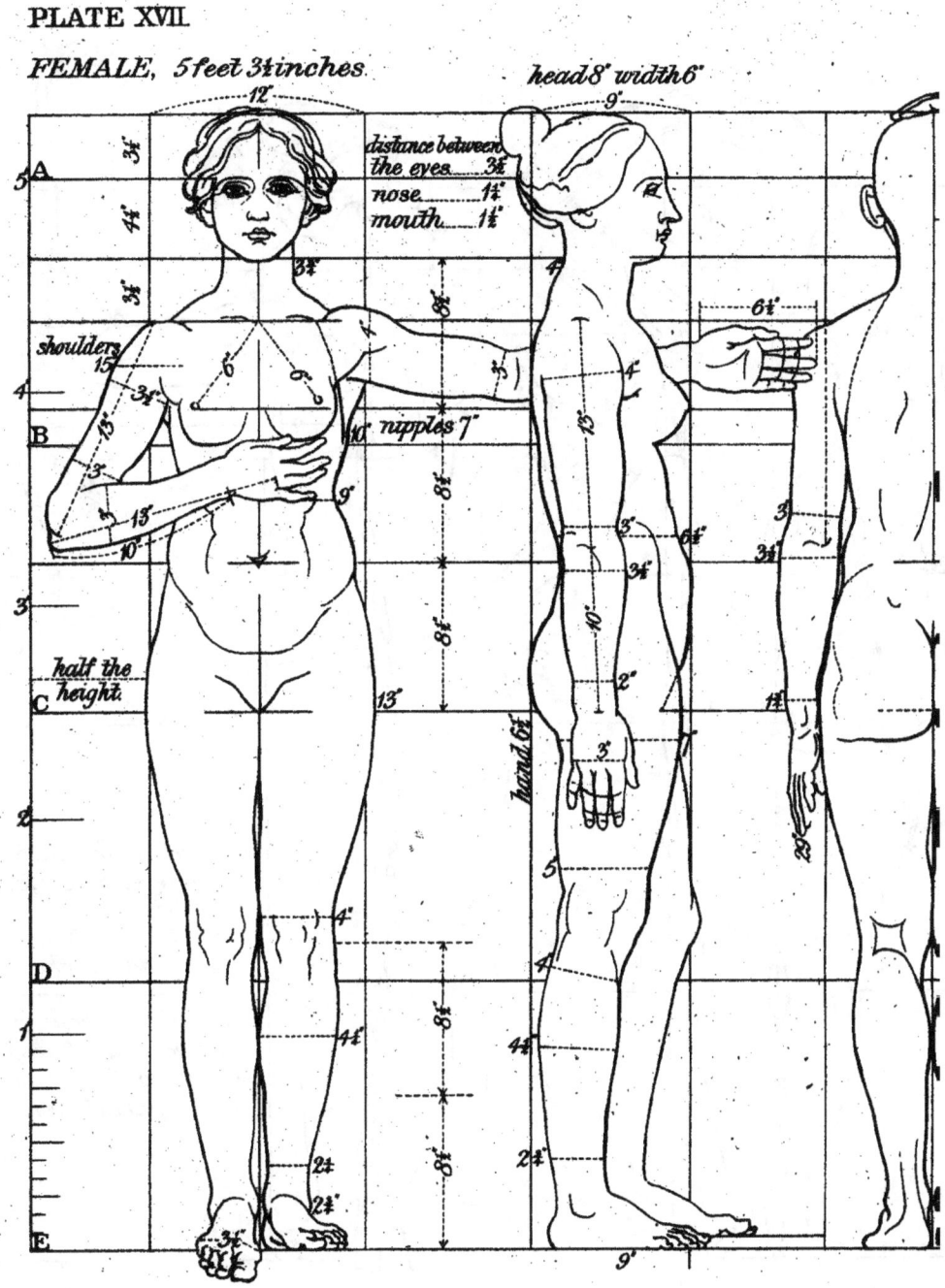

PLATE XVII

FEMALE, 5 feet 3¼ inches.   head 8" width 6"

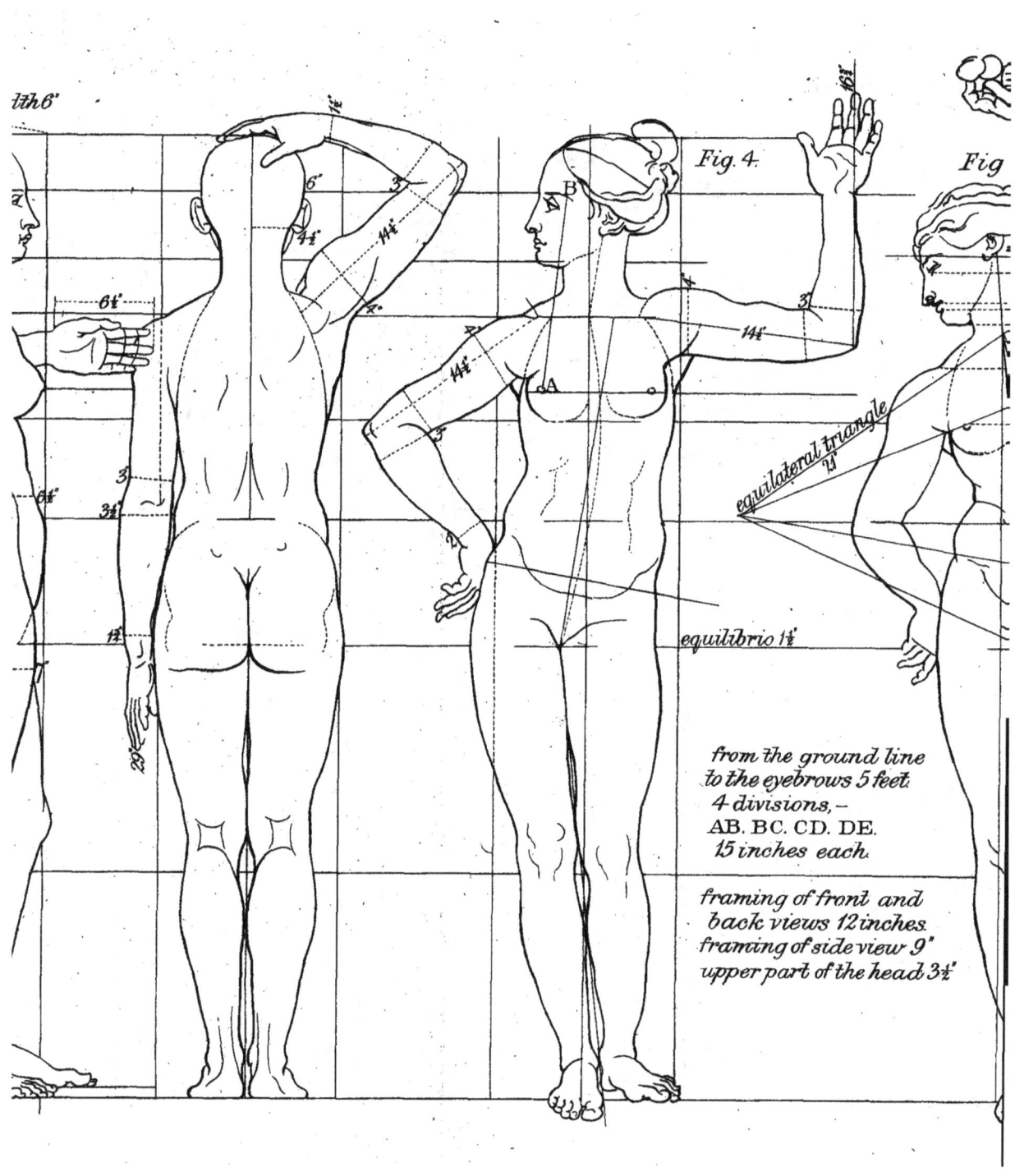

Fig. 4.

Fig

equilateral triangle

equilibrio 1¼

from the ground line
to the eyebrows 5 feet
4 divisions, —
AB. BC. CD. DE.
15 inches each.

framing of front and
back views 12 inches.
framing of side view 9"
upper part of the head 3½"

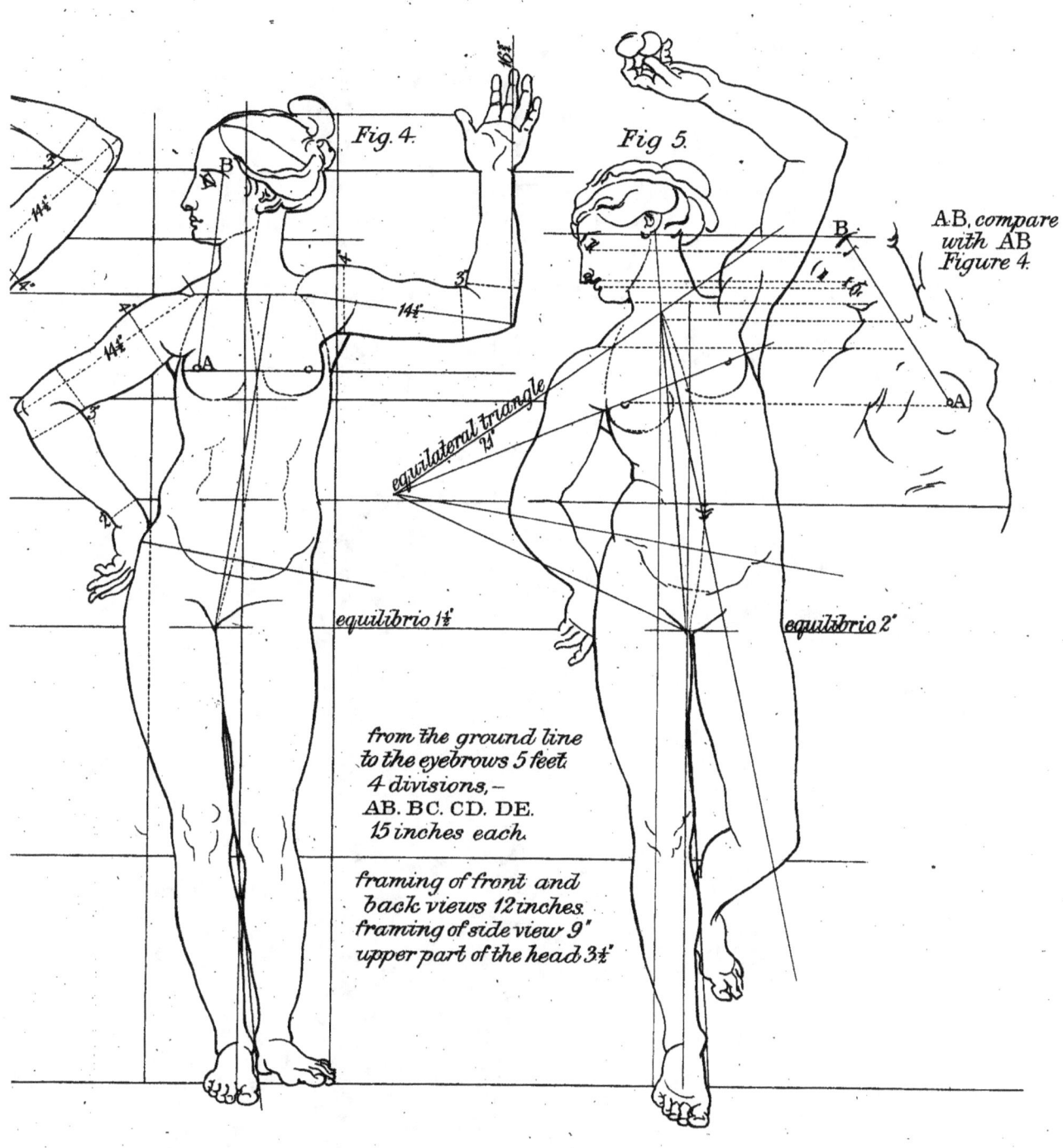

Fig. 4.

Fig 5.

AB, compare
with AB
Figure 4.

equilateral triangle

equilibrio 1½

equilibrio 2"

from the ground line
to the eyebrows 5 feet.
4 divisions, —
AB. BC. CD. DE.
15 inches each.

framing of front and
back views 12 inches.
framing of side view 9"
upper part of the head 3¼"

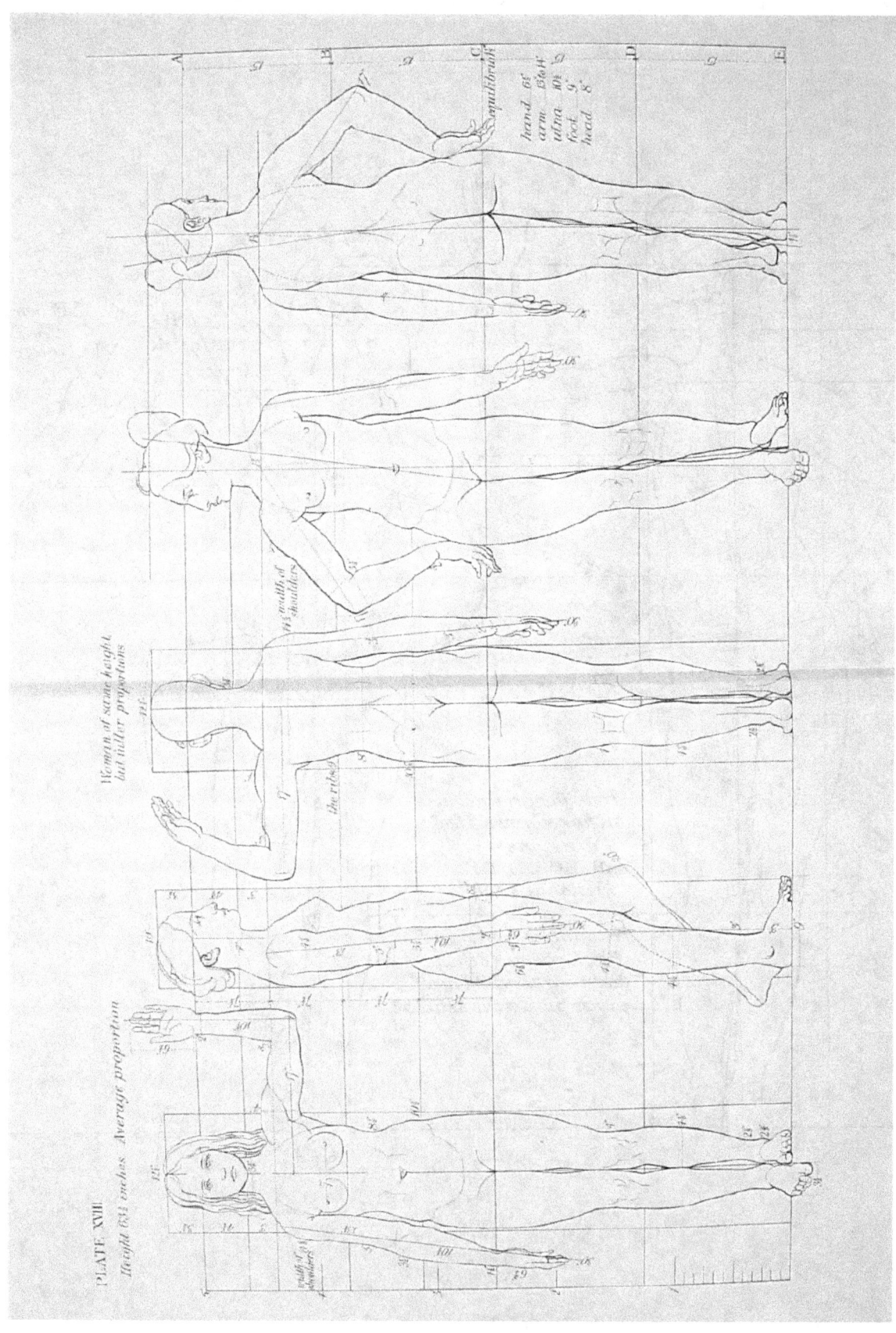

PLATE XVIII.

Height 63¼ inches. Average proportion.

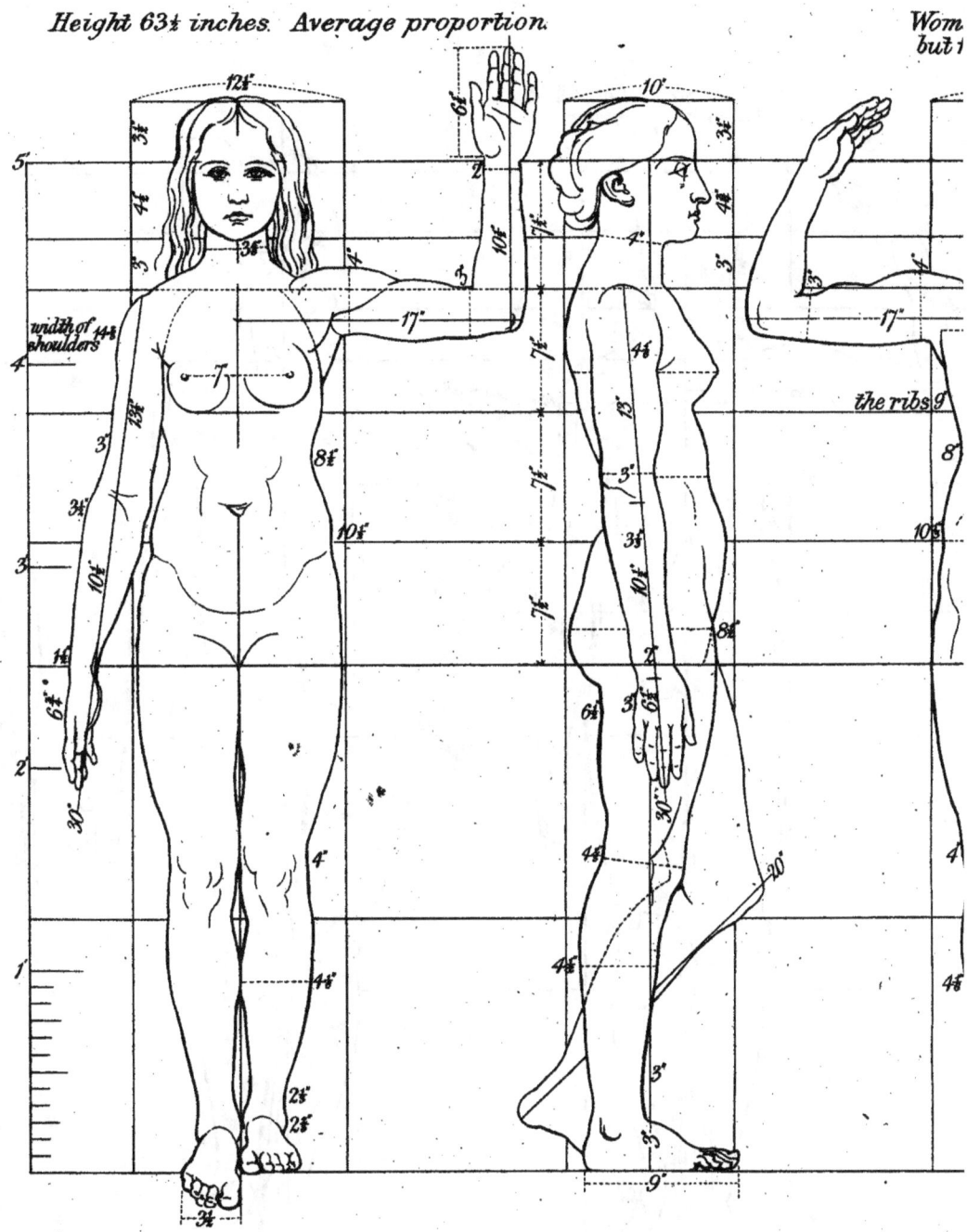

Wom
but t

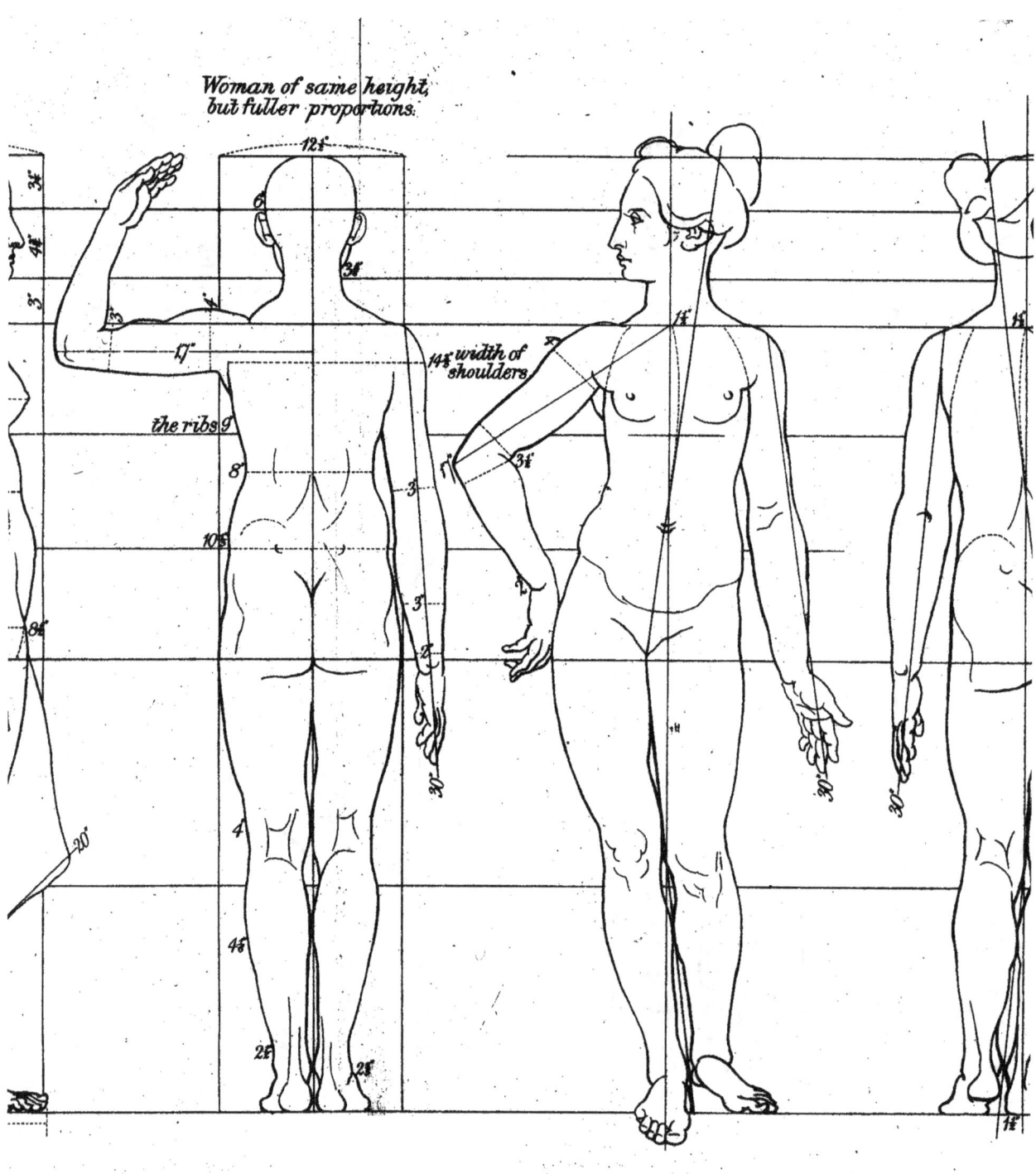

Woman of same height,
but fuller proportions.

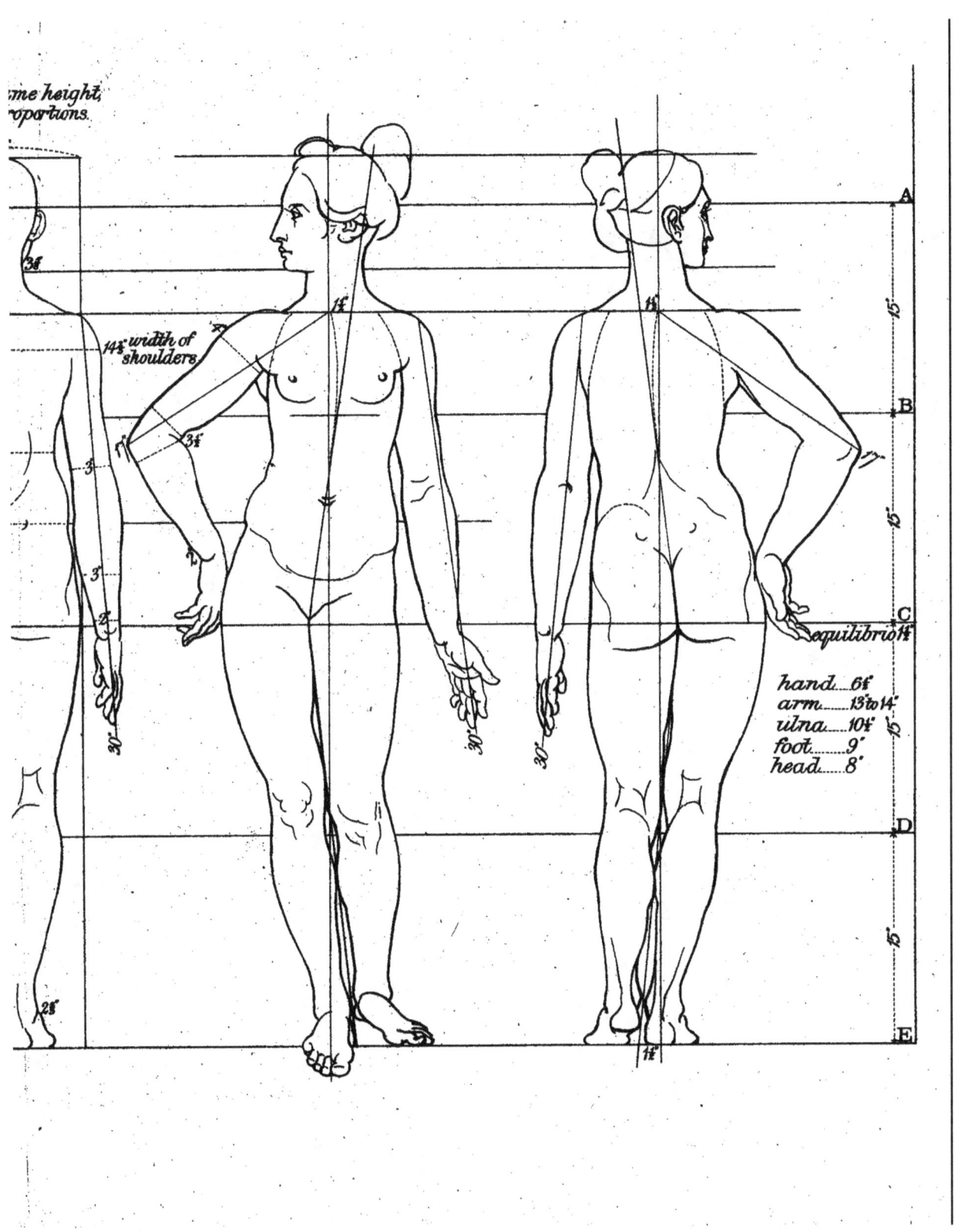

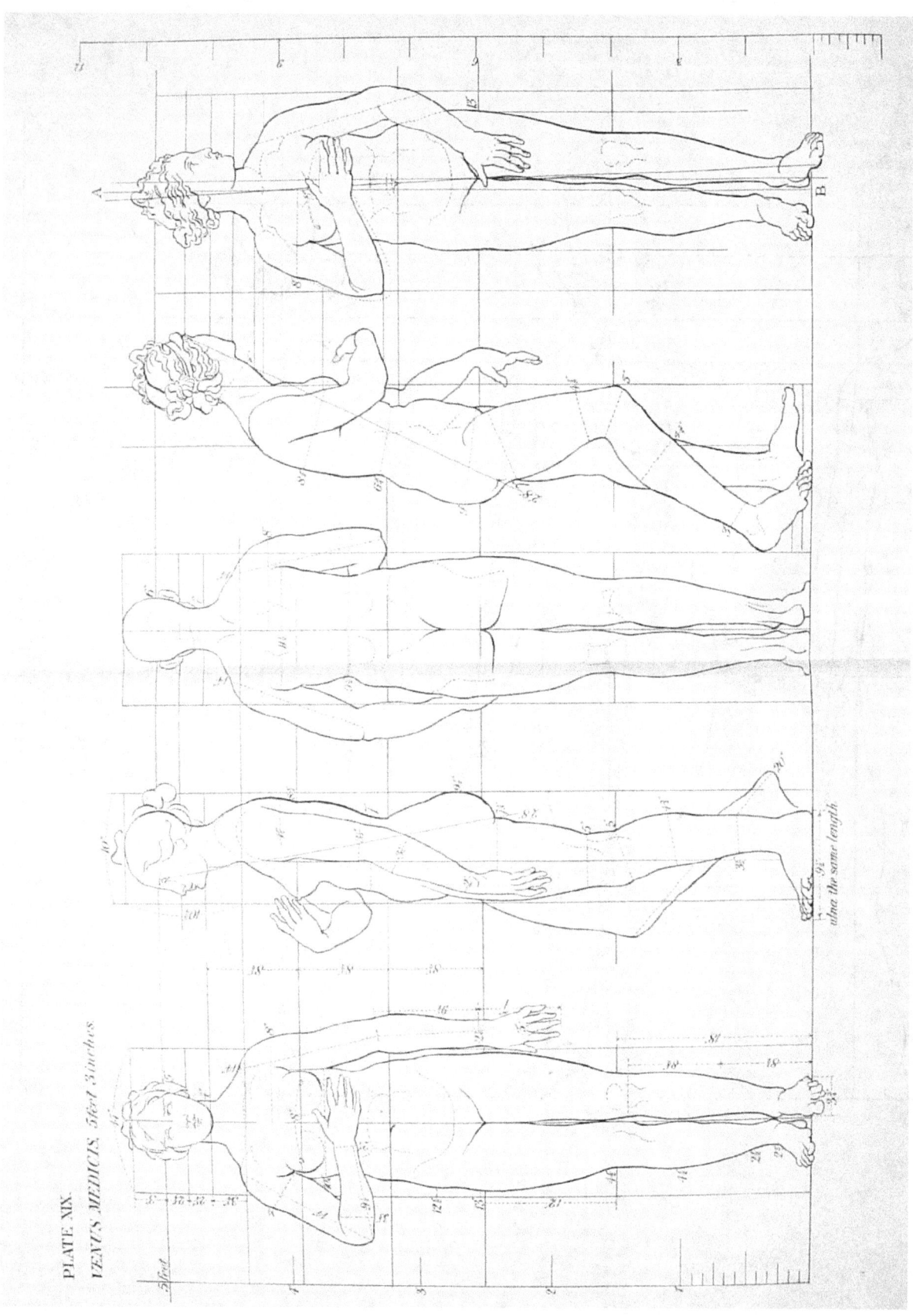

PLATE XIX.
VENUS MEDICIS, 5feet 3inches.

PLATE XIX.

VENUS MEDICIS, 5feet 3inches.

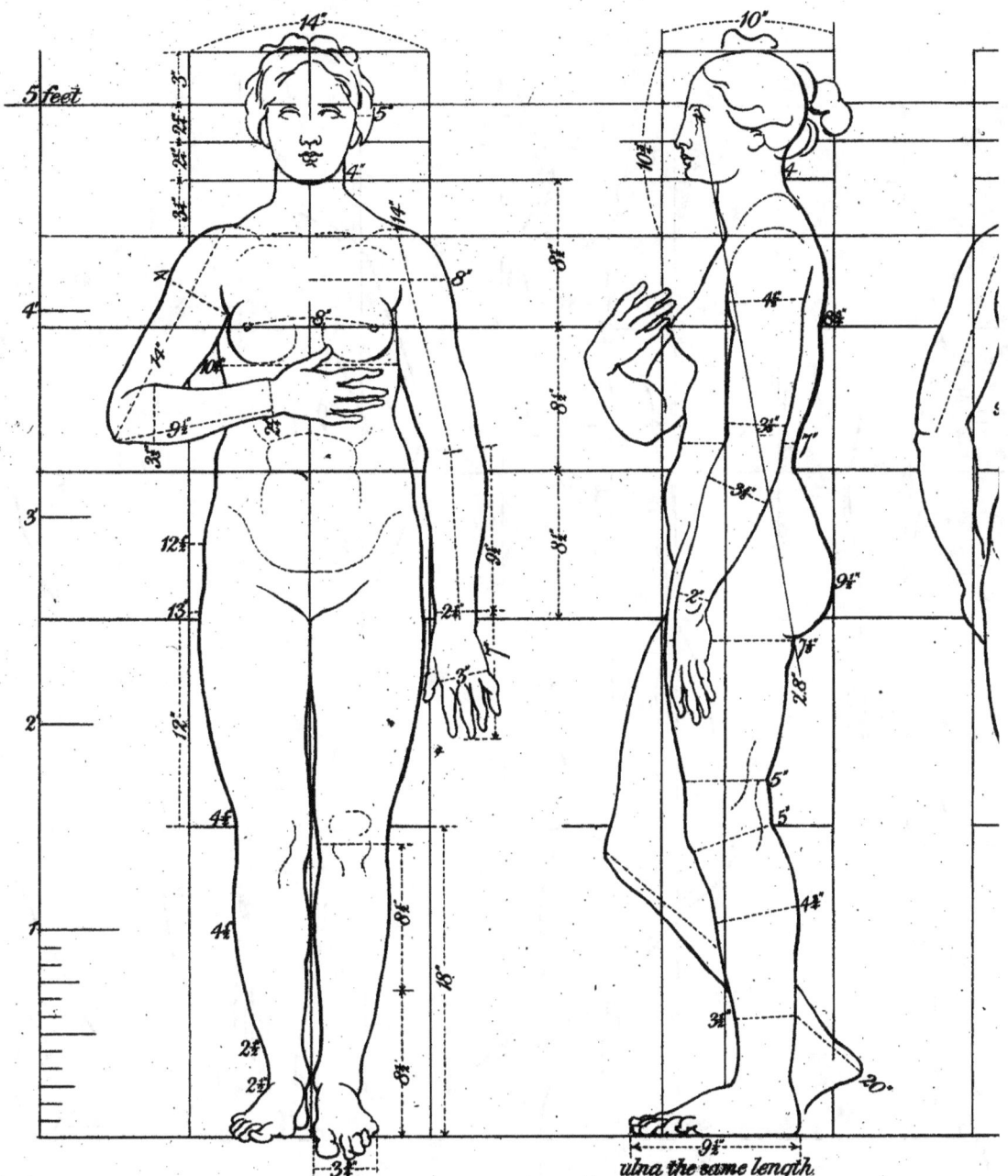

ulna the same length.

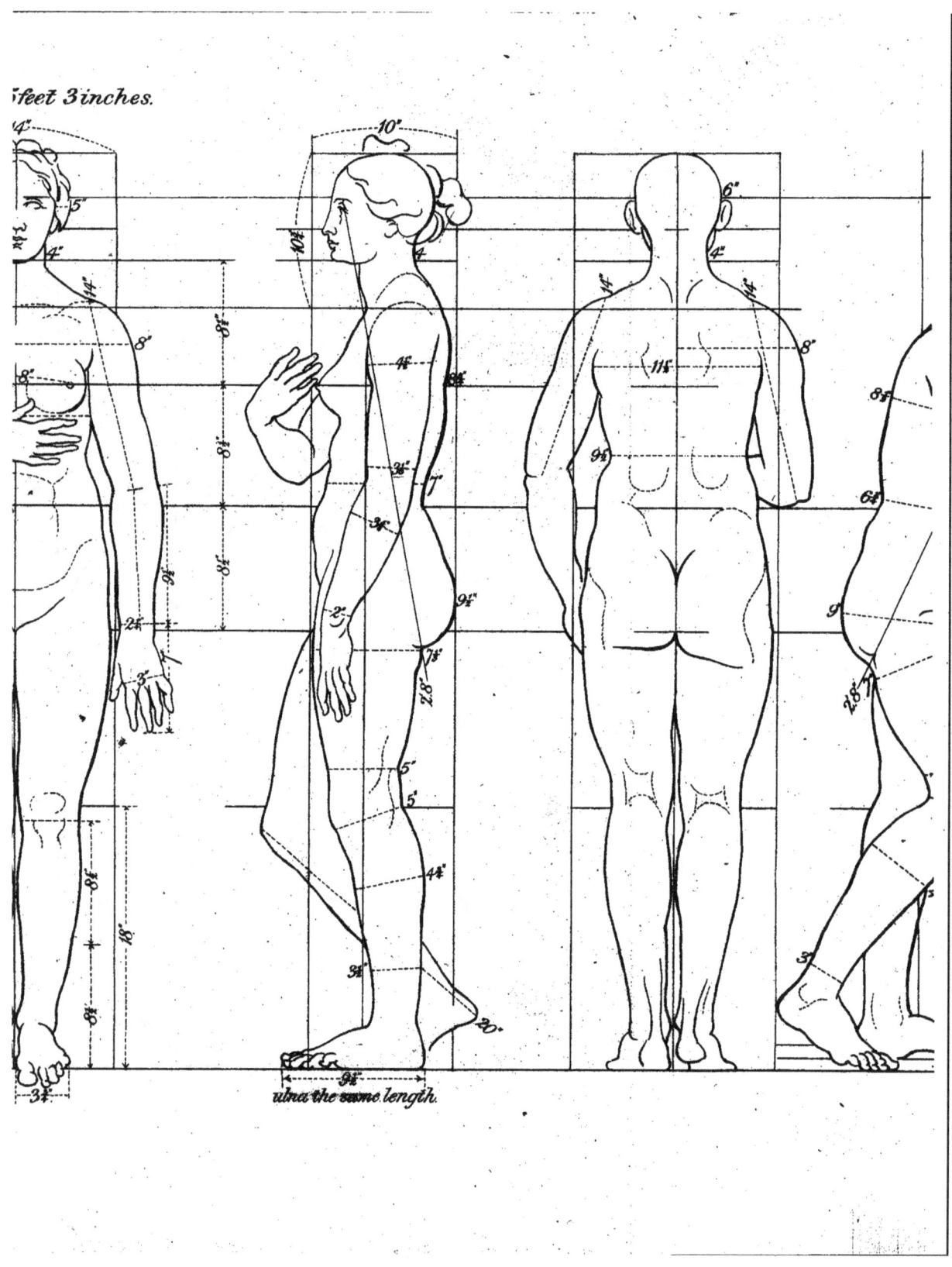

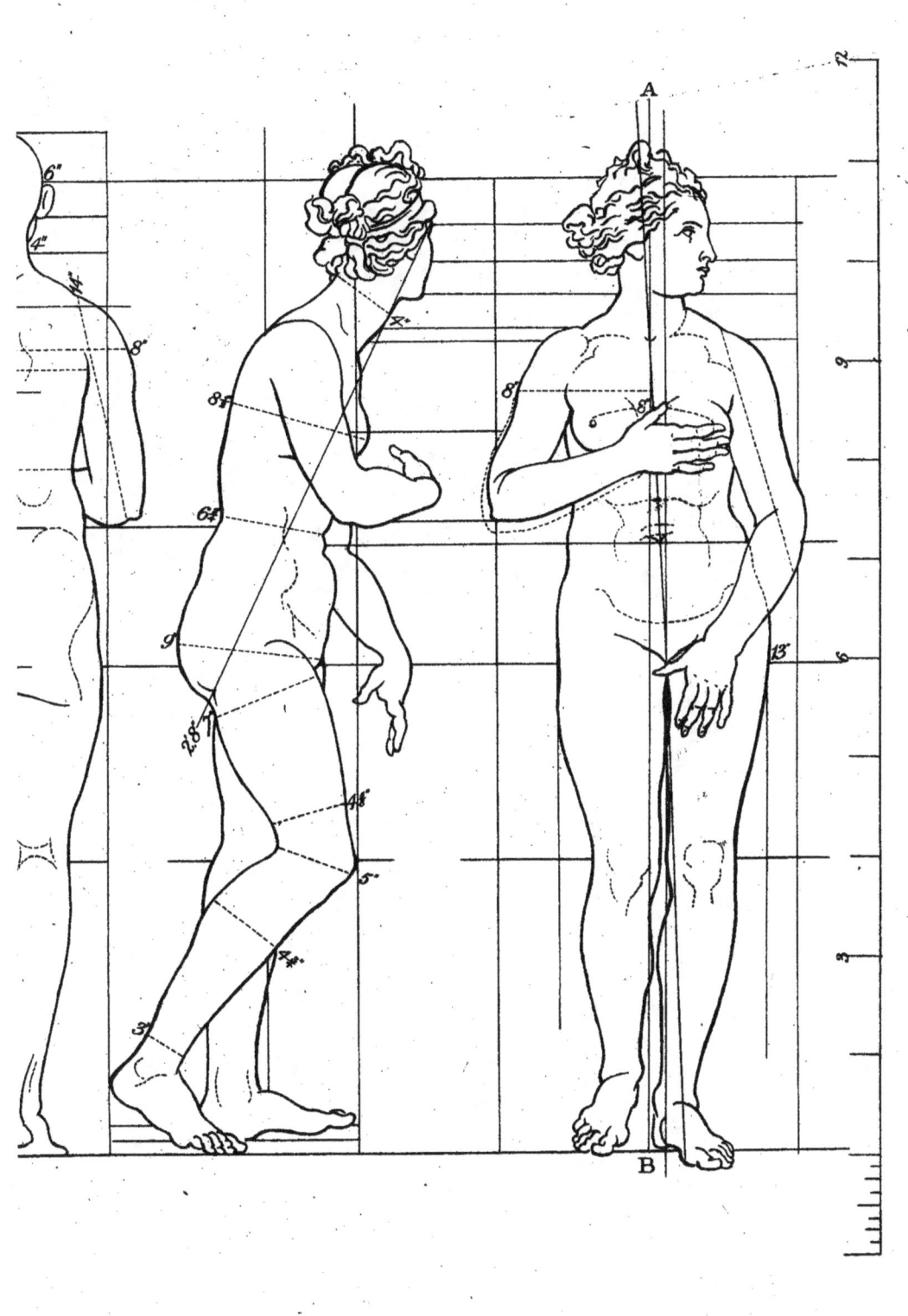

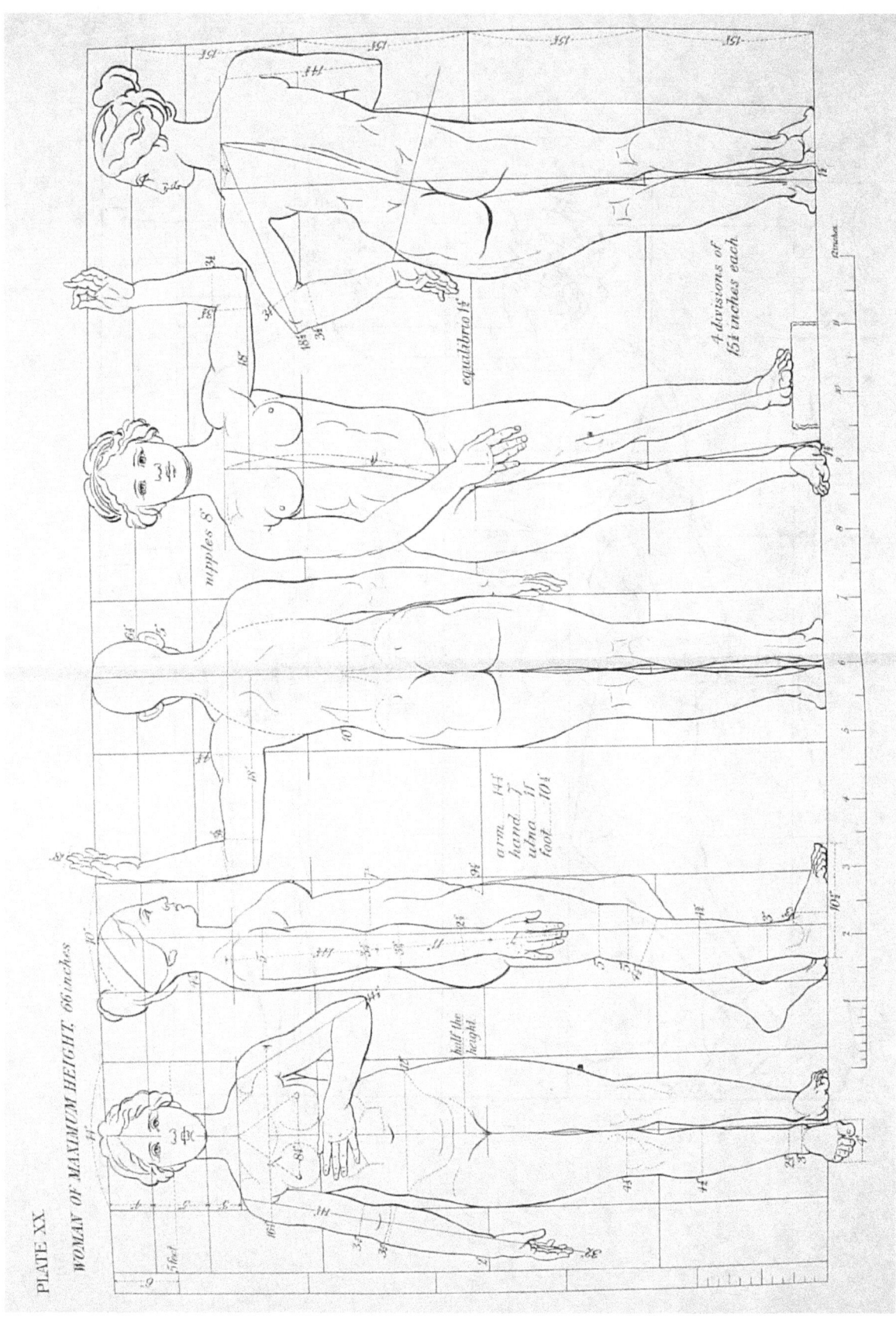

PLATE XX.

WOMAN OF MAXIMUM HEIGHT, 66 inches.

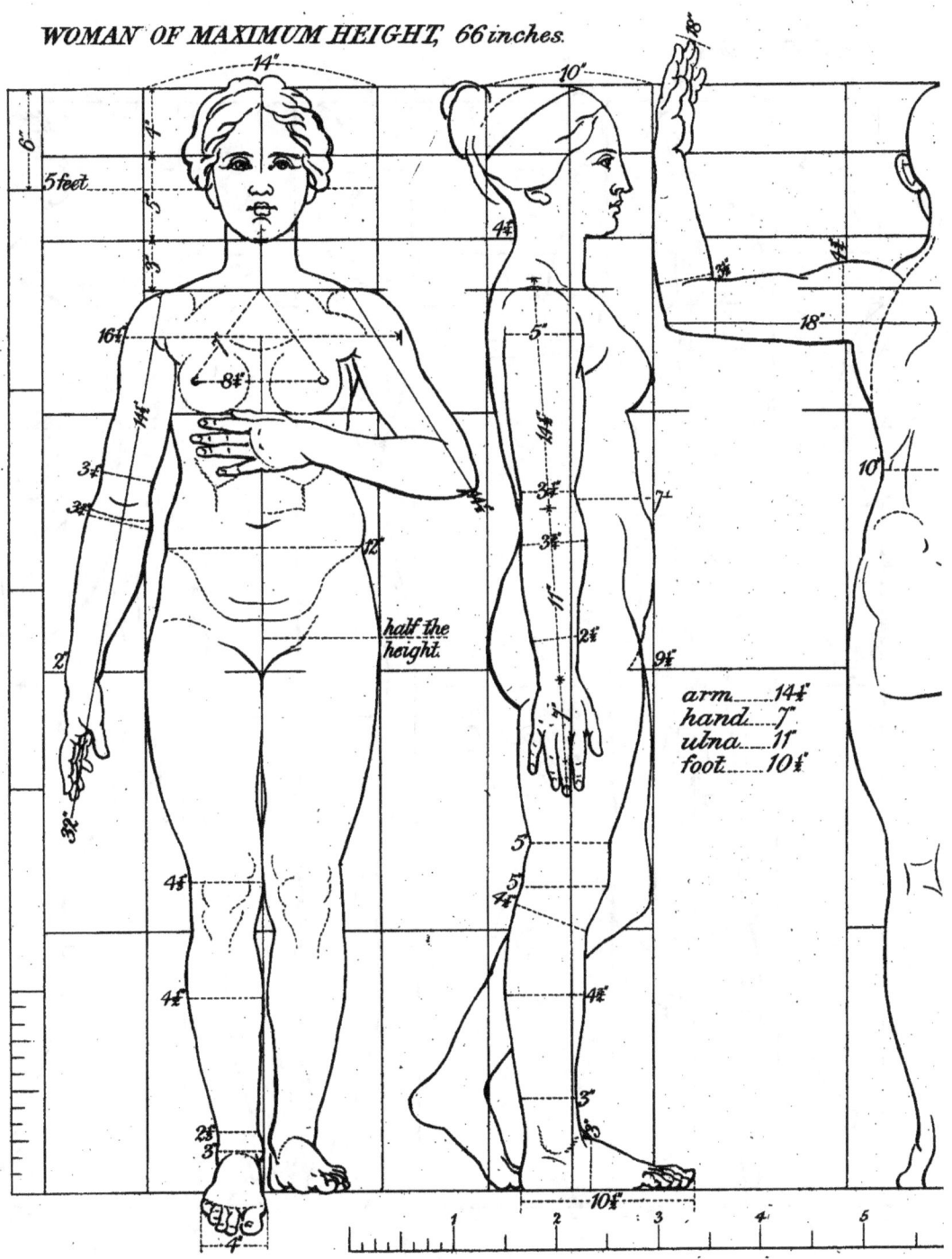

half the height.

arm...... 14¼
hand..... 7
ulna..... 11
foot...... 10¼

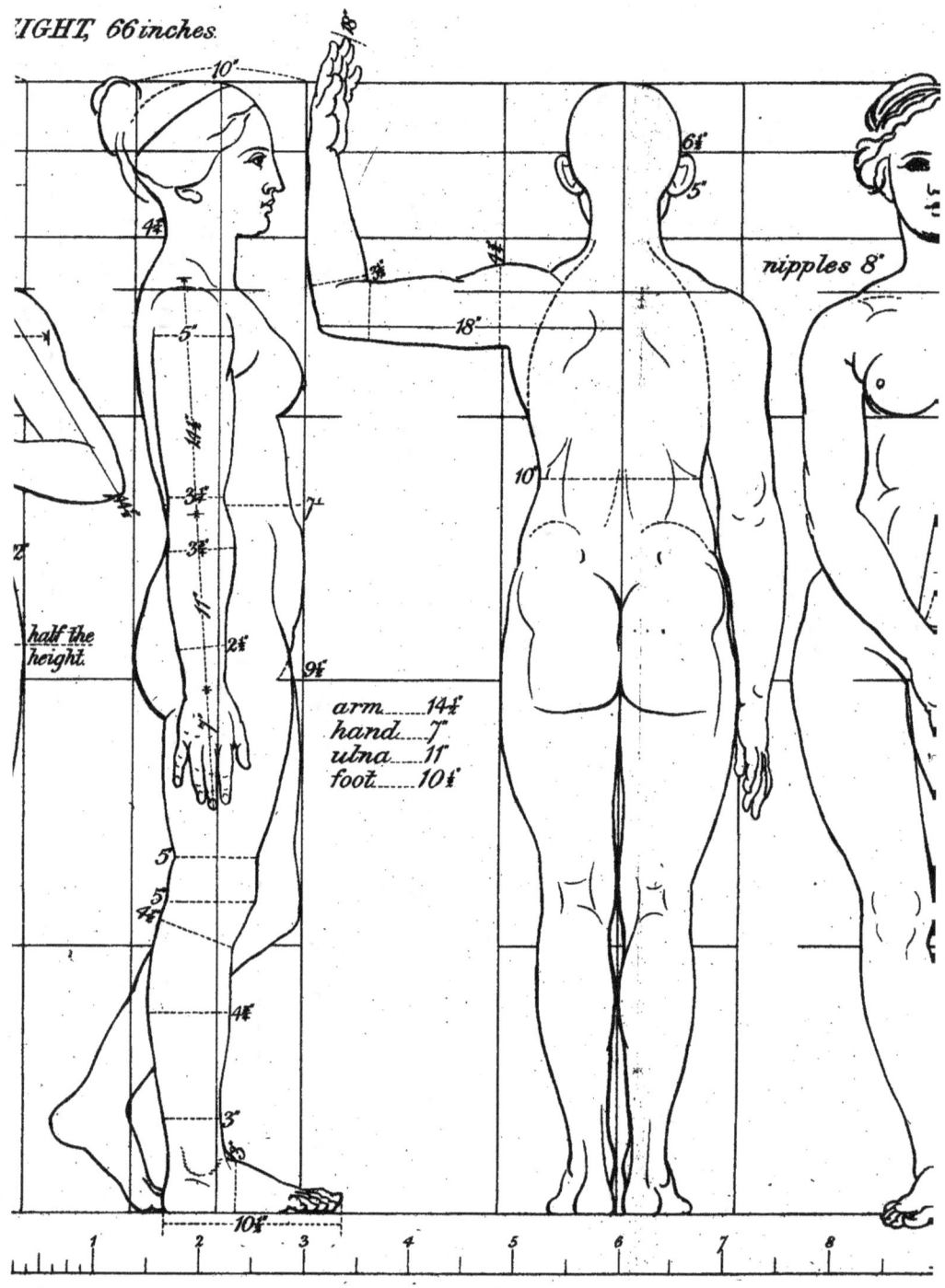

IGHT, 66 inches.

10"

4½

5

4½

3¾

3½

11

2½

half the height.

5

5
4½

4½

3"

10½

nipples 8°

6½

5°

18"

10"

arm........14½
hand.......7"
ulna.......11"
foot.......10½

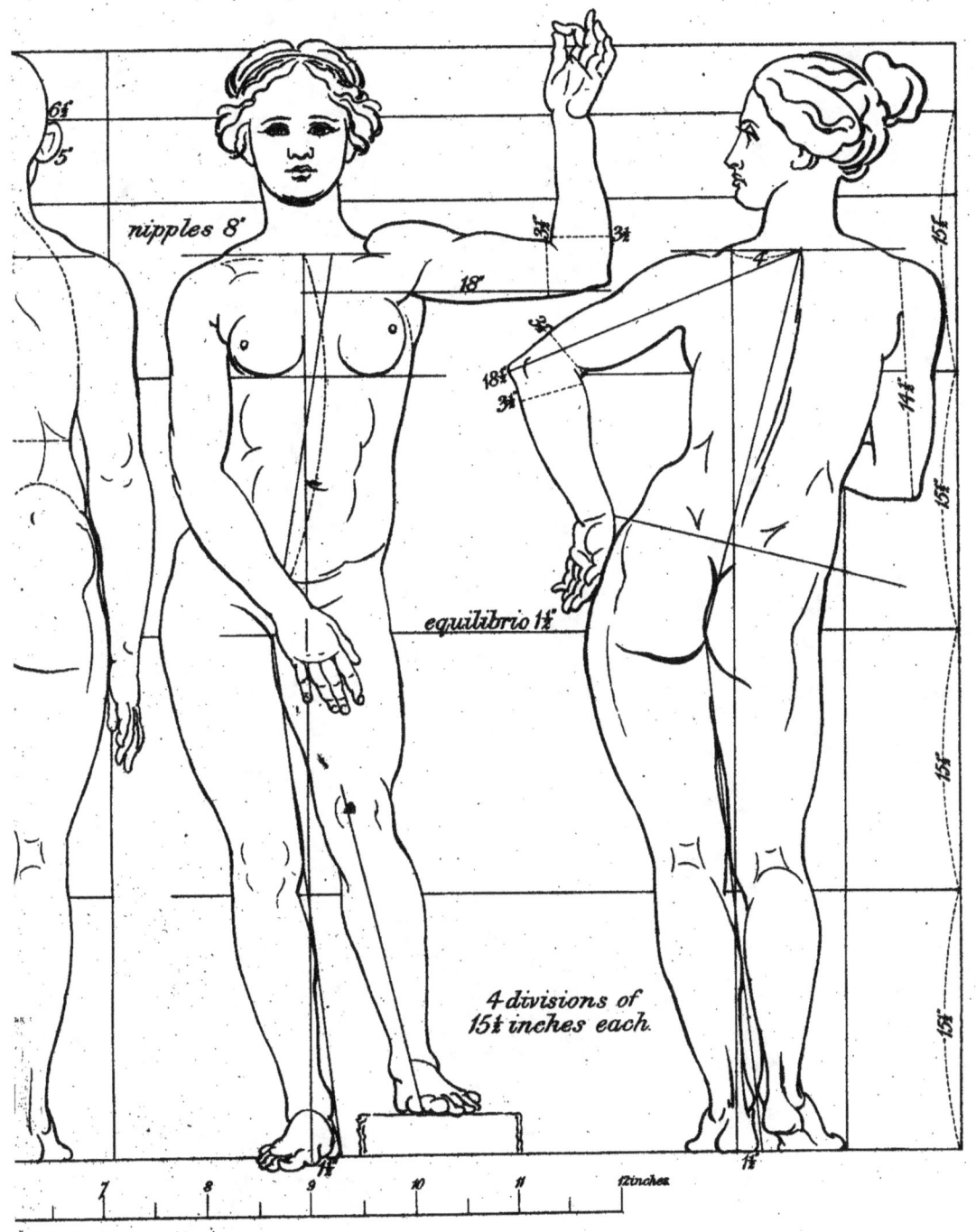

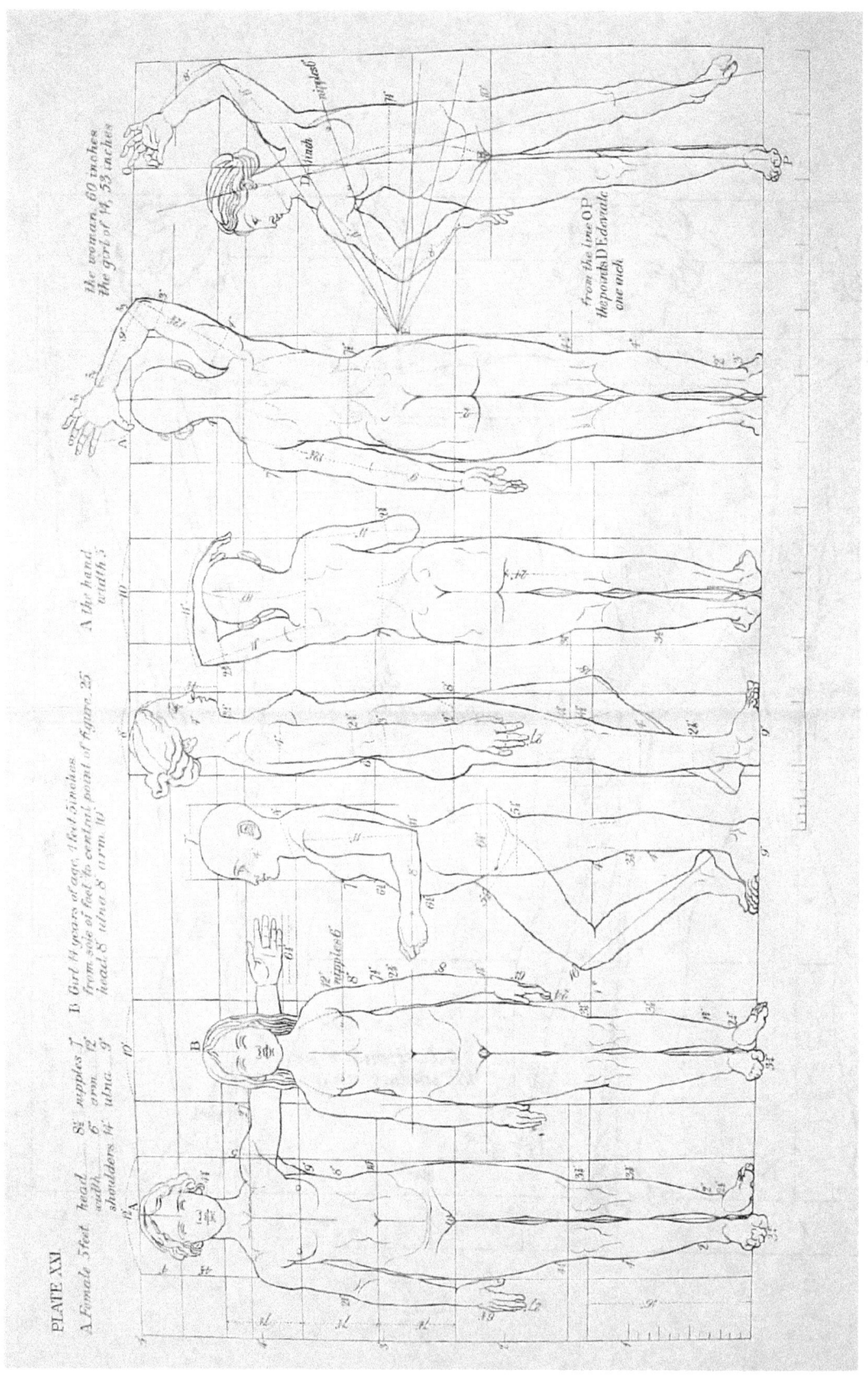

PLATE XXI.

A *Female 5 feet.* head............8¼ nipples....7   B *Girl 14 years of age, 4 feet 5 inc*
width............6" arm......12   *from sole of foot to central po:*
shoulders...14" ulna......9"   *head.8" ulna.8" arm.10"*

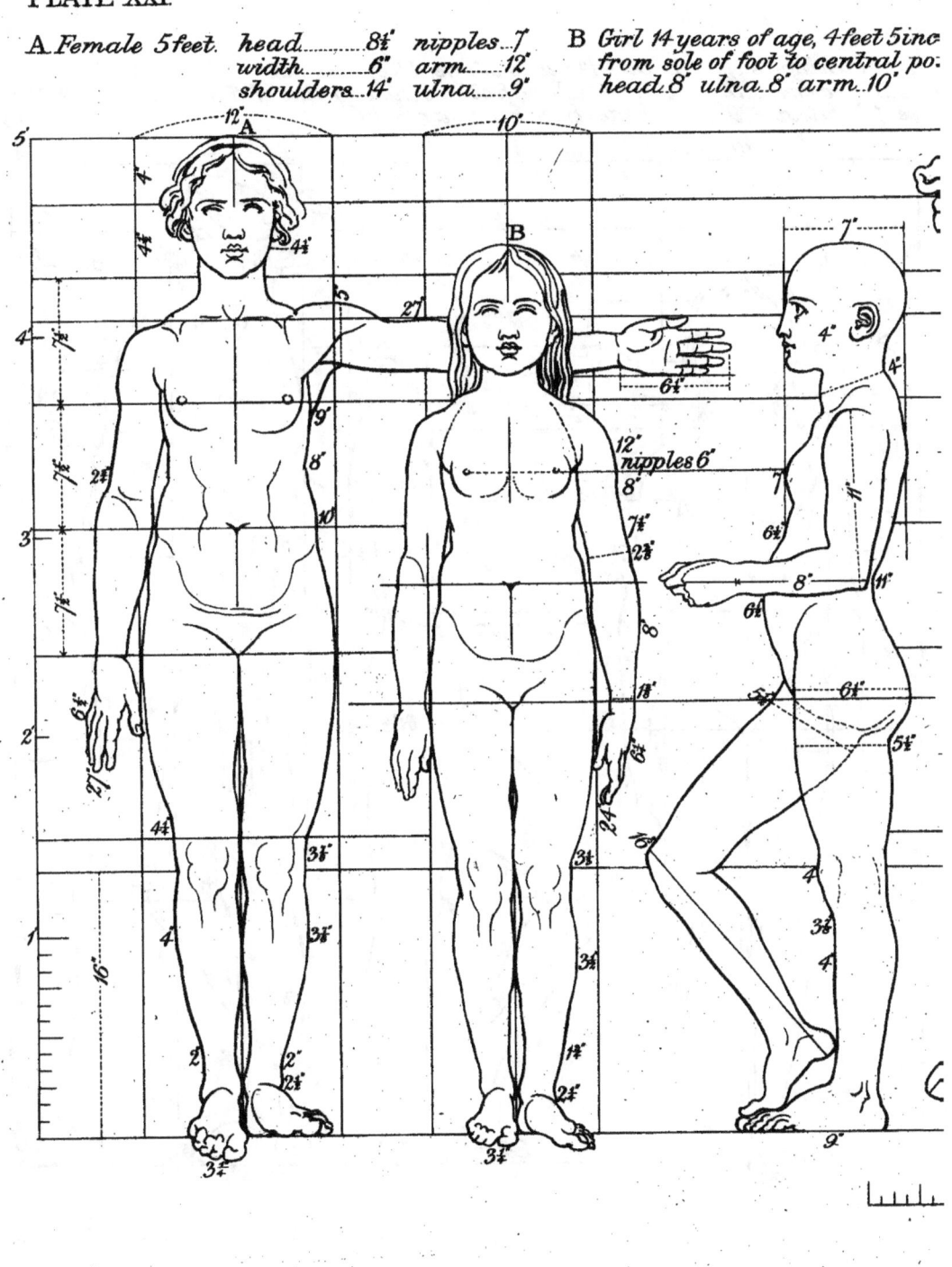

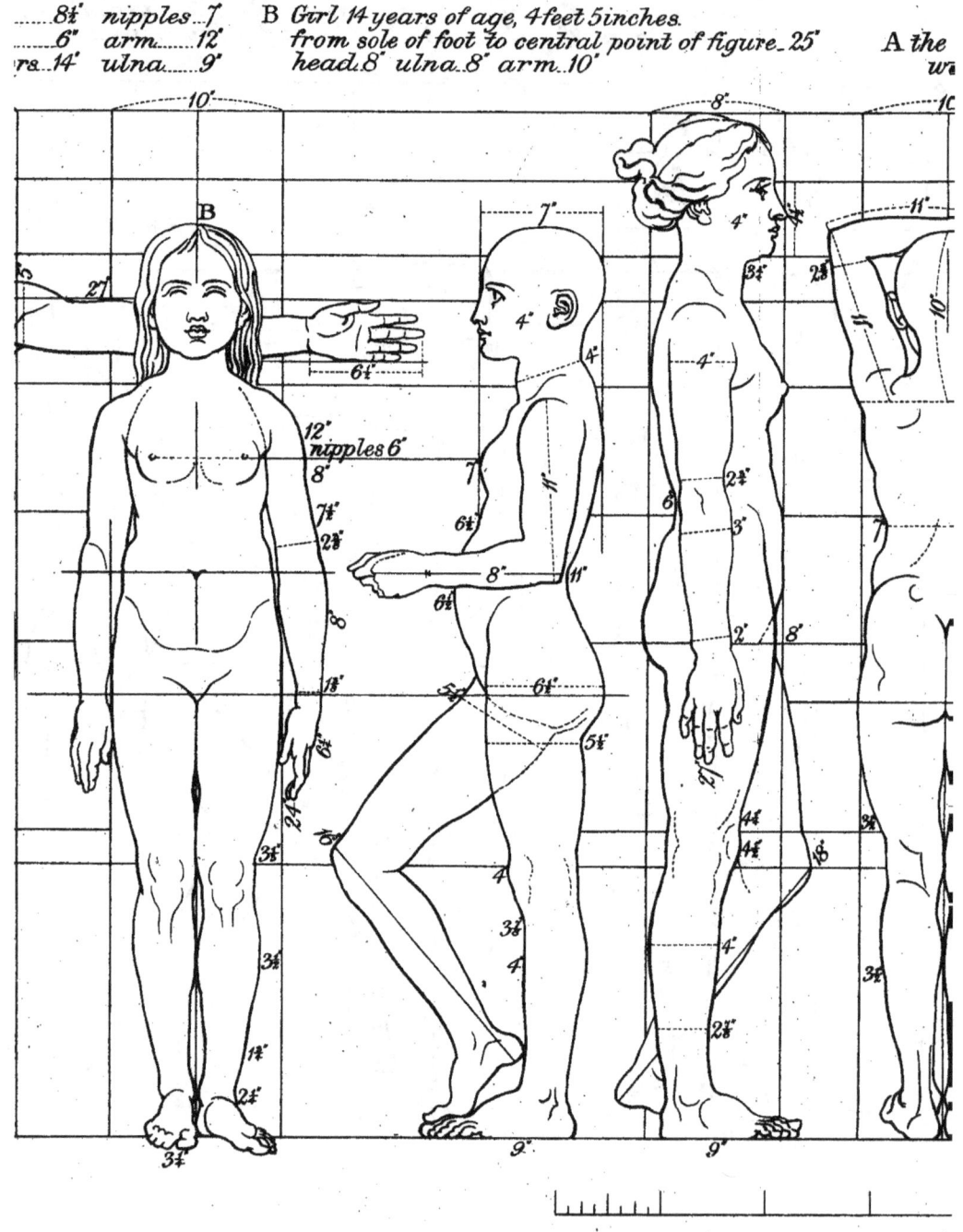

......8¼"   nipples..7"   B *Girl 14 years of age, 4 feet 5 inches.*
.......6"   arm.......12"   *from sole of foot to central point of figure_25"*   A *the*
rs..14"   ulna.....9"   *head.8" ulna.8" arm.10"*   *w*

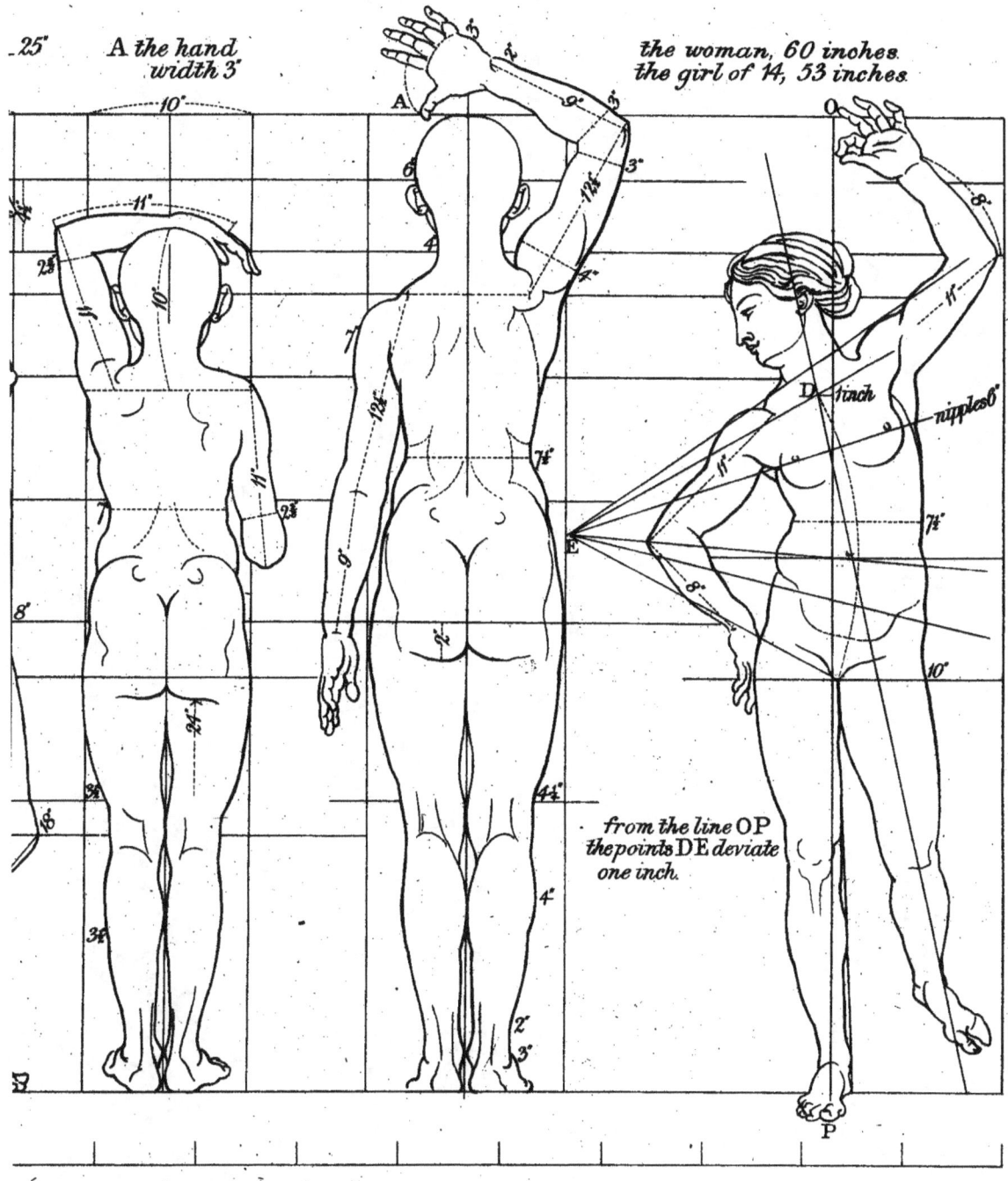

_25"   A the hand
width 3"

the woman, 60 inches.
the girl of 14, 53 inches.

from the line OP
the points DE deviate
one inch.

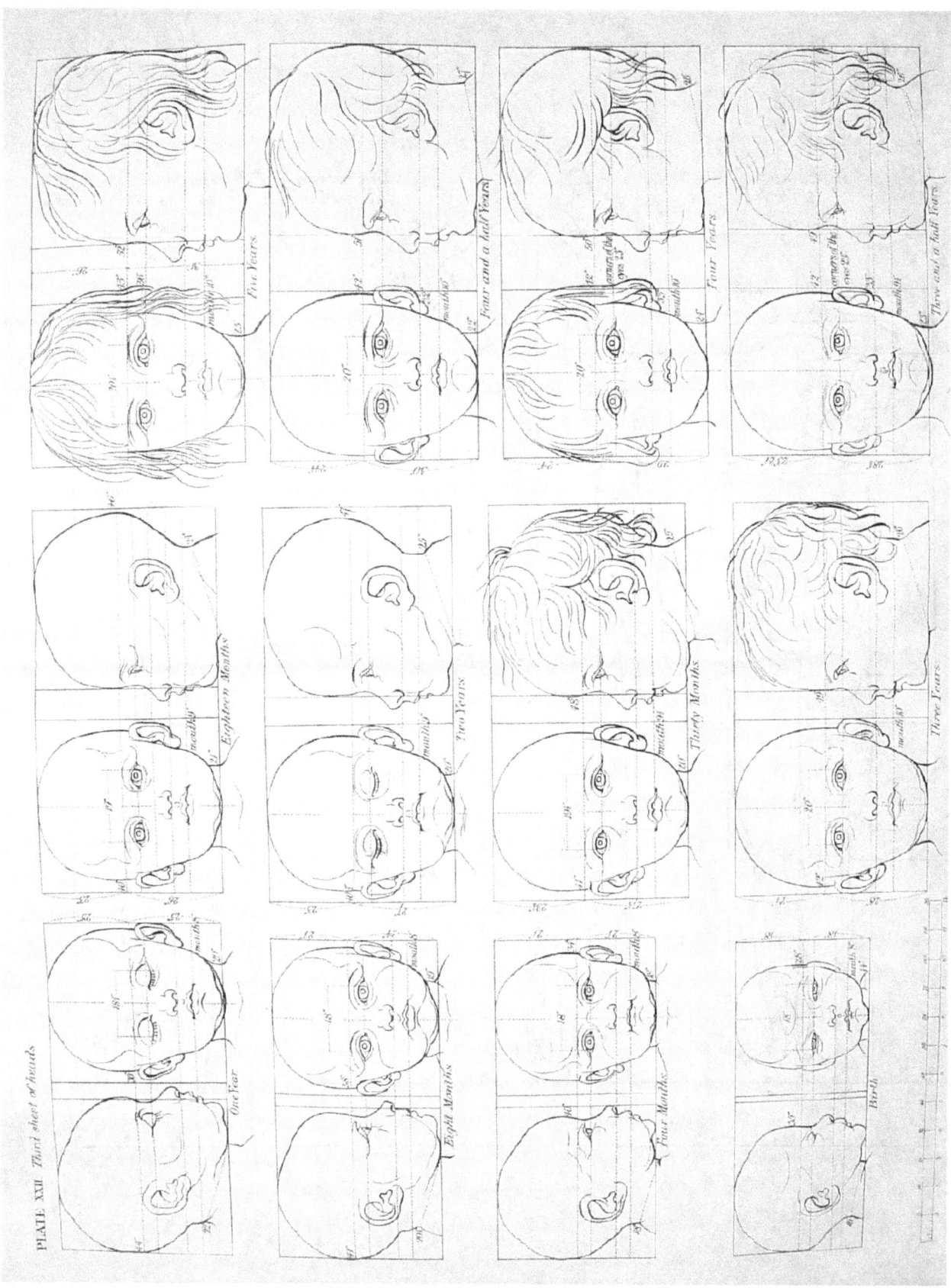

PLATE XXII. *Third sheet of heads.*

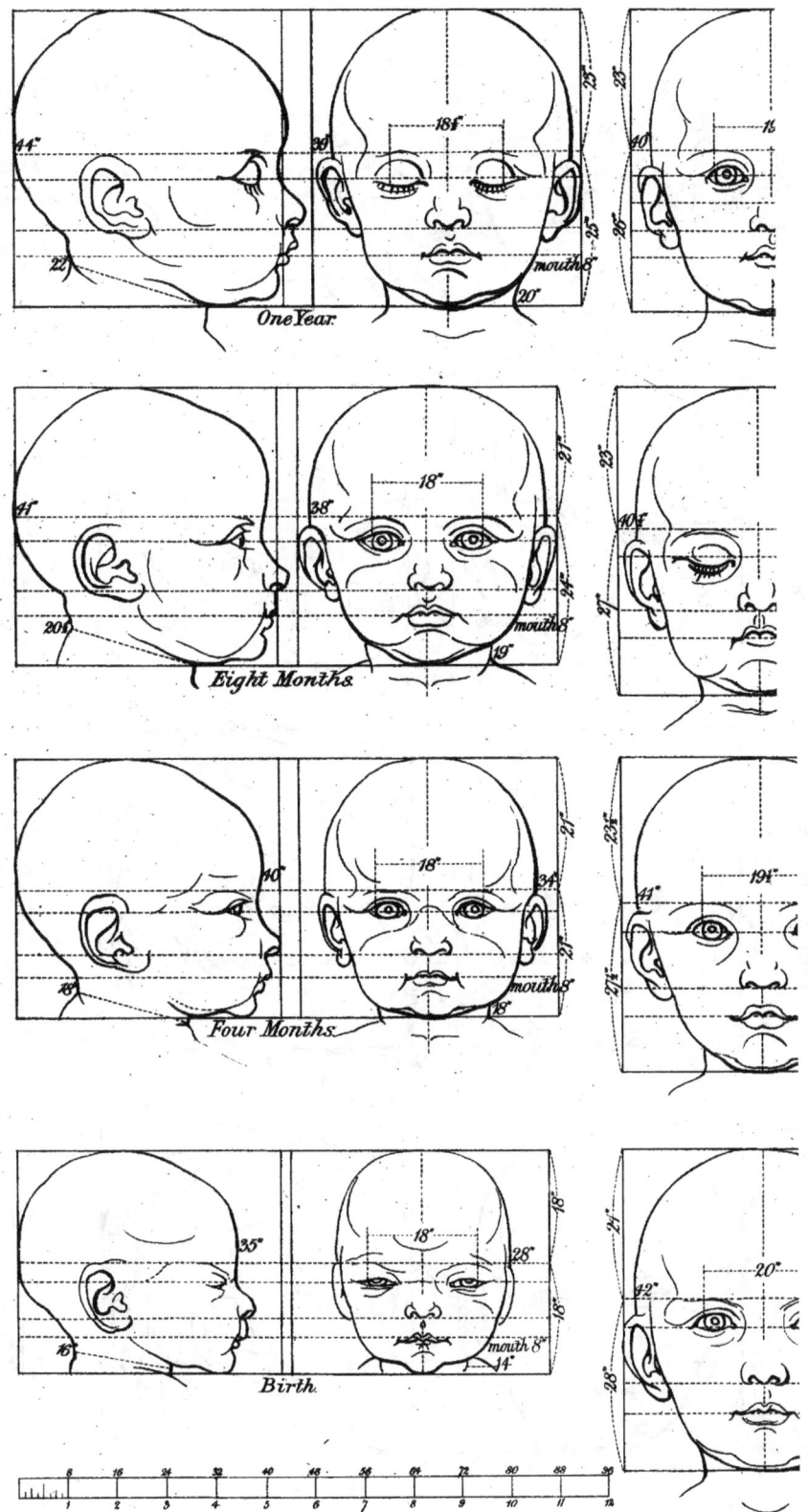

One Year.

Eight Months.

Four Months.

Birth.

105

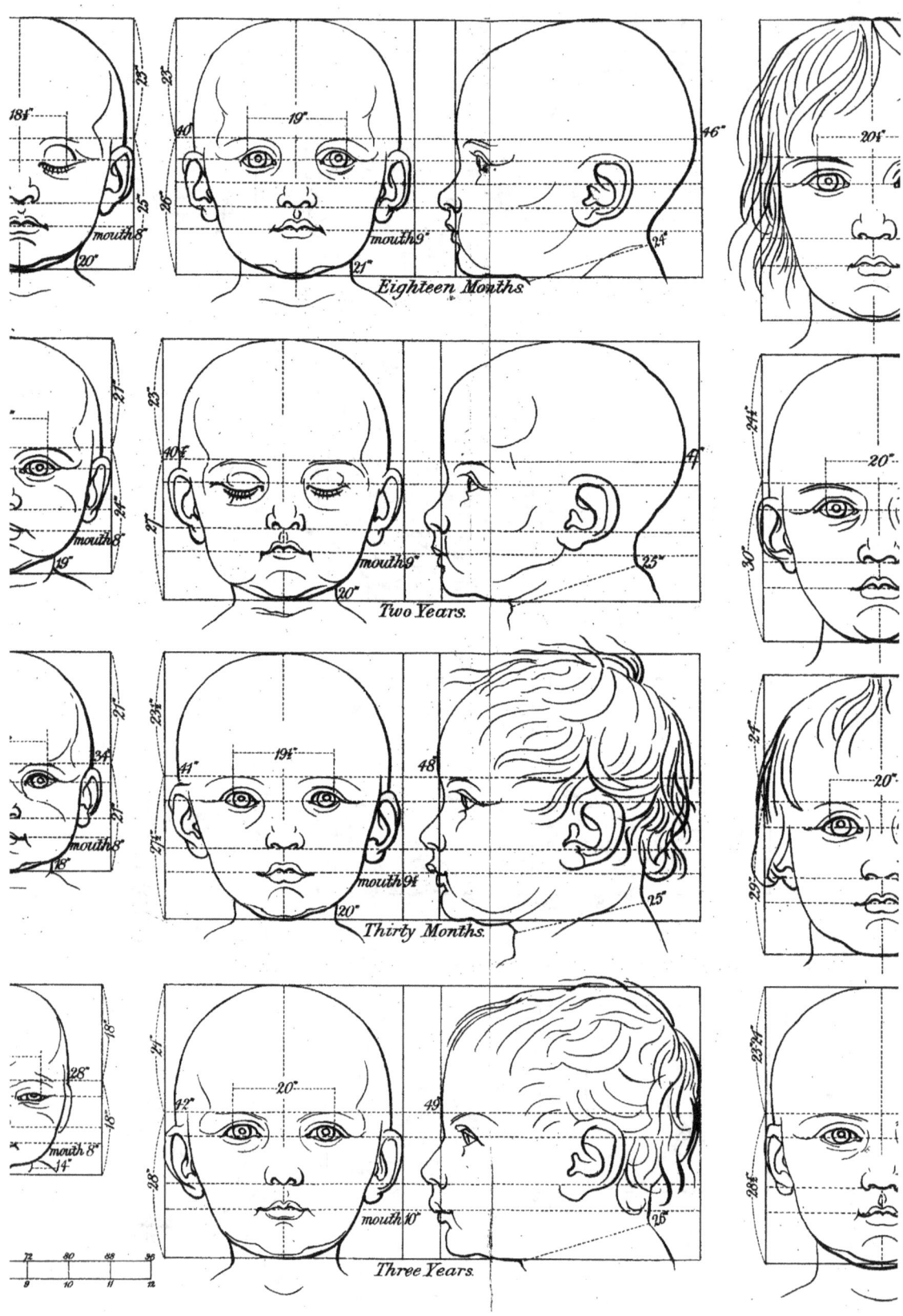

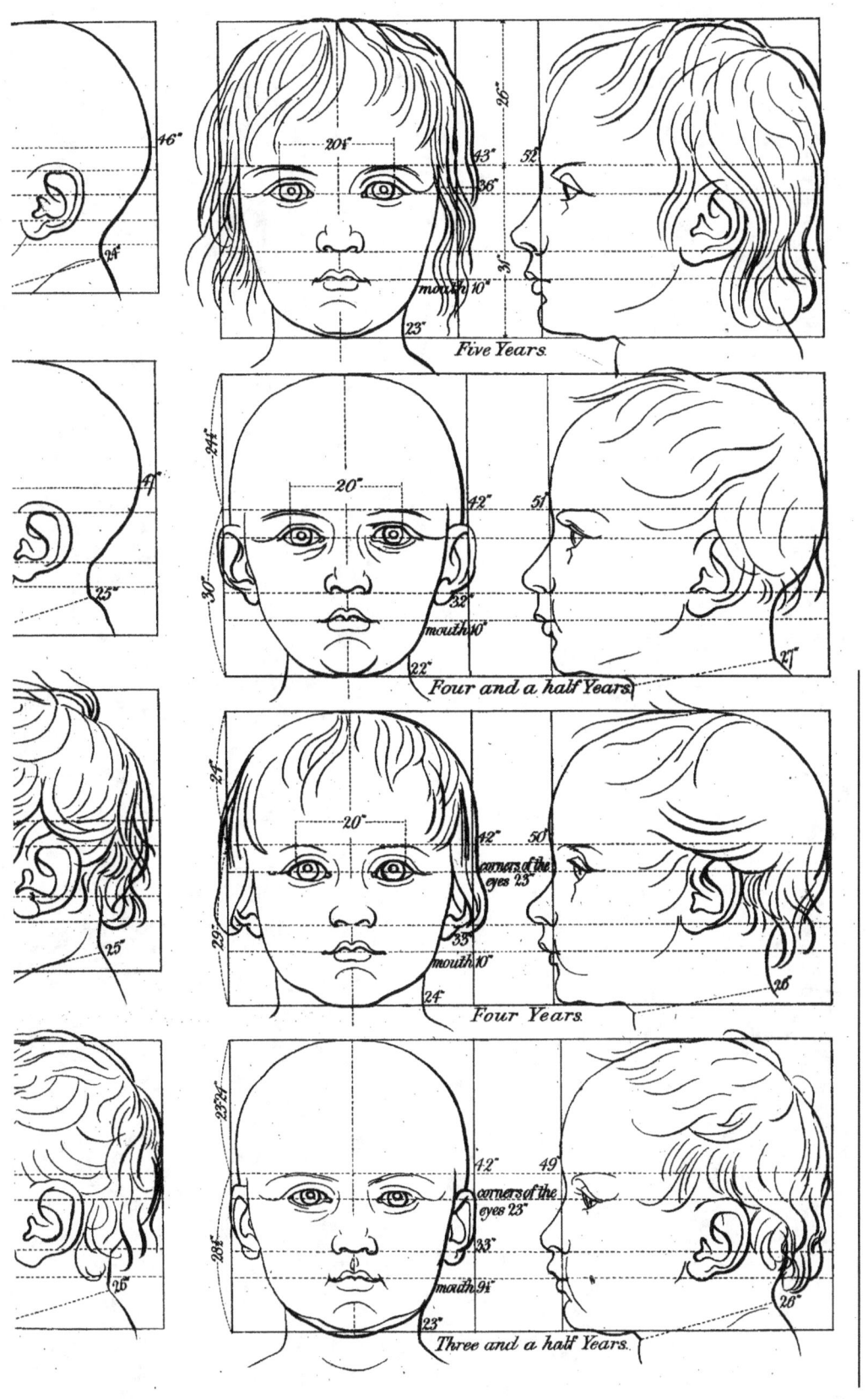

Five Years.

Four and a half Years.

Four Years.

Three and a half Years.

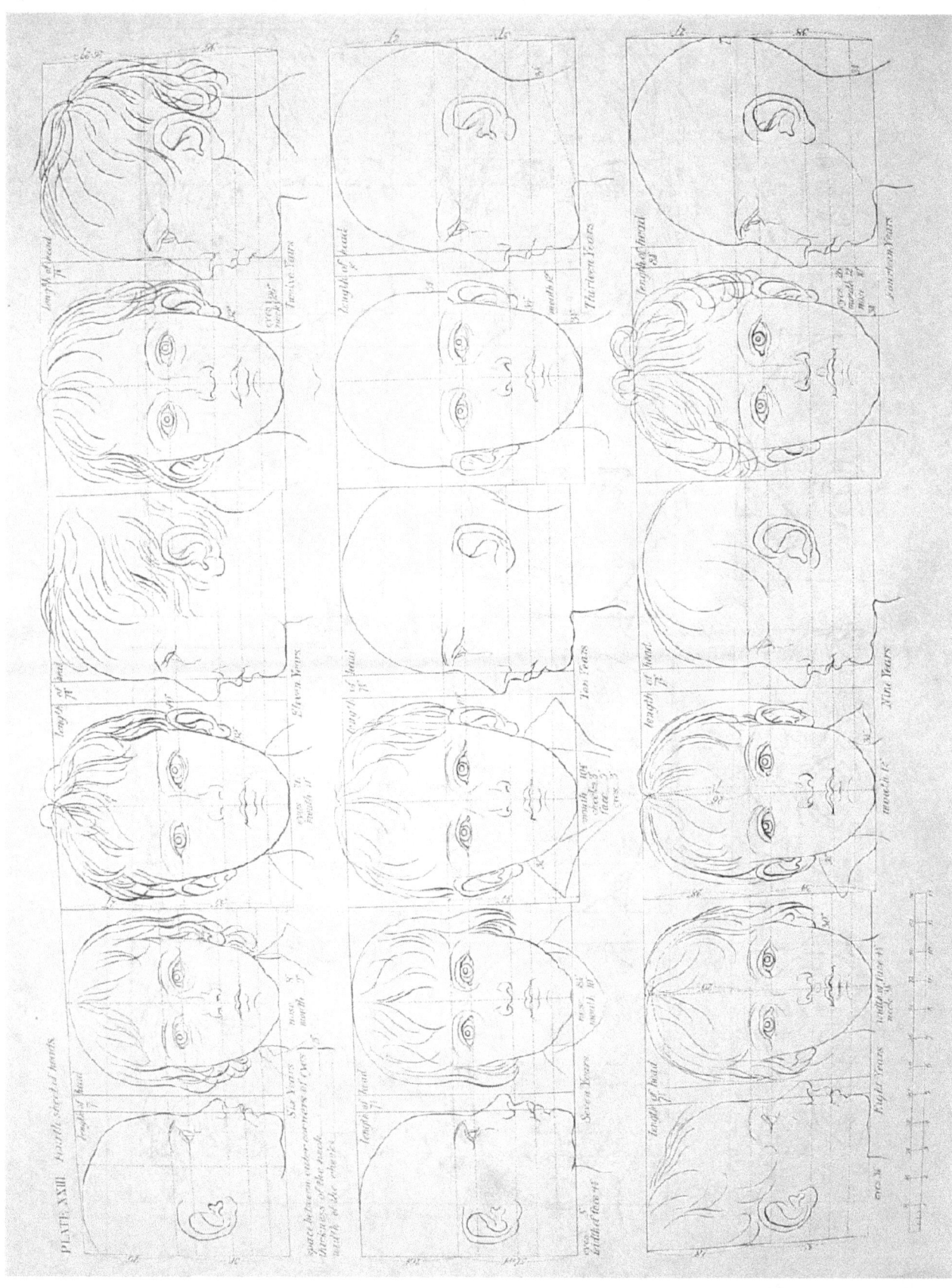

PLATE XXIII. *Fourth sheet of heads.*

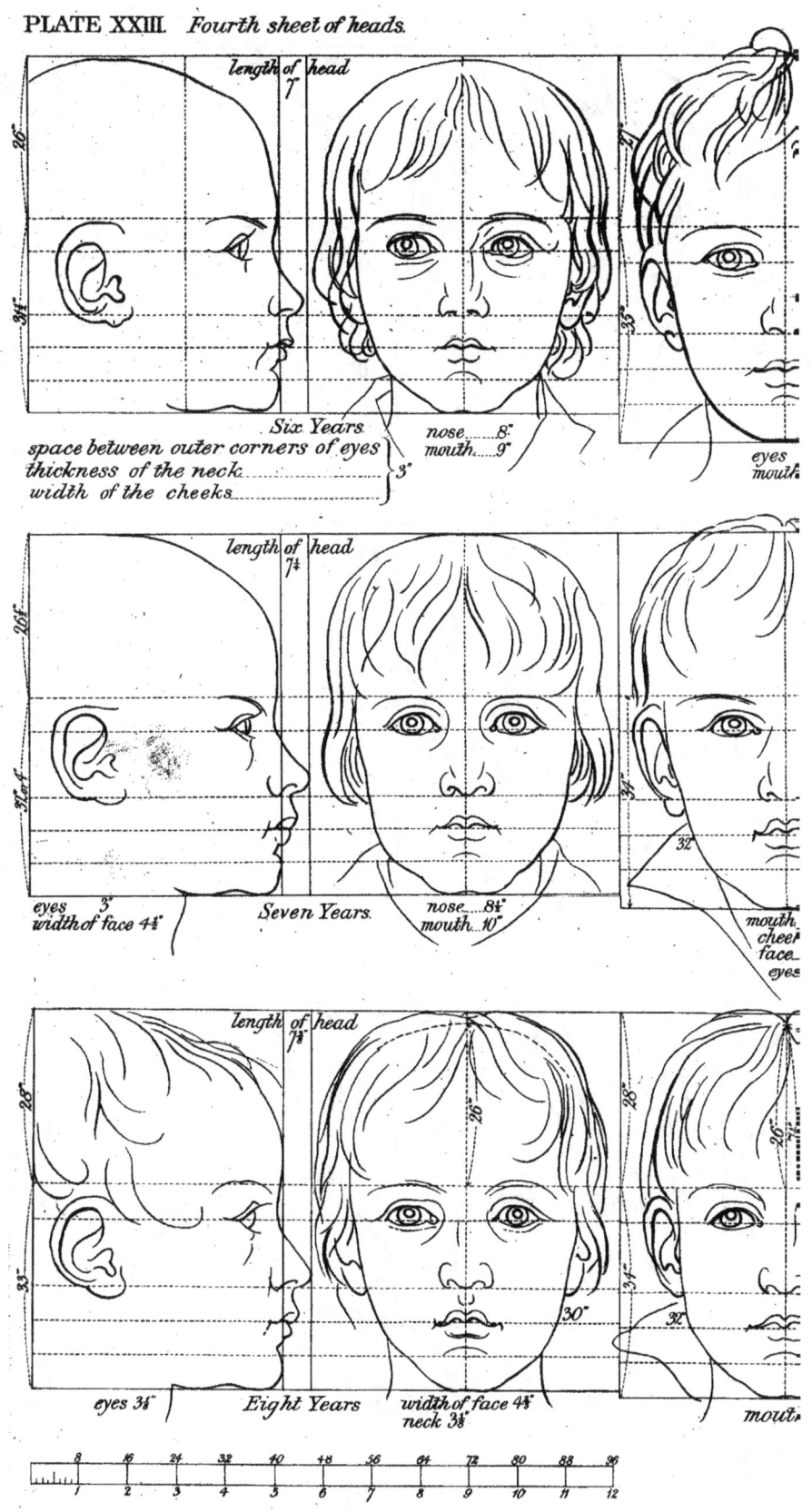

length of head
7"

Six Years
space between outer corners of eyes
thickness of the neck................................3"
width of the cheeks..................

nose   8"
mouth 9"

eyes
mouth

length of head
7¼

eyes   3"
width of face 4¼"

Seven Years.

nose   8¼"
mouth 10"

mouth
cheek
face
eyes

length of head
7⅜"

eyes 3¼"   Eight Years

width of face 4⅝"
neck 3⅝"

mout

109

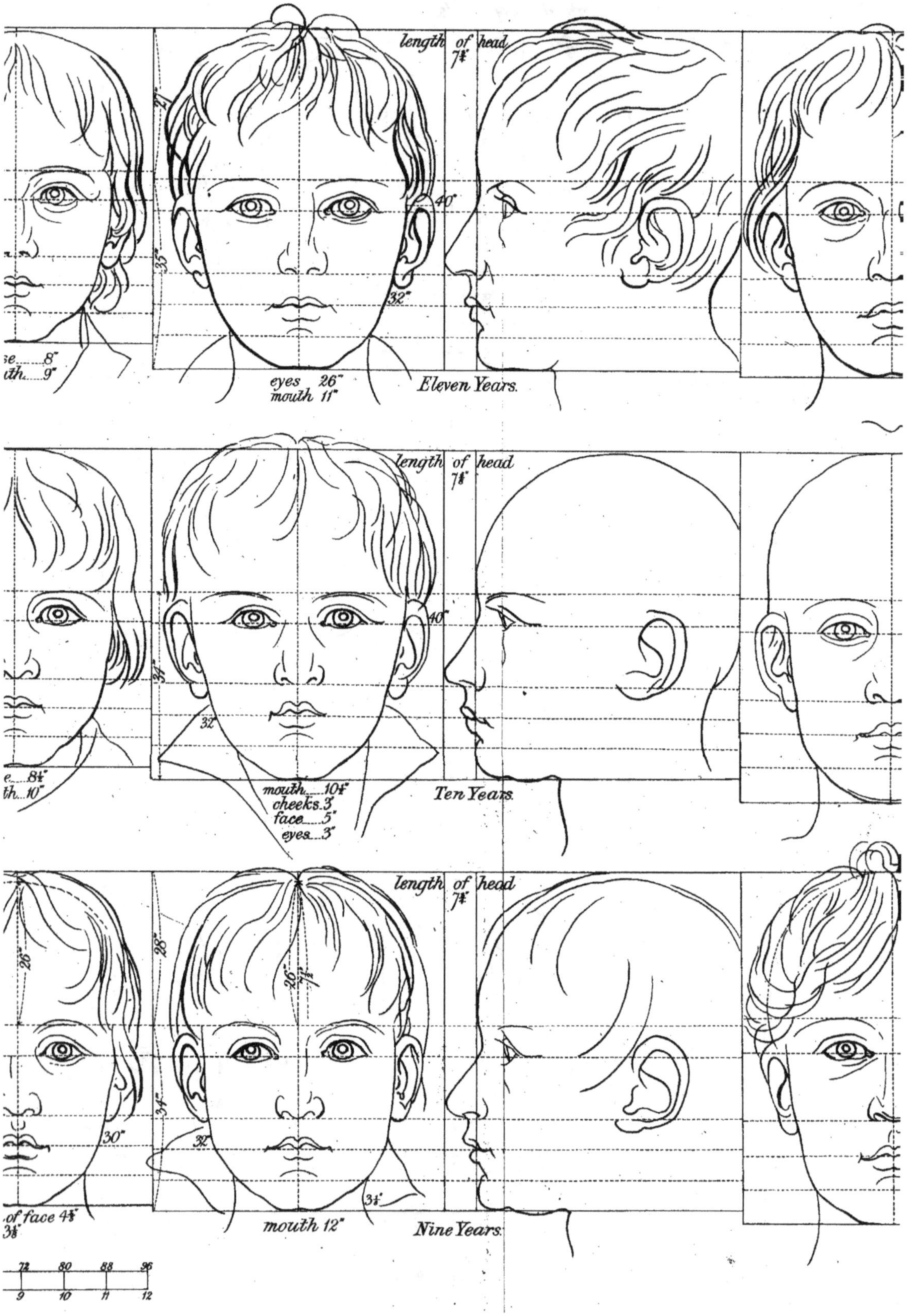
length of head
40"
35"
32"
eyes 26"
mouth 11"
Eleven Years.
length of head
40"
34"
32
mouth 10¼"
cheeks 3"
face 5"
eyes 3"
Ten Years.
length of head
28"
26"
34"
30"
32
3¼"
mouth 12"
Nine Years.
of face 4⅛"
72 80 88 96
9 10 11 12

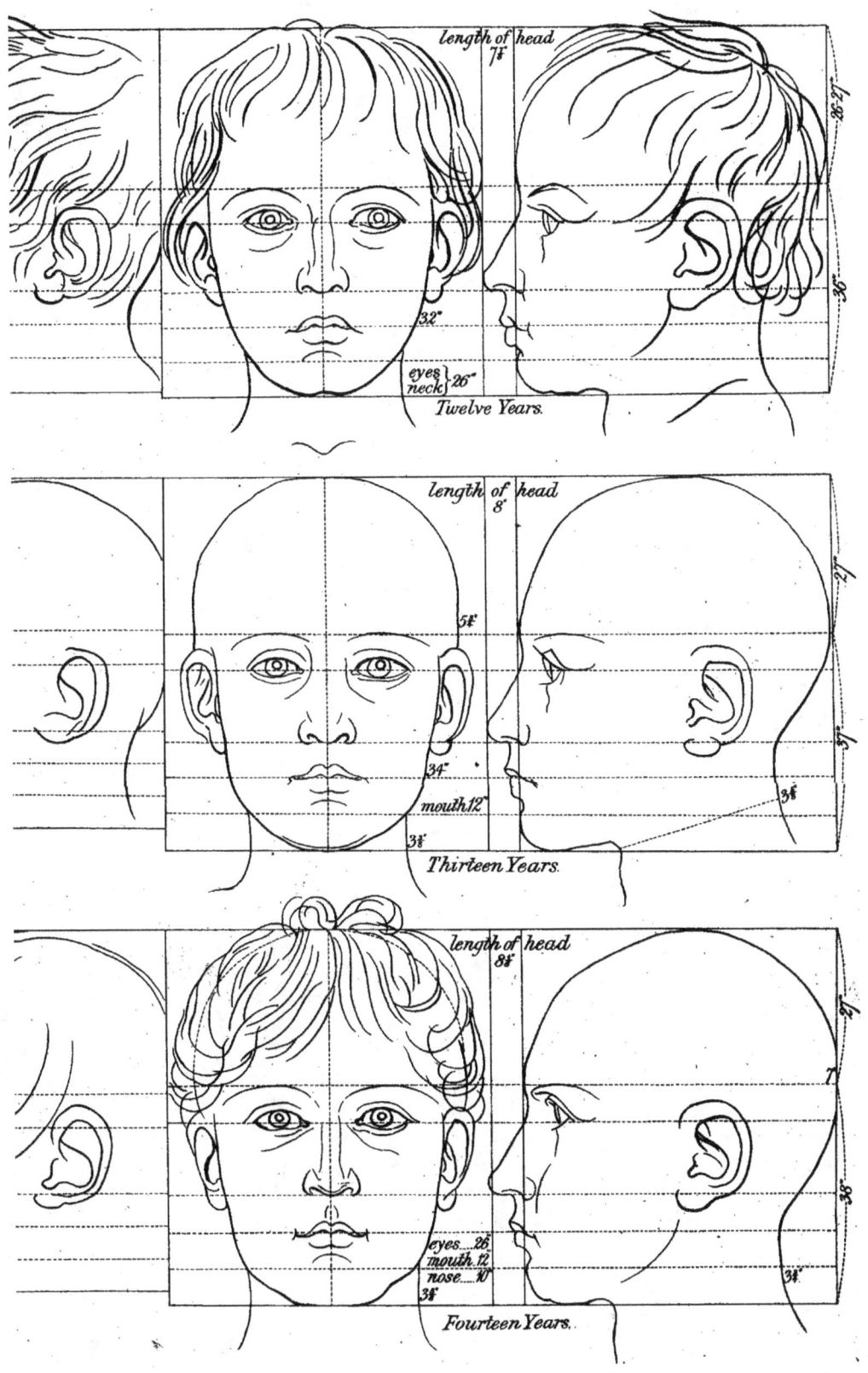

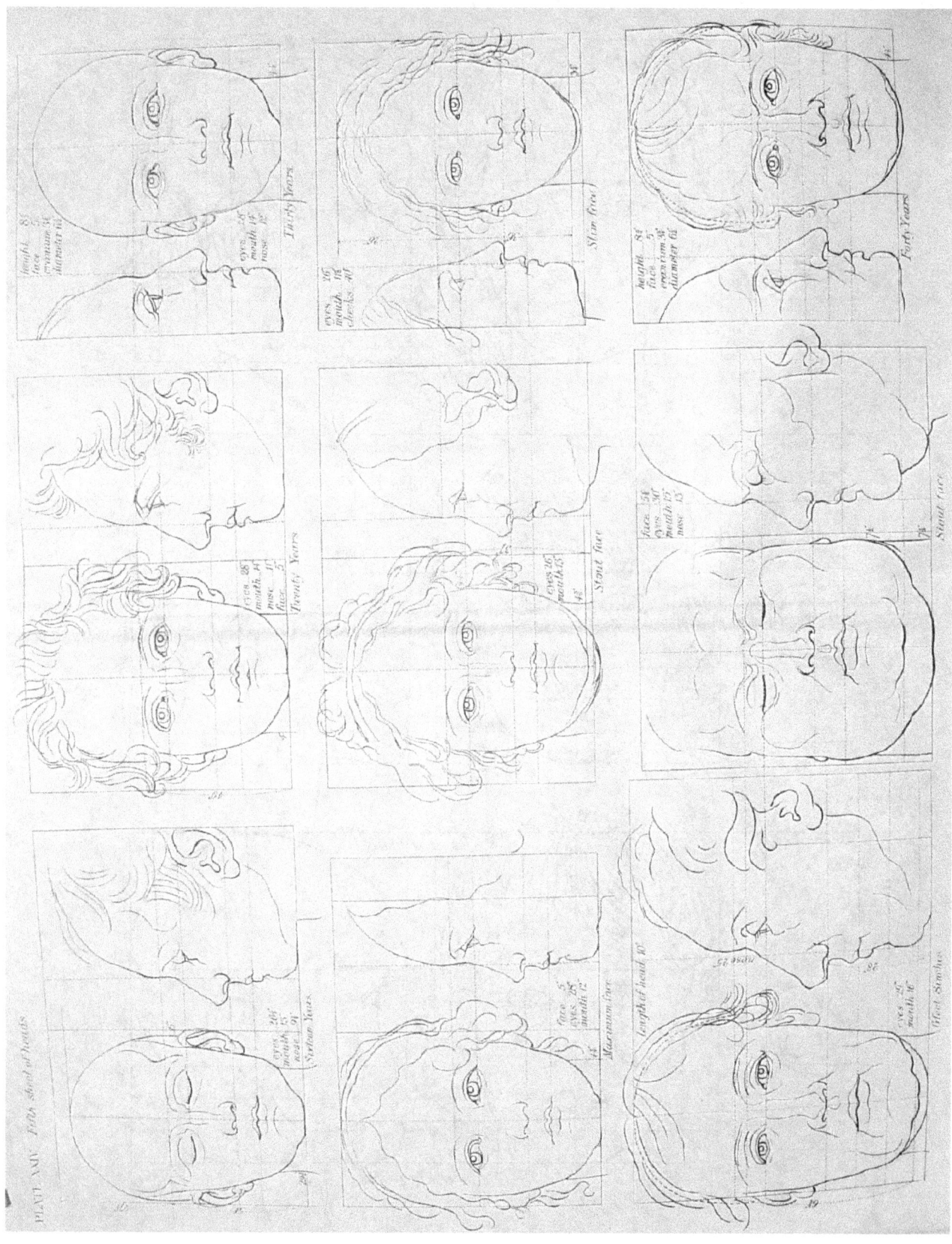

PLATE XXIV. *Fifth sheet of heads.*

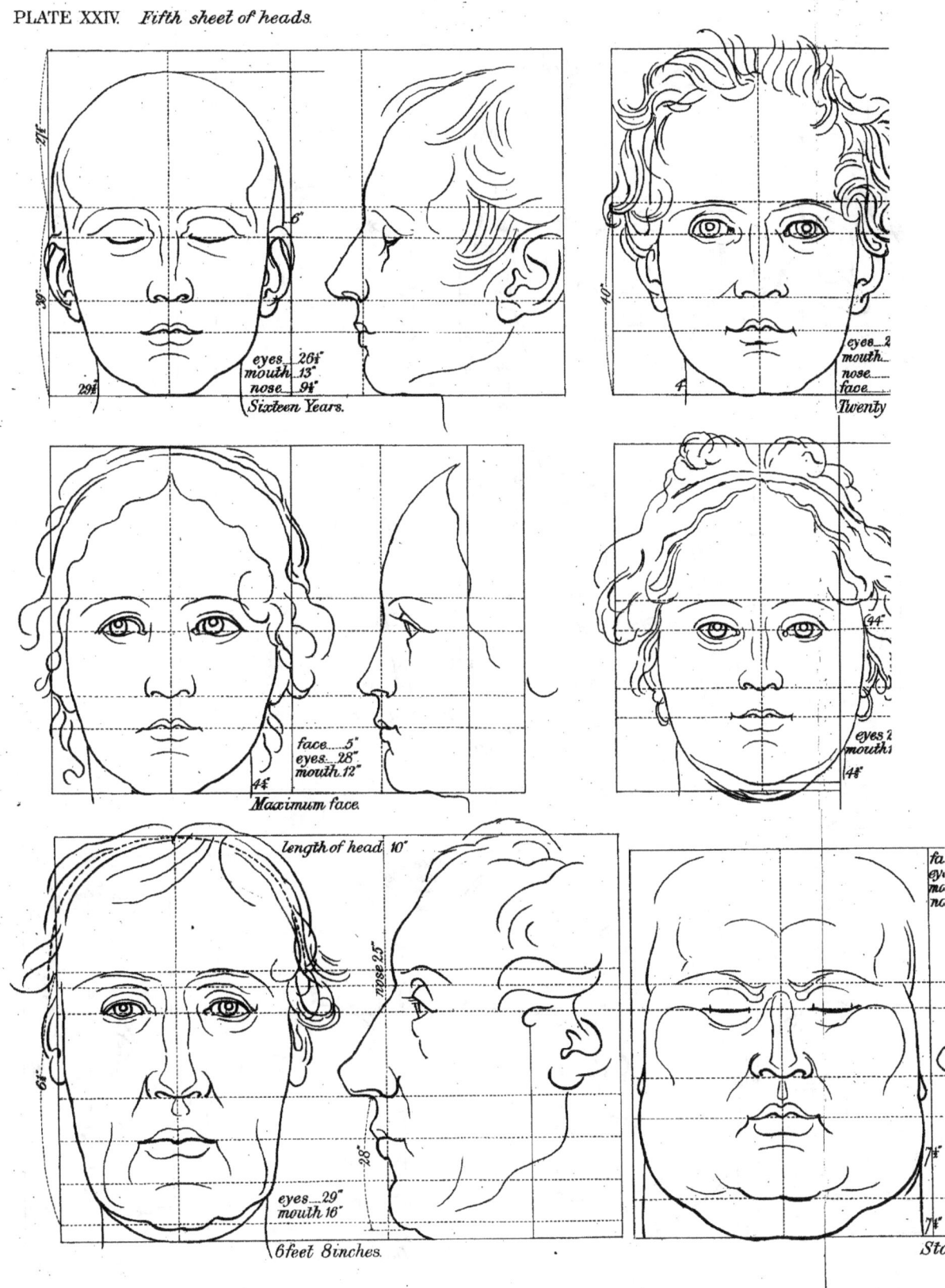

eyes....26½"
mouth...13"
nose....9¼"
(*Sixteen Years.*)

eyes....
mouth...
nose....
face....
Twenty

face....5"
eyes....28"
mouth..12"
Maximum face.

eyes....
mouths...

length of head 10"

nose 2.5"

.28"

eyes...29"
mouth..16"
6 feet 8 inches.

fa
ey
m
no

St

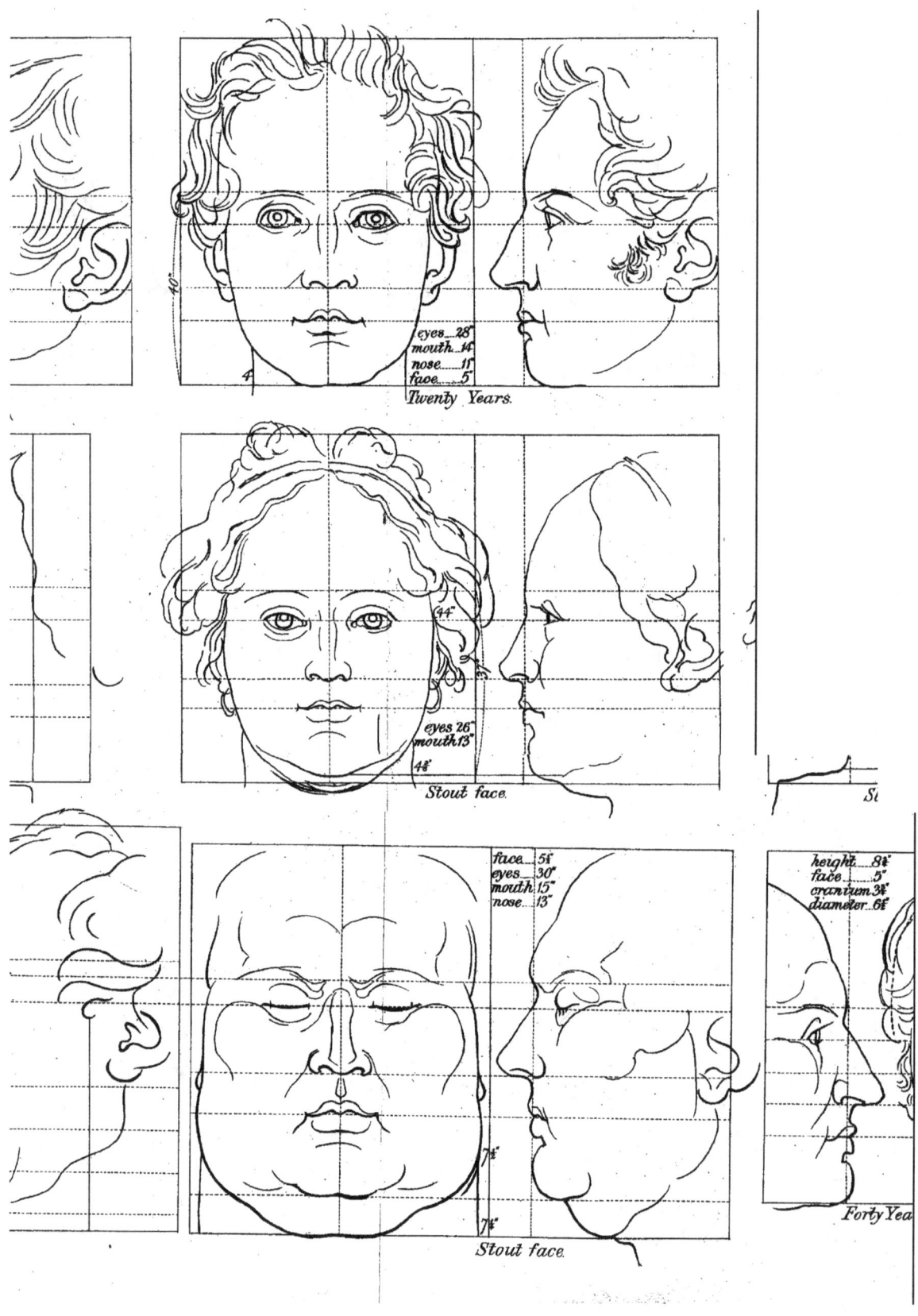

eyes __ 28
mouth __ 14
nose __ 15
face __ 5
Twenty Years.

eyes 26″
mouth 13″
Stout face.

face __ 5⅓
eyes __ 30″
mouth 15″
nose __ 13″

Stout face.

height __ 8⅓
face __ 5″
cranium 3⅓
diameter 6⅓

Forty Yea

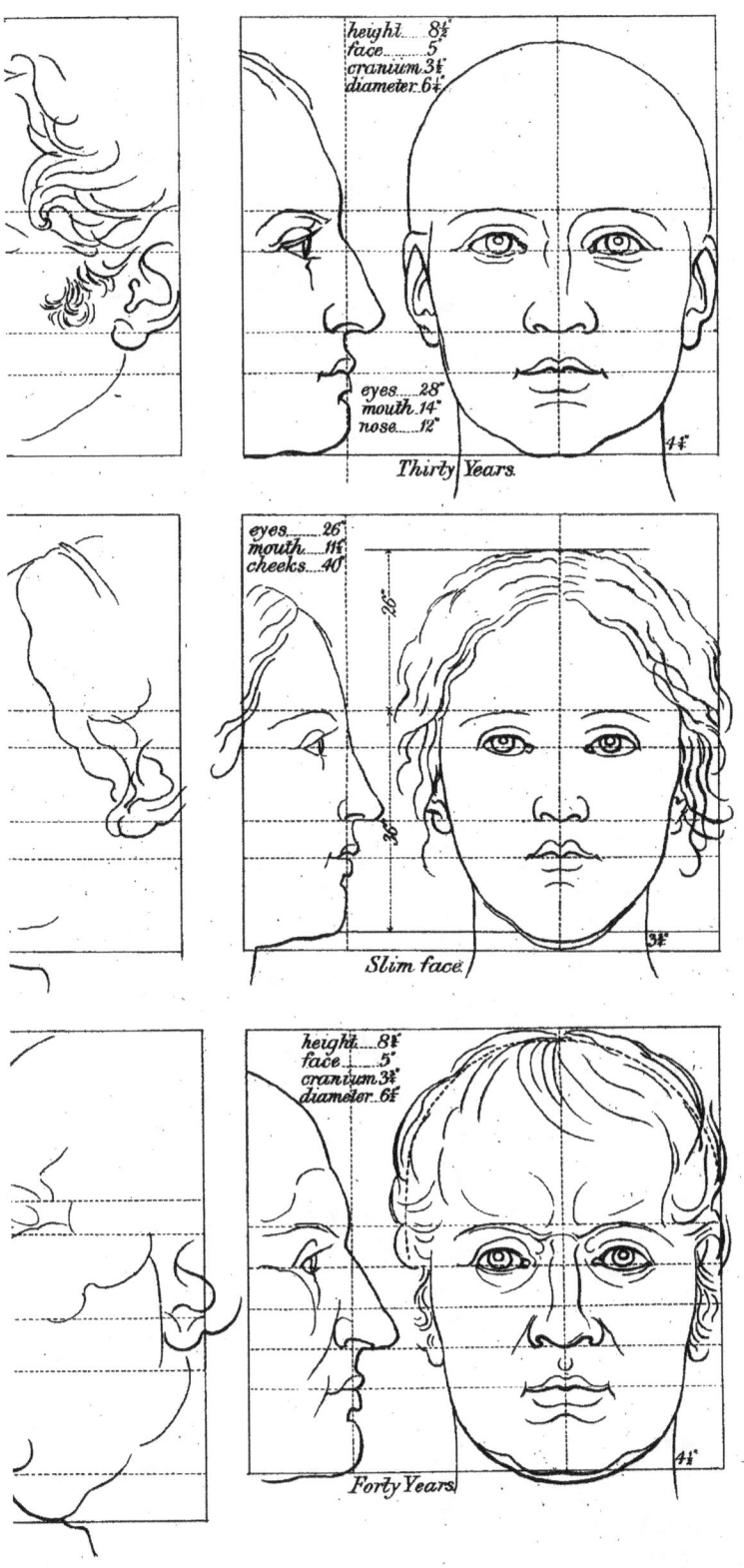

height   8¼
face   5
cranium 3½
diameter 6¼

eyes   28"
mouth 14"
nose   12"

4¼

Thirty Years.

eyes   26"
mouth 11½
cheeks 40"

26"
26"

3¼

Slim face.

height   8¼
face   5
cranium 3¾
diameter 6¼

4¼

Forty Years.

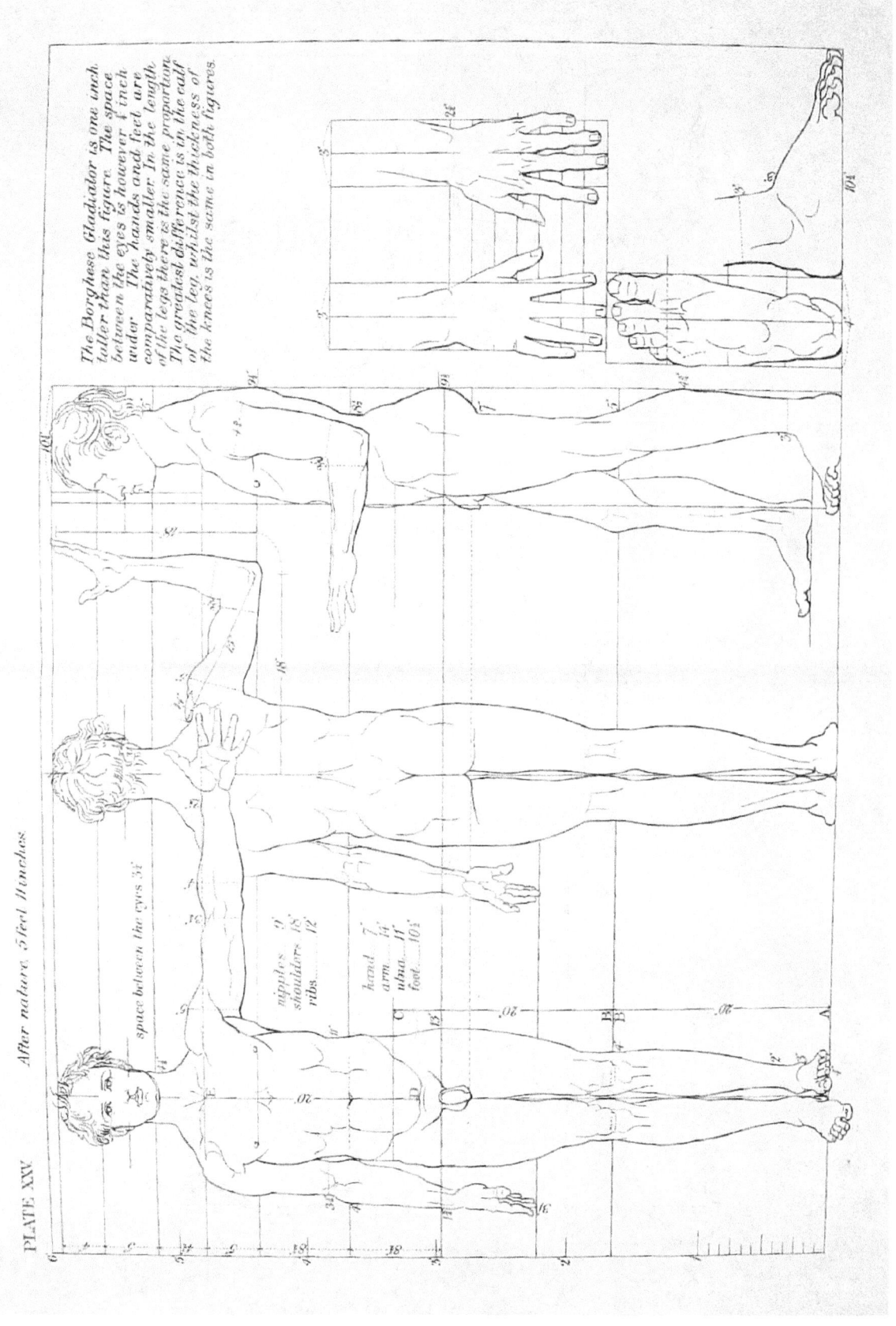

The Borghese Gladiator is one inch taller than this figure. The space between the eyes is however 1 inch under. The hands and feet are comparatively smaller. In the length of the legs there is the same proportion. The greatest difference is in the calf of the leg, whilst the thickness of the knees is the same in both figures.

PLATE XXV

After nature, 5 feet 8 inches

space between the eyes 3¼

nipples....9
shoulders..18
ribs.......12

head....7
arm.....1¼
ulna....11
foot....10½

PLATE XXV. *After nature, 5 feet 11 inches.*

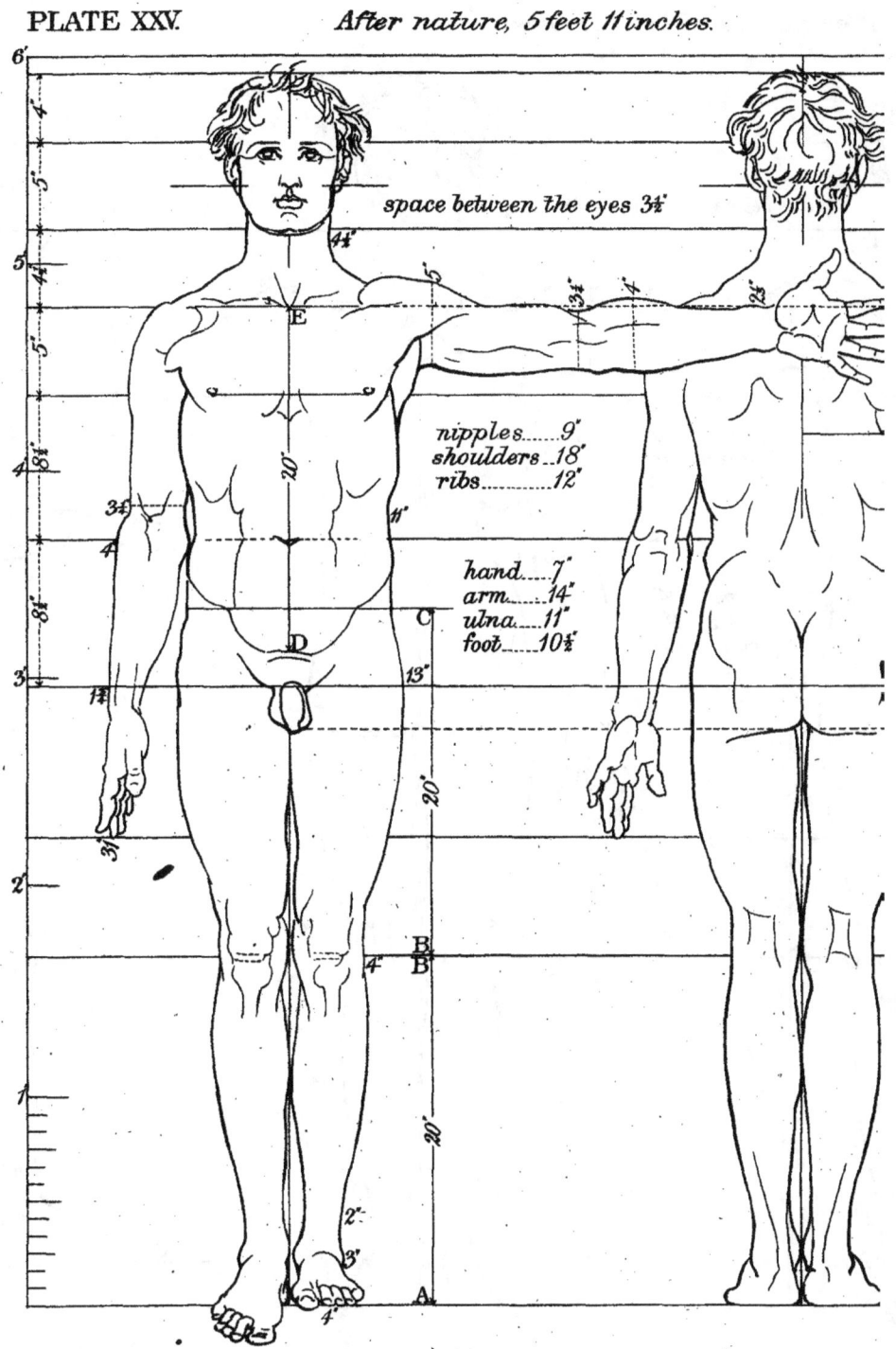

space between the eyes 3¼″

nipples.......9″
shoulders...18″
ribs............12″

hand.....7″
arm.......14″
ulna.....11″
foot.....10½″

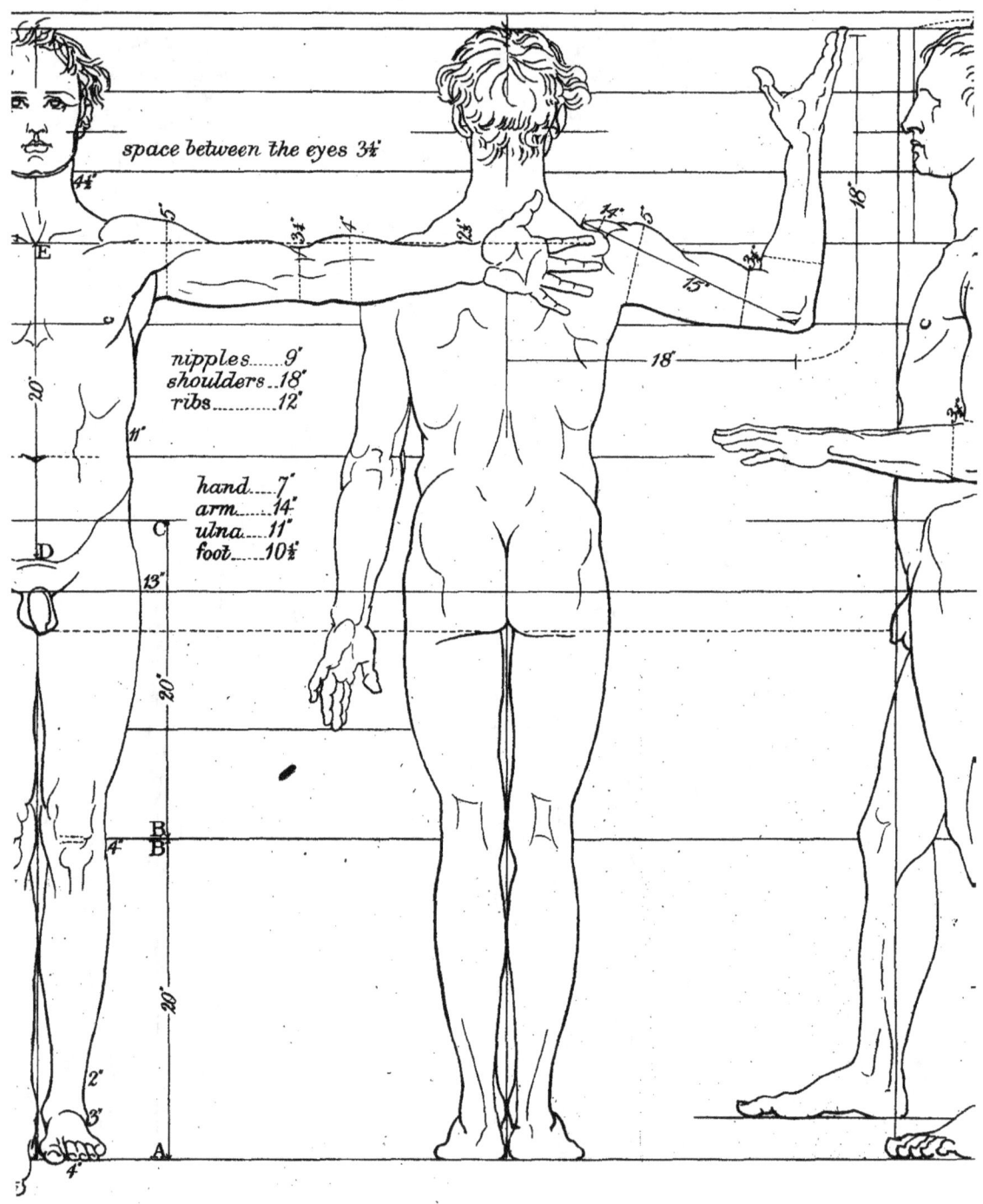

After nature, 5 feet 11 inches.

space between the eyes 3¼"

nipples......9"
shoulders..18"
ribs..........12"

hand......7"
arm........14"
ulna.......11"
foot.......10¼"

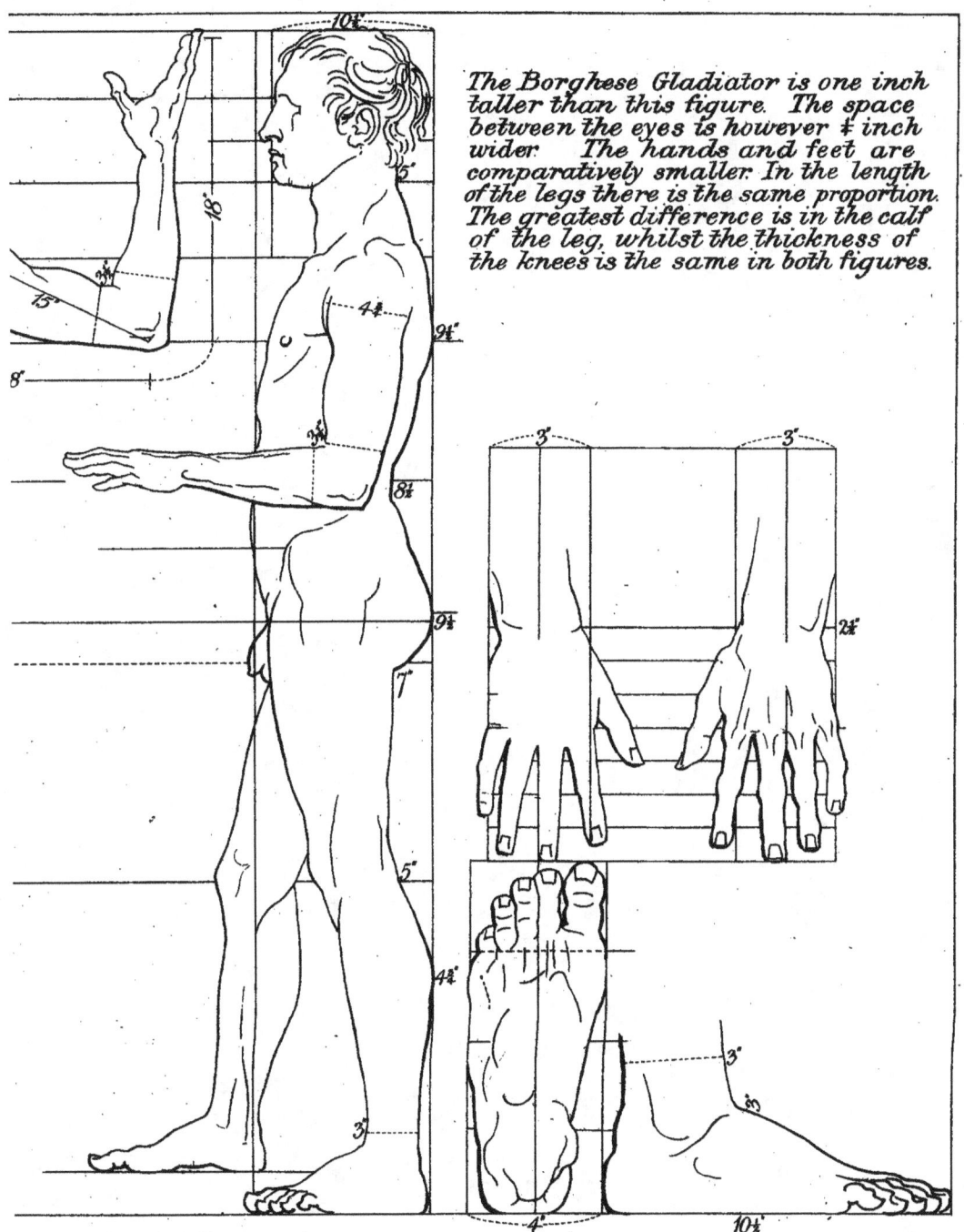

The Borghese Gladiator is one inch taller than this figure. The space between the eyes is however ¼ inch wider. The hands and feet are comparatively smaller. In the length of the legs there is the same proportion. The greatest difference is in the calf of the leg, whilst the thickness of the knees is the same in both figures.

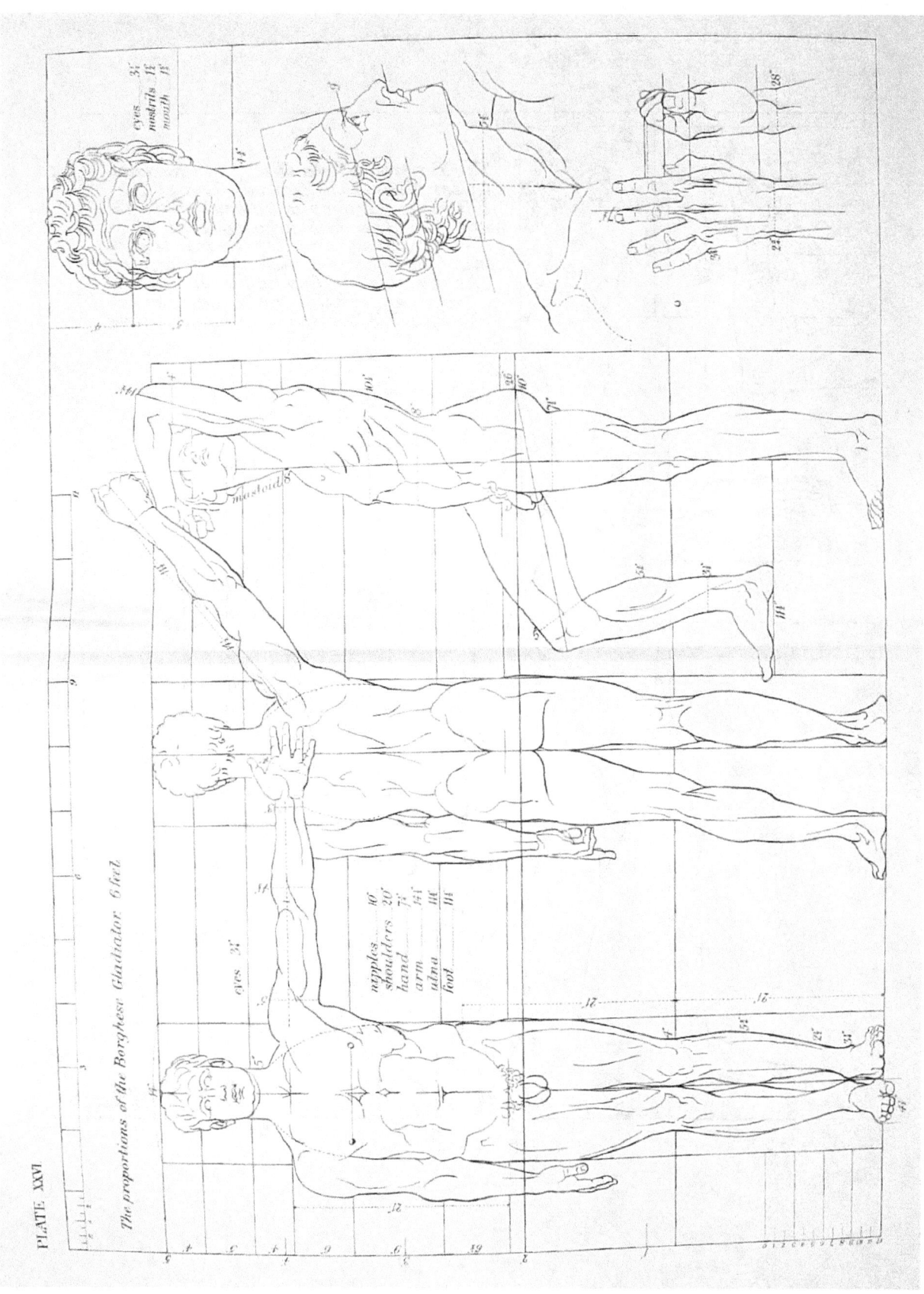

PLATE XXVI.

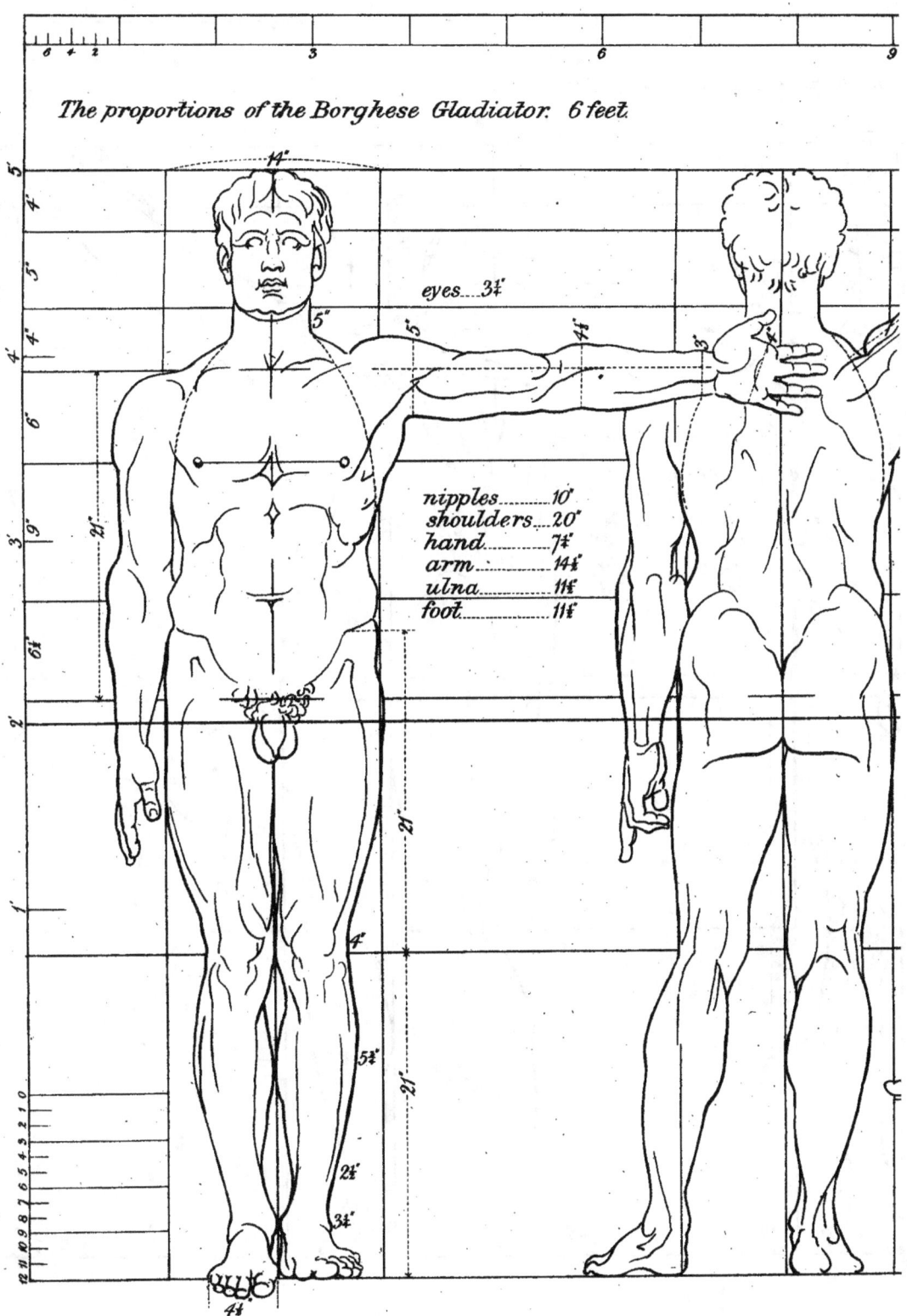

The proportions of the Borghese Gladiator. 6 feet.

eyes....3¼"

nipples	10"
shoulders	20"
hand	7¾"
arm	14½"
ulna	11½"
foot	11½"

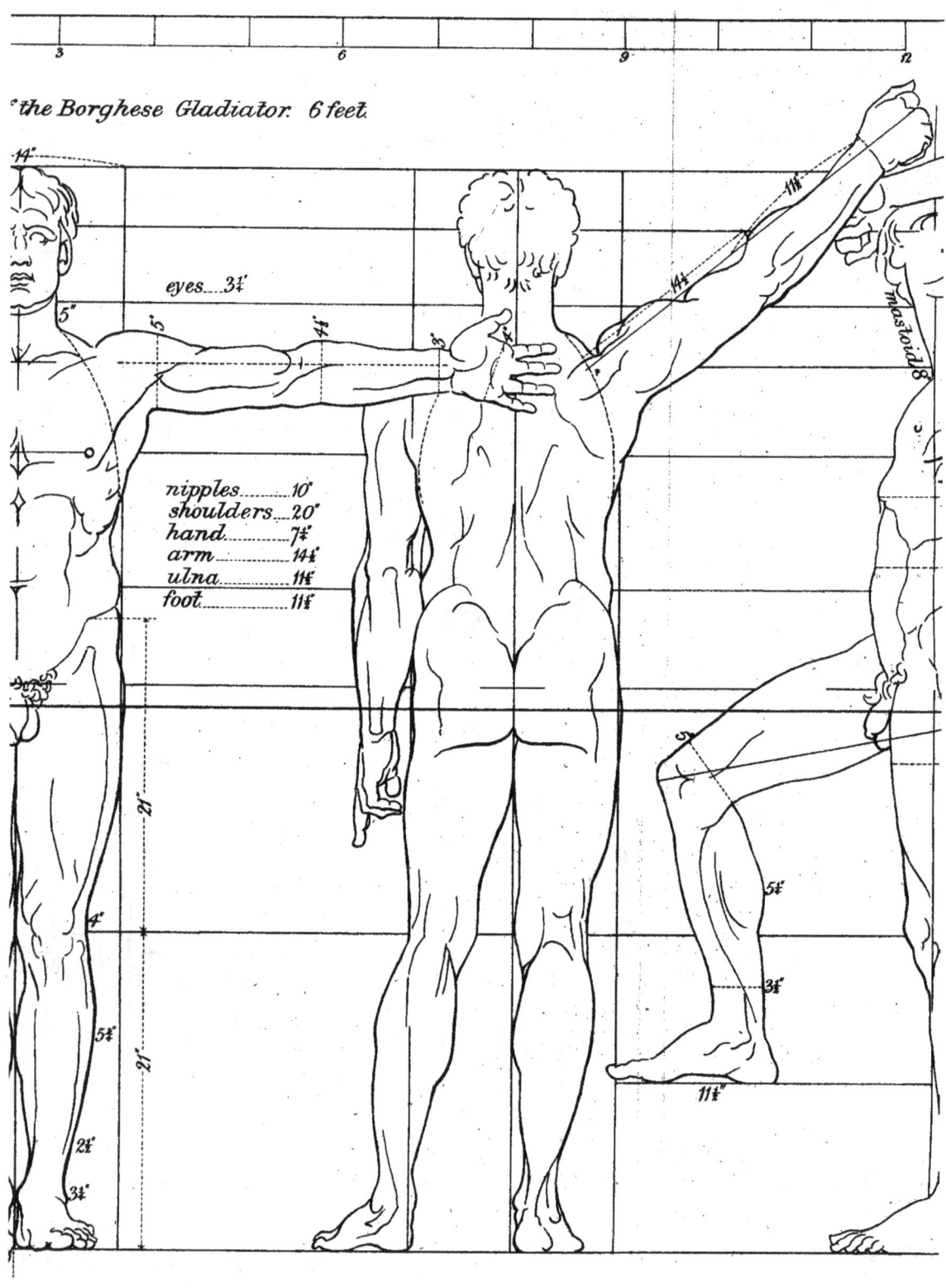

the Borghese Gladiator. 6 feet.

eyes___3¼"

nipples_____10"
shoulders__20"
hand_____7¼"
arm_____14¼"
ulna_____11¼"
foot_____11¼"

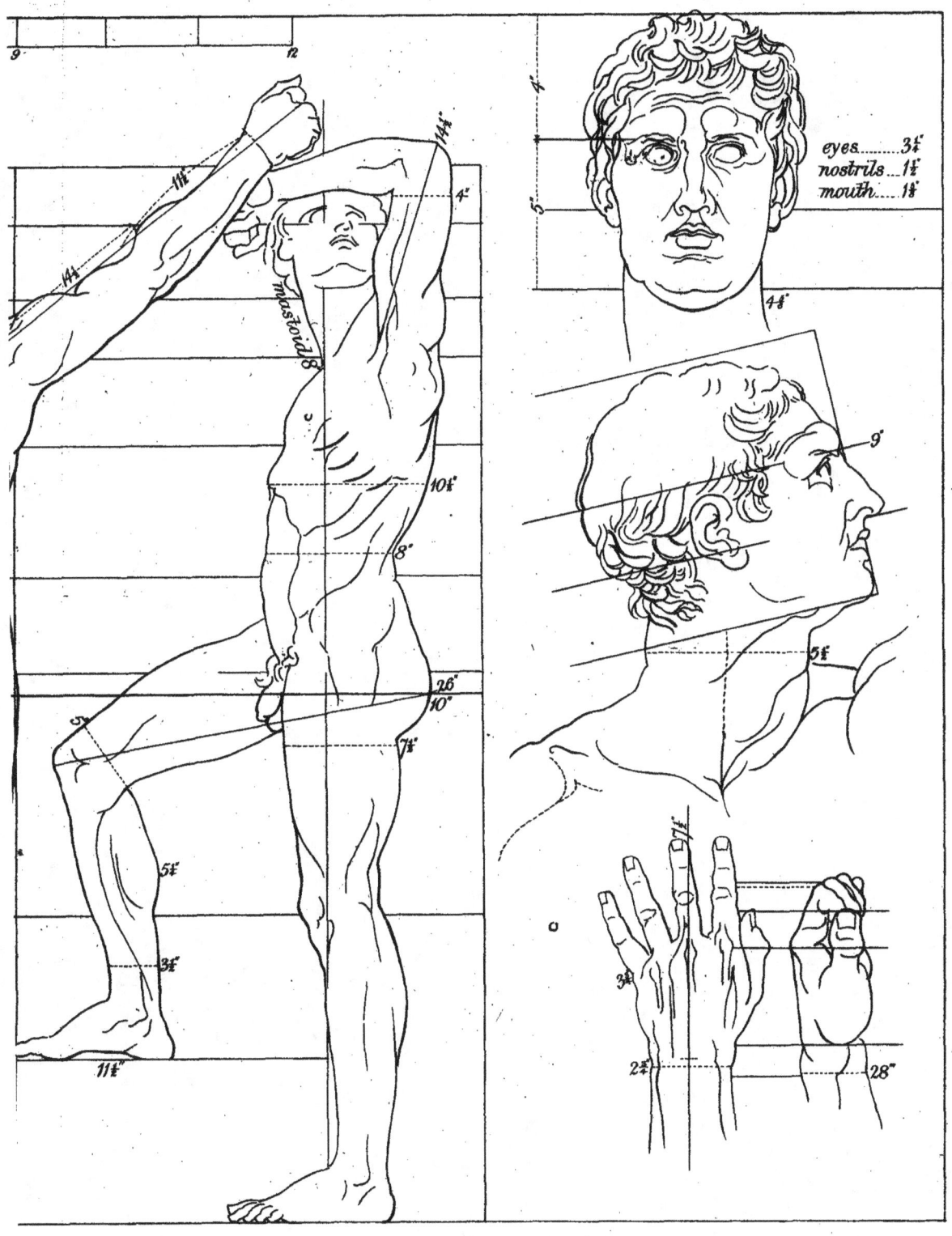

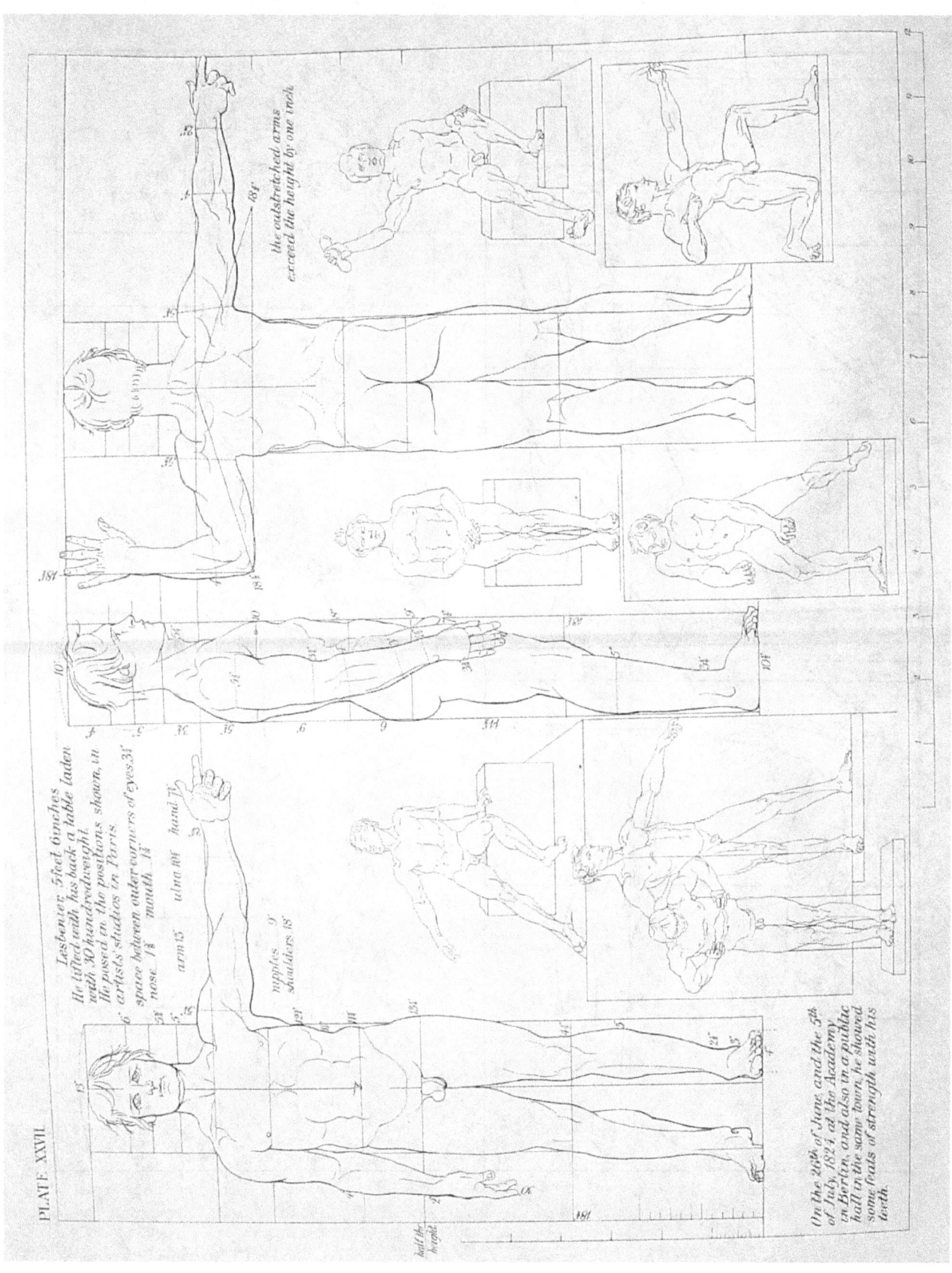

PLATE XXVII.

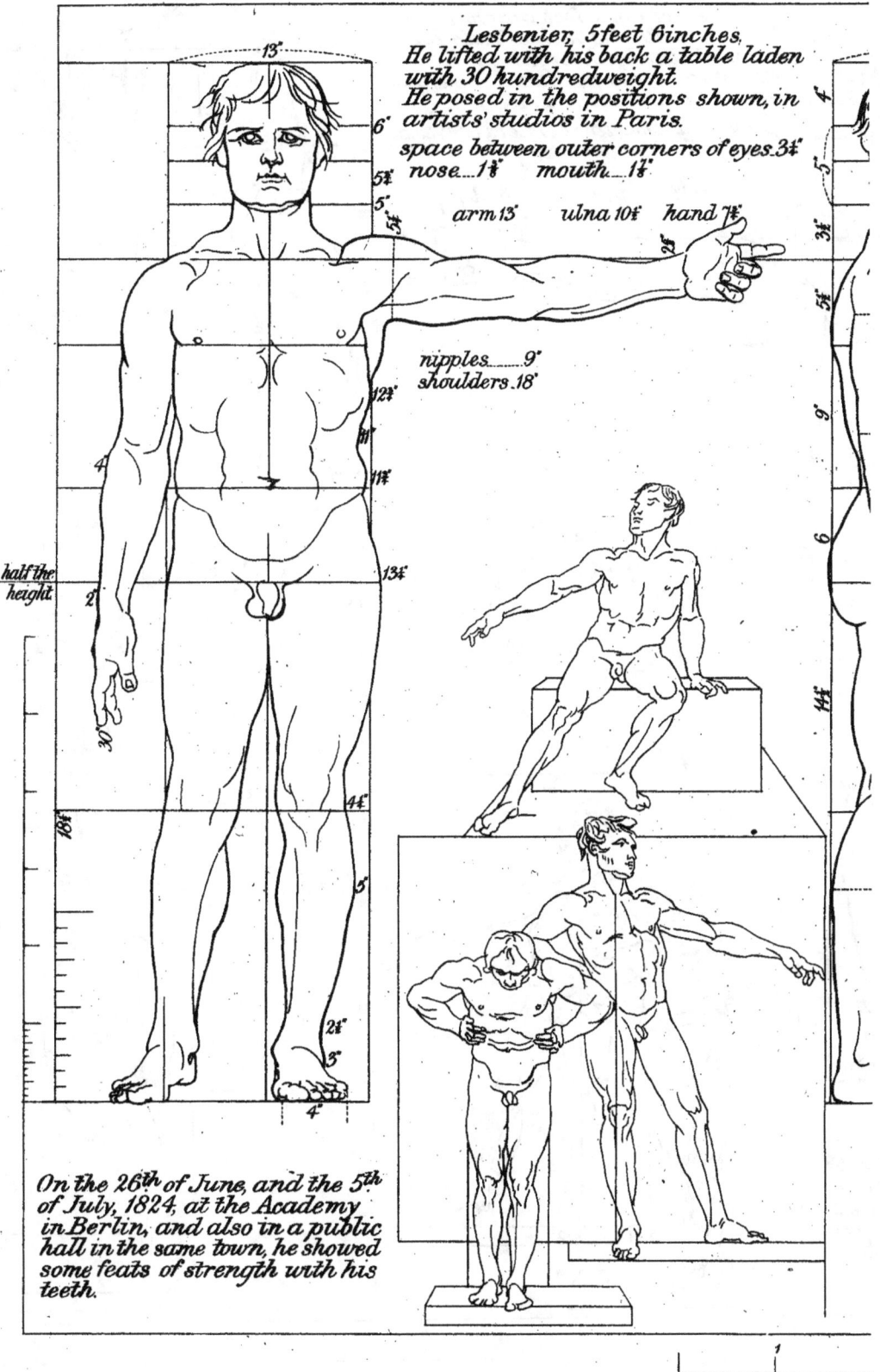

Lesbenier, 5 feet 6 inches.
He lifted with his back a table laden
with 30 hundredweight.
He posed in the positions shown, in
artists' studios in Paris.

space between outer corners of eyes 3¼˝
nose...1⅞˝   mouth...1⅞˝

arm 13˝   ulna 10⅜˝   hand 7⅞˝

nipples...9˝
shoulders.18˝

half the
height

On the 26th of June, and the 5th
of July, 1824, at the Academy
in Berlin, and also in a public
hall in the same town, he showed
some feats of strength with his
teeth.

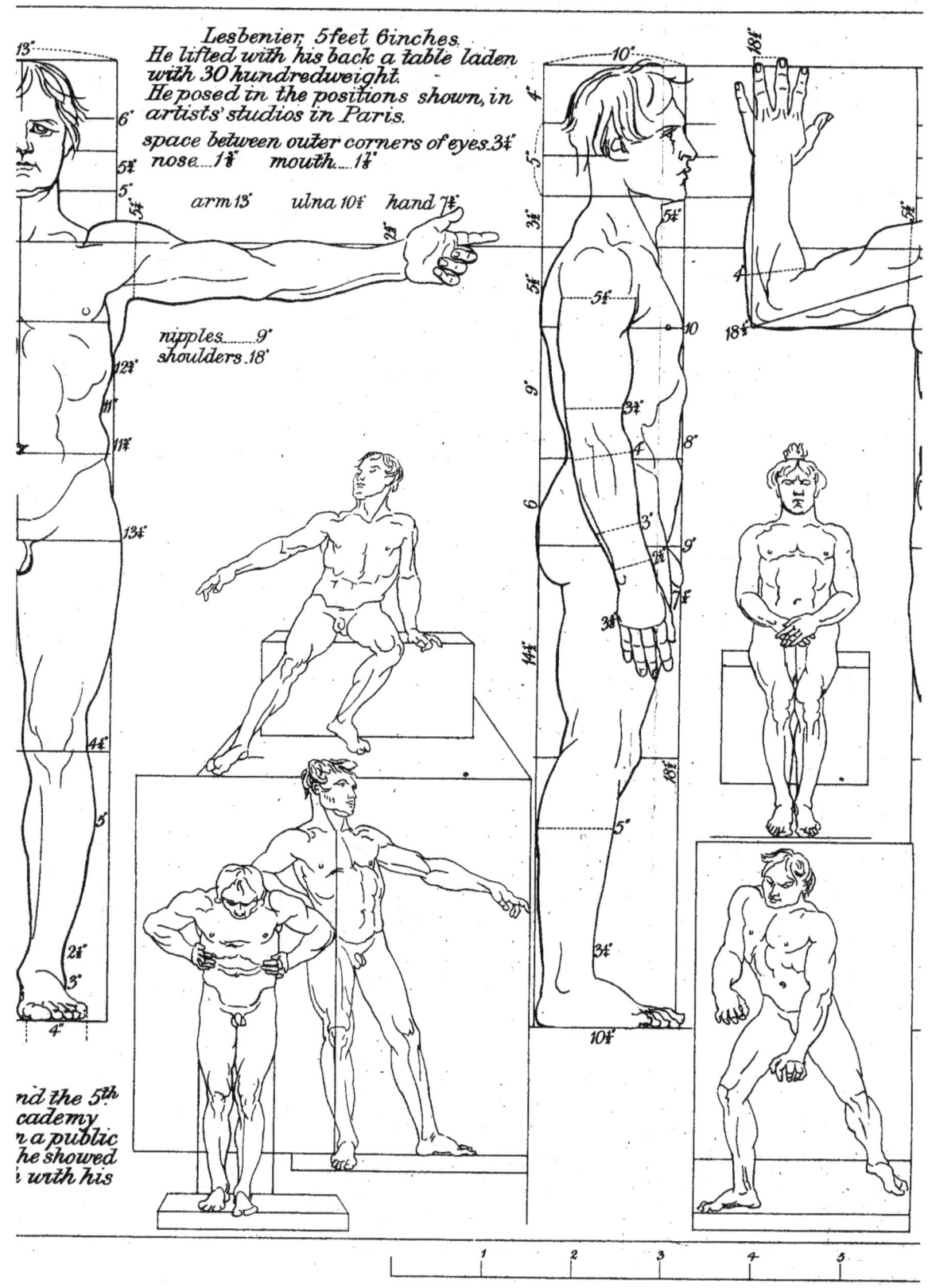

Lesbenier, 5 feet 6 inches.
He lifted with his back a table laden
with 30 hundredweight.
He posed in the positions shown, in
artists' studios in Paris.

space between outer corners of eyes 3¼
nose 1⅜   mouth 1½

arm 13   ulna 10¼   hand 7½

nipples 9
shoulders 18

nd the 5th
cademy
r a public
he showed
 with his

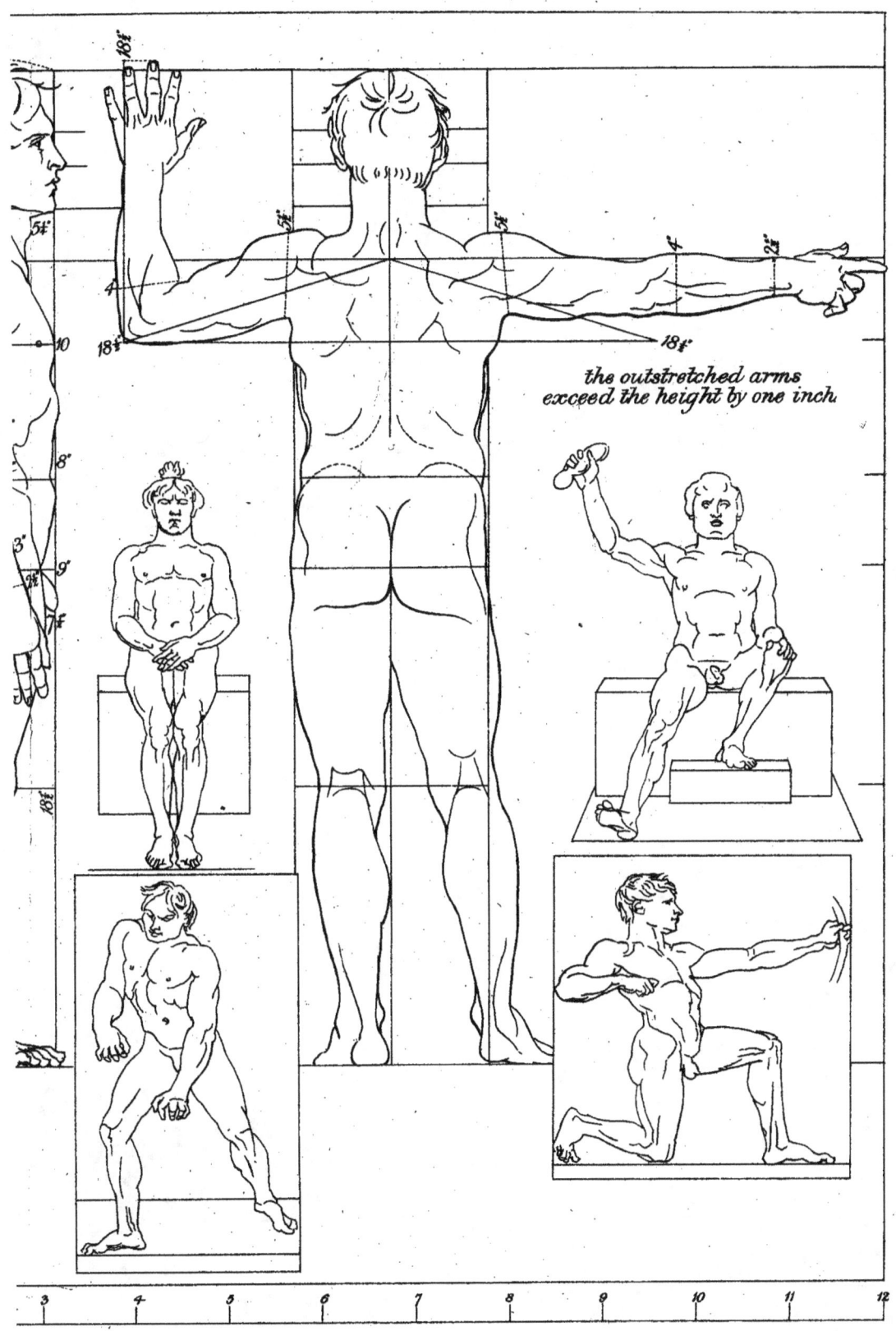

the outstretched arms
exceed the height by one inch

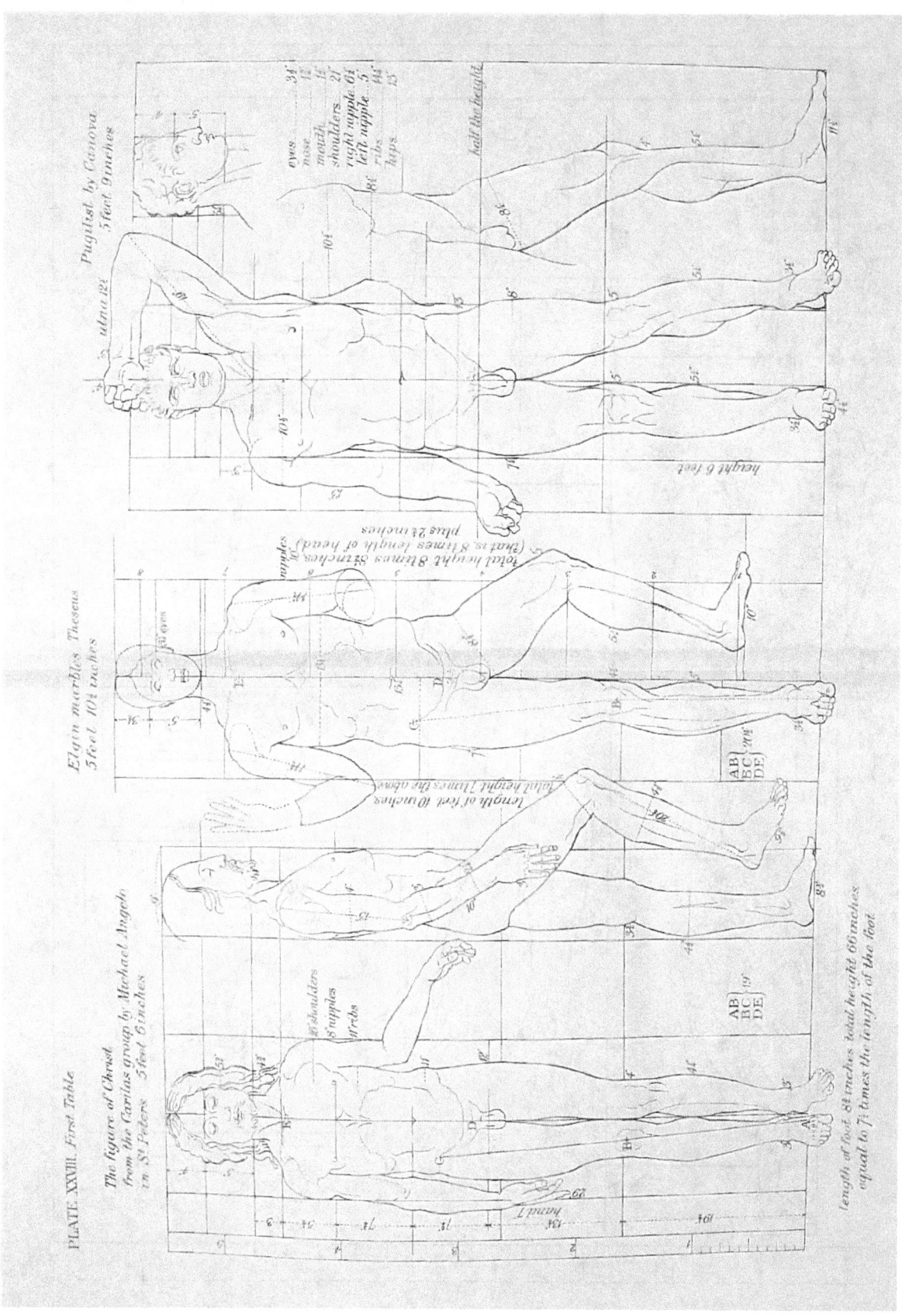

PLATE XXVIII. *First Table.*

The figure of Christ,
from the Carilas group by Michael Angelo,
in St Peter's.   5 feet 6 inches.

Elgin m
5 feet 10

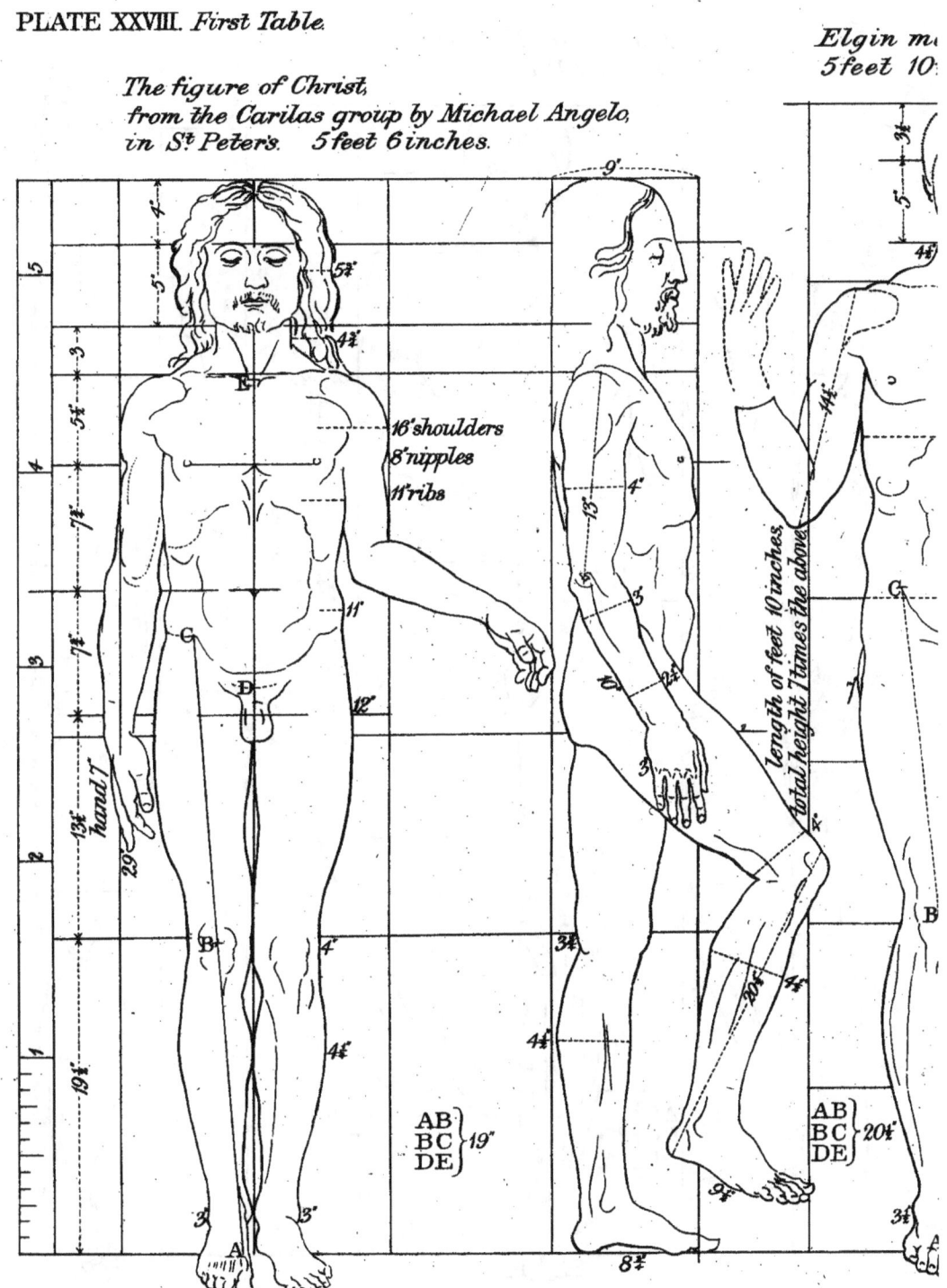

16' shoulders
8' nipples
11' ribs

length of foot 8¾ inches total height 66 inches,
equal to 7½ times the length of the foot.

129

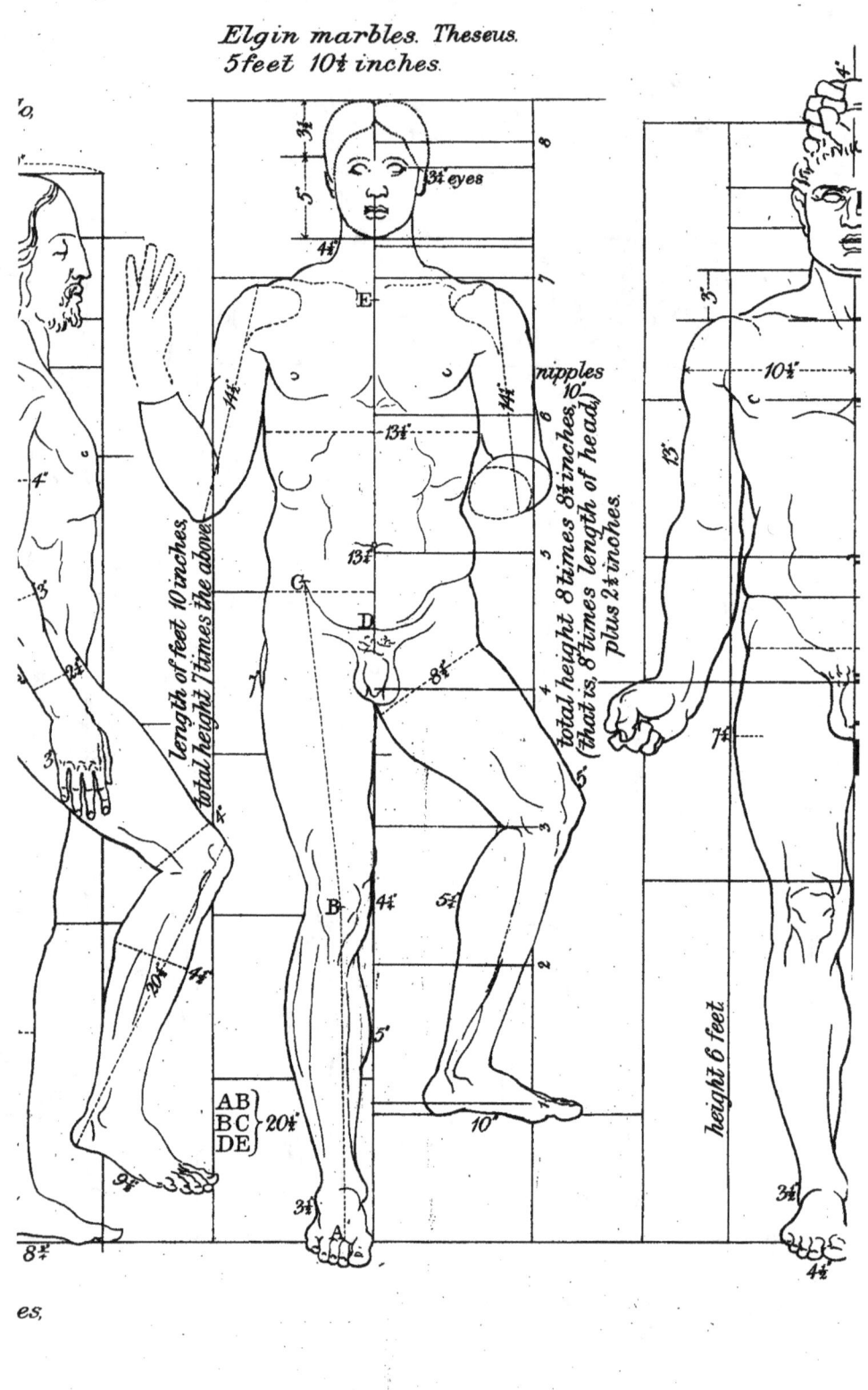

Elgin marbles. Theseus.
5 feet 10¼ inches.

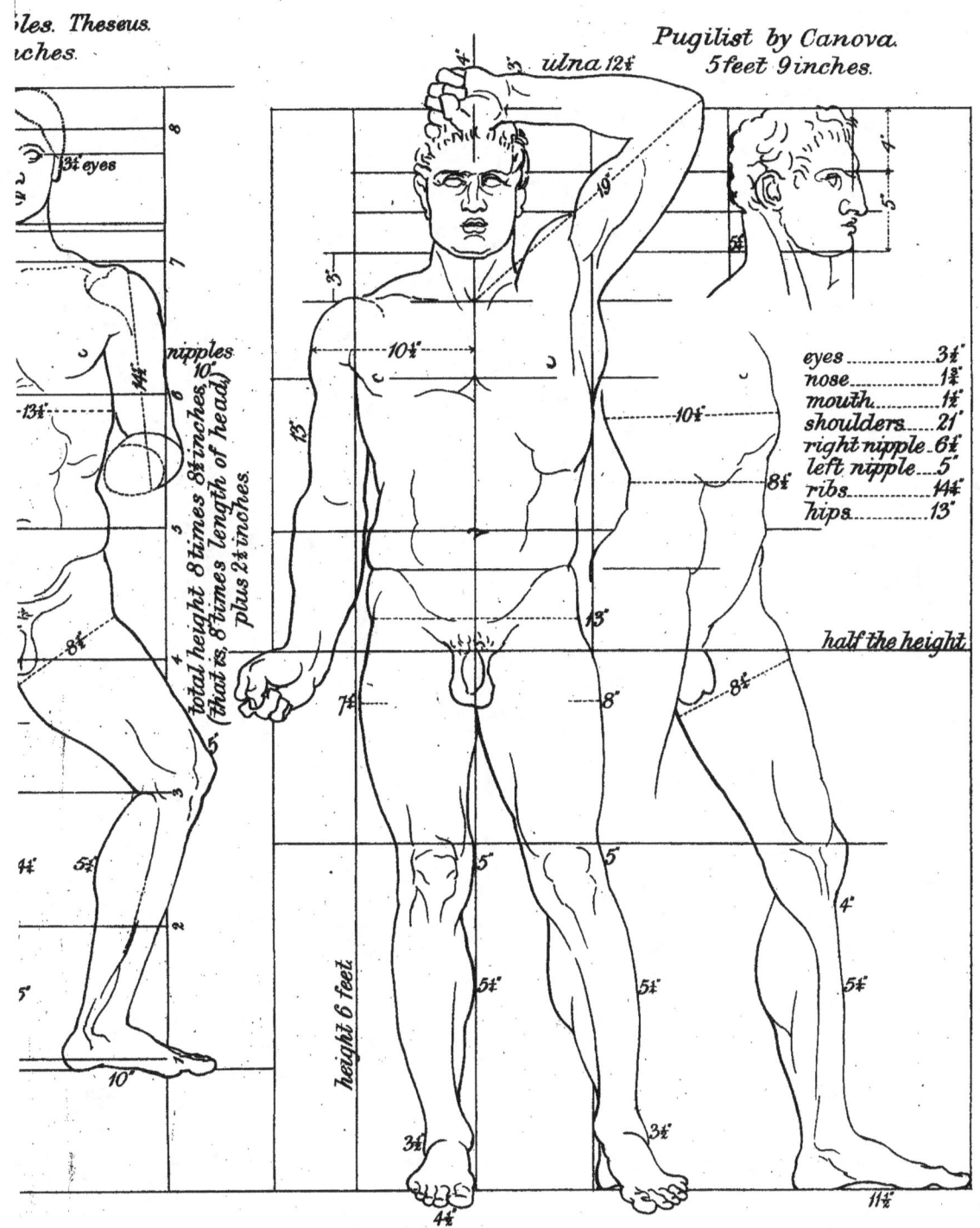

les. Theseus.
ches.

3¼ eyes

nipples
10″
13¼″

total height 8 times 8 inches, (that is, 8 times length of heads) plus 2¼ inches.

Pugilist by Canova.
5 feet 9 inches.

ulna 12¼

19″

10¼″

eyes............3¼″
nose...........1¾″
mouth........1¼″
shoulders....21″
right nipple 6¼″
left nipple....5″
ribs............14¼″
hips...........13″

10¼″

8¼″

half the height

8¼″

13″

13″

7¼″

8″

height 6 feet

5″

5″

5¼″

5¼″

4″

5¼″

3¼″

3¼″

4½″

11¼″

10″

4¼″   5¼″

2

5″

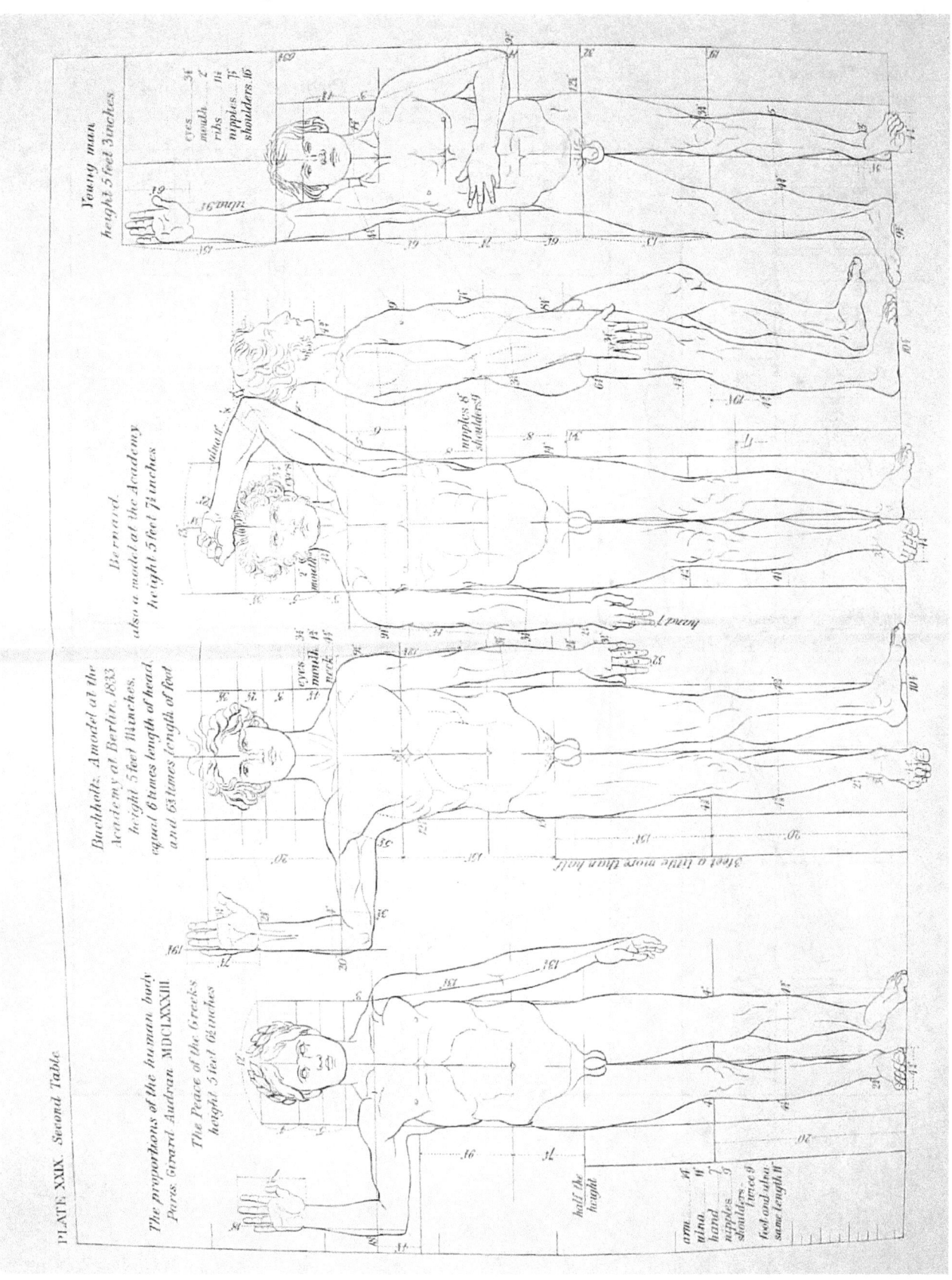

PLATE XXIX. *Second Table.*

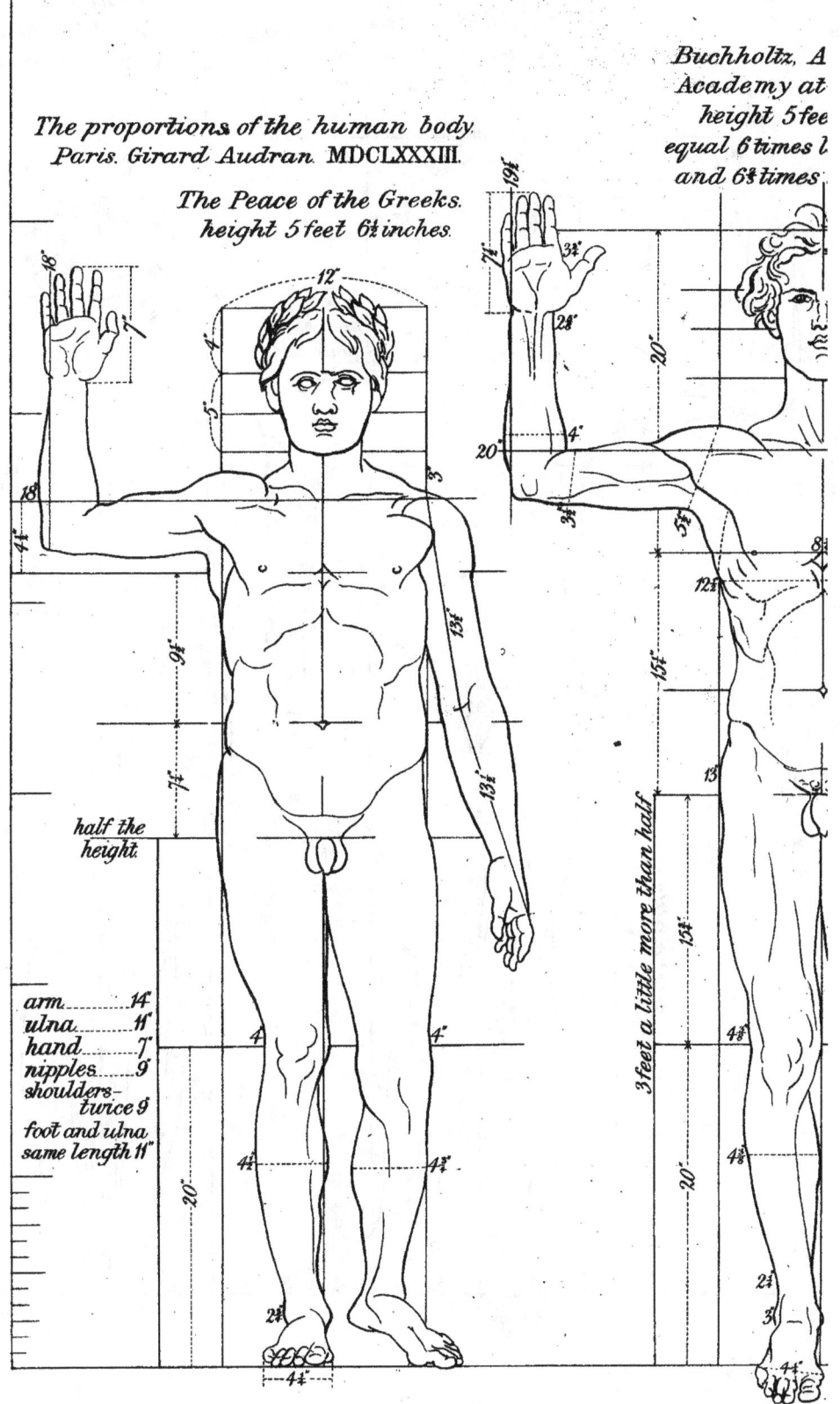

*The proportions of the human body.
Paris. Girard Audran. MDCLXXXIII.*

*The Peace of the Greeks.
height 5 feet 6½ inches.*

*Buchholtz, A
Academy at
height 5 fee
equal 6 times l
and 6½ times*

half the
height.

arm..........14"
ulna..........11"
hand..........7"
nipples..........9"
shoulders–
twice 9
foot and ulna
same length 11"

3 feet a little more than half

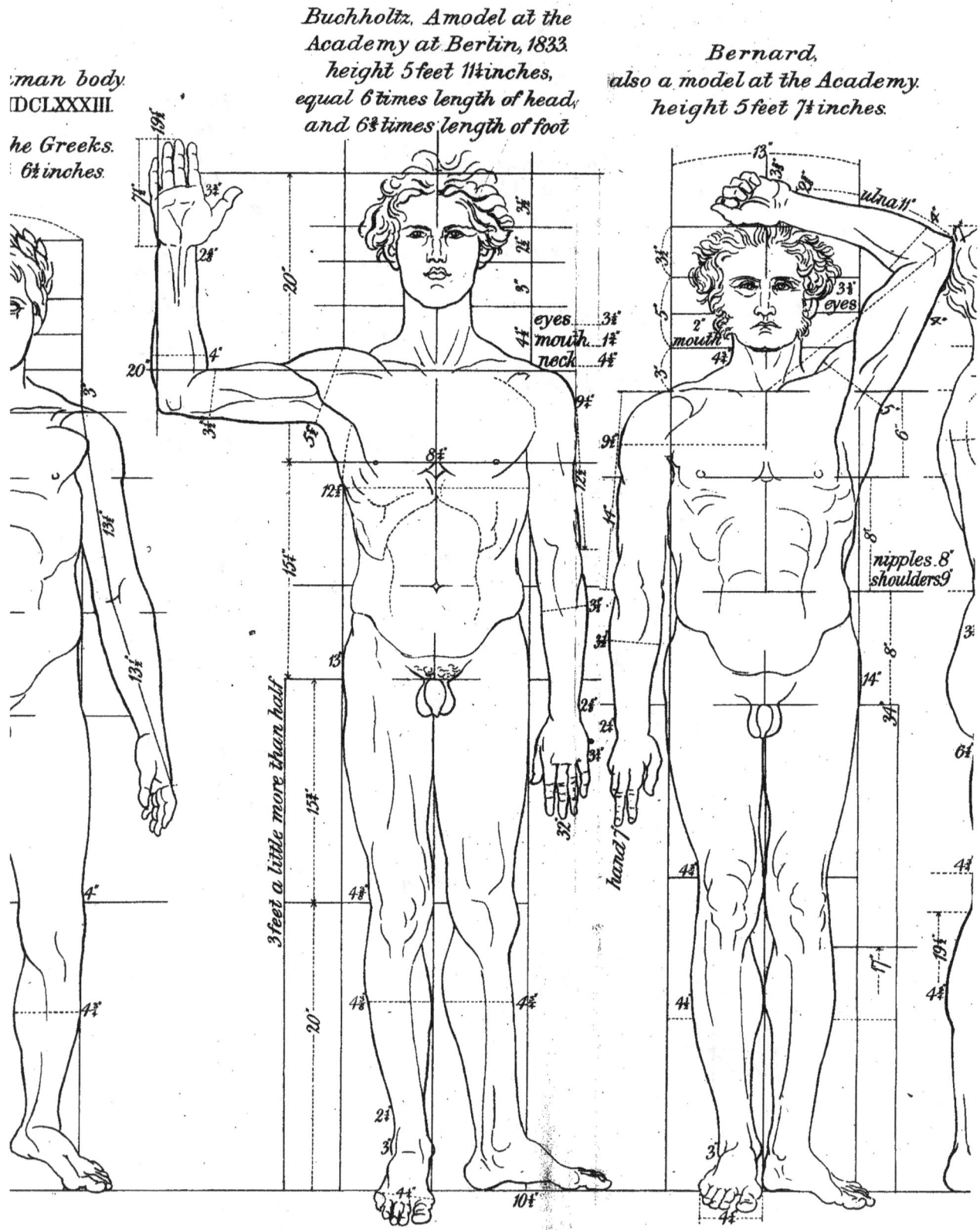

Buchholtz, A model at the
Academy at Berlin, 1833.
height 5 feet 11¼ inches,
equal 6 times length of head,
and 6⅜ times length of foot

Bernard,
also a model at the Academy.
height 5 feet 7¼ inches.

:man body.
:DCLXXXIII.

:he Greeks.
: 6¼ inches.

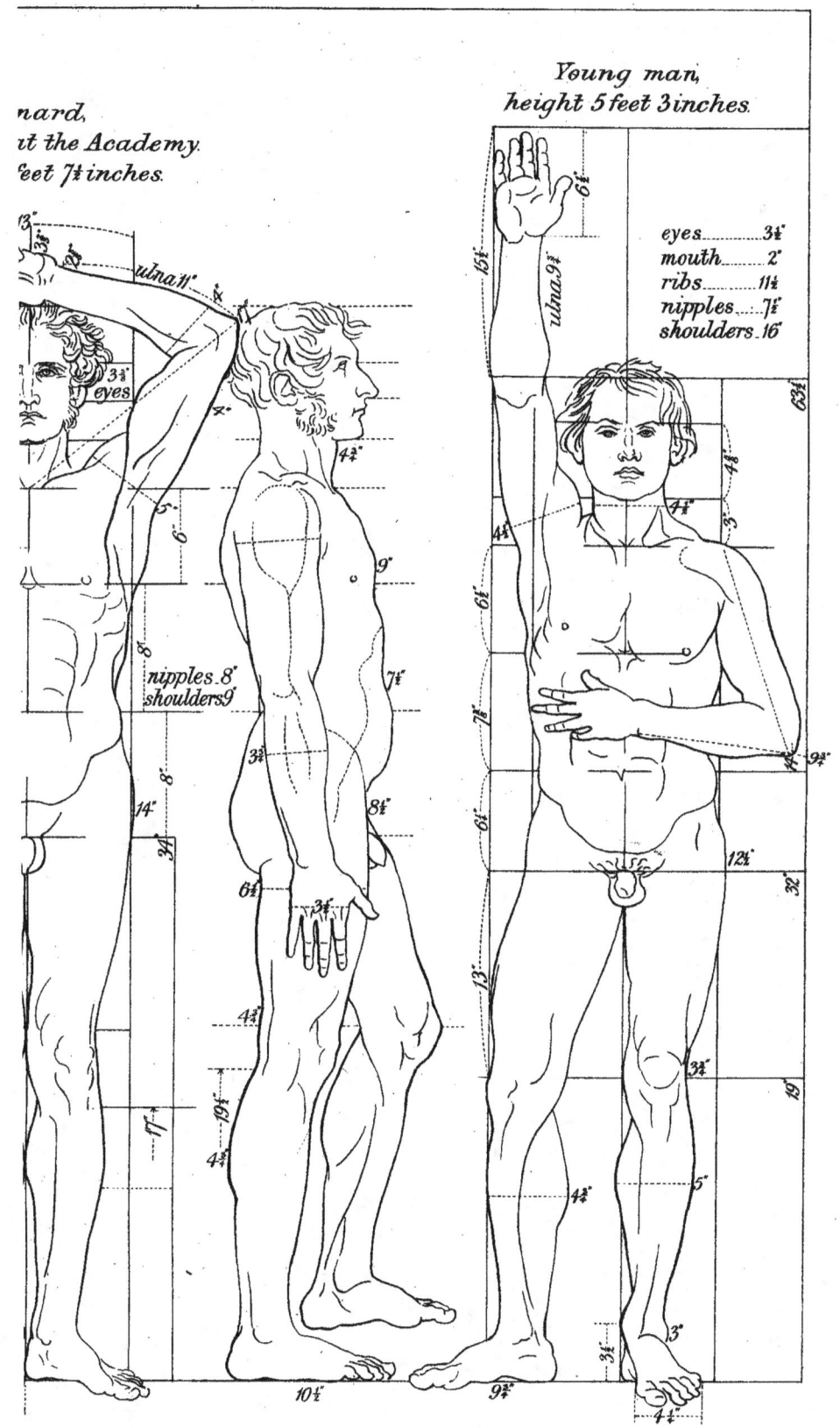

nard,
it the Academy.
eet 7¼ inches.

Young man,
height 5 feet 3 inches.

eyes............ 3¼"
mouth.......... 2"
ribs............. 11¼"
nipples .... 7¼"
shoulders .16"

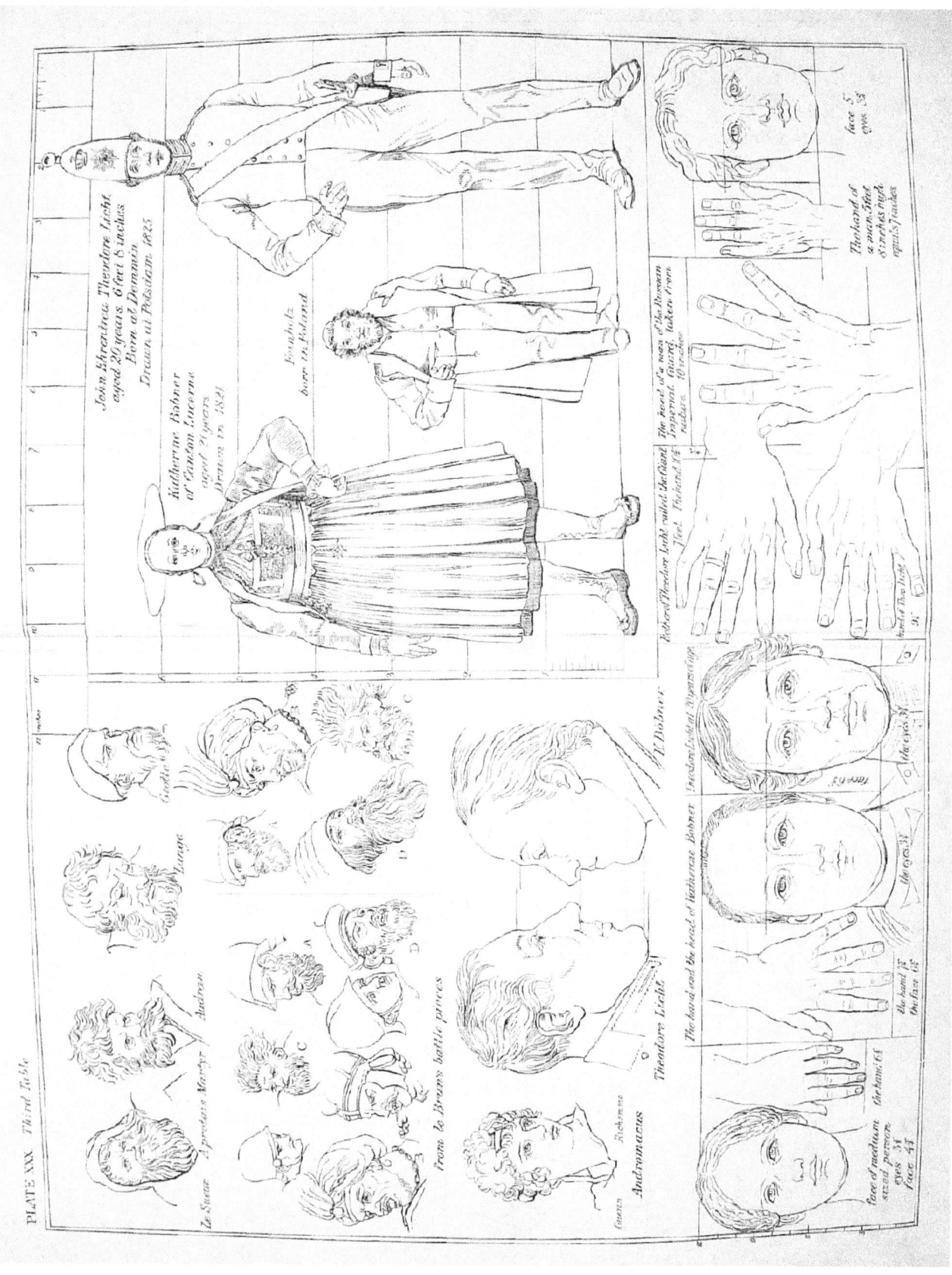

PLATE XXX. *Third Table.*

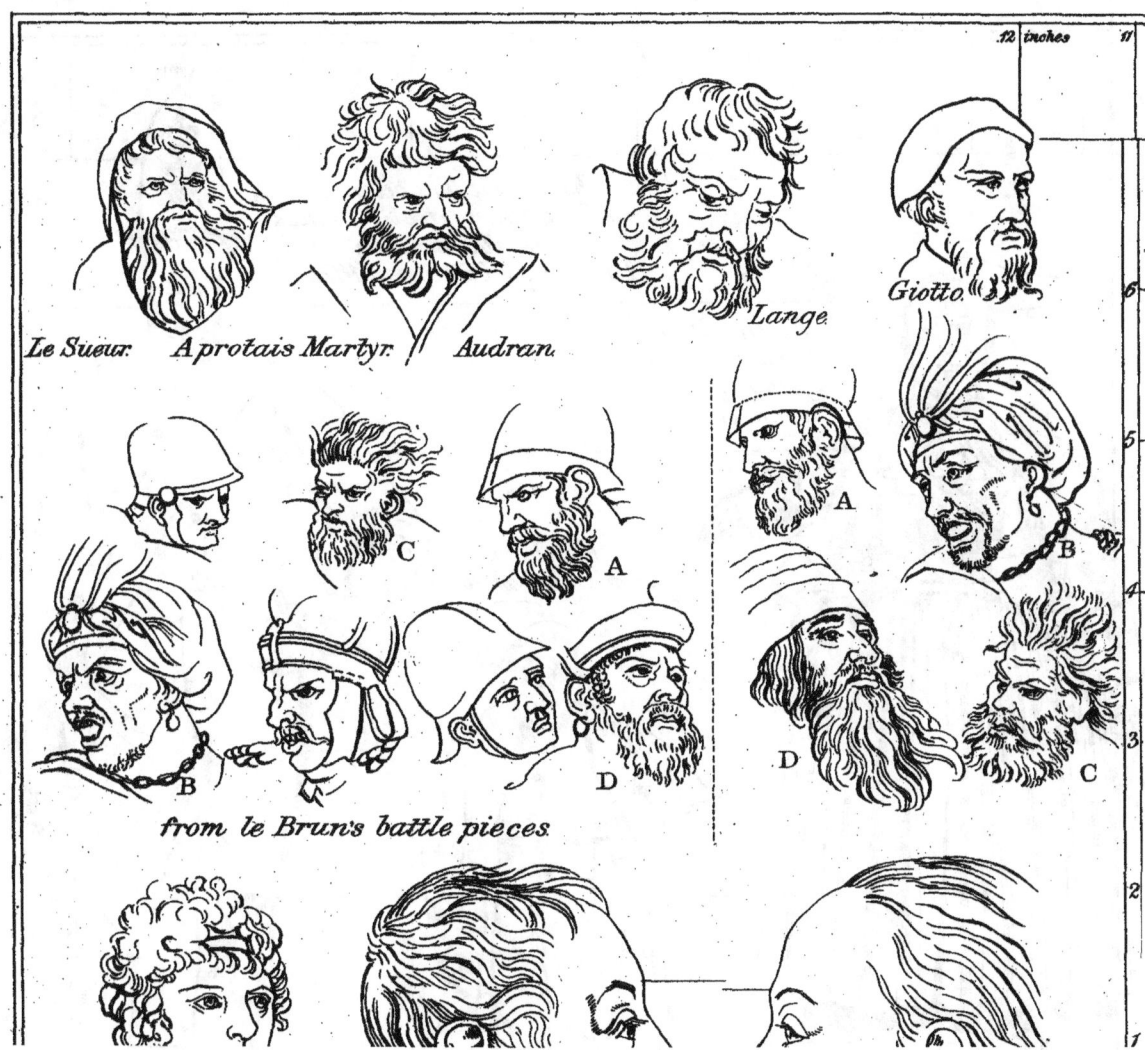

Le Sueur. Aprotais Martyr. Audran.

Lange.

Giotto.

from le Brun's battle pieces

137

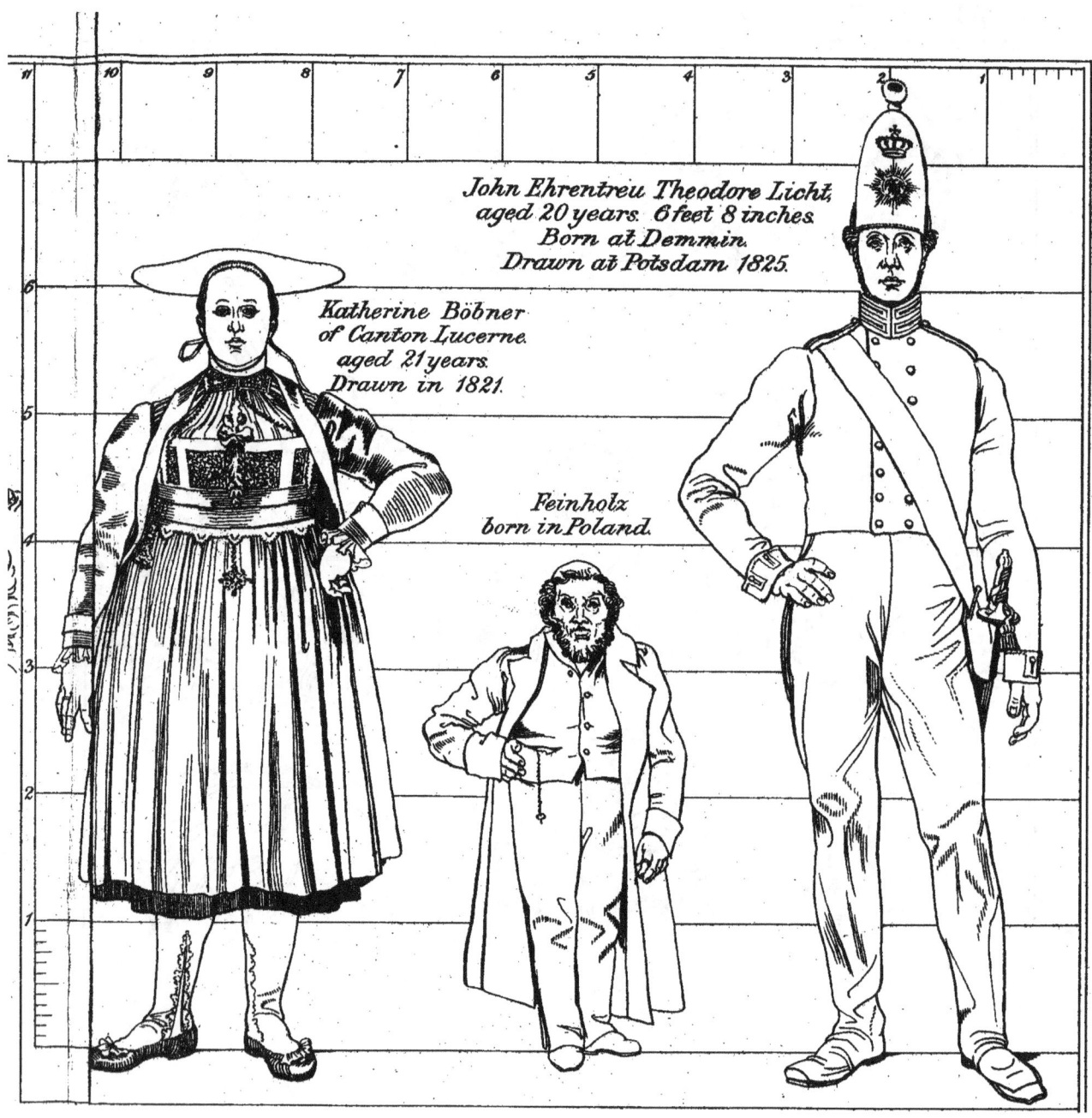

John Ehrentreu Theodore Licht,
aged 20 years. 6 feet 8 inches.
Born at Demmin.
Drawn at Potsdam 1825.

Katherine Böbner
of Canton Lucerne.
aged 21 years.
Drawn in 1821.

Feinholz
born in Poland.

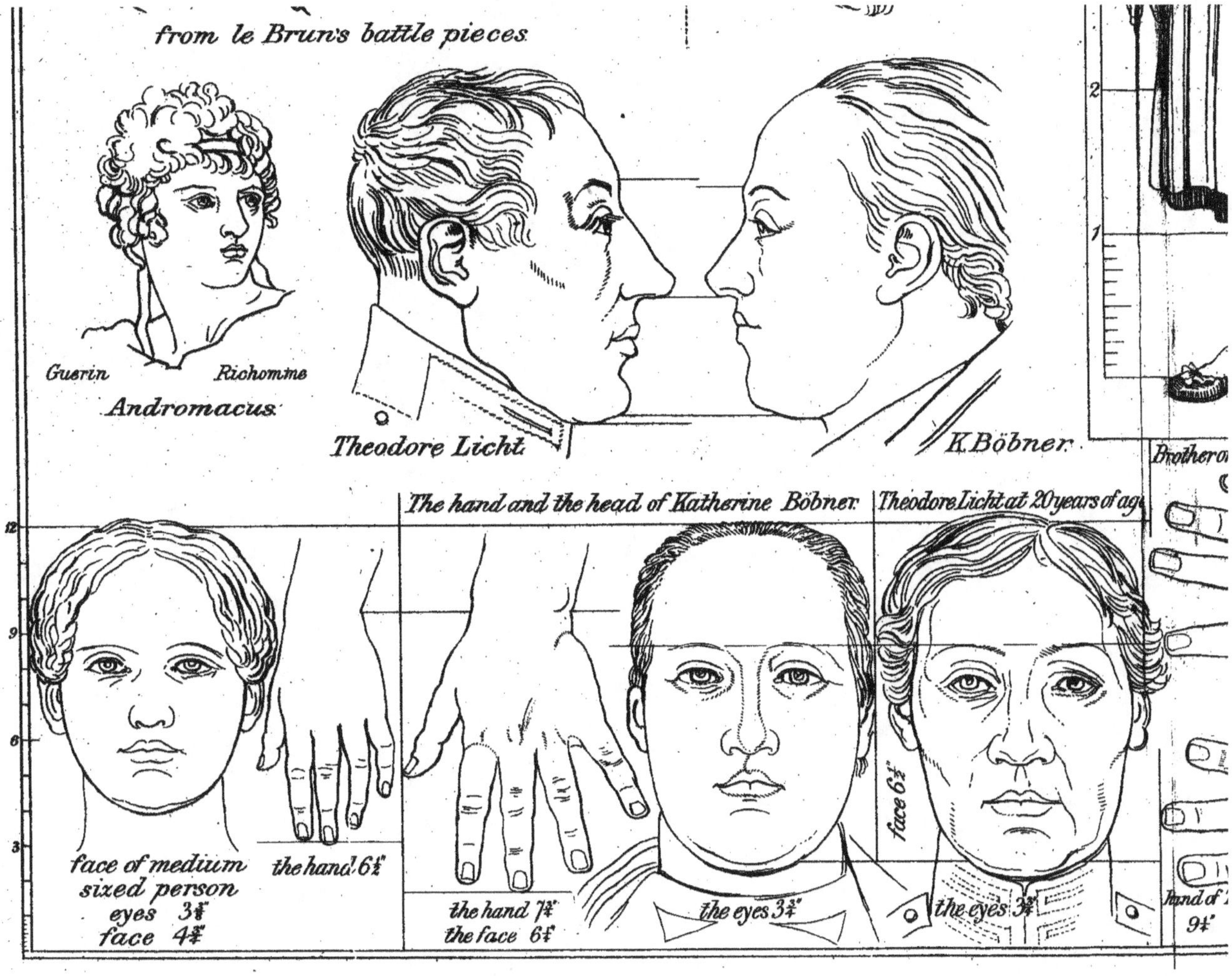
from le Brun's battle pieces
Guerin
Richomme
Andromacus
Theodore Licht
K.Böbner
The hand and the head of Katherine Böbner
Theodore Licht at 20 years of age
face of medium
sized person
eyes 3¼"
face 4¾"
the hand 6½"
the hand 7¼"
the face 6¼"
the eyes 3¾"
face 6½"
the eyes 3¾"
9¼"

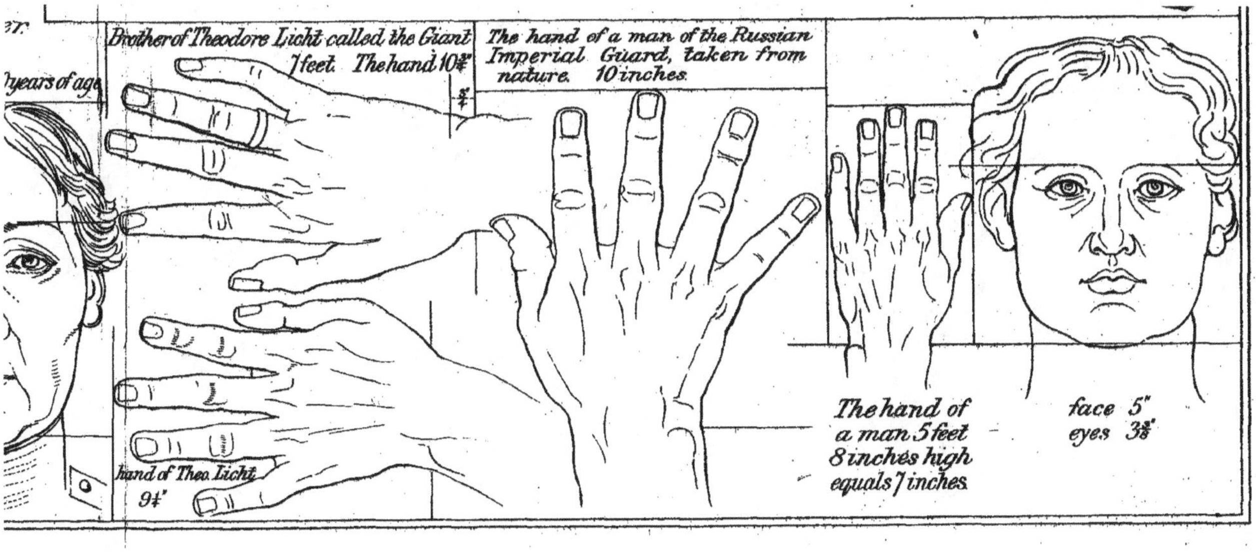
Brother of Theodore Licht called the Giant
7 feet. The hand 10¾"
The hand of a man of the Russian
Imperial Guard, taken from
nature. 10 inches
hand of Theo. Licht
9¼"
The hand of
a man 5 feet
8 inches high
equals 7 inches
face 5"
eyes 3⅜"

APPENDIX I.

(From the minutes of proceedings of the Royal Academy of Sciences in Berlin: Lecture by Counsellor Hirt, illustrated by a diagram showing the proportions of a man.)

The knowledge which we possess of the work of Polycletus, leads us to the belief that his so called "Canon" consisted of a statue designed principally to show the beautiful proportions of the human body; the statue represents the figure of a youth who has attained maturity, Pliny (34, 19, 2) remarks, when referring to the works of Polycletus, "One of the productions was designated by artists 'The Canon,' because they worked in accordance with its proportions, and were bound by it as by a law." In virtue of this great work, "Polycletus" was regarded-as a master, whose canon of art was accepted as a standard of excellence.

The following passage from Galenus, "De Temperencia," (1, 9) has reference to the same work :—

"Carvers, painters, sculptors, and artists in general, strive to paint and represent the most beautiful forms they can find, whether of human beings or animals. Such a form is exemplified by the 'Canon.' of - Polycletus. This statue owed its name to the fact that its parts are of perfect proportions, and in harmony."

In Lucian's "De Saltat" (p 946), a comparison is made between the figure of the dancer (designated perfect) and that of the "Canon" of Polycletus. The description, which is somewhat of a negative character, is couched in the fol
lowing words :—

"The dancer must neither be long nor short and dwarf-like, neither fleshy nor fat, but not so lank and thin as to resemble skeleton covered with a skin. His build and proportions must, in a word, combine accuracy of form with the most perfect symmetry."

The statue of Polycletus has been called by some the Doryphorus or Lance-bearer, instead of the "Canon." Cicero (do clar. Orat. a. 86) has noticed the work in the following passage :—

"You have taken as an example the oration in favour of the laws of Servilius in the same way as Lysippus, for his work, chose the Doryphorus."

In a passage of his orations (ad Brut. c. 2) be remarks that :—

"Other artists did not allow the perfections of such statues as those of the Olympian Jupiter and the Doryphorus to discourage them from the attempt to produce something greater."

Quintilian also cites the Doryphorus as a standard work (5.12) in the following terms :—

"The most celebrated sculptors and painters, when representing the most beautiful figures, have never taken as their model either a Bagoas or Megabyzus, but have chosen the Doryphorus, whose form is as suitable for the figure of a warrior as for that of a gladiator."

These latter extracts imply that the Canon and the Doryphorus were one and the same statue. Pliny, however, was of a different opinion, and wrote of them as two statues; still, there is little doubt that this is either an error (many such occur in his art jottings), or an incorrect sense has been given to the text through false punctuation. Pliny's words are: "Polycletus" "Diadumenum fecit molliter juvenum, centum talentis nobiliatum:. idem et Doryphorum viriliter puerum. Feint at quem Canona artifices vocant, lineamenta artis ex eo petentes, velut a lege quadam, etc."

It is possible that Pliny's meaning was that the Doryphorus is the statue which artists call the Canon, and, in order to express this idea clearly, the full.stop after the word puerum would have to be struck out and a comma placed after the word fecit. This view of the matter is supported by passages from other writers, who refer to both titles as belonging to the same statue. Again, the statue of the Canon must have been made to represent as erect a position as possible, and that of a lance-bearer would, no doubt, be the simplest and most suitable for the purpose. It should also be borne in mind that, in all probability, the appellation of Canon was rather a nickname than the actual title which had been given to the statue. The real Canon of Polycletus consisted- of some writings, in which he explained the laws of proportion, and the statue was, no doubt, intended to illustrate these laws. The following passage from Galenus (de Placit Hippocr. et Plat 5, p. 288 ed Basil) gives further information on this point :—

"The beauty of the human body is shown in the symmetry of the various parts, as clearly explained in the Canon of Polycletus. In these writings the master has described-his law of all the proportions of the body, and has illustrated this by means of a statue made in exact conformity with his rules. The name of Canon was given by him both to the writings and the statue."

Polycletus, the Sicyonian, who gave such eminence to the ancient schools of art by means of his "Canon," was a pupil of Ageladas. He lived in the age of Pericles, which may be termed the most flourishing epoch of Greek art. Polycletus, in addition to his fame as a sculptor, had that of an able architect. The theatre and the temple of Epidaurus, designed by him, were both considered as examples of symmetry and beautiful proportions (Paus 2.27). He was, however, not the only man of his time who acquired eminence, as regards the study of proportion. Myron, his fellow pupil and rival, is said to have given even more attention than Polycletus to symmetry of form in his works (see Plin. 84.19, § 3). The painters Parrbasius and. Zeuxis, contemporaries of the above-named sculptors, were the first to introduce into painting a symmetrical treatment. Zeuxis, in particular, deviated considerably from the Canon of Polycletus. The limbs and beads of his figures are larger; the dimensions generally seem to have been chosen of an undue size, possibly in imitation of Homer, who had a love for figures of stupendous proportions, whether male or female (Plin 85, 36, § 2 and 5, Conf. Quint 12.10).

At a later period Euphranor, a celebrated sculptor and painter, wrote on the subject of proportion in the 104th Olympiad. The dimensions of the torso prescribed by him are slight, but be gave somewhat nobler proportions for the head and limbs (Plin. 35.40, § 25).

Lysippus acknowledged that he. had taken the Doryphorus as his teacher and example (Cicero de clar. Orat. c. 86), but in the study of symmetry he went even farther than Polycletus. The head and torso of his figures are smaller and harder in style than those in the works of more ancient masters. He imagined that by this treatment his statues gained in appearance, and, in order to avoid the squareness of style which characterized the works of the older masters, he diverged considerably from the canons of art then prevailing. Euphranor's words were, "The old masters represented men as they were, but he portrayed them as they appeared to him" (Plin. 84.19, § 6). It should not, however, cause surprise that, in a matter so dependent on individual feeling and optical experience, Euphranor, as well as many other artists, declined to adopt the instructions of Polycletus in their entirety.

The want of some law of proportion was, no doubt, felt in the schools of art which existed anterior to the time of Polycletus, and it may be taken for granted that some efforts were made to supply the deficiency; there is no record left of any previous works, but Diodor (1.98) gives some interesting particulars about two very old masters, Taleclos and Thedorus of Samoa (sons of Phoecus), whose work appears to have had some bearing on this subject. These men had studied art in Egypt, and had brought from that country a special method of measuring the human body. By means of this devise, they completed on their return the statue of the Apollo Pythius for their native town; one of these sculptors worked at Ephesus, on one half of the statue, and the other half was completed by his coadjutor at Samos. When the halves were placed together they fitted perfectly, and showed that no mistake had been committed with regard to the dimensions. In accordance with the laws of Egyptian art, the brothers had divided the entire figure into 21¼ parts, and each worker had given to his portion of the figure. the exact number of parts it required; in this way the entire work was brought to a successful issue.

The Egyptians, from whom the Greeks learned their art, appear, therefore, to have had some kind of law for the proportions of the body, and to have made their statues in conformity therewith. This law could, however, only have been a technical makeshift to enable the workman to model quickly a statue in clay and afterwards copy it in wood or other material. An examination of Egyptian sculptures suffices to prove that the canon of art above referred to was certainly not the outcome either of a feeling for, or a knowledge of, the beauty of the human form; which is so inseparably connected with the graceful symmetry of each part. It is true that the art which the Greeks received from the Egyptians was of a rude description, but it is only fair to add that, even their primitive method of measuring the limbs gave an impetus to the further development of artistic principles amongst the Greeks, whose love of the beautiful soon taught them to choose from the graceful forms they were able so closely, to observe, the one which was the most suitable for their art, and which could be accepted as a standard for all time.

DESCRIPTION OF THE PLATES.

Before proceeding to a description of the Plates at the end of this work, a few words about the scale, employed for the measurements will be necessary.

The Rhenish foot is divided into 12 inches, and the inch into eight parts. The scale of twelve inches was derived from the foot of an unusually big man; that of, a man of medium size measures 10 inches.

When using compasses it is found that twelfths of a foot are better than tenths, and that errors are avoided by a further division of the inch into eighths.

The Plates, which show in a conspicuous manner the proportions of the human body, represent the various stages from the new-born child to the full-grown man of a medium height of 5 feet 6 inches. In order, however, to show the infinite variety of nature, and the aids which art requires for its highest works, some figures of larger dimensions have been added.

In drawing it is customary to commence with the head, and in this work it has been deemed advisable to follow this practice. Students have; in fact, to draw the separate parts of the head at first, so as to prepare them for the difficulties of representing it as a whole. Draughtsmen, however, of some experience will find no difficulty in working according to the rules given herein.

PLATE I.

The upper half of Plate I. contains five heads, belonging to three different periods of life, viz., childhood, manhood, and old age.

The head may be taken to consist of two parts :—

1. The skull or upper part, containing the brain.
2. The face or lower part, from the top edge of the eye- cavities to the bottom of the chin.

The lower part of the head contains the organs of four senses exclusively, viz., sight, hearing, taste, and smell. The skin of the cheeks is the most flexible part of the whole body.

In order to determine a law for the proportions of the head, only three periods of life have been chosen, as a greater number might have caused some confusion.

The line cutting the upper edge of the eye-cavities is taken as a fixed one.

The full-grown face of a man has a length of 5 inches. Two vertical lines, at a distance of 5 inches from each other, enclose the full face in this case and form the basis of measurement for all the other faces.

The space between the outer corners of the eye is taken as 3 inches, and this measurement is adopted as a standard for all faces.

The proportion between this measurement (including a slight increase, owing to growth), and the length of the face, shows the essential difference of age; for instance, on Plate I.:—

Distance between Outer Corners of the Eye	Length of Face
Child's face, 3 inches.	3½ inches
Man's face, 3½	5 inches

A woman's head is shown between the child's and the man's. The length of the face is 4½ inches, or 1 inch shorter than that of the man. The eye-space in both cases being the same, viz., 3½ inches, it follows that the oval of the woman's face is rounder than the man's.

The forehead has hitherto been included in the division of the face, and in consequence of the uncertain boundary line of the hair, no standard of measurement has been applied to it.

The slight increase in the size of the child's skull and the woman's (see Plate I.) is :—

In the breadth, from 5½ in. to 6 inches.
In the height, from 3 inches to 3½ inches.

For the man's skull an unusual expansion has been taken, viz., 4 inches in height and 6½ inches in breadth; it will be seen from this that the growth of the part enclosing the brain is less than that of the various parts of the face.

The face for each age and sex is divided into six equal parts; counting downwards from the fixed line already referred to, we have

The first part, crossing the corners of the eyes.
The third part crossing the lower edge of the nostrils.
The fourth part crossing the cavity of the mouth.
The sixth part crossing the edge of the chin.

In the full-grown male head, the four squares have an equal width and height of 2½ inches, but in the woman's and children's beads the height of the squares is less than the.width, for example:—

Child ......Width, 2½ inches. Height, 1¾ inches.

In general, the eyes of children are somewhat smaller than those of adults, but the coloured part, or iris, attains its full size in the third year, and is often larger than that of old people, in whose eyes a good deal of white is seen surrounding the iris. New-born and young children show very little of the white. The diameter of the iris is somewhat less than ½ inch.

THE PROFILES.

The profiles of the five heads are shown in the middle of Plate I.

The basis of measurement for the profile of the man's head is as follows :— -

Height (same as before), 5 inches; breadth, 7½ inches.

In the breadth, one square has been added to the two mentioned above.

A vertical line touching the lower edge of the forehead may be termed "line of profile."

The child's head is enclosed in three squares of the same dimensions as in the former case, and the figure shows that the expansion is much less than in the head of the adult.

From the contour in dotted lines it is seen that the growth of the face is greater than that of the skull. The profile line (see man's head) touches the upper lip, lower lip, and chin, but in the child's head the upper lip projects beyond this line, and the chin does not touch it.

In the profile of the woman's head, the ear stands at the same distance as in the man's head, viz., 3¾ inches, although the face is ½ inch shorter than the male's. The female profile consequently appears. rounder than that of the male.

The nose can stand in relief a distance equal to one of the six parts, in which the lower part of the face is divided. This gives the necessary prominence to this feature both for the male and female face.

The breadth of the female nose, seen from the front, can be equal to the space between the inner corners of the eyes, that is, 1¼ inch. Breadth of male nose, 1½ inch. Breadth of female mouth, 1½ inch. Breadth of male mouth, 1¾ inch.

The eye, both male and female, can be drawn of equal size— namely, 1 inch.

The man's head differs from the woman's as follows :—

1. The greater width and prominence of the nose.
2. A larger cavity of the mouth.
8. A longer face.
4. A broader lower jaw, and consequently a thicker neck.

The neck increases in size, through growth, more than other parts. The increase from the third year to the period when growth ceases is almost double.

For example :— 2½ inches to 4½ inches.

The diameter of the skull increases from 5½ inches to 6½ inches.

These two instances are a further proof that the face becomes larger by growth than the skull.

OLD AGE.

The same division of the face as heretofore is adopted, and the Plate shows the essential differences produced by age.

As the vertebra becomes curved the skin at the back is distended as far as the upper edge of the eye-sockets, the eyebrows are drawn upwards, and, to a certain extent, the upper eyelids, hence the fixed look of old people.

The loss of teeth causes the lower jaw to rise, the cavity of the mouth and the edge of the chin are drawn up, the face thereby becoming shorter.

The diameter of the harder parts, such as the skull and the temple-bones, remains the same; on the other hand, the lower jaw shrinks on account of a decrease of power in the masticatory muscles.

The want of teeth causes the lips to recede and the upper lip draws down the tip of the nose. The chin, as seen in the Plate, projects beyond the profile line, on account of the lower jaw being drawn upwards.

The loss, of power in the muscles of the face is accompanied by a similar effect in those of the neck

In many works of art, the heads of old men and women are badly drawn, owing to the want of a knowledge of the foregoing principles

THE HAND AND FOOT.

The foot has served as a standard of measurement for a considerable time, on account of the facility with which its exact length could be taken.

The Germans and other nations have made use of the elbows (whence the ell), each one when measured separately having usually the same length as the foot.

A well formed foot, however, of a man of medium height, viz., 5 feet 6 inches, has a length of 10 inches (Rhenish scale); the ulna and foot are the same length.

The male foot on Plate I. is drawn according to this proportion, and has a length just double that of the face, which is 5 inches.

Measurements taken from nature, authorize us in adopting the same rule for the female foot.

For example :— Woman's face, 44 inches in length, or for the foot, 9 inches in length.

Plate I. shows the correct width.

These examples teach us that the length of the foot must exceed that of the face.

The proportion in the case of a child, three years old, is different. For instance :—

Length of head—6½ inches; length of foot—5½ inches.

The breadth of the foot in this case, in comparison with the length, is greater than in the foot of an adult.

Feet 12 inches long are rare, and only men of unusual stature have feet of this size.

THE MALE HAND.

The length of the male hand is taken as 7 inches, or 2 inches more than that of the face.

The three largest fingers measure 3½ inches.

In Plate I. the hand is shown spread out. From this form the Italians derived a measure, termed a Palm, which is equal to 9 inches when the hand is spread out to the utmost. In the drawing a point is given, from which circles passing through the finger-joints can be described. The width of the hand can be measured with exactitude only at the base of the four fingers; taken in this the width is 3¼ inches.

THE FEMALE HAND.

The length of the female hand is taken as 6½ inches. In proportion to the face, the woman's hand is somewhat longer than the man's. In Plate I, the hand is enclosed in a space 3 inches in width, but across the base of the four fingers the measurement must not be quite so much. The child's hand is 4 inches long, and at the base of the four - fingers the width can be a little more than one half, or 2¼ inches.

These natural laws were studied by Rafael and others. It often happens, however, that the hands are drawn smaller, consequently, the outstretched arms, which should equal the length of the entire figure, do not fulfill this law. Again, when the legs are drawn the full length and the torso somewhat short, the arms are made too short as well. These inattentions to the laws of nature are practiced not alone by bunglers but also by renowned living masters.

PLATE II.

Containing four Representations of Greek Gods and two Portraits *from the Antique.*

Plate I. gives the proportions, which are in harmony with those of well-formed living beings. The same proportions can be employed for figures from the antique, which are intended to represent forms taken from actual life, but careful study has proved that the division of the face into six parts is not applicable to mythological personages, who require a division of the same space into eight parts. The application of such a division to natural faces is so extremely rare that the forms, which must be represented by its aid, may with propriety be termed "ideal forms."

The faces of Meleáger and the Apollo (see Plate II.) have the same length as in the man's head, viz., 5 inches. Those of Niobe and Venus are shorter by one part of the eight into which the face is divided.

The space between the outer corners of the eyes is 3½ inches for both sexes; the faces of the goddesses consequently appear rounder.

As Meleáger is shown somewhat larger than in nature and Apollo smaller, a special scale has had to be adopted for each. The eyes are placed higher, on account of the division in eight parts, and the space between the eye-lid and the eye-brow becomes small. The cavity of the mouth is likewise higher; the upper lip becomes shorter and the lower jaw so much stronger.

The lower jaw of the male heads and the neck are broad, the latter being inch larger than in the female. The proportion of the mouth to the eyes is as 3 to 2; or 1½ inch. This law is frequently neglected, presumably with the object of "gilding refined gold." In Nature the size of the eye is almost always 1 inch, whereas. the mouth is often twice as large, or 2 inches, without lending any appearance of deformity to the face.

The eyes of the Apollo are large and fully opened, and the space between the outer corners the same as heretofore. The space between the inner corners s, in consequence, so much smaller.

In the Venus Medicis, the eyes are small, space between outer corners the same, and, consequently, that between the inner corners larger. The cheek-bones and the skull are very small— on this account this head is not considered in conformity with Nature. The cheek-bones are 4 inches and five-eights.

In the bottom row (see Plate) is the head of Faustina, with cheek-bones 5⅜ inches apart.

Above these two heads, in the top row, is the head of Niobe's daughter, whose cheek-bones are 5 inches from each other.

The eight divisions of the face are shown by themselves in two of the heads, without additional lines, as in the Apollo and Faustina the difference however, between the Ideal and the Real is sufficiently marked.

The great breadth of the cheek-bone of Roman women arose from intermarriage with men of Gallic and Germanic origin. In busts of these women, by old sculptors, this unusual-breadth is apparent.

The Niobe heads represent a conception of 'beauty adopted by Guercino and Guido Reni, but the old Flemish and German painters remained within the confines of the Real, as, for instance, in the Faustina.

In the profile of Niobe; which is one eighth shorter than that of Meleáger, the ear is the same distance from the standard line, as in the latter, vz., 4½ inches, In the profile of Venus, the ear is 3⅝ inches front the line, and in-that of Faustina, 3¾ inches.

The lower jaw of the Venus is the shortest; and the edge of the upper lip is within the standard line.

The position of these parts in the Faustina is similar.

The space between the outer corners of the eyes is the same for all these heads, and measures 3½ inches.

On Plate II. is the head of Seneca, which is likewise divided into eight parts, so as to show the differences between it and a head from real life; for instance, the nose does not quite reach the fourth line, yet the tip of the ear stands below this line; the whole of the ear is in consequence very low. An arc drawn from the cavity of one ear to that of the other, and passing over the forehead, would, owing to the low position of the ear, be larger, and represent, accordingly, large mental capacity. In passing down the scale of life, from intellectual beings to fish, this arc gets smaller and flatter.

The cavity of the mouth is double the size of the eye, viz., 2 inches, and is below the fifth line, so that the upper lip becomes longer.

The temple-bones are prominent, as shown in the profile, giving the face a fiat appearance. This is a special characteristic of northern faces.

In the cases of the Apollo and Meleáger, the scales which were used to measure the marble have been appended; the former figure being somewhat smaller than Nature, and the latter a little larger.

In one of the following Plates the entire figure of the Apollo is given, the dimensions being from the Same scale.

Three other Plates of male heads are included in the set, in order to show the growth of the head.

Although the science of Dr. Gall, and the minute observations of Dr. Spurzheim, are not generally believed, there is no doubt that to them belongs the merit of having established the precise place amongst the sciences which should be accorded to Lavater's doubtful and uncertain doctrine of physiognomy.

The observations of Peter Camper will always meet with the attention they deserve, though they are, to some extent, marred on account of his weak drawing. The data respecting national physiognomy, which will be found further on in this work, are intended -as corrections of the defects in Camper's studies. -

NOTE.—Special attention is here called in measuring to the point already remarked upon, that the word - "FACE" in the present Treatise is intended to mean the distance from the chin to the upper edge of the cavity of-the eyes, or vice versa.

PLATE III.

THE NEW-BORN CHILD AND. A CHILD FOUR MONTHS OLD.

BIRTH.

Most healthy children are found to be 1 ft. 6 ins. A new born child, according to Buffon, 1 ft. 9 ins. In this case the child is said to have remained a longer time in the womb, A new-born child, according to Horace Vernet, 1 ft. 6 ins, The same authority gives 2 ins. less for a girl.

NOTE.—The measurement of new-born children can only be taken with accuracy when the nurse stretches out by force the arms and legs.

The head is taken, as heretofore, 4½ ins., or the fourth part of the height. The width of the head 3¾ ins. The heads of children of the Mongolian and Negro races, are smaller: this is possibly the reason that the women give birth to these children with greater ease. Body or torso: This is almost round, and the diameter of the ribs in front is 4 ins. The diameter in profile is 3¾ ins. Arm and legs: The equal gradations in the dimensions of these parts are worthy of attention. The hand is 2 ins.; the elbows are 3 ins. the upper part of the arm is 4 ins.; the lower part of the leg, with outstretched heels, 5 ins.; the foot and elbows have the same length, 3 ins.; from the navel to the pit of the neck, 6 ins.

CHILD FOUR MONTHS OLD.

Scale—Eighths of an inch are here noted in order to make a comparison of the dimensions easier and the differences more apparent.

Framing.—This term may be applied to distinguish the space enclosed by the ground line and the top of the head (2 ft. or 24 ins.) on the one hand, and on the other by the ribs (5 ins. or 40 eighths). This framing will admit of a rapid comparison of the front, side, and back views of the figure. The drawings are made on the same principle as that adopted for plans of buildings, so as to show the entire length of each part.

Height, 24 ins. Well nurtured boys of 3 months sometimes attain. this height, but it is better to adopt a medium growth on which to base a law. Navel: This is situated at half the height, or 12 ins. Arms: The outstretched arms are equal to the whole height, 24 ins. In the new-born child the outstretched arms exceed by a little the height. Legs The upper part of the legs has increased a good deal in length, and the hips have extended. The space between the nipples has increased from 2½ to 3½ ins., or 28 eighths. Profile: The profile of the back has now a curvature, which is almost entirely absent in new-born children. The length of the ulna and that of the foot, 3¾ ins.

PLATE IV.

CHILD OF EIGHT MONTHS AND TWELVE MONTHS.

Eight months, height 26 ins. Increase in 4 months, 2 ins. Framing: This has a width of 6 ins. The expansion of the ribs is 5 ins. The width of this part of the body, and that of the space between the nipples, is somewhat less in proportion. There may, however, be cases in which the width between the ribs is greater than that given above. Navel: This is somewhat above the middle of the entire length of the body. Face : The space measured from the eyebrows to just beneath the chin is greater than the upper part of the head, in the ratio of 23 to 22 eighths. The ulna and foot are of equal length, 3⅝ ins,, or 29 eighths. The size of the body and limbs of healthy well-nurtured children is, at this period of life, frequently such' as would give a much greater width than that taken above.

BOY OF TWELVE MONTHS.

Twelve months, height 28 ins. Framing: The ribs have now almost attained-the width of the framing, 6 ins. The upper part of the head has still the same height, 2¾ ins. or 22 eighths. Face: This part, on the other hand, has considerably increased 3½ ins., or 28 eighths. The upper part of the head, in' profile, has not extended, but is 5½ ins., or 44 eighths. Division of the body: The easiest plan is to take the length as FOUR EQUAL PARTS, each measuring seven inches, or 56 eighths. For example:—

1. From the crown of the head to the pit of the neck A B.
2. From pit of the neck to the navel   B C.
8. From the navel to the knee   C D.
4. From the knee to the bottom of the foot   D A.

The middle of the space between C and D touches the testicles.

Face: The length is as above, 3½ ins,, or 28 eighths. This length is measured from underneath the chin. The length of the bead is then 6 ins. Hand: The length of the hand is precisely one half, or 3 ins. Space between the nipples, length of the ulna and foot, each four inches. At this period the boy begins to stand and walk, and in some cases does so even at 10 months.

PLATE V.

CONTAINING BOYS OF ONE AND A HALF, TWO AND TWO AND A HALF YEARS OF AGE.

One and a half years, height 30 ins. Increase in 6 months, 2 ins. Framing: Same as for boy of 12 months; width 6 ins.

Division: In four parts, each of 7½ ins. Navel: This is situated a little above the middle of the entire height, 16 ins. Head: Height of the entire head, 6¼ ins. Length of the face, 3⅛ ins. Length of the skull, 3½ ins. These parts have been made equal to show that, at this age, this is sometimes the case, although it happens but seldom. Arm: The upper arm is double the length of the hand, or 6 ins. The ulna and foot are of equal length, viz., 4½ ins. Remark: A dotted line from the ribs across the breast carries the eye to the first rib. Many artists have given such extension to the ribs below the breast that they bear no resemblance at all to the form they bear in nature.

BOY OF TWO YEARS OF AGE.

Height, 32 ins. Increase in 6 months, 2 ins. Framing: The width of the framing is taken in this case one inch more, or 7 ins. The ribs and shoulders have expanded in proportion . . . . The shoulders are 9 ins. Division: In four parts, each 8 ins. The pit of the neck is now above the line. The breadth of the head and the length of the foot are equal, viz., 5 ins. The ulna is likewise of the same length, 5 ins. Head: The length of the head is 6⅜ ins. Profile: The diameter of the head, 6 ins. Thickness of neck, one half, or 3 ins. The length of the hand is half the length of the upper arm, which is 7 ins.

BOY OF TWO AND A HALF YEARS OF AGE.

Height, 34 ins. Nipples: The space between the nipples is 4½ ins. Shoulders: The breadth between shoulders is a little more than double, or 9¼ ins. Ribs: The ribs in this case just touch the framing, the breadth being 7 ins. Neck: In the drawing the neck has 3½ ins. At this age such a size is seldom attained. Foot: The foot is a little longer than the ulna, or 5¼ ins. This length often occurs in boys of this age. Arms: The space between the outstretched arms, measured from the tips of the fingers, is equal to the height of the body, or 84 ins. Division: The five lines A, B, C, D, E, are distant from one another 8½ ins. Remarks: At this age most parts of the body will not have increased much in thickness, the growth being principally in the length. A boy of 80 months can be said to have attained half the height of a full grown man. It had been thought hitherto that this was not. the case till the age of three years had been reached.

PLATE VI.

SHOWING BOYS OF THREE,. THREE AND A HALF, FOUR, AND FOUR AND A HALF YEARS.

Three years, height 36 ins. Head: The length of the head is the same as in the preceding case, viz., 6½ ins. The parts of the face are, however, larger, or 3½ ins. This gives for the upper part of the head a length of 3 ins. Division: The division from A to G comprises 6 parts, with a total length of

29½ ins., 5 of them from B to G (5 being equal to 25 ins., that is 5 ins, each, and the sixth part from A to B is equal to 4½ ins. We then have the following division: From the chin to the seat of the heart; from the seat of the heart to the navel; from the navel to the middle of the pubis; from the middle of the pubis to the upper edge of the knee-cap; from upper edge of knee-cap to a little below the calf of the leg.

Framing: The breadth of the framing remains the same, viz., 7 ins. Ribs: The ribs are shown with a still smaller covering of flesh on them. Eyes: The distance between the outer corners of the eyes increases so slightly that the dimensions of this space given on Plate I. of the heads may be taken as a standard. These dimensions are 3 ins. This measurement is at times found even in full grown persons. Head: The diameter of the head, from the front, is 4¾ ins. This is less than was given for the head of a boy of 30 months, and has purposely been taken, to show that there are such differences in Nature. Shoulders: The breadth of the shoulders is taken as 9 ins. The distance between the nipples can be made one half of this, or 4½ ins. This proportion can remain the same till full growth is attained. In the full-grown body the breadth of the shoulders is sometimes 18 ins., and the distance between the nipples, consequently,. 9 ins. Middle line: This line, drawn vertically through the middle of the body, comes into contact with three different parts, viz. :—

1. With the upper part of the thigh.
2. With the knee.
3. With the inner part of the ankle.

At the age of manhood the inner part of the calf of the leg touches this line.

THREE AND A HALF YEARS OF AGE.

Height: 37½ ins. Growth in 6 months amounts to 1½ ins. Framing: Breadth the same as in former case, 7 ins. Head: Length as before, 61 ins. Shoulders: Breadth, 9½ ins. Width between nipples, 4¾ ins. Neck: The neck is made longer, and now has 2 ins. Division: Taken from the ground line, from H to A, each part measures 5⅛ ins. The top line A cuts the middle of the forehead; the drawing shows the remaining divisions. Foot: The length of the foot is taken as 5½ ins. Ulna: The length of the ulna is shown as 6 ins. This length would, however, scarcely be met with in Nature; the foot being usually equal in length to the nina.

BOY FOUR. YEARS OLD.

Height: 89 ins. Increase in 6 months, 1½ ins. Framing: Width as heretofore, 7 ins. Head: The head has now attained a length of 6¾ ins Three Plates, on a larger scale, give the details of the head with more exactness. Division: The division is, in this case, formed by 7 lines from A at the chin to G, each part being 5¼ ins. From the ground line G is 1 in. Although there is an increase of length in the lower limbs, the line giving the middle height of the figure is still above the upper part of the pubis, as is the case in nature. Foot: The foot in this figure is taken as somewhat shorter than the ulna, or 5¾ ins., the ulna itself being 6 ins. Shoulders: The breadth of the shoulders is the same as before, viz., 9½ ins.

BOY FOUR AND HALF YEARS OLD.

Height: 40½ ins. Increase in 6 months, 1½ ins. Head: The height same as before, 6¾ ins. Division: The figure is divided into 6 equal parts, from A to G, each being 6¾ ins. This division is equal to six times the length of the head; the lines do not, however, cut any fixed points as in the other figures. Neck: The length of the neck in this case, as well as in the others, is taken as 1¾ ins. This length, although shorter than is sometimes the case, may be adopted for boys; but, in the case of girls, it would make the shoulders too high. Upper part of the arm: This part can be made double the length of the hand, or 8½ ins. Ribs: The drawing shows that the ribs do not yet touch the sides of the framing, although in this figure they might be allowed to do so. The breadth of the framing is still 7 ins. The front view shows the lower part of the legs somewhat too long. It would be better for the student to adopt the length given in the profile of the same figure.

PLATE VII.

BOYS OF FIVE AND SIX YEARS OF AGE.

Five years: Height, 42 ins. Division: From A to G, each part being 6 ins. Head: The length of the head as before, 6¾ ins. Framing: Width of the framing, 7 ins. The ribs might be made slightly to exceed this width. Shoulders: The width across the shoulders is only 9 ins. The drawing shows this figure to be of slender proportions, in order to form a contrast with those of the other boy on the same Plate. The dimensions of both have been taken from Nature. Neck: The length of the neck is 2½ ins. The length is different in the two figures, without, however, being detrimental to the characteristics of either. Arm: The length of this part is 8½ ins. Hand: The length of the hand, half, or 4½ ins. Ulna: The length of the ulna is 6 ins. Lower part of leg: This part, measured from the ground line to the upper part of the knee-cap, occupies two of the seven divisions, or 12 ins. The length from the skull to the seat of the heart is the same. The expansion of the nipples shown on the line passing through the pit of the neck is 4½ ins. If the half of this be added to the entire length of the arm, which is 18¾ ins., the result is 21 ins., or one half the entire height of the figure. Profile and back view: For the lowered arm in the profile, and the outstretched arm in the back view, the same dimensions are given, it was therefore necessary to show the distance of the nipples on the line passing through the pit of the neck by means of point marks. From the same points measurements are taken of the upper part of the right arm (see front view) and the upper part of the left arm (see back view). The length in each case being 9½ ins. The additional half-inch arises from the projection of the elbow- joint in these positions of the arm.

EQUILIBRIUM OR PONDERATION.

In these figures the action of equilibrium, or ponderation, is shown. Leonardo da Vinci was the first one who paid attention to this matter, and, after him, Gerard Lairesse. They did not, however, employ any special method, but were guided in their measurements simply by the eye. As their labours in this direction became known, the difficult task was attempted to represent ponderation in accordance with rules and definite proportions. Further on, figures will be shown which are better adapted to lllustrate the laws of ponderation than those on this Plate Framing: The height is the same as in that of the other three figures, 3 ft. 6 ins. Breadth of framing likewise the same, 7 ins. The line just above the pubis is taken as the centre. This method answers as well for the full-grown man, as this part is situated just at half the height of the whole figure. When the figure is supported on one leg, the old rule is retained, viz., that the vertical line passes through the middle of the neck to the supporting limb.. In order to give repose to the active limb (in this case the right leg), the centre is placed 1 in. from the vertical line, that is, a 42nd part of the entire height. On the horizontal line passing through the pit of the neck and on the ground line, two points are marked opposite to each other, and 1 in. to the left of the vertical line; from these points lines are drawn to the centre. The upper line, from the pit of the neck to the centre, must be curved till it reaches the naveL The lower line from the centre to the ground indicates the direction which the inner side of the supporting limb must have. The dimensions appertaining to the width of the torso must be measured from the above- mentioned curved line. Further instructions on this subject will follow.

BOY SIX YEARS OF AGE.

Height: 3 ft. 8 ins., or 44 ins. Increase from the fifth year, 2 ins. The framing is widened to 8 ins. The width across the hips fills out this space, the ribs are slightly drawn in. The upper edge of the knee-cap can be above the ground line, a little more than 12 ins. The upper part of the pubis is a little below half the height, or 22 ins. This is taken as the centre line. The following dimensions are all equal, viz.: From the chin to the seat of the heart, 5 ins.; from the seat of the heart to the navel, 5 ins.; from the navel to the pubis, 5 ins. The head in this figure has 7½ ins. The upper part of the head is made exceptionally high, viz., 3½ ins. If the upper part of the bead were made somewhat shorter, and the neck a little longer, the head would stand higher from the shoulders, and a more graceful form would result. The space between the nipples, 5½ ins. The width of the shoulders is 11 ins. This is double the measurement between the nipples. The width across the shoulders is therefore one-fourth of the height. The hand is large, and measures 4½ ins. When the arm is bent (see profile) so that the elbow joints project, the upper part is 9 ins. The length of the ulna and that of the foot is 6½ ins. The space between the outer corners of the eyes is equal to the thickness of the neck, or 3 ins. In the profile, however, the neck is taken as 3½ ins., and one fourth of an inch might be added to the neck in front view.

EQUILIBRIUM OR PONDERATION.

The figure, showing the boy of 6 years, supported on one leg, is constructed according to the. rules previously given. The head is in profile, and turned at a right angle to the body; this position is not a natural one, but the geometrical principle of the rules given herein oblige us to employ this method of representation. A careful observer will, however, at once detect any anomalies of the kind. As in this work no fore-shortening has been permitted, it is surprising that the life and action of the human form have been delineated with such fidelity. The left arm resting on the hip, the measurement from the centre of the figure to the elbow is 12 ins., and from the elbow to the pit of the neck 12 ins.

PLATE VIII.

TWO PROPORTIONS—SHOWING BOYS OF SEVEN AND EIGHT YEARS OF AGE.

BOY OF SEVEN YEARS.

Height: 3 ft. 9 ins., or 45 ins. Increase from the sixth year, 1 in. A slowness of growth occurs to the tenth year, but at the twelfth year a rapid increase takes place. In the present case the head is taken about the same, viz., 7½ ins. In the figures drawn to a larger scale a greater difference is made. From the chin to the seat of the heart, 5¾ ins.; from the seat of the heart to the navel, 5¾ ins. The neck is longer, the chest larger, although the width across the shoulders is a little less than in the last figure, or 10¾ ins. There is an increase in the length of the hand and foot. The hands and feet may, in this figure, appear large to such artists as have paid too much attention to works of art, and too little to the dimensions of these parts in the living form. Many modern artists have, in fact, neglected the laws of Nature, and have consequently drawn the hands and feet too small. Profile or side view: A vertical line (the middle line) touching the neck and the shin gives the correct upright position. The size of the body (in profile) across the stomach is 6 ins. In the front view this part is 7 ins., or in the proportion of 3 to 4. The dimensions across the ribs (front view) 8 ins. The right leg in its raised position is slightly increased in length; if the measurement be taken to the upper. part of the knee-joint it is 13½ ins. Back view: The left arm in a raised position. The elbow in this case is not level with the crown of the head, as it is in adults, when the arm is raised. The part of the arm above the head is 10 ins. The right arm in its bent position: From the middle line to the elbow the dimensions are 12 ins. From the elbow to the finger-tips 11 ins. In adults these measurements are equal. The left thigh in the position shown can, as regards its inner line of support, be drawn according to the same rules that apply to the right leg.

EQUILIBRIUM.

In the fourth figure *equilibrio* is shown with two points of support, viz., the right leg and the left shoulder. The pit of the neck: The divergence from the middle line amounts to 4 ins. The supporting limb (the right leg) retains the vertical position. The distance from the pit of the neck to the navel is increased by ½ in. The dotted line between these two points, or the vertebral line, is curved more than in the previous case; the line forming a right angle with the straight vertical line gives the depression of the hips and of the knee-joints. These parts are therefore parallel. The depression of the profile is parallel with the line through the hips. The mastoid retains its upright position. The ear is between the same division lines in the other figures, and the remaining divisions are alike, The left arm shows two points at the elbow, as the latter is, owing to its position, somewhat fore-shortened; the same thing applies to the joint of the left leg, which is shown full length in the drawing.

BOY OF EIGHT YEARS.

Height: 3 ft. 10 ins., or 46 ins. Increase from the seventh year, 1 in. The head is of the same size, viz. 7½ ins. The lower jaw can, however, project slightly below the line of the chin. In the drawing the neck is taken as 3 ins. The space between the outer corners of the eyes and the width of the neck is increased in Three of the divisions are equal, viz. :—From the chin to the seat of the heart, 6 ins.; from the seat of the heart to the navel, 6 ins.; from the navel to the scrotum, 6 ins. The ribs now reach quite to the sides of the framing, the dimensions being 8 ins. The seat of the pubis is lower than in the previous figure. The width across the shoulders is 11 ins. The figure in profile: In this figure the proportion of 3 to 4 is exactly applicable; for instance, the body in profile, 6 ins., and the ribs, in front view, 8 ins. The foot has a length of 6½ ins. The ulna is ¼ in. longer, or 6¾ ins. These parts are very frequently of the same length. The back: On the line passing through the base of the neck the distance between the nipples is marked by two points, and is 5 ins. The length of the upper part of the arm is measured from these points; with projecting elbows, this length is 10 ins. The dotted line, which indicates the projection of the ribs, runs also through the same points.

EQUILIBRIUM.

The figure in *equilibrio* is constructed according to the rules previously given. The deviation A amounts to 1 in. The deviation B and C on the opposite side of the middle line is the same, viz., 1 in. The vertical middle line is also the middle of the neck, the vertebral column of which is curved backwards. The line forming a right angle with the vertical line A B is dotted, and gives the depression of the hips and knee. The distances from the base of the neck to half the height; from the dotted line (at the point touching the right hip) to the middle of the right knee and from the middle of the right knee to the point a on the ground line are equal, each distance being 13½ ins. From the crown of the head to the seat of the heart the distance is the same.

PLATE IX

SHOWING BOYS OF
NINE AND TEN YEARS OF AGE.

BOY OF NINE YEARS.

Height: 3 ft. 11 ins., or 47 ins. Increase from the eighth year, 1 in. It would have been superfluous to have given a new figure for the sake of this increase of 1 in., but the variety of Nature offers sufficient deviations to admit of the character belonging to this age being retained without overstepping the limits of a healthy and natural growth. The head is still the same size, viz., 7½ ins., but the face itself is larger, or 4¼ ins. The width of the head in front view is somewhat less, and measures only 5⅜ ins. The base of the neck, measured from the chin, is 3 ins. The three following measurements are equal :—From the chin to the seat of the heart; from the seat of the heart to the navel; and from the navel to the seat of the pubis, each measurement being 5½ ins. The hand is ⅛ in. larger, or 4⅞ ins. The foot is equal to the ulna, viz., 6¾ ins. The width across the shoulders is 11½ ins.. The distance between the nipples is not the half of this measurement, but 5 ins, This is consonant with the higher position of the nipples. The altered position of one leg, shown in the front and back views, pushes out the opposite hip, and this slight divergence suffices to give some life to the figure. The parts which fall to some extent along the same straight line are shown in the figure, for instance: the index finger of the outstretched hand; the edge of the radius, the biceps, and the acromion, when the arm is in the lowered position; also some parts of the leg, as the heel, the inner part of the ankle, the knee-joint, and the inner part of the thigh beneath the posterior.

EQUILIBRIUM.

This is drawn by the same rules as apply to the boy of 7 years of age. The divergence of the neck from the middle vertical line amounts to 3 ins, The right arm (the supporting one) shows the hand lowered; in this case fore-shortening could not be prevented. In place of the vertical position of the supporting leg, a line 1 in. from the middle vertical line is drawn, against which the heel rests, as in the upright position. Lines of deviation; A point 1 in. is set off from the centre line of the neck, and from this point a line is drawn to the centre of the figure; a cross-line at right angles gives the lowered position of the hips and that of the knee. Curved lines The dotted curved line, indicating the curved position of the vetebral column, serves as the middle line from which the width of the body is measured.

Remark: The artistic sense must now be brought into play, in order that a satisfactory figure may result from the application of the rules. The movements of nature cannot, in every respect, be represented by mere rules, such as may be applied to architectural drawings, and even the latter, when shown in perspective, must be treated with artistic talent, so as to bring all the parts in harmony.

BOY OF TEN YEARS.

Height: 4 ft., or 48 ins. Increase in one year, 1 in. The framing is widened 1 in., and is now 9 ins. The length of the head is the same, 7½ ins. The distance between the eyes is increased, and is now 8¼ ins. The base of the neck, measured from the chin, is 3 ins. Chin, to seat of the heart, 5½ ins. Seat of the heart to the navel, 5½ ins. Navel to the pubis 5½ ins. The legs, from the knee downwards, have increased to 14 ins. The band is long; it measures 5 ins, The ulna and foot are equal 7½ ins. The width of the shoulders is 12 ins, The distance between the nipples might be taken as the half of this, but they should then be placed somewhat lower. In the figure this distance is only 5¼ ins., a measurement according to life. The width of the ribs is 8 ins. They could be wider, but the body would then have to be drawn longer and the, legs shorter. In this figure the elbow is on a line with the crown of the head, with the arm stretched upwards.

EQUILIBRIUM.

The deviation from the middle line is, in this case, for the neck and on the ground line, 1½ ins. This deviation must be taken as the maximum. The arms appear too small, and the one which is raised may be, in place of 9 ins. from the shoulder to the elbow, increased to 91 ins. And the left arm, in the lowered position as well as the raised arm, can be, for the entire length, 22 ins.

PLATE X

TWO PROPORTIONS—BOYS OF
ELEVEN AND OF TWELVE YEARS

BOY OF ELEVEN YEARS.

Height: 4 ft. 2 ins., or 50 ins. Increase in one year, 2 ins. Law of Nature: In the preceding 4 years the boy grew each year 1 in., and after this period follows one of 4 years, in which the growth per year is at the rate of 3 ins. Remark: These periods of slow and rapid growth of the human body are as varied in character as other phenomena of animate nature. Some boys are at this age considerably bigger than in the case given above: they grow rapidly to the full height of manhood, and then increase in this direction ceases. The framing in this case is 9 ins, The length of the head is the same, 7½ ins. The ulna and foot, each 7½ ins. The hand, 5 ins, The upper part of the arm, 10½ ins, The width across the shoulders, 12½ ins. The thickness of the body in profile scarcely half of the preceding measurement, or 6 ins. With regard to the lower, part of the legs, the thickness of the calf is 3 ins., the ankle 2 ins. It has been found that the same thickness of 2 ins. is met with in the ankles of full-grown men, whilst the calf of the leg can attain a thickness of 5 ins. This may be the reason that artists seldom give to the knee and lower part of the leg the character properly appertaining to them at this period of life.

EQUILIBRIUM.

The figure resting on a staff. The upper part of the left arm has had to be foreshortened, and a three-quarter view of the head is given. The dimensions given on the Plate can be employed for the other parts of the body.

BOY OF TWELVE YEARS.

Height: 4 ft. 5 ins., or 58 ins. Increase in one year, 3 ins. The head is of the same length as before, 7½ ins. The face is however larger, viz., 4½ ins. Distance from the base of the neck to central line, 16 ins. The lower part of the leg is the same length, 16 ins. In the front view the width of the figure has increased. Across the shoulders, 13½ ins. In profile, however, only the thighs are bigger. On this account, the body as seen in aide view looks spare in comparison with the size of the thighs.

PLATE XL.

TWO PROPORTIONS—BOYS OF
THIRTEEN AND FOURTEEN YEARS.

BOY OF THIRTEEN YEARS.

Height: 4 ft. 8 ins., or 56 ins. Increase in the last year, 3 ins. The framing is widened, and is 10 ins. The length of the head, 8¼ ins. The length of the face, 4¾ ins. From the chin to the central line there are 8 divisions, each 6½ ins. This arrangement is the most simple that could be adopted, and is in conformity with the natural division of the body; the seat of the heart and the navel may, however, be placed somewhat beneath the lines of the divisions. The hand is 6 ins. The upper part of the arm, 12 ins. The ulna and foot, each 8½ ins. The distance between the nipples, 6½ ins. Width across the shoulders, 13 ins. The thickness of the knee, 3½ ins. The thickness of the calf, 3½ ins.

EQUILIBRIUM.

The figure is leaning on the right arm, which is, however, not intended to act as a support. The pit of the neck is in a vertical line with the small toe of the left foot, the object being to show that the body can bend the same distance backwards, although a moment before its weight was resting in the forward position on the right arm.

BOY OF FOURTEEN YEARS.

Height: 4 ft, 11 ins., or 59 ins. Increase since the thirteenth year, 3 ins. Variation I.: The length of the head is, in order to give some variation, taken less than 3 ins. The division of the head is altered in this figure, a line is drawn through the corners of the eye, dividing the head into two equal parts, each of 4 ins. Variation II.: The length of the lower limbs has been taken from a well-formed living form. The base of the pubis is from the ground line, 80½ ins. This is 1½ ins, higher than prescribed by the rule. In the following eases the rule will be maintained, but it has been thought advisable to show that a deviation therefrom may be allowed, without risk of delineating an unnatural form. The width of the framing is the same, but the ribs are 10 ins. The distance between the nipples has been increased ½ in.; and is 7 ins. The ulna and the foot have also increased ½ in., each being 9 ins. The hand is of the same length, viz., 6 ins. The width across the shoulders is 14 ins. The upper part of the arm 12 ins. The outstretched arm, measured from the vertical middle line, does not quite equal half he height of the figure, as the rule prescribes. Profile: The upper part of the arm is ½ in. longer, owing to the projection of the elbow, 12½ ins. The distance from the point of-the elbow to the joint of the middle finger is the same, viz., 12½ ins. The lower part of the right leg is increased in length by the projection of the heel, as shown in the drawing, the length being 19 ins. The length of the upper part of the leg, measured to the extreme outer part of the posterior, is 19 ins, Profile: The diameter across the stomach is 7 ins. Across the lower joints of the spine only 6 ins. These parts appear spare in comparison with the thickness of the thighs. The size of the latter occurs in the living form, and has therefore been retained. Remark: If the breadth of a living figure, as seen from the front or back, should be large, the dimensions of the body in profile are correspondingly small. On the other hand, if in Nature the measurement around the ribs is small, the size of the body from the breast-bone to the vertebra is large. The inner volume of the body is thus in each ease equal.

EQUILIBRIUM.

The upraised head in this figure causes the back part to meet the nape of the neck. The neck itself maintains its position with regard to the middle vertical line. The drawn up position of the right arm and shoulder, and of the left supporting leg, causes the extension of the right side of the figure. If an equilateral triangle be formed on the line connecting the central point of the figure with the base of the neck, the segment drawn from the apex of the triangle gives the middle line of the torso, and from the apex the lines indicating the sides can also be drawn. The straight lines from the apex give the divisions of the torso; the line C, however, passing through the seat of the heart, must be parallel with the line N, touching the base of the neck.

PLATE XII.

TWO PROPORTIONS.
YOUTH OF FIFTEEN YEARS OF AGE
AND THE YOUNG APOLLO.

Height: 5 ft. 4 ins., or 64 ins. Remark: The measurements correspond to those actually taken of a youth of this age, although it rarely happens that the increase of height in one year amounts to 5 ins. The usual growth is 3 ins., consequently the figure of the Apollo at 15 years of age has been drawn on the same Plate, the increase in this case being exactly 3 ins The width of the framing is in both figures the same, viz., front view, 12 ins.; in profile, 10 ins. The base of the pubis is in the two figures exactly on the line representing half the height. The height of the youth's head is 8½ ins. The face is 5 ins. The face of a full grown person has the same dimensions. The width across the shoulders is the same in both figures, or 16 ins. The space between the nipples is only 7½ ins., or less than half the breadth of the shoulders. The length of the hand is 6¾ ins. The upper part of the arm is not quite double this, 13 ins. The length of the foot is 10 ins. The length of the ulna a little more, or 10½ ins. Note: If our inch rule was divided into 10 ins., in place of 12 ins., it would correspond in length with the majority of full grown feet of medium size, as it is only seldom that the foot of a living person is 12 ins, long. The lower part of the legs of the youth, 18 ins, in length, are not longer than in the Apollo, but the upper part of the youth's legs are proportionately longer. The knee joints of the youth are bigger, and the calf of the leg smaller than in the Apollo. Remark: The fulness of the calf of the leg is attained when a man is in the prime of life. Artists have imitated this fulness from the representations of the Greek Gods, but this imitation is not in harmony with Nature. The breadth of the two figures in front view is almost the same, but the difference in the dimensions in profile is considerable. Profile: The knee-joint is 5 ins.; on this account the calves and the upper part of the thighs appear smaller. Remark: The difference of 2 ins, in the length of the whole figure suffices to give the figure of the youth an appearance of spareness. With the exception of the measurement across the trochanter, which makes the upper part of the leg in the Apollo larger, the other dimensions of thickness are almost the same.

EQUILIBRIUM

In the youth of fifteen years the points of deviation from the normal lines of the base of the neck, the privities, and the ground are 2 ins. This deviation is a maximum, and is an approach to what may be termed an affectation.

THE APOLLO.

It is a matter of conjecture whether the artist modeled this figure from a material which shrunk on drying, or purposely made the Apollo smaller than the natural form would have been. Height: The length of the face from the eyebrows to the chin is scarcely 4 ins. If a scale be made, giving a length of 4½ ins, for this part (as it actually is in Nature), the whole figure would have a height of 5 ft. 2 ins., which is in accordance with the age taken for it, viz., 15 years. The fulness of the limbs, and their flowing curves, may be attributed to that innate love of the Beautiful which the Greeks possessed; but Nature gives to the living form at that age another character, which is also met with in the works of the ancients, as, for instance, in the "Boy Extracting a Thorn."

EQUILIBRIUM.

The figure rests on the supporting leg and on the left elbow. The deviation of the base of the neck is, in this figure, 3 ins. In order to determine the depression of the hips, a point, the same as on the ground line, with a further deviation of 1½ ins., is taken; from this point a line is drawn to the central point of the figure, and on this line another at right angles gives the true depression. It may be remarked that the torso, in its inclined position towards the left, should measure less than the upright figure, but the difference, as the figure shows, is too little to be visible.

PLATE XIII.

WITH ONE PROPORTION.

A YOUTH OF SEVENTEEN YEARS.

Height: 5 ft. 4 ins. (same height as the youth of 15); and, in conformity with the medium height, 5 ft. 6 ins. This is everywhere regarded as a medium height. In Nature, however, it may be difficult to find individuals corresponding between the ages of 15 and 19 to this height. The development at the age of puberty is so varied that accurate tables of height have not been put together. Although only a representation of the true natural form is here given, still such standard dimensions as could be adopted are noted down, for instance :— The length of the head, 8 ins.; from the chin to the seat of the heart, 8 ins.; from the seat of the heart to the navel, and from the navel to the centre line, the same, 8 ins. The width can also be amplified. Space between the nipples, 8 ins. Width across the shoulders, 16 ins. The figure has this peculiarity, that the outstretched arms measure 1 in. less than the entire height. In Nature they often measure more. Width across the ribs, 11 ins. Across the trochanter, 11 ins. Width over the knees, 4 ins. Width over the calf, 4 ins. Either of these measurements, when doubled, gives the same figure, viz., 8 ins., which has been applied to so many parts of this figure. Remark: It must be noted that the dimensions given here for the breast, the shoulders, and the ribs, give almost the same character to the youth of 17 as to the one of 19.

EQUILIBRIUM.

The pit of the neck is, from the vertical central line, 4½ ins., and the upper part of the body leans over as much. The figure supports itself on a staff held in the lefthand. The deviation on the ground line for the supporting leg is 2 ins, A point 2 ins, from the central point of the neck is taken, and from this point a line is drawn to the centre of the figure. Another line at right angles determines the depression of the hips and-knees. In the figure the thighs appear heavy; this was the case, however, in the living form from which the dimensions were taken. The torso looks thinner than in the first figure (front view). The extended position of the left side is, no doubt, the reason thereof.

PLATE XIV.

WITH ONE PROPORTION—THE MAN.

Medium height 5 ft. 6 ins. NOTE—The scale, according to H. Vernet's rule, is 5 ft. 4 ins. This is measured with the French foot. The height is divided into equal parts, each of 9 ins. The entire height is about 7½ times that of the head. This is in conformity with the proportions of most antique statues. It is usual to take the length of the head as the unit of measurement for the other parts of the body. As the crown of the head is so round, it is, however, difficult to get the exact height of the head, and the hair renders this difficulty greater. The human foot, according to Vitruvius, is the sixth part of the entire height, therefore 11 ins.

As this corresponds with the length of the foot in Nature, it would be a better unit of measurement than the head. The foot has, however, in full, well-grown living forms, very frequently only 10 ins.

This length has been adopted in the present case. The ulna is a, little longer, or 10½ ins.
The foot and the ulna are often of equal length.
The hand has a.length of 7 ins.
The upper arm is twice as long, or 14 ins.
Vitruvius gives the length of the face as 7 ins., and remarks that the height of the body is 10 times this length, or 70 ins.

PLATE XV.

This Plate represents a man whose height is 8 times the length of the head, and the figure is of the following proportions:—

1. The entire height (the length of the outstretched arms) equals 8 times the length of the head, or 64 ins.
2. Framing of front view. Framing of side view, equals 1½ times the length of the head, or 12 ins.
3. Space between the nipples. Space between the collar bones. Width across both knees when pressed close together. Half of the width across the shoulders. Each equals the same length as the head, or 8 ins.
4. Neck seen from the front. Neck in profile. Upper part of the deltoid. The deltoid in profile. Each equals the 4½ eighths of the length as the head, or 4½ ins.
5. Length of the neck. Height of the foot to the ankle. From the face of the outer ankle to that of the inner one - Each equals ⅜ of the length of the head or 3 ins.
6. Length of the upper arm (front view) Length of the upper arm (in profile) each -1⅝ length of the head, or 13 ins.
7. Length of the ulna. Width of the framing (side view). Width of the body beneath the ribs (front view). Length of the foot (side view), each 1¼ times the length of the head, or 10 ins.
8. Width across the thighs (front view). Width from the shoulder blade to the breast

(profile).Width from the posterior to' the pubis, each 1⅛ times the length of the head or 9 ins.

9. Length of the hand. Width from the lower part of the spine to of navel. Width across upper part of the loins (profile), each ⅞ of the length head, or 7 ins.

10. Length from wrist joint to the point of finger. Width of arm above the elbow joint. Width of arm below the elbow joint each 8½ eighths of the length of head, or 8½ ins.

11. breadth of the foot ½ the length of the head, or 4 ins.

In the following Plate of the Heros it will be seen that this latter measurement is exactly right; but in a figure of medium size this breadth is not attained.

Referring again to the preceding Plate, showing the man of medium height, we find that if the head should, according to Vitruvius, be one eighth part of the entire height of the body, the length of the head would be 8½ ins. This is in conformity with the heads of many men when the upper part is somewhat short. In order to divide the upper part of the body into 4 equal parts, each of 9 ins., half an inch has been added to the upper part of the head, as shown in the figure. Two divisions, each of 9 ins., are, likewise measured from the ground line. The top line of these divisions touches the lower edge of the knee-cap. The notes on the Plate show how well the dimensions harmonize this harmony is more evident in the figure of a full grown man of medium height than in one of any other proportions. For instance, the thickness of the calf and that of the neck (see front view) is 4½ ins., and double this is 9 ins., or one of the divisions referred to above. There are also in the figures several equal measurements, each being 19 ins.

EQUILIBRIUM.

The three points of deviation from the central vertical line are those of the neck, the pubis, and ground line, each from the centre 2 ins. The thirty-third part of the whole height may be taken as the maximum of this deviation. To facilitate the drawing the profile is shown at right angles to the breast. This position cannot be quite attained in Nature. The neck must, however, always come on the vertical central line. The calves of the leg: This is the first figure in which the inner part of the calf touches the supporting line, as it is only in full grown men that this size of the calf is attained.

PLATE XVI.

PROPORTION OF THE HEROS.

Height: 5 ft. 10 ins. In representations of the Gods by the ancients, this proportion has never been exceeded, even in the largest works. It is uncertain whether this arose from their not having observed any living figures of greater stature, or from their sense of beauty, not permitting them to adopt bigger forms. At the present day it is evident that men of a greater height than this are frequently met with. Experience proves that strength is not proportional to size, and men of medium height (such as Lesbenier, Frank, and Rapps) have performed the most astonishing feats of strength.

If the head is divided into two parts the line of division passes through the eyes, each part is 4½ ins. The easiest division for the whole height is one of 7 parts, each being 10 ins. The width of the framing is increased to 13 ins.; twice 10 ins., = 20 ins., is the measurement from H to I, from I to K, and from K to H. Same from ground line to the knee L and from the knee to. The calves each 5 ins., give together 10 ins.

EQUILIBRIUM.

The deviation in this case is 1½ ins. The head: With the exception that the jaw is somewhat wider, the dimensions of the head are the. same as those in the man of medium height of 5 ft. 6 ins.

PLATE XVII.

PROPORTIONS OF THE FEMALE FORM.
THE WOMAN.

The height of the woman is taken as 63½ ins. Although most women are shorter than this, a smaller stature cannot be chosen for art purposes.

Taking the man of medium height at sixty-six inches, we have a difference of two-and-a-half inches.

The difference causes a notable decrease in the entire volume of groups, especially in sculpture. The most prominent difference in the proportions of a man and a woman are:

1. The shorter face for the woman.
2. The smaller width across the ribs, 16ins.
3. The shortness of the legs; The measurement from the ground line to the pubis is 30 ins.

This difference of 3 ins. is considerable when we reflect that the dimensions of the same parts in a man, and especially in many antique statues, are the same. In Nature, however, the width across the ribs in the male is slightly 1ess than across the upper part of the thighs. A, B, C, D, E, from four convenient divisions, each 15 ins; From the chin to the pubis there are three divisions, each 15 ins. The length of the face is 4½ ins. The three divisions of 8½ ins. and the length of the face when added, give 30. ins. The space between the nipples, is 7 ins. The width across. the shoulders, 15 ins. Another difference between the man and the. woman shown here. In the man the space between the nipples is the half of the breadth across the shoulders.

The Woman: Front view, side and back views; fourth figure, right arm resting on the side of the body, left arm raised; fifth figure, left arm raised, dancing position.

When the two. arms are stretched. out horizontally, their length is equal to that of the entire, figure. The space between the nipples is 7 ins. 'The length of the hand, 6½ ins. The ulna has a length of,.10 ins. The length of the foot is 9 ins. Remark: In most women of small stature the ulna and foot are equal. The length of the upper arm is double that of the hand, 13 ins. It measures more when the arm is bent and the elbow projects. Length from the elbow to base of The fingers, 13 ins. Width across the upper part of thighs, in front view, also 13 ins. Profile: The profile view is enclosed in a' framing of 9 ins. This. width is attained at two parts of the body, viz., the breast and the posterior. The upper part of the thigh is larger in this view (7 ins.) than the .width of the body across the lower part of the vertebral column, this being only 6½ ins. The base of.the neck, measured from the chin, is 8½ ins. This gives the sloping shape of the shoulders, which in the male form stand higher. Back view: The length of the arm taken from the shoulder blade to the point of the elbow is 14½ ins: The. entire length of the arm in the lowered position is 29 ins.

Figure 4: The length of the upper part of the right arm and of the left arm is 14½ ins.

EQUILIBRIUM.

Figure 5: In this representation it is shown that the science of measurement can be applied even to figures whose limbs are in energetic action. The base of the neck is deviated from the central vertical line 2 ins. The width of the body must be taken from the dotted curved line. The left nipple is at the same height as in the other figures. Distance from central horizontal line to base of neck, 21 ins.

With the compasses set to the same length, the apex of She triangle is found; and from this point lines ate drawn, giving the direction of the shoulders and hips. On account of foreshortening, the width across the hips is less by 1 in., the drawing shows clearly how other parts of the figure must be foreshortened.

PLATE XVIII

WOMAN OF STOUTER PROPORTIONS
(FIVE FIGURES)

The height same as in the previous figure. Framing is wider 12½ ins. Figure 1: The left arm in the raised position. Distance from middle vertical line to the elbow, and from this to the finger tips is equal, each, being 17 ins. When the arm rests on the side as in Figure 4; the length from the base of the neck to the elbow is also 17 ins. Thickness of the joints same as in preceding figure. The arms are somewhat too large in the drawing; in practice, this error should be avoided. Width of the body just under the ribs is, in front view, 8½ ins. Same part of the body in back view, 8 ins.. This is given as the minimum size: of his part in Nature. On account of the parts being fleshier the space from the ribs to the edge of the pelvis is shorter; and the position of the hips apparently higher.

PLATE XIX.

THE VENUS DE MEDICIS.

The length of the face is the same as in the other female forms, viz., 4½ ins, Height of the upright figure, 5 ft. 3 ins. — equal to 68 ins. Profile: In the marble statue the distance from the inner edge of the posterior to the eyebrow is 2 ft. 8 ins., equal to 32 ins. This distance is the same in the profile, showing the right side of the figure. The bent position of the figure causes a decrease in the entire height of 3 ins. The principal divisions of the body, viz., from the chin to the nipples, from the nipples to the navel; and from the navel to the central point, are each 8½ ins. If the head, were of the right size, a fourth division of 8 ins, would be taken. It may be remarked that, in Nature, so small a head as in this statue is not met with—its size, in fact, indicates a want of intellectuality. The four divisions, from the ground line to the knee, from the knee to the centre, from the centre to a line below the breast, and from this line to the eyebrows, can each be 15 inches. Those divisions show, however, that the lower part of the legs is longer than in the preceding female figures.

The shortness of the upper part of the right leg, and the length of the lower part, are especially noticeable. On account of this disproportion between the, two parts of, the limb, the knee does not sink. The space between the nipples is 8 ins. Twice this distance gives the breadth of the shoulders, 16 ins. The foot is, in this case, ½ an inch longer than in the previous. figures, 9½ ins. From the ground line two divisions, each of 8½ ins., give the position of the bend of the knee (in profile view), and that of the knee-cap in front view.

Profile of the marble statue.—Figure 4: The base of the neck in Figure 1 is in a vertical line with the joint of the foot. In Figure 4 it projects forward until it stands in a vertical line with the point of the foot, which is, from the central line, 5½ ins.

Front view, of the marble statue.—Figure 5: The vertical line A B falls close to the heel of the left, or supporting leg. By means of the inclined lines the, easy pose of the figure is accurately represented. The length of the hand is 7 ins. In comparison with the length of the face the hand is too long, but it is in proportion with the length of the foot, which is correctly given as 9½ ins.

PLATE XX.

MAXIMUM SIZE OF THE WOMAN.

Height: 5 ft. 6.ins., or 66 ins. The length of the face is considerably more in this. figure, 5 ins. The hand is the aims. length as before, viz., 7 ins. The space between the nipples is 8 Ins. The breadth across the shoulders is a little more than double or 16½ ins.. The ulna is 11. ins. The foot, 10 ins., there being a little difference between the two. The calf of the leg is 4½ ins. The knee-joint is slightly less, viz., 4⅛ ins. This is, however, necessary, in order to maintain the womanly character of the figure. The figure is divided into four equal parts, each of 15½ ins. The breadth of the shoulders is exactly a fourth of the entire height, or 16½ ins The statue of the Venus of Milo may be cited a an example of the large proportions which the ancients gave even to this goddess.

PLATE XXI.

THE WOMAN OF FIVE FEET IN HEIGHT.

Height, according to Horace Vernet, 4 ft. 8 ins., or 56 ins. Paris scale is meant, which gives the height as 5 ft., or 60 ins. The height of the head is 8½ ins. The upper part of the head is of maximum length, or 4 ins. According to the above length of the head, it would be contained 7 times in the whole height. If the upper part of the head were taken as 3½ ins. (this size being more in conformity with Nature), the height of the figure would be 7½ times the length of the head. The outstretched arms are equal to the height. The measurement from the chin to the nipples, from the nipples to the navel, and from the navel to the centre, is in each case 7½ ins. The shoulders are placed somewhat lower than the base of the neck, viz., 2½ ins. The width across the shoulders is 14 ins., or less than a fourth of the height. Framing: In front view the framing is 12 ins, in width; the upper part of the thighs does not quite touch the sides of the framing. The ribs are only 9 ins. The foot and the ulna are each 9 ins. The hand, is 6½ ins. Profile: The framing of the profile view is 8 ins. wide, and is to that of front view as 2 to 8. The posterior, however, projects slightly beyond the framing. Back view: The upraised arm is 12½ ins. from the shoulder to the elbow, which is on a level with the crown of the head. The forearm, from the elbow to the base of the fingers, is 12 ins. The entire length of the outstretched arms is 27 ins., or three times the length of the foot, which in consequently 9 ins. The width across the part of the body just beneath the ribs is 7½ ins. The same part in front view is 8 ins. The. difference shows that, owing to no hard parts being underneath, the dimensions of this part of the body vary.

THE MAIDEN OF FOURTEEN YEARS.

Height, 4 ft. 5 ins., or 53 ins. The length of the head is taken as 8 ins. This is about the 6½ part of the whole height. Framing; Width of the framing is only 10 ins. The part of the body just beneath the ribs is the same width as in the larger figure, or 7½ ins. The width across the ribs is less than in the previous figure by one inch, 8 ins. The width of the shoulders is 2 ins. less than in the former case, 12 ins. The measurement from the chin to the nipples is less than from the nipples to the navel; and, less than from the navel to the central point of the figure. The hand has a length of 6¼ ins. The foot, however, is 9 ins. This was the length of the natural figure from which' the dimensions were taken; in practice the foot might be taken ½ in. shorter, as the ulna is very little more than 8 ins. Back view: The part of the body just beneath the ribs is taken as 7 ins. This is somewhat less than the same part in front view.

EQUILIBRIUM.

The base of the neck deviates from the vertical central line by 1 in. From the point of the deviation D to the point N a line is drawn forming one side of an equilateral triangle, the length of the line is 18 ins. The lines drawn from the apex E touch the shoulders, the centre of the breasts, the hips, and the central point of the figure. The lines bounding the figure, both in length and breadth, are drawn as much as possible with the compasses. This plan has hitherto not been considered practicable.

PLATE XXII.

THE THIRD SHEET OF. HEADS.

An explanatory table has been given with the two first sheets of heads, but only three different ages were then shown. A repetition of the foregoing remarks on heads will not be out of place here, as they will lead to a clearer idea of the sizes of the head at different periods of life, and will complete the data already given of the full-length figures. Great attention must, in fact, be paid to the human head. It is true that the first studies given to pupils are parts of the face, and that these are more studied than the other parts of the body; yet, in drawings of the entire human frame, the head is usually the most unsatisfactory part. The law by which the face is divided from the eyebrows to the chin into six equal parts (as shown on the Plates) has been adopted for all periods of life from birth upwards. The first line passes through the corners of the eyes; the third through the nose, and the fourth through the mouth. The second sheet of heads shows eight divisions, but this number can only be applied to ideal heads. The few cases in Nature in which such a rule would be applicable, do not admit of a departure from the standard number of divisions—viz., 6—which is in conformity with Nature. In comparing the head of a newly-born child and that of the biggest man, and confining the attention simply to the face, from the eyebrows to the chin, we find that in the new-born child the space, between the outer corners of the eyes is 2½ ins., or 20 mins. The length of the face is 2 mins. less than this, which is 18 mins. These dimensions, in the case of the biggest man, are :—Space between the corners of the eyes, 8 ins., or 80 mins. Length of the face, 6½ ins., or 52 mins. The increase in the case of the eye-space being only 1¼ ins., or 10 mins., whilst the face shows an increase from 18 to 52 mins., that is to say, 4¼ ins., or 84 mins. This remarkable difference of growth in the length of the face, when compared with that of the width, gives the key to the whole system, and must be carefully remembered, as this key is likewise applicable to the growth of the whole body. It is superfluous to refer' to every application of the rule, as the artist, by careful study of the figures given herein, will readily make these observations himself. The skull, or receptacle for the brain, must be treated by itself, because the slow growth of this part differs materially from the growth of the face.. For instance, during the time that the growth of the face increases in length fourfold, the increase of the skull is only 2½ times its original height; in width it may increase from 3½ ins, to 6½ ins, at the most. This latter increase is rare, and would be met with only in the European race. The three sheets of heads are to serve as a completion of the full-length figures. Owing to the small scale to which the latter have been drawn, the separate dimensions of the heads, could not be given with exactitude. The male head is given in the majority of cases. A special representation of female heads would have been necessary to show the differences of growth from the age of five upwards, as it is only at this age that the differences commence to be apparent.

In the male sex the maximum length of the face in Nature is 6½ ins., or 52 mins. In the female sex the same part should only have, as maximum, 5 ins., or 44 mins. Even with this length of face it is difficult to preserve the female character of the face.

BIRTH.—The height of the head from birth to full growth is double, viz., 4½ ins, to 9 ins., or 72 mins. At birth the face and the skull are of the same length, each being 2¼ ins., or 18 mins. After full growth is attained, the face is 5½ ins., or. 44 mins.; the skull, 8½ ins., or 28 mins. This is only the case, however, when the entire head is 9 ins, high; This length is seldom met with.

FOUR MONTHS' GROWTH—In the first four months the most remarkable increase is observed, and the skull expands in height and breadth, in the same proportion with the face. After the age of four months this is no longer the case; the skull in front view is wider by in., or 6 mins. In profile it is larger by 5 mins., and in height 8 mins.

EIGHT MONTHS.—In the following four months the skull shows no increase in height, but in the width the increase is ½ in., or 4 mins.; in profile, 1 min.; in, the face, 3 mins.

ONE YEAR.—When the child is a year old, the face has increased by 7 mins.; the height of the skull by 5 mins.

EIGHTEEN MONTHS—In the next six months the increase in the height of the skull is imperceptible. The increase of the skull in width (front view) is 1 min.; in profile, 2 mins. The increase in the length of the face is 1 min.

TWO YEARS.—In the following six months—that is, at two years of age—the face has increased by min. The increase of the skull (front view) is min., and in profile 1 min.

TWO AND A HALF YEAR5.—In another six months the increase is the same, and a like increase occurs in the succeeding six months.

THREE YEARS.—The face has now a length of 3½ ins., or, 28 mins. The width of the skull is 5¼ ins., or 42 mins. The space between outer corners of the eye, 3 ins., or 24 mins.

THREE AND.A HALF YEARS.—In the six months no change is apparent in the skull, but, the face has increased in length by min.

FOUR YEARS—At the fourth year the face has increased another ½j min. There is, however, no perceptible increase in the skull.

FOUR AND A HALF YEAR5.—At this age there is a slight increase.

FIVE YEARS.—At five years of age, the increase, reckoning from the third year, is in the height of the scull, ¼ in., or 2 mins.; in the width of the skull, 1 min. The face in the same time has become longer by 8 mins. On comparing the head of the new-born child with that of a child, of 5 years of age, it is apparent that a considerable difference has occurred despite the small increase in the size of the head. If all parts had suffered the same increase the difference would not be visible in a drawing; it is, in fact, the slight additional increase of the space between the eyes which gives prominence to the different character of the two heads, although the said increase is only 2 mins.

PLATE XXIII.

FOURTH SHEET OF HEADS.

The first head is that of a child of 6 years of age. The intervals of time in these cases are taken as twelve months, as the differences of growth in a shorter period of time than this would not be perceptible.

SIX YEARS.—From the fifth to the sixth year the increase of the face amounts to ½ min. No difference is visible in the height of the skull, and the mouth is even a little smaller than at five years of age. This is to show that the age of a child cannot be determined by any reference to the size of the mouth.

SEVEN YEARS.—The mouth in this case is 1¼ ins., or 10 mins. The width of the nose is 1⅛ ins., or 9 mins. The nostrils in particular expand as the child gets bigger. The face has in one year increased by min.

EIGHT YEARS.—At the eighth year the increase of the face is taken as 1 min.

NINE YEARS.—At the ninth year also 1 min.

TEN YEARS—At this age no increase for this part is given. From the seventh to the eighth year the height of the skull is increased by 1½ mins. At the tenth year the width of the skull in front view is 5 ins., or 40 mins. By means of two outlines the height which may be given to the skull is shown.

ELEVEN YEARS—At the eleventh year the face is increased by 1 min. In this has it is seen how the base of the upper lip approaches the line of the profile (see profile view), later on in life this part of the lip stands within the line of the profile.

TWELVE AND THIRTEEN YEARS.—In the four years from the tenth to the fourteenth the face grows each year 1 min. It thus approaches with rapid growth the size it attains to in manhood. From the third year to the fourteenth the space between the eyes (which is 8 ins.) has increased by 2 mins.

FOURTEEN YEARS—The mouth (1½ ins.) has increased from the sixth to' the fourteenth year 8 mins; and the thickness of the neck in the same time, 4 ins. The width of the skull in front view has increased in the same period 4 mins. Although these measurements are small in the series of heads, and only perceptible by means of the compasses, still, on comparing the heads at such different periods of life as those of 6 and 14 years, the difference is sufficiently well marked.

PLATE XXIV.

FIFTH SHEET OF HEADS.

SIXTEEN YEARS—This gives an interval of two years. In this time the length of the face has increased by 1 min. It has now attained almost 5 ins., or 40 mins., which is the size of the face in a full-grown person. The diameter of the skull is nearly 6 ins., or 48 mins. The head shown has been drawn from Nature, and in profile the approach of the lips to the line of profile is noticeable. The height of the skull has increased ½ min. As the effects of growth are after this age less apparent, and more difficult to show by means of measurements, the following heads are divided one from the other by a greater interval of time :—

TWENTY YEARS—An interval of four years has now elapsed, the face having at this age it full length of 5 ins., or 40 mins. The nostrils have expanded, and in profile view the tip and bridge of **the** nose project more. The frontal bone above the eyes is more curved; this is also the case with the chin. The edge of the lower jaw is fuller, and the neck has expanded considerably.

172

THIRTY YEARS.—At the age of 30 most of these distinctions are still visible.

FORTY YEARS.—At the age of forty the point of the nose is a little lower, and the nostrils are somewhat higher. The lower jaw commences to project beyond the line of profile; the upper lip touches this line; the edge of the lower jaw gets bigger, producing thereby what is known as a double chin, and the neck attains its greatest size, viz., 4½ ins., or 36 mins. Having now shown the appearances appertaining to persons of middle age, it will be well to give an example of a face of unusually stout proportions.

STOUT FACE.—The front view and profile have both been taken from Nature. The face is, as shown by the division lines, of the same size as the one of a man of forty. The eye cavities and the mouth occupy the same positions as in the other face. The edge of the chin is lower; the mass of fat around the lower jaw quite transforms this part of the face, but the skull is only a little larger than in the previous case, owing to a covering of fat. The increase in the size of the neck is the most striking, and the massive double chin gives the neck its appearance of shortness. The position of the base of the neck remains the same. It has been deemed necessary to give the above particulars, because many artists, in dealing with a case of this kind, not only increase the width of the whole face, but also enlarge the various organs. This is contrary to the facts observed in Nature, as the harder parts and bones of the head do not increase in size.

THE THREE FEMALE HEADS.

MAXIMUM.—The woman's head placed underneath that of the youth of sixteen. The length of the face (see youth's head) is 39 mins. The length of the woman's face is 40 mins. The space between the eyes in the woman's head is greater by 2 mins. The mouth is smaller by 1 min. The upper lip is shorter by 1 min. The lower jaw is smaller, but the neck bigger than the youth's. In profile the woman's nose projects far less, and it has a feminine character. The length of the face may be taken as the greatest which can be given in the case of a woman. In Nature longer faces are certainly met with, but they are then said to have a manly appearance.

A STOUT FACE.—The woman's head, placed underneath the head of a men of 20, is of the proportions hitherto given; on account of fulness of flesh the length of the chin is increased 1½ eighths, consequently the face is 37½ eighths instead of 41 inches, or 36 eighths. The double chin and full cheeks increase these dimensions still more. On comparing the man's face and that of the woman it will be seen that, despite the increased dimensions on account of stoutness, the distinctive character of each face is well preserved.

A SLIM FACE.—The head of a slim woman is placed between the heads of men of 30 and 40. The size of this head is in conformity with the proportions of a tall and slim figure. The length of the oval formed face is due to the extension of the lower jaw by 2 eighths beyond the usual line of division. The more delicate nose, the smaller mouth, the slimmer neck, and lower jaw give the face its girlish aspect.

THE LARGEST MAN'S HEAD.—This has been taken from Nature, and is the face of a man, whose height was six feet eight inches, or eighty inches.

The space between the eyes is .... 3⅝ ins., or 29 eighths.
The length of the face is ... 6½ ins., or 52 eighths.
The diameter of the skull is only 50 eighths.
The height of the skull is 25 eighths.

The man had a remarkable appearance when his head was uncovered, and the small circumference of the skull was especially noticeable. This man's brother was 4 inches taller, and was called the Giant. Although his height was 7 ft., or 84 ins., the muscular system of his body was weak. His hands were very large, but the head was of the same proportions as in the other case. In both instances. the truth of the statement is proved that, in Nature, the part of the head which increases least is the space between the eyes, for example :—

At birth this space measures 20 eighths.
This is greater, than the length of the face by 18 eighths.
In the case of the biggest man the space between the eyes is 29 eighths,
And the length of the face 52 eighths.

Thus during, the time that the space between the eyes increases 9 eighths, the length of the face increases 34 eighths, or from 18 to 52 eighths.

Through neglecting these principles, some of the greatest masters have, especially in their historical works, given to the heads of the male characters a fanciful character, which has made them appear quite unnatural, although the artists imagined that by their treatment an air of grandeur was given to the figures.

Rafael has drawn most of the heads in his frescoes from Nature; in this way the natural character of each is maintained, and a rich variety introduced into his works.

His successor and scholar, Giulio Romano, appears to have paid little attention to this, consequently the same head frequently recurs in his works. Amongst Rafael's predecessors, Masaccio may be mentioned as one who studied this branch of his art. In the works of Masaccio, and in those of the best of his contemporaries, there is a reflex of Nature, in consequence, most of the figures in these works are regarded as representations of persons living in that age. After Rafael's time less attention was given to this point, and, in the age of Luca Giordano, Pietro di Cortona, &c., three figures, forming as it were, a standard, were introduced into historical works. These figures were a man, a woman, and a child. The youthful male heads were drawn of the same proportions as those of the female heads; male heads' of an older type were characterized by a beard. These artists, with the genius which really belonged to them, were thus able to paint with extraordinary facility the ceilings of the palaces and churches in Italy. French artists worked in the same manner, and in Germany the artists who painted the ceilings in palaces and churches permitted themselves even greater freedom in their treatment of the figure.

PLATES XXV., XXVI. & XXVII.

THREE SHEETS OF FULL LENGTH FIGURES.

Two of these figures are drawn from Nature, while one shows geometrically the proportions of the Borghese gladiator. The first figure (Plate 25) has above it the inscription :—" After Nature. Height, 5 ft. 11 ins." The second (Plate 26) :— " The proportions of the Borghese gladiator 6 ft." The third (Plate 27) :—" Lesbenier, 5 ft. 6 ins, high." The latter is also taken from Nature. In the first sheet the measurements from the ground line to the middle of the knee-cap A B, from this line to the region of the groin C, and from the base of the stomach to the neck D E are equal, each being 20 ins. It is found that this proportion is applicable to the majority of male antique figures, and it has been adopted for the Borghese gladiator. There is, however, a considerable difference in the length of the foot, in the two figures; although the Borghese gladiator is only 1 in. taller, his feet are quite an inch longer. As regards the length of the feet and hands, modem artists have paid but little attention to the laws of Nature. Even Michel Angelo has erred in this respect. It is seen that the feet of the figure, "Lesbenier," on the third Plate, are of same length as those of the man of 5 ft. 11 ins., although the "Lesbenier" is only 5 ft 6 ins, high. The height of the head in each figure has been taken as 9 ins., although this height is rarely met with in Nature, and only in cases where the upper part of the head is high. The biggest men of 7 ft. and upwards have not a greater length of head than that above given. The mode in which Nature restricts the dimensions of certain parts, serves in art as a means of representing the differences of form both on a small and large scale. When artists therefore draw the hands smaller than Nature prescribes, the arms must be drawn proportionately longer, in order that when stretched out they may be equal to the height of the figure, in conformity with the laws of Nature. The small dimensions of the calf of the leg are copied from Nature, but it is not advisable to imitate this deviation from a well proportioned form. In this case the dimensions of the calf were maintained, in order to preserve the equality and harmony subsisting between this part and the other dimensions of the figure If the feet may be termed small, so may the hands, and for a man of this size it would be difficult to find a hand shorter than 7 ins. The width of the space between the eyes is 3½ inches. In the head of the Borghese gladiator this space is only 3¼ ins. Although the difference of height between the Borghese gladiator and the man of 5 ft. 11 ins, is only 1 in., the width and size of the parts in the former figure are very different The shoulders are less depressed. In the man of 5 ft. 11 ins. the width of the shoulders is a fourth part of the whole height, but in the gladiator the height is 3½ times the width of the, shoulders. The thickness of the knee-joint, 4 inches, is the same in both figures. Salvage based his analysis of the human form on the figure of the gladiator, and no other work of the old sculptors is more suitable for the purpose. A great many of their works appear to have been made in accordance with the teaching of schools, and appear, consequently, conventional, although a spirit of beauty pervades them all. On account of their customs, the ancients were prevented from studying the anatomy of the human form from dead subjects, but their customs gave them better opportunities of observing and copying the nude figure. The so-called "Dying Gladiator" bears also a natural character, but in this figure the movement is wanting which brings into prominence the whole of the muscular system.

The faults of the ancient masters, already referred to, have been brought into special prominence by our celebrated anatomist, Walter, in his observations on the Laocoon group. The parts he criticizes most severely are: the clavicle, the intercostal spaces, the serrati, the knee, and the faulty phalangeal joint of the small toe. On the other hand, it is no doubt the pain, which is expressed in the entire body from the crown of the head to the feet, that excites so much admiration.

In the majority of male figures by the ancients the size of the body over the ribs and across the trochanter is equal, but the results of a great number of measurements of man of medium size and of the biggest proportions show that the dimensions over the ribs should be somewhat less.

The confinement of the neck amongst Europeans is the reason that this part is seldom seen in its full proportions. The mode in which the feet are confined is a still greater drawback as regards the development of this part of the body, and in order to see perfect freedom of form, we must turn either to the works of the ancients or to the figures to be found amongst uncultivated peoples.

PLATE XXVII.

PROPORTIONS OF LESBENIER.

Height, 5 ft. 6 ins. The herculean men of the present day, who combine bodily strength with a degree of dexterity that enable them to perform in public the same as actors, are all of the same build. The proportions of one or two of them may be taken as a standard, for instance, those of Frank, called the Northern Hercules, or of Mathevet, Rappa, and others. The proportions of the so-called group of the Commodus Hercules (an ancient work) may be cited as corresponding with those of the modern figures mentioned above. This work does not belong to the highest class, but the forms are good and of a natural type. Corneille included this work in his measurements. His opinion of the group is recorded in a book by Antoine Jombert, entitled, "Method of Learning Drawing." Lesbenier was the least dexterous of the strong men, whose names are given above, but he could lift a large table with his teeth, and raise a load of 30 cwt. on his back. The others were acrobats as well as prestidigitateurs, and they proved that it is possible for Such men not only to bear heavy loads but to perform the neatest sleight of hand tricks. Although Lesbenier was much smaller than the Borghese gladiator, the dimensions of parts of his body were the same, some parts, for example, the shoulders, being even stronger. In Potsdam, where, from an early period, the biggest men in Germany have been found, it is well known that colossal size is no criterion of great strength. In the case of two brothers, one being 7 ft. high and the other 4 ins, shorter, this fact is clearly shown by reference to their hands, which have been drawn from Nature, and are represented on Plate 80 of this series. Amongst the works of the ancients no men of greater proportions than those of the Borghese gladiator can be found. The Farnese Hercules is of the same dimensions, likewise the Colossi of Monte Cavallo. The immense vase on which the sacrifice of Iphigenia is represented, as well as the Homeric heroes, are of elegant rather than colossal proportions. The Elgin marbles are likewise of proportions which harmonize with those of Nature. We are consequently led to the belief either that the ancients never saw such tall figures as live in modern times, or a sense of beauty made them disinclined to represent men of unusual size. Taeitus has mentioned the surprise of the Roman soldiers when they saw men of great stature in Germany. In these three Plates it will be seen that the distance between the nipples is one half the breadth across the shoulders. This measurement is a minimum in the case of the Sleeping Farm, which is now in Munich, but was originally in the Barbarini Palace. The broad chest of the Antinous of the Capitol and of other Roman figures must have resulted from a fashion of the period, which artists followed. These exaggerated dimensions of the chest and ribs are to be seen in Canova's Pugilists (see Plate 28) and in other heroes of his modelling. The narrowness across the hips is thereby rendered more striking. In this respect, as well as in the abnormal projection of the frontal bone, Canova has had numerous imitators, not only amongst indifferent artists but also amongst men of talent, whose works have consequently lacked a natural character. There are now so many opportunities offered to artists to acquire a knowledge of the structure of the human body, that the works of talented men leave in this matter nothing to be desired; but as regards the skin it might almost be said that this covering had been removed altogether, judging from the little attention which has been paid to it. In effect, it should be the aim of every artist to exercise his imitative faculties by copying as truthfully as possible the movements of tim wondrous covering. A neglect of this branch of art is plainly seen in the incomplete treatment of the flesh in modern statues.

PLATES XXVIII., XXIX. & XXX.

The method of finding and determining the proportions of the body by measurement has, up to this point, only been applied to the living form, which admits of such suitable positions as have been given, viz., the upright one, front view, and profile. The question now is: Can this method be applied to figures in a sitting or lying-down posture?

On the first and second tables will be found some attempts to solve this problem, the figures being taken from ancient and modem sculptures. It would be difficult to show any such application of the method to paintings of the modern schools, for a nude male or female figure, representing with clearness and accuracy the human form, can rarely be met with even in the largest picture galleries. The ancient paintings, on the other hand, which are still to be found in Rome, Herculaneum, and Pompeii, prove that painters in those days strove to represent the figure as dearly as possible. As soon as perspective became a science, it was employed not only by artists for drawing in their backgrounds, but by sculptors. The success of its application is seen in the door of the Baptistry at Florence, by Lorenzo Ghiberti. The ancients regarded its use in the representation of the human form as a great piece of legerdemain; and Vasari gives prominent notice to those artists who foreshortened the feet of their figures (when seen from the front) in place of drawing them full length, as if standing on a sloping floor. The same writer also refers to the artifices, as he calls them, practiced by Michel Angelo in his work in the Sistine Chapel, and by Rafael in his "Transfiguration." These two artists must certainly have seen in old bas-reliefs and paintings that neither the Greeks nor the Romans had ever introduced such bold foreshortening in their works of art. Liberties of this kind had been practiced before, and the predecessors of Michel Angelo and Rafael had endeavoured to represent the features foreshortened as they appear when the head is bent forwards or backwards. This sort of foreshortening is essential to the study of the figure.

The differences in full-grown figures are shown on three Plates at the end. They are represented by figures from modern and ancient sculptures, and a few from Nature.

On the first of these three Plates is "Christ," by Michel Angelo, the Theseus from the Elgin marbles, and "A Pugilist," by Canova.

The best method to arrive at the height of the human figure with certainty is to take the length of the face as 5 inches. According to this rule, the height of the figure of Christ was found to be 5 feet 6 inches. This figure is one of the finest works of this master, and differs materially from his "Christ" in the temple of Minerva at Rome. The head is bent backwards, and the neck is on this account somewhat expanded. The breadth of the shoulders is double the distance of the space between the nipples. This further confirms the law, which has already been referred to several times. The entire figure is divided into two equal parts, and the thickness of the legs arms are in perfect harmony. The hands are of the length prescribed by Nature, but the small size of the feet is unnatural. This error is the more remarkable, as the left foot, which is raised in the original group, is a whole inch shorter than the right one, which touches the plinth. This figure forms however, part of one of the best groups of modern sculpture, and the treatment of the skin is delicately worked out

The next figure on this Plate is that of Theseus, from the collection of Lord Elgin, now in the British Museum. The length of the face, viz., 5 ins., gives a total height of 5 ft. 10½ ins. This is not an exceptional height in the present age, but the Greeks appear to have regarded it as ample for the figures of their heroes. The heroic character is represented by the strength of the limbs; the width across the ribs, cheat, and shoulders. The ravages of time have no doubt destroyed the surface of the figure, as the neck appears short and thin. This part has in general the same thickness as the calf of the leg, which in this instance is 5 ins. The width across the ribs, 13½ ins.; across the hips the dimensions are the same. These are the smallest dimensions which could be given to these parts, as the outer points of the trochanter are always separated from each other by a greater distance than the width across the ribs. The feet, which are wanting in the original, are here taken as 10 ins, long. This length, however, is not in conformity with Nature.

The third figure, Canova's pugilist, has a height of 5 ft. 9 ins., and is of natural size. Although the figure is smaller than that of Theseus, the width across the ribs is 1 in. more, or 14½ ins. Across the hips this figure measures 1½ in. less than across the ribs. The space between the nipples measures 11½ ins.; the dimensions across the shoulders should therefore be 28 ins.

These data show that the leading idea in the production of this figure was to improve on Nature, as a consequence the proportions are entirely contrary to the laws of Nature. This error has, no doubt, been caused by the artist having taken his forms and proportions from the works of various Masters, in place of working from the nude figure. Again, it is frequently in the nature of young artists to pay greater attention to works of art than to Nature, who, it is true, sometimes presents herself to their eyes not unaccompanied by blemishes. The heed of this figure is drawn in profile, a vertical line touches it, end shows how the upper edge of the eye cavity projects. If this profile were drawn in conformity with Nature the forehead should be within the vertical line. The exaggerations seen in this head are likewise to be found in the beet works of modern masters, both in sculpture and painting. The ideal forms they produce are in fact treated in the same style, and when to this are added thin knee-joints and ankles, and small hands and feet, an elegance, which even the Greeks did not attain, may be the result, but the truth of Nature is sacrificed. It may be further remarked that, as the nose of the pugilist is wider than the mouth, the unnatural appearance of the heed is still more striking.

Second Table—On this Plate (29) there are four figures. The first is from the antique by Audran, and the other is from Nature. The figure from the antique, called "La Paix des Grecs," gives one the impression that it may have been formed in accordance with the canon of Polycletus, and frequently copied. No particulars are given as to the place where this example may be found; but, according to Audran's measurements, the figure is not life size. The position given to the "Paix des Grecs," in his work on proportion, taken in connection with the spear and shield in the left hand, seems to indicate that this figure was intended to represent one of the bodyguard of the King of Persia. The proportions of this youthful figure of medium height are exceedingly harmonious. The only modification which has been introduced in the figure on this Plate, is to make the length of the face 5 inches. Audran himself employed the method used in the schools of his time, viz., that of dividing the head into four parts, two for the face and two for the upper part of the bead. This mode of division is, however, contrary both to Nature and to the antique. In adults it is seldom found that the upper part of the head is to the face as 4 to 5. On reference to the heads on Plate 30 (the last Plate), showing physiognomies of different nationalities, this fact can be verified. In general the upper part of the head has a height of 3½ ins., and the majority of the heads of male adults are 8½ ins., and many female heads are in. less. In order to give the dimensions clearly we have not shown the figure in the picturesque attitude given to it by Audran, but have drawn it in one more suitable for measurement. Notwithstanding the stiff appearance of the figure, the beauty of the proportions is apparent. The broad shoulders, measuring 18 inches across, and the strong torso, 12 inches wide, do not deprive the figure of its youthful aspect. The distance from the seat of the heart to the navel is in this instance greater than usual, but it agrees with the dimensions which are observed in well-formed figures of the present day. The hips are a trifle broader than the ribs.

Bucholz.—The figure at the side of the one already described is that of a big man who posed as a model. The imperfections of his form are given as they actually were in Nature. The length of his lower jaw makes the face quite half an inch longer. The breadth and height of the upper part of the head do not, however, measure more than in men of medium height, and the eyes do not occupy more space. The upper parts of the legs are exceedingly long, and, considering the narrowness of the space between the nipples, the shoulders are too broad. On this account, the part which artists call the "bust" appears too large. In spite of these defects the man was a useful model. The hands and feet did not harmonize, the lower parts of the legs and the feet were small and the hands large. A youthful fulness of the muscles made his figure a contrast to that of another model, who was about 4 ins, shorter, and is also shown on the same Plate. This man's name was Bernard. In his case, the shoulders and hips were in conformity as regards breadth, and the upper and lower parts of the leg likewise. The hands and feet are 10½ ins, long. Between the ribs and the upper joint of the arm, stands the continuation of. the shoulder' blade (*processus coracoideus*). On reference, however, to Canova's pugilist it is seen that the ribs gradually lessen upwards till they border on the region occupied by the vertebral column of the neck, leaving no space for the processus coracoideus. In several figures of Canova this fault is still more striking than in the example before us.

The ulna (see Bernard) is only half an inch longer than the foot, these measurements being as a rule equal. In the case of small women, the foot is in fact often longer than the nina. In the profile view the arm which is lowered, shows a. decrease of one half in thickness, taking the upper part at 6 ins. and the part at the wrist at 2½ ins. From the shoulder blade to the breast bone the greatest diameter was found to be 9 ins. The ancients made the *os pubis* project further forward, and the base of the stomach less confined; they also gave greater fulness to the upper part of the legs. The dimensions of the posterior in profile were likewise full, and the fulness of this part was rendered more apparent by the spareness of the region between the lower part of the vertebral column and the stomach, as seen in profile.

The young man of 5 ft. 8 ins, high was employed as model on account of the well defined and strong muscular system be possessed. His outstretched arms measured a little more than the entire height of his body, but this cannot be termed a fault, as it often occurs in small people. The celebrated sculptors of our day, however, have committed an error in the opposite direction, for the outstretched arms of their figures when measured from one finger tip to the other do not equal the total height. They make, in fact, the torso too short, and the arms are modeled short to give an appearance of harmony to the figure.

The arm, when held vertically upwards, increases the length of the body by one-fifth part, if the height from the ground line to the crown of.the bead be divided into four parts. The thickness of the calf of the leg has, in this case, been taken from Nature, but is too great for a well- formed figure. The height of the biggest of these figures is almost 7 times the length of the foot, and the height of the smallest only 6½ times. This difference in the proportion of the separate parts of various individuals enables the artist to represent, both on a small and large scale, human beings of both sexes, whether of insignificant or imposing stature, and to give to each a clearly defined characteristic. A glance at the few figures on these two tables shows at once that only a very small portion of the endless varieties' of types met with in Nature has been given. In spite of the variety of human forms, one has only to look attentively at some of the most imposing works of art, which represent an almost incalculable number of figures, to become convinced how poor Art really is in this respect.

In the battle-pieces of Le Brun, or in the enormous painted ceiling by Pietro Cortona in the Barbarini Palace, the figures differ from one another principally in pose and in the view presented to the spectator. It is true that King Porus is drawn larger, and Alexander smaller, than the rest of the figures; but, with these two exceptions, the figures are so much alike that they lead to the belief that Le Brun must have painted them from one model only. In Pietro Cortona's pictures the same man, woman, and child are repeated an indefinite number of times. The great Michel Angelo even has, in his painted ceilings and in the "Last Day of Judgment" in the Sistine Chapel, shown very little variety in his figures. A pleasant contrast is offered by such Greek works as the groups of the Menelaos and Patroclos, of the Apollo, Pan, &c., even greater by such works as the "Dispute del Sacramento,""Heliodor,""The Miracle of Bolsena," and others, by Rafael. His favourite pupil, Julio Romano, had followed in the footsteps of M. Angelo. The picture of the Titans was the favourite subject of Romano, as he was enabled to give all the figures therein a family likeness.

The frescoes of Dominichino, in the Grotta Ferrata, are deserving of mention on account of the beautiful variety to be observed in the figures. Painters, however, like Ciro Ferri, Luca Giordano, and others, could with ease fill large canvases with figures, as they never attempted to give varied proportions to the forms they represented.

The want of variety in these rich compositions, which have been painted with astonishing celerity, shows that there is still a vast field for artistic talent, which can have no worthier aim than that of doing homage to the boundless richness of Nature in her highest works, and no truer' aspiration than that of recognizing character as a universal law, whilst the artist retains to the fullest degree his esthetic perceptions. A master alone can attain these conditions, as the faintest semblance of caricature must at the same time be carefully avoided.

The third of these Plates completes the entire series, which has been put together to illustrate this work on the proportions of the human frame. On this Plate, the scale which has been adopted for the drawings is given once more, so that the dimensions can be checked and compared with those of living forms.

In order to show the errors, which arise from faulty principles, and the use of the unaided vision, some heads are represented which have been taken from well known copper plate engravings. Two of these heads are by Audran, after Le Sueur, and belong to men of good stature, but, even if they were heads of short men, the distance between the eyes is so great that, if the other parts were properly proportioned, there would be no space left for the cheek bones and the jaw. The other two heads in the same row are by Lange and Giotto; they have the same fault. The heads beneath are taken from Audran's "Battles of Alexander." Taking the size of each face as correct, it is seen that some of the separate parts, such as the eyes, nose, and mouth are too large. With a view to making these errors clear, a head, A, has been drawn of natural size in all its parts, and is shown close to the other head A, and to the right hand of it. The head B, also to the right, is that of a Persian, and a similar head B, is added of more natural proportions. The head of a rude barbarian is represented, and is marked C; another head of the same kind, but drawn correctly, is also shown.

It should have been the duty of the artist to portray the difference of features of the various races represented. In Trajan's column the Dacians are distinguished from the Romans, nOt only in dress, but also in the character of the heads.

The head D is in close proximity to that of King Porus, and should have an oval forth to be in conformity with the excessive length of the body. The same division has, however, been applied in this case. The accompanying head D, is shown merely as an illustration of this remark. The above observations only refer to the engraving, as the original drawings by two such masters as Le Sueur and Le Brun would certainly not deviate so much from the natural dimensions.

Many more examples could have been given, but those above will be sufficient to illustrate the method of treating the human head; another example is, however, on the same Plate, and represents the head of Phyruss, son of Achilles, engraved by Richomme from the painting by Guerin. The proportions of this head would have been equally as suitable for the head of a boy of 12 years of age. There is a series of splendid portraits by Holbein, in which the characteristics of the male and female heads are faithfully portrayed. Historical painters have, however, seldom taken the trouble to derive knowledge from this source, otherwise the beads of their old women would not be so very nearly like those of their old men.

On the same Plate there are three figures, the dimensions of which have been taken from life. The contrast in these figures does not represent the extremes which can be found in Nature, as no example is given of the giant and the dwarf. The first of these figures (the Swiss woman) is only 6 feet 8 inches high; she weighed 330 pounds. Her corpulence arose principally from the size of the bones and muscles. The hands were hard, owing to the work she had been compelled to do. She is described as having a pleasant type of face, which was confirmed as regards the full face, but was less apparent in profile. The head is drawn on this Plate according to the actual dimensions taken by the compasses, the distance between the corners of the eyes being a maximum. This space in the heads of females of medium height is 3½ ins.; the difference in the case of the Swiss is therefore only in., although the face is quite 2 ins longer than in other cases. The width between the eyes is seldom found to be more than 4 ins. The examples referred to above will show how frequently this law of Nature is abused. The length of the face (see Swiss woman) is principally owing to the long under jaw; notwithstanding this, the female character of the face is quite apparent. On comparing the head and hand of this woman with those of a female of medium height, it will be at once seen of what imposing proportions the Swiss was formed: Women of still greater stature have been exhibited, but they have 'not been given here as examples, owing to the want of gracefulness in their figures. When the head of the Swiss was bare, the smallness of the upper part in comparison with the size of the face was especially noticeable. This will be at once apparent on looking at the profile drawn on the same Plate. This woman was said to possess mildness of character and a good deal of native humour. The conformation of her skull is in conformity with this description, its form being very superior to that of the big man, who had very little of these qualities. The brother of this man, who served in the Prussian Grenadiers, was 4 ins. taller, but had so little physical strength that it exerted him considerably to stand upright for 5 minutes. The hands of these men are drawn to a smaller scale, and shown together on the Plate. The hand of the so-called giant is 1 in. longer than that of the grenadier, Theodore Licht. Another hand of equal length is shown, viz., that of a man of the Imperial Russian guard. From the length of this hand it may be concluded that this man was also 7 ft. high. The head and hand of a person of medium height are also shown, so that the colossal size of the others may be visible at a glance.

It is difficult, by means of the eye alone, to perceive the difference in the size of the male and female hand when of the ordinary size. Measurements made with the aid of the compasses are therefore not so unnecessary to the artist as is generally maintained.

The very little man between the two big figures cannot be classed among the dwarfs, as men of this size are found in every large town. It is remarkable that amongst such men, the upper part of the head frequently exceeds that of the biggest men.

A great many more data could be put together on the subject of proportion, and there. will doubtless be found a number of young and talented artists willing to collect with care the facts which they observe in studying from the life, and in this way assist the completion of a science that fails to further the progress of art in this country.

The numerous measurements of heads which have been taken for the purposes of this work, prove the incomplete character of the publications that treat upon this part of the human body. Peter Camper's treatise on national physiognomy seems to have been, after the lapse of several years, the best attempt to collect accurate data respecting the noblest portion of man's structure.

In conclusion, it is hoped that, in spite of its short. comings, this work will be of some assistance to artists, and smooth many of the difficulties inseparably associated with the correct representation of the living figure.

Appendix II.

Original German Plates from an 1886 Edition.

ATLAS

OF

POLYCLET

OR

THE PROPORTIONS OF THE HUMAN BODY

OF FIGURES OF BOTH SEXES AND VARIOUS AGES

BY

DR. GOTTFRIED SCHADOW

BERLIN

ERNST WASMUTH PUBLISHER

MARKGRAFEN STRASSE

1886

ABOUT THE APPENDIX

The first part of this book consists of photographs of full double wide pages of *The Sculptor and Art Student's Guide to the Proportions of the Human Form* that are 24 inches by 19 inches, and of large reproductions of portions of those pages. Is is arranged in the order of the original book. *The Sculptor and Art Student's Guide to the Proportions of the Human Form* was published in 1883 and is an English translation of the work by Dr. Johann Gottfried Schadow, the German Sculptor. The text was translated by James J. Wright and lithographs were made by John Sutcliffe.

The appendix consists of reproductions of a reduced size German edition of 1886. This edition was 8.5 inches by 12 inches. The original edition by the same publisher was 12 inches by 18 inches with double sized plates of 24 inches by 18 inches tipped in just like the English edition.

The original edition was titled *Polyclet oder von den Massen des Menschen nach dem Geschlect und Alter, mit Angabe der wirklichen Naturgrösse nach dem rheinländischen Zollstocke und und Metermass Mit einem Atlas von 30 Tafeln*, Berlin, 1834.

I cannot tell what method was used to produce the smaller plates but there is some evidence of distortion - particularly in Plate XV. - Der Mann - 8 Kopflängen (Male Adult — 8 Heads) - indicating the possibility of the use of photolithography to make the new plates.

The fortunate thing for the modern reader is that finding this edition makes it possible to present full page views of the giant prints in this form.

-Tom Richardson, 2008

ATLAS

ZU

POLYCLET

ODER

VON DEN MAASSEN DES MENSCHEN

NACH DEM GESCHLECHTE UND ALTER

VON

DR. GOTTFRIED SCHADOW

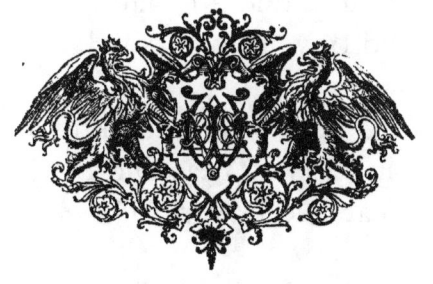

BERLIN

VERLAG VON ERNST WASMUTH

35 MARKGRAFENSTRASSE 35

1886

LIST OF PLATES

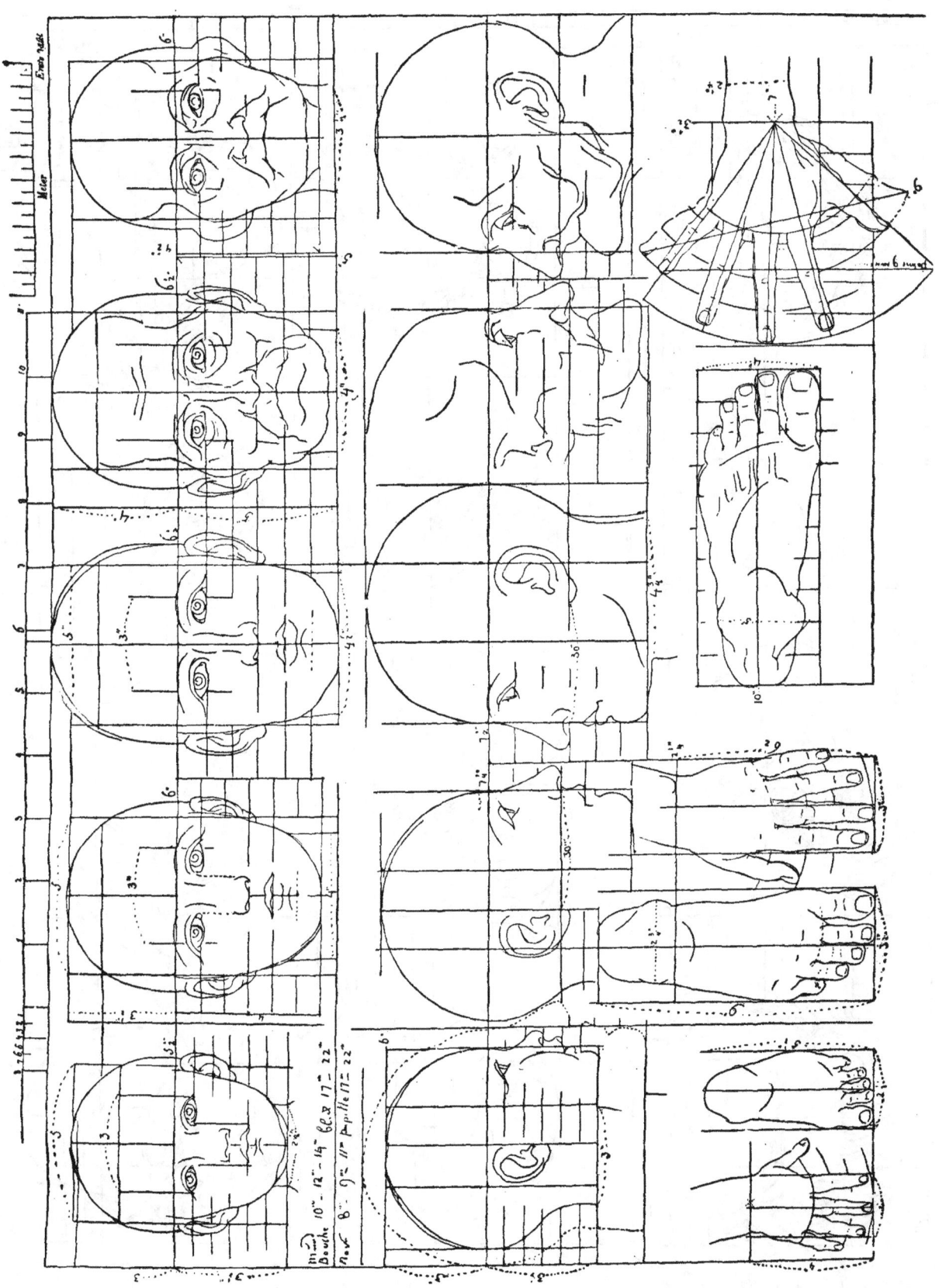

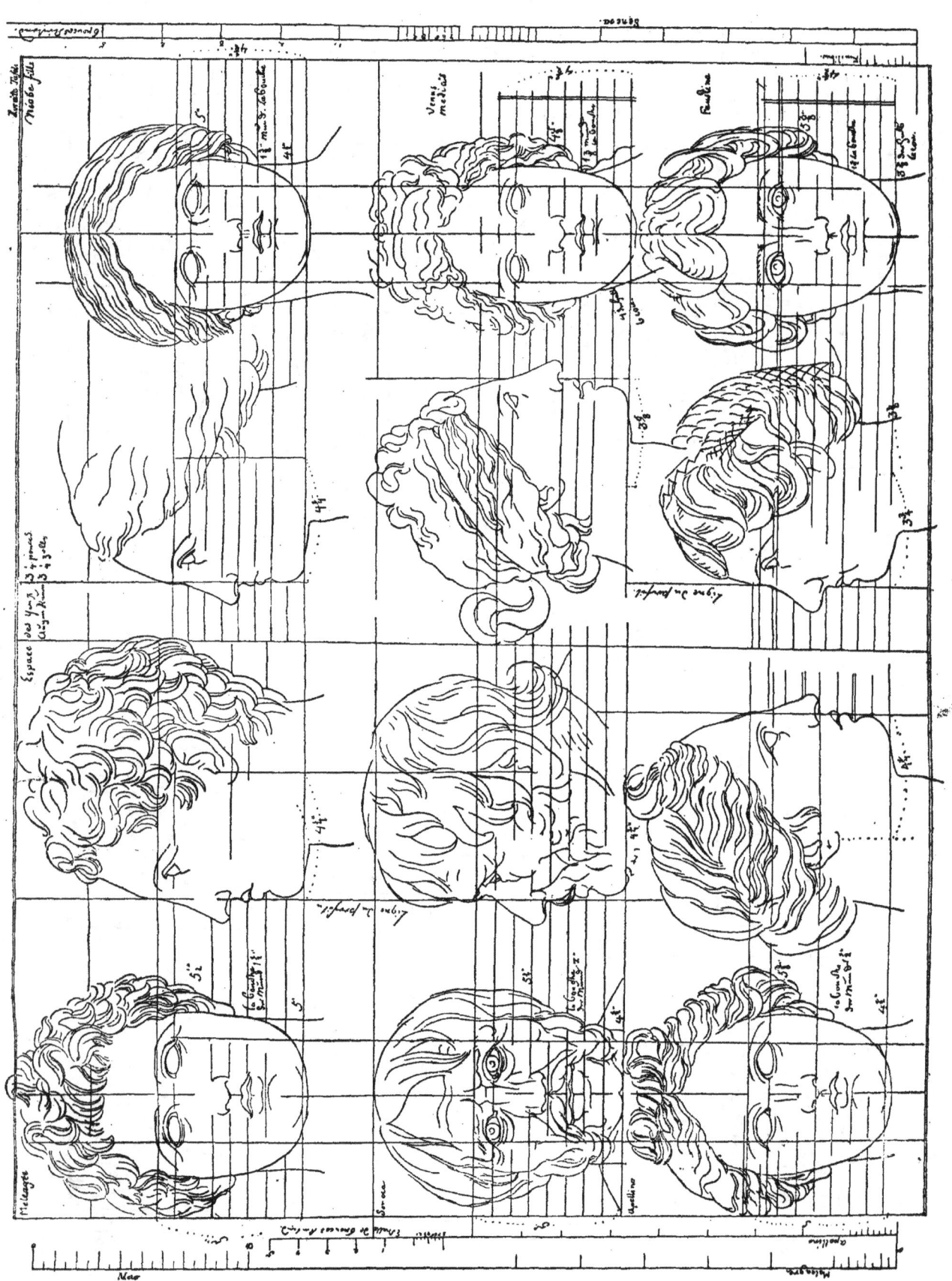

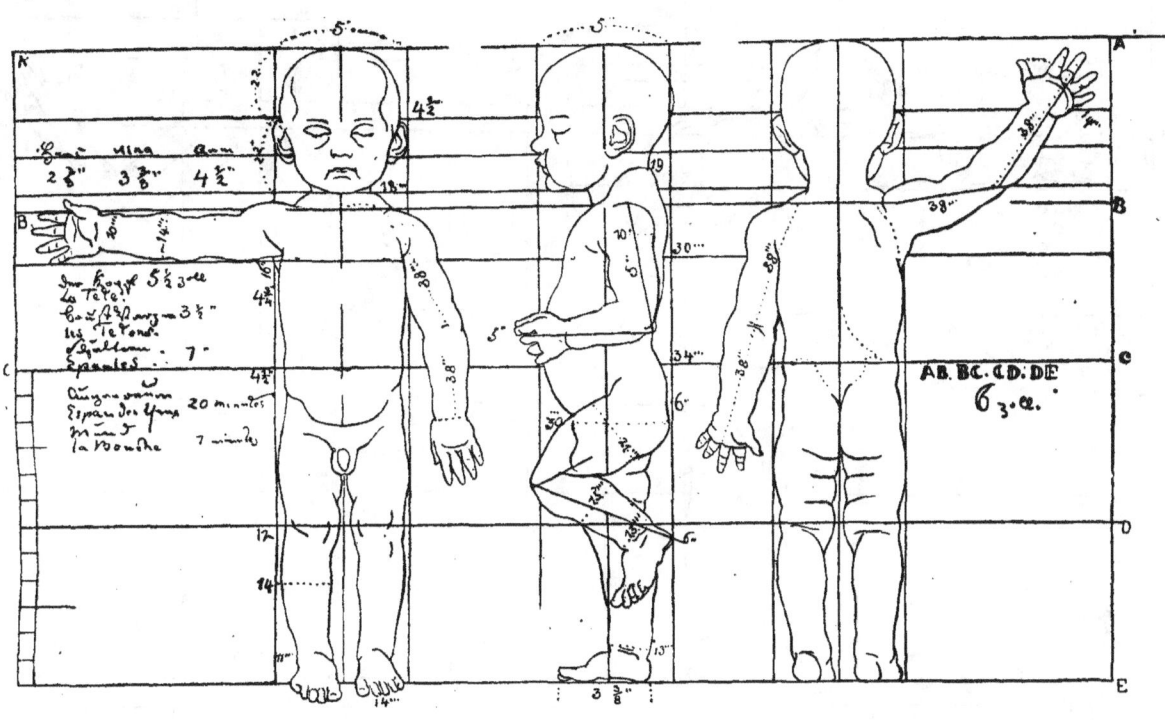

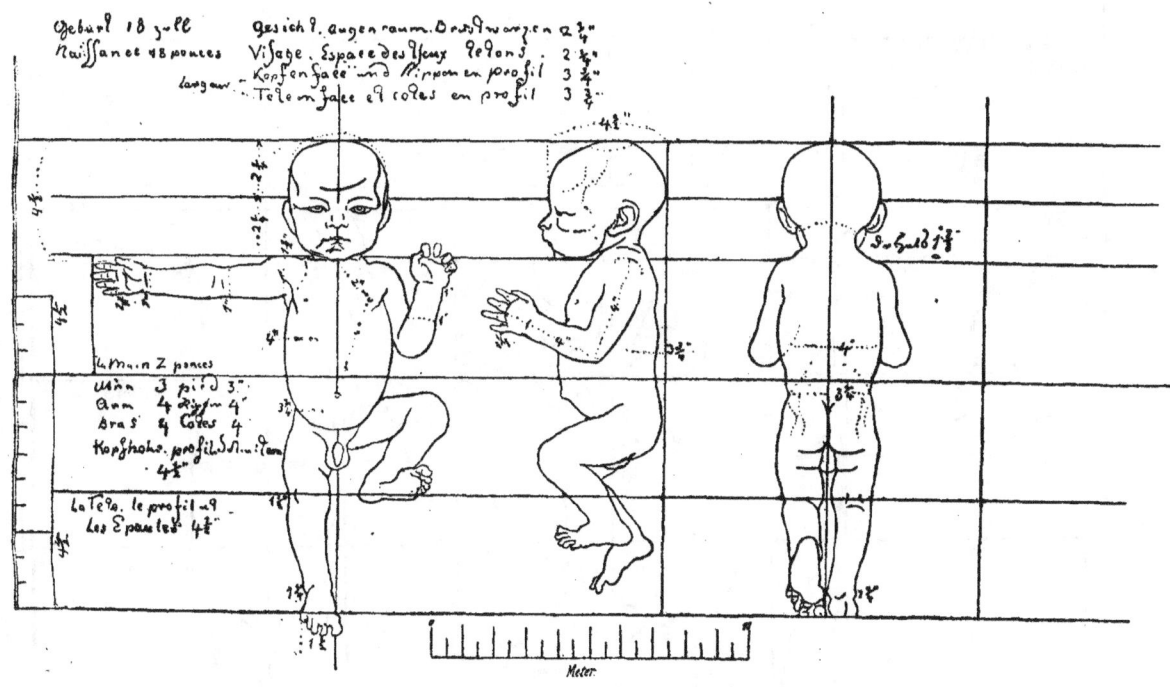

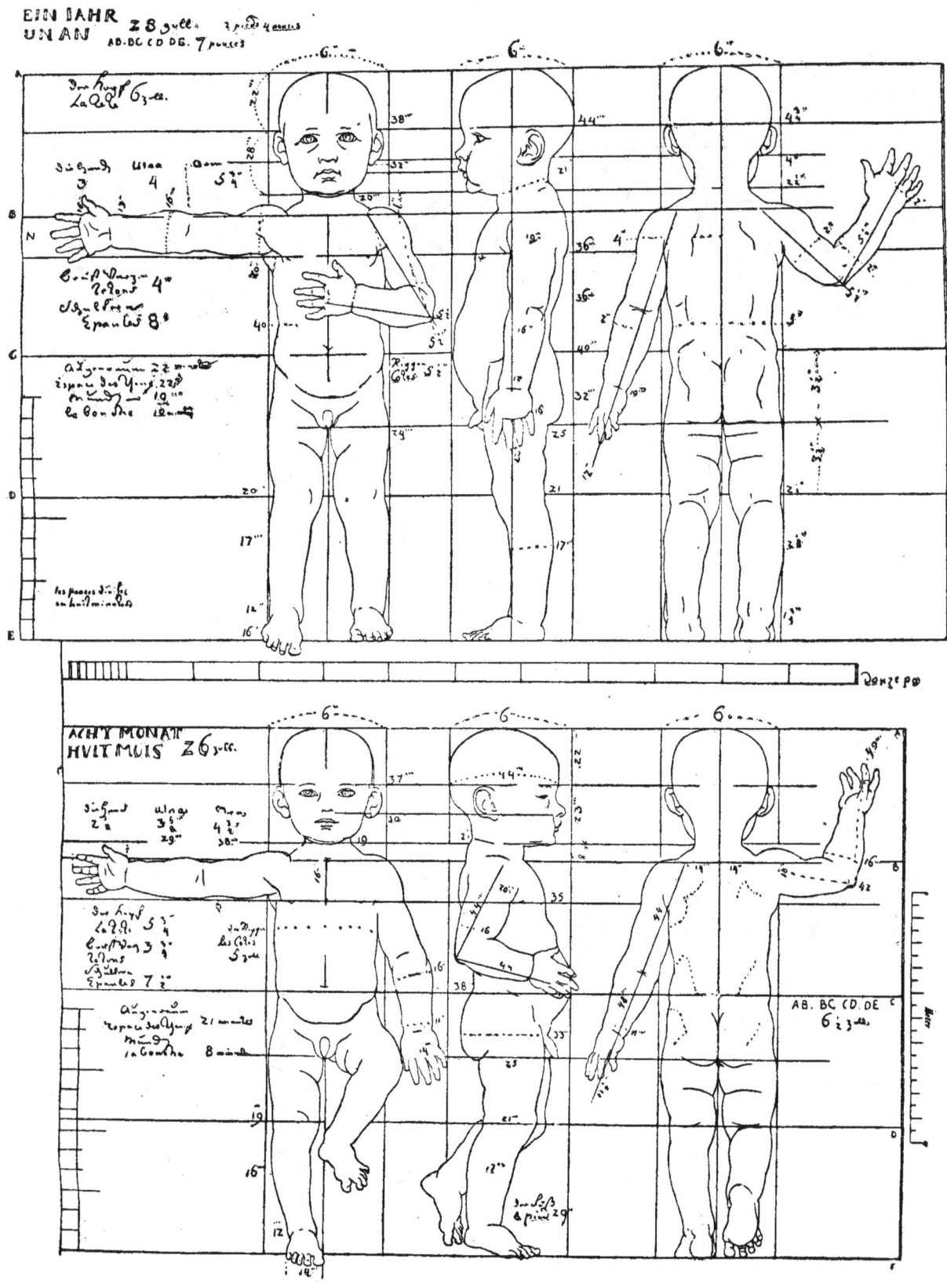

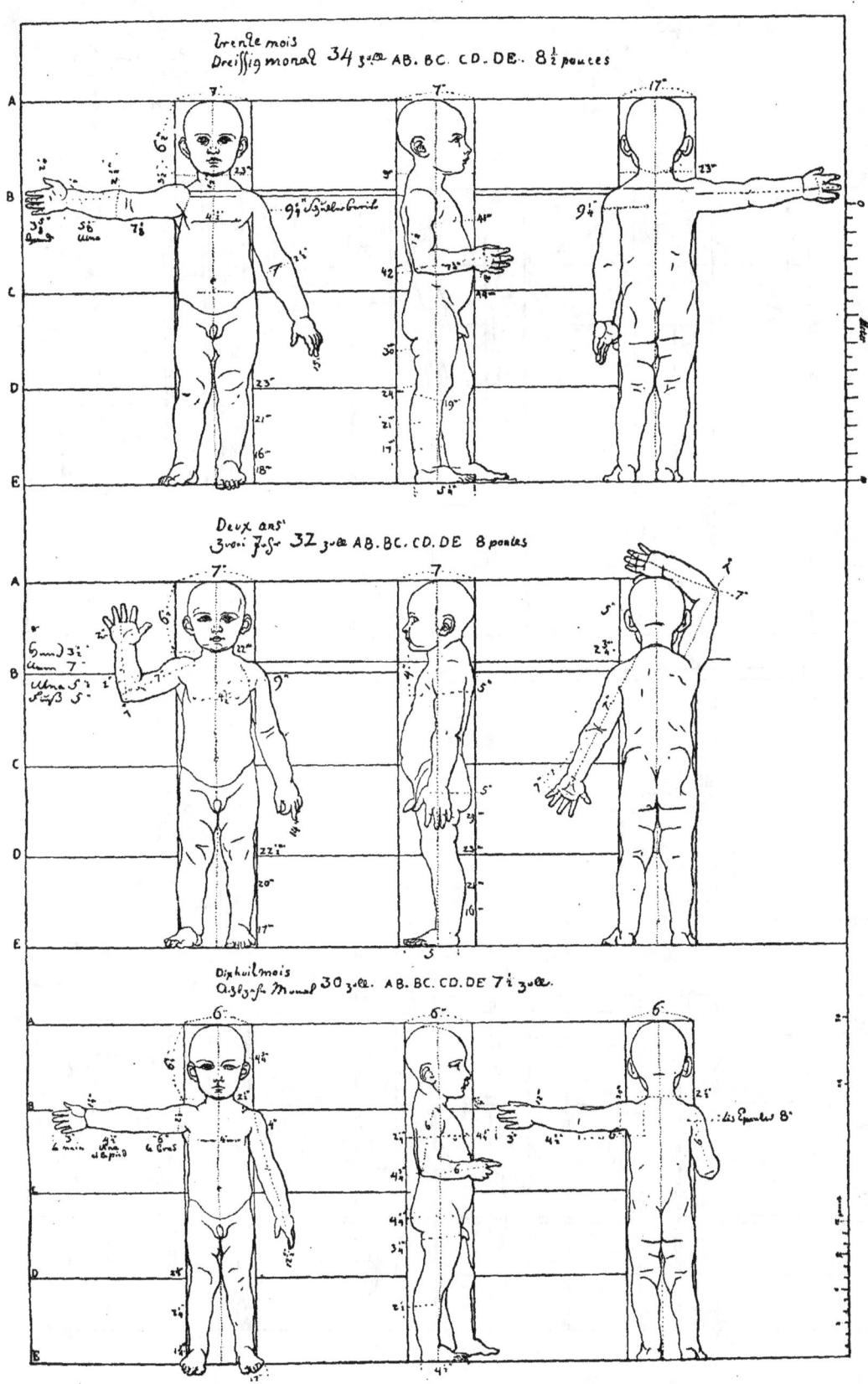

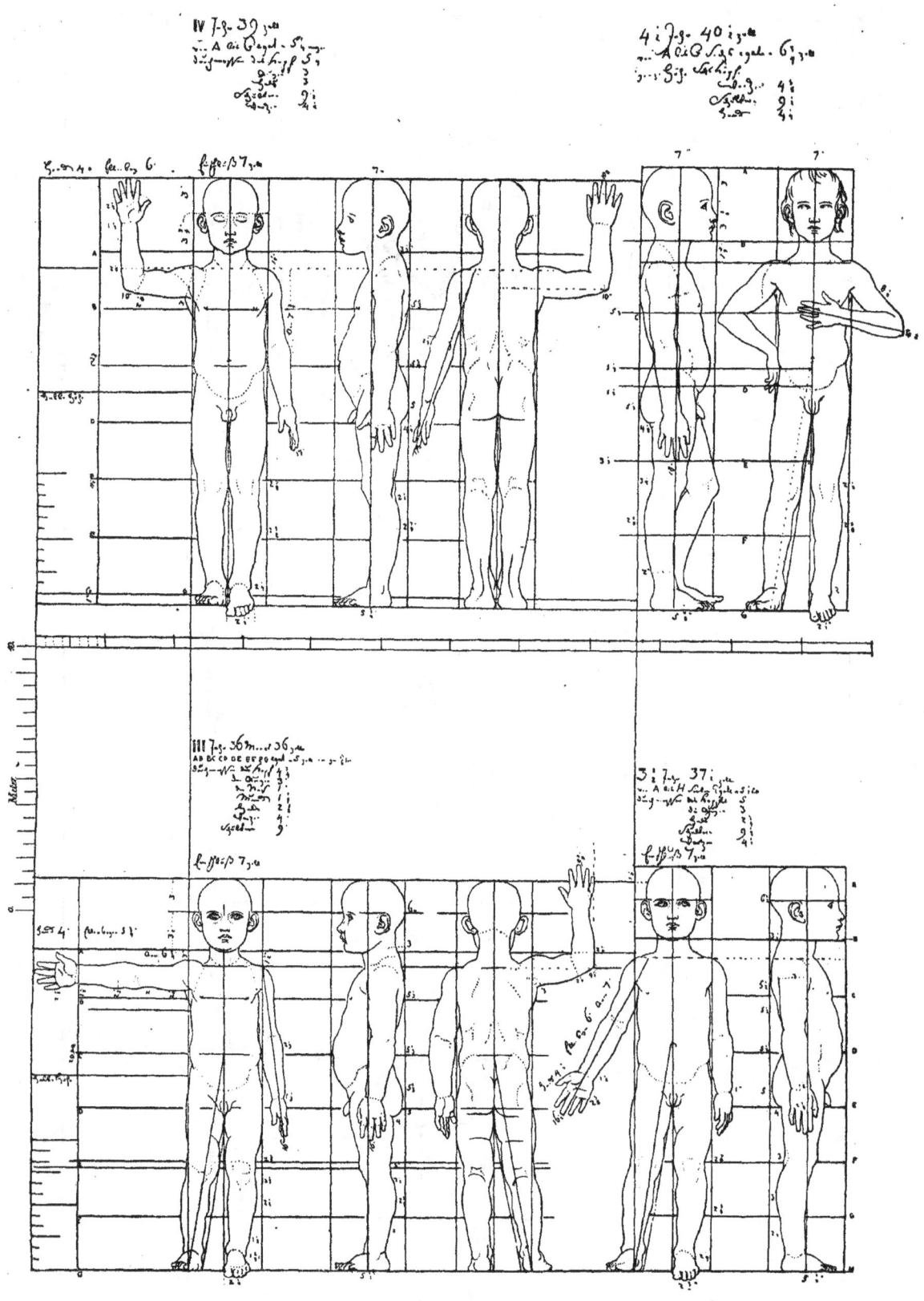

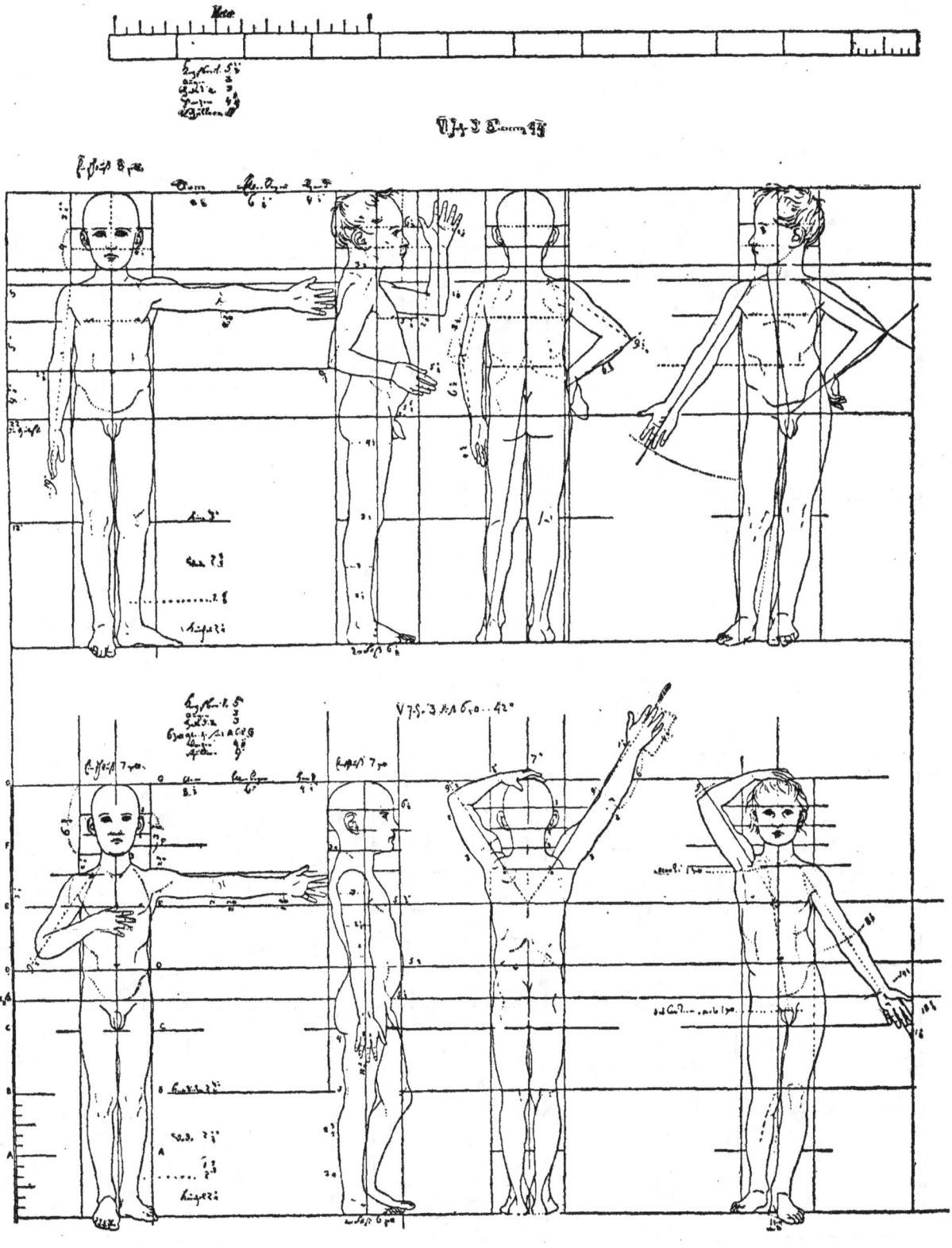

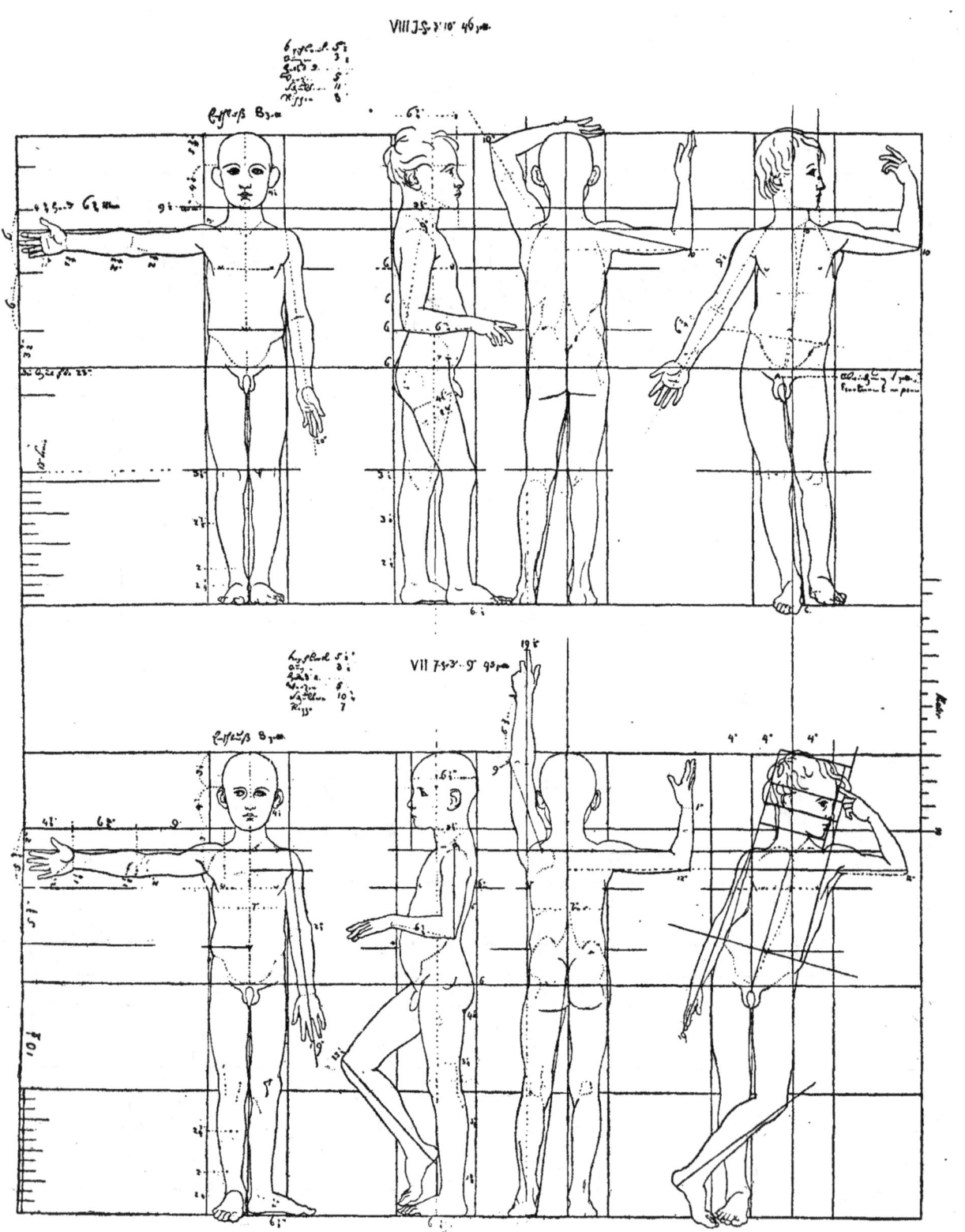

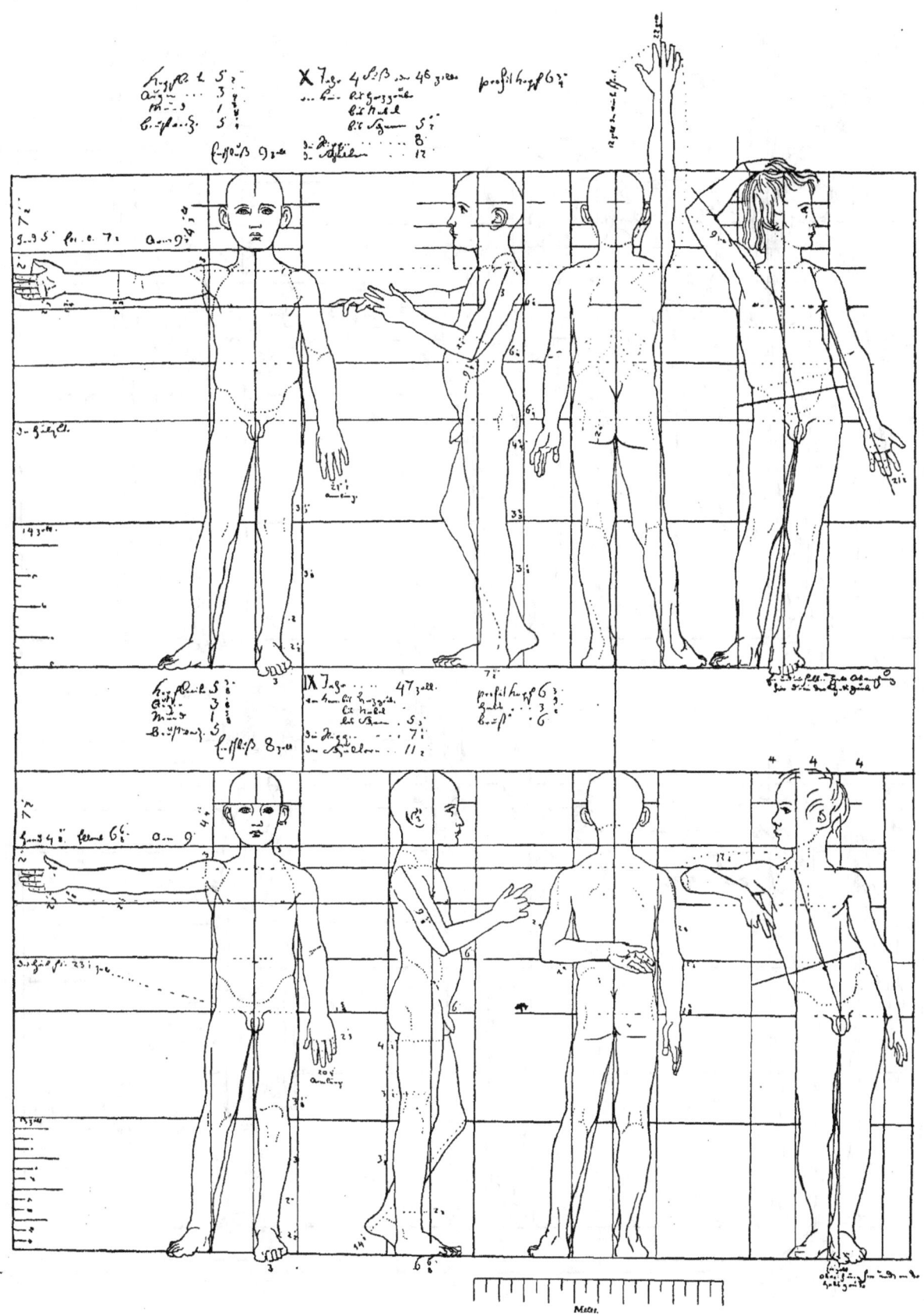

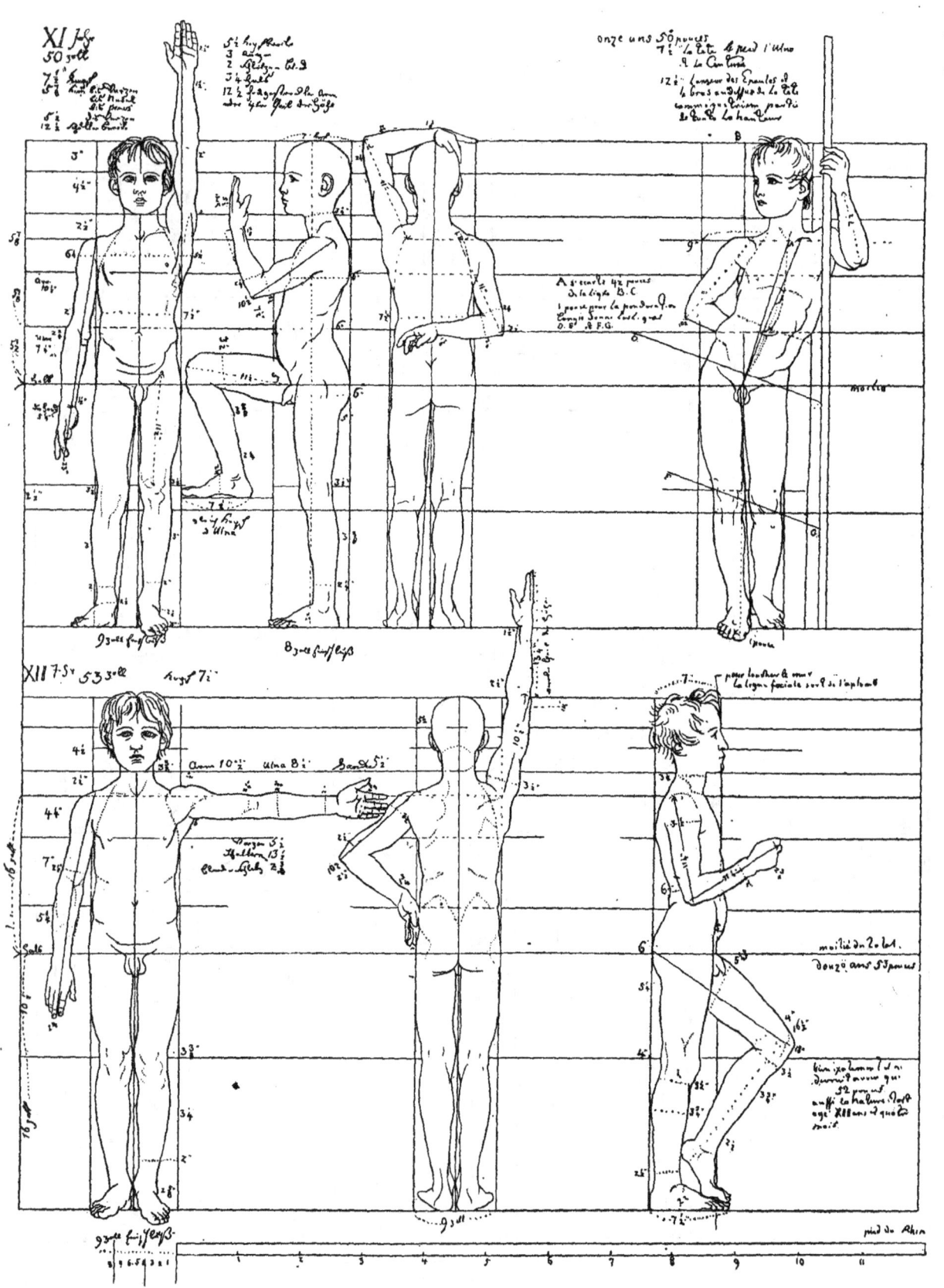

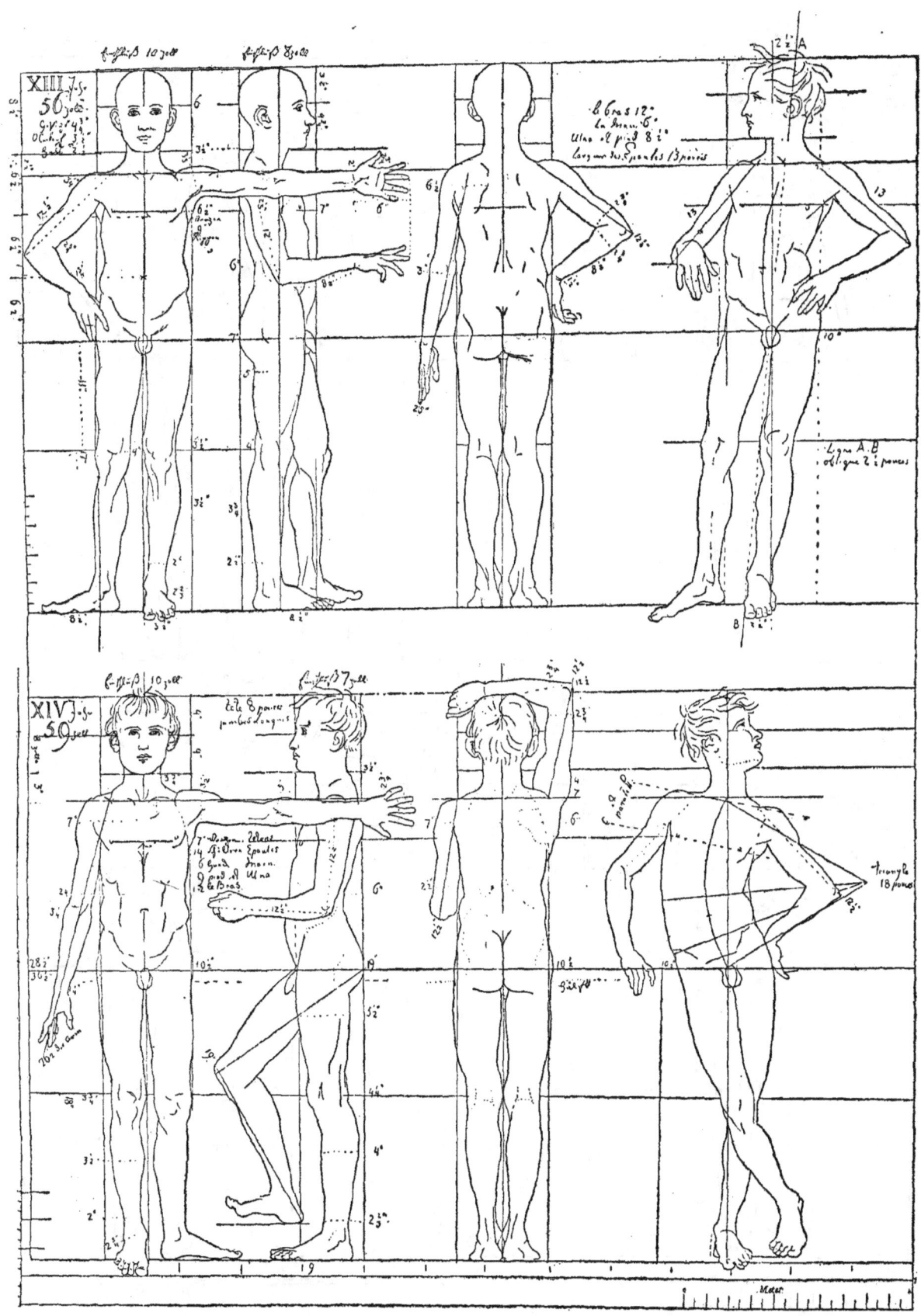

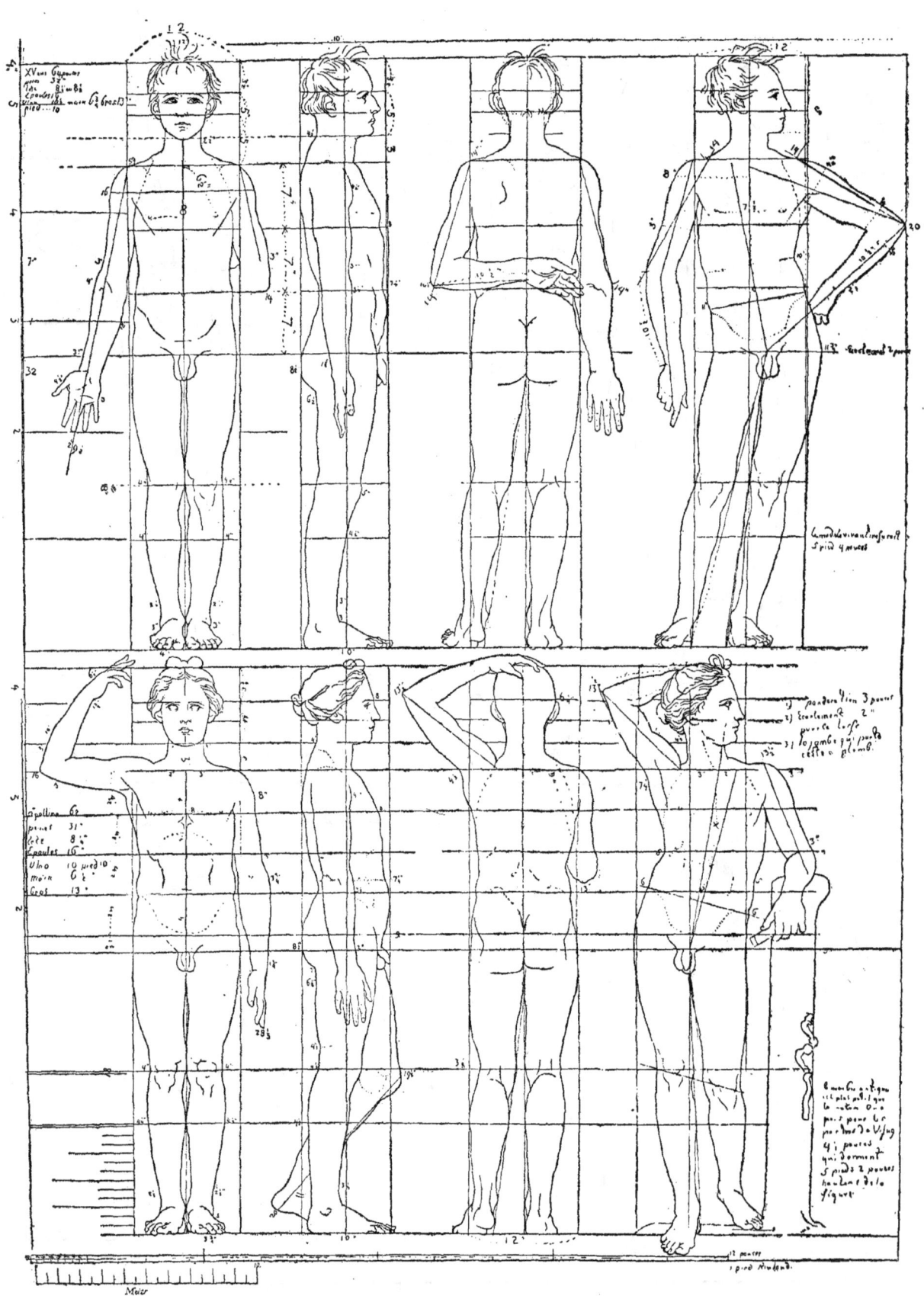

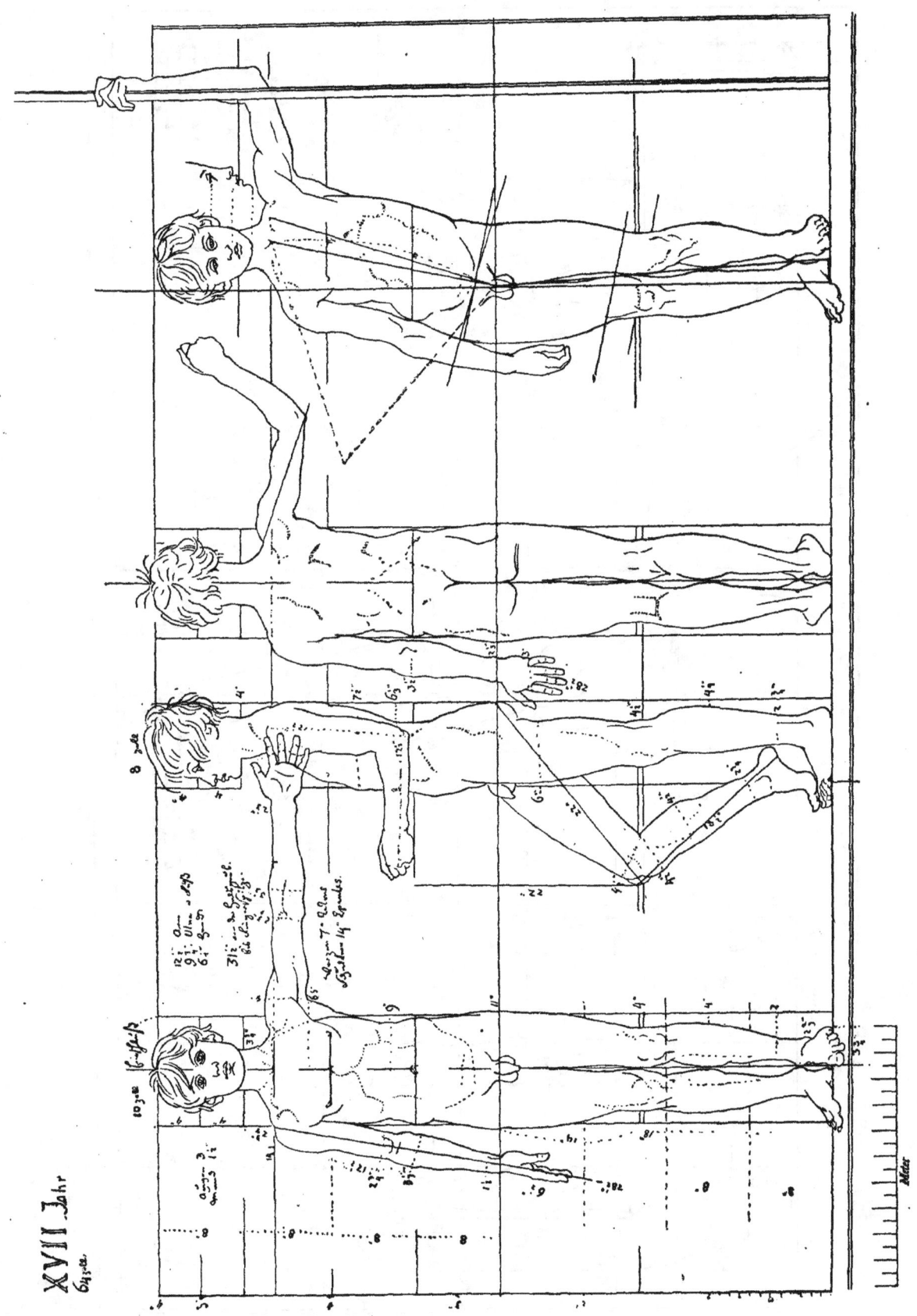

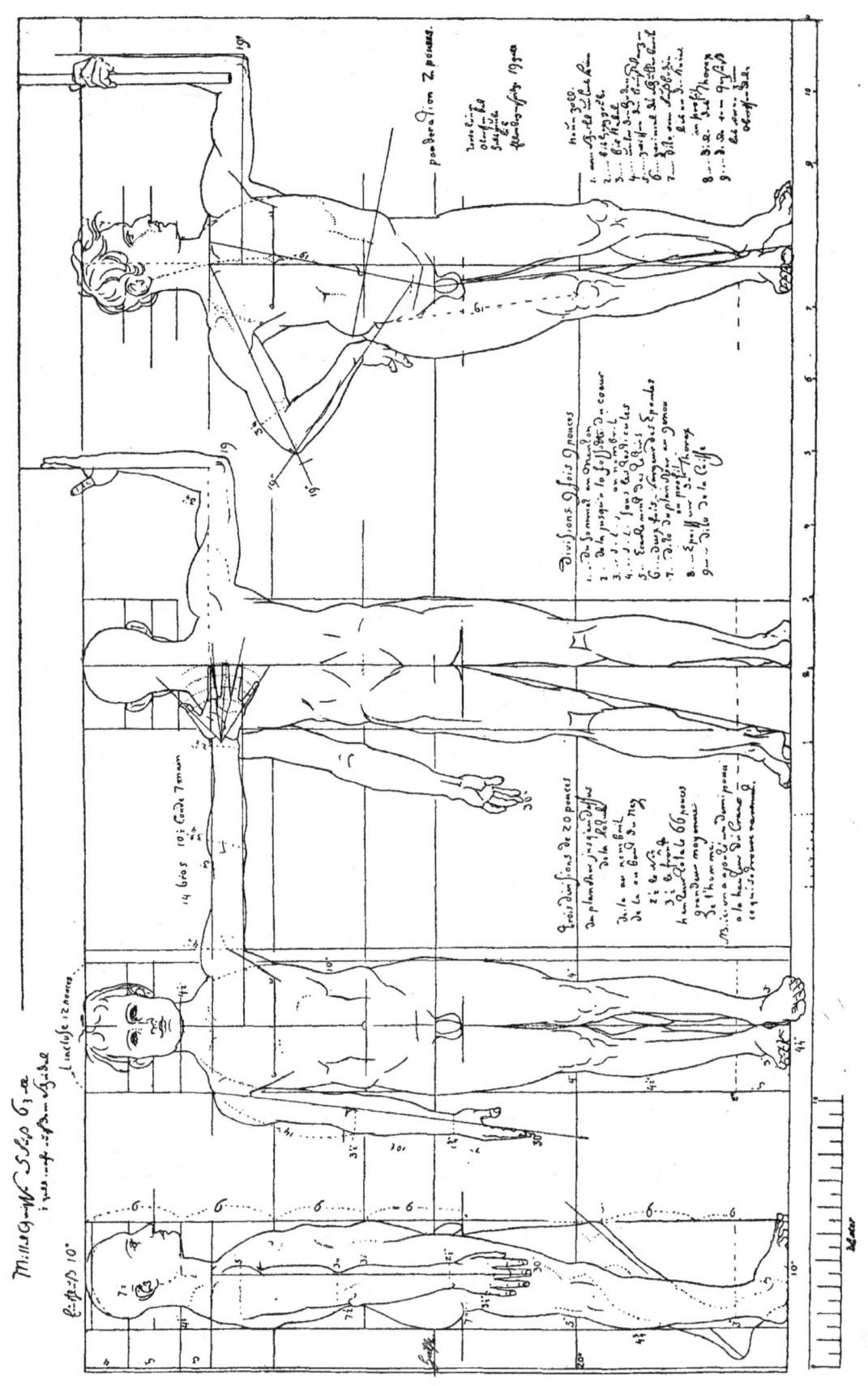

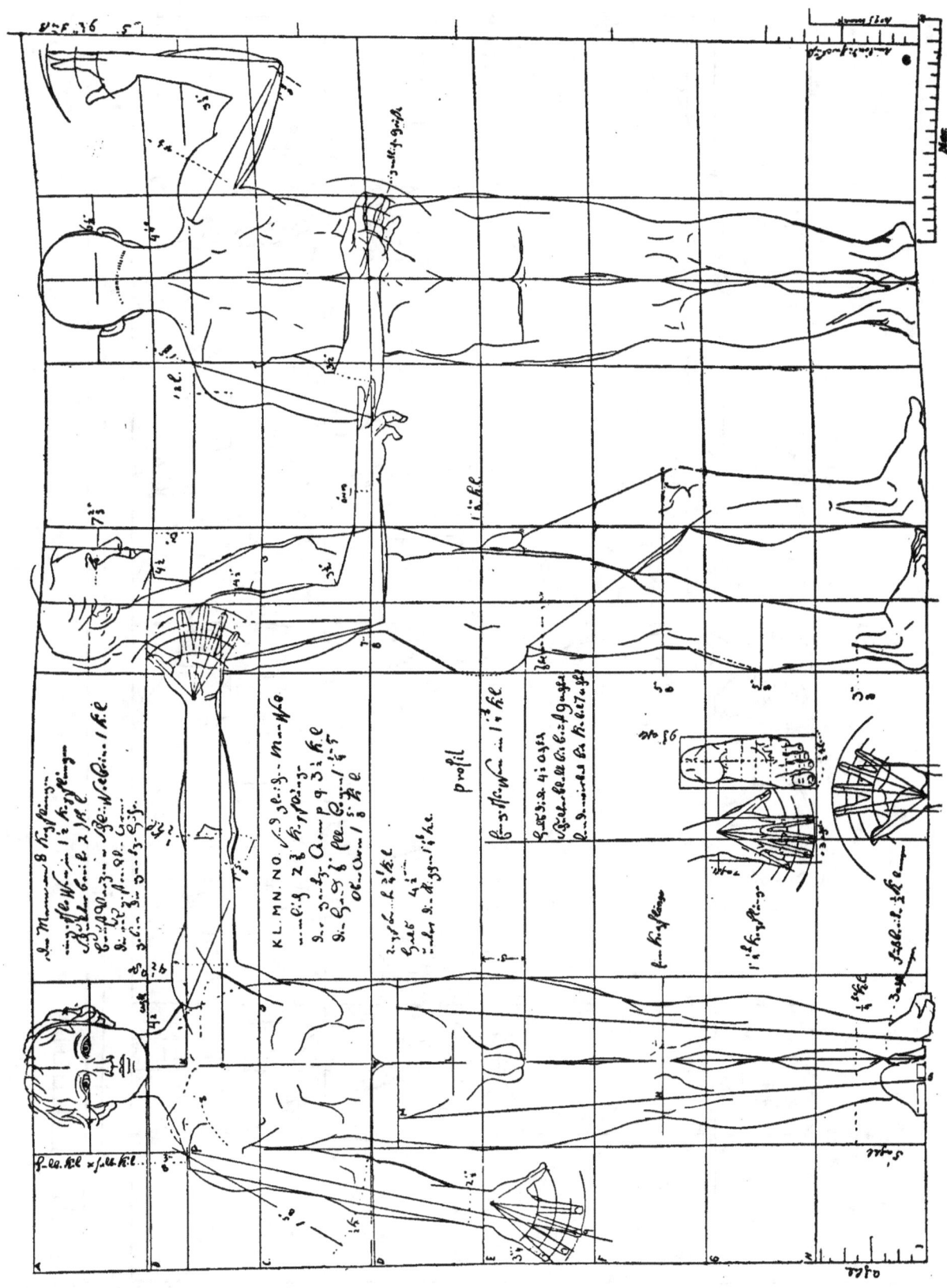

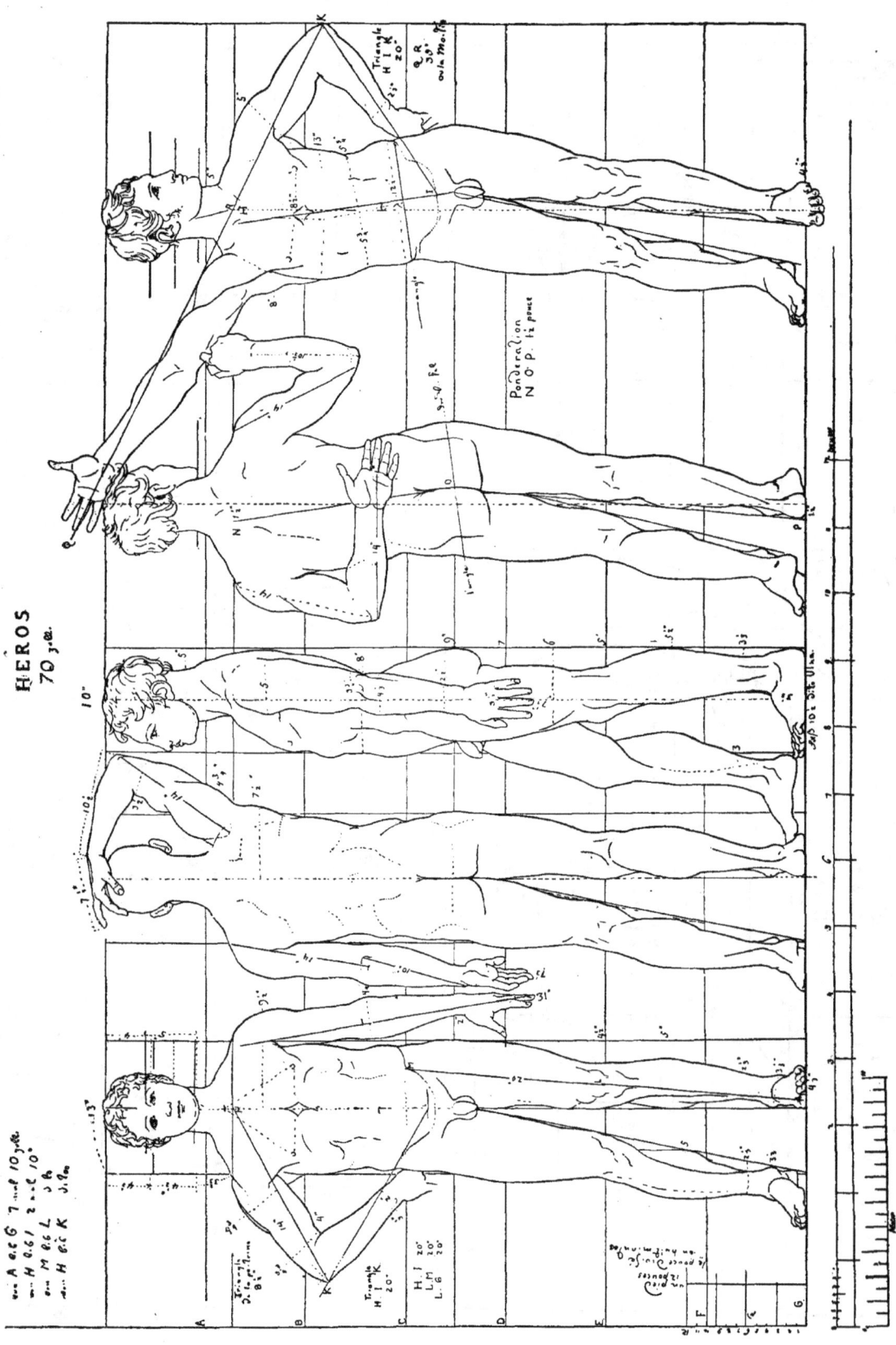

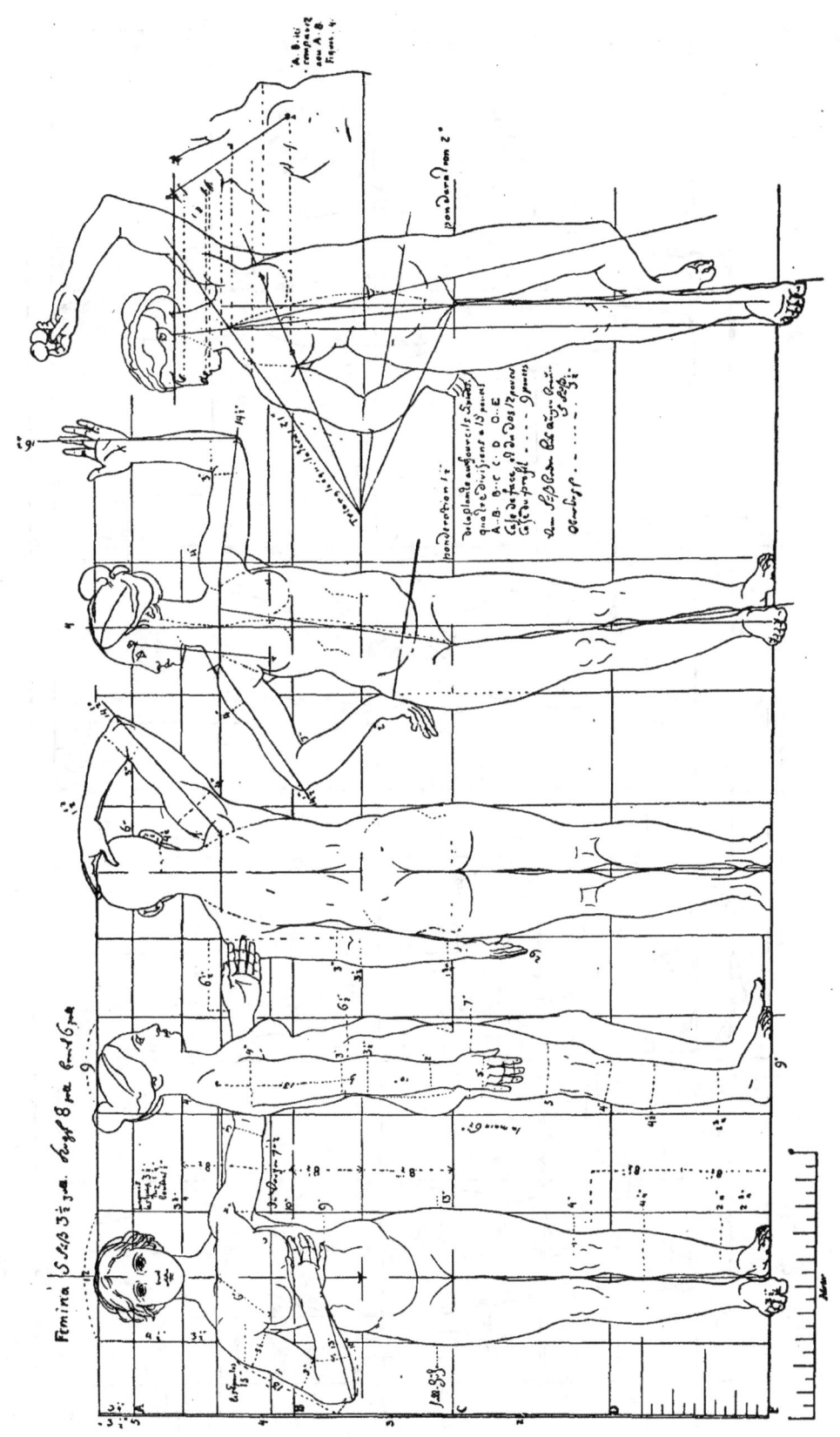

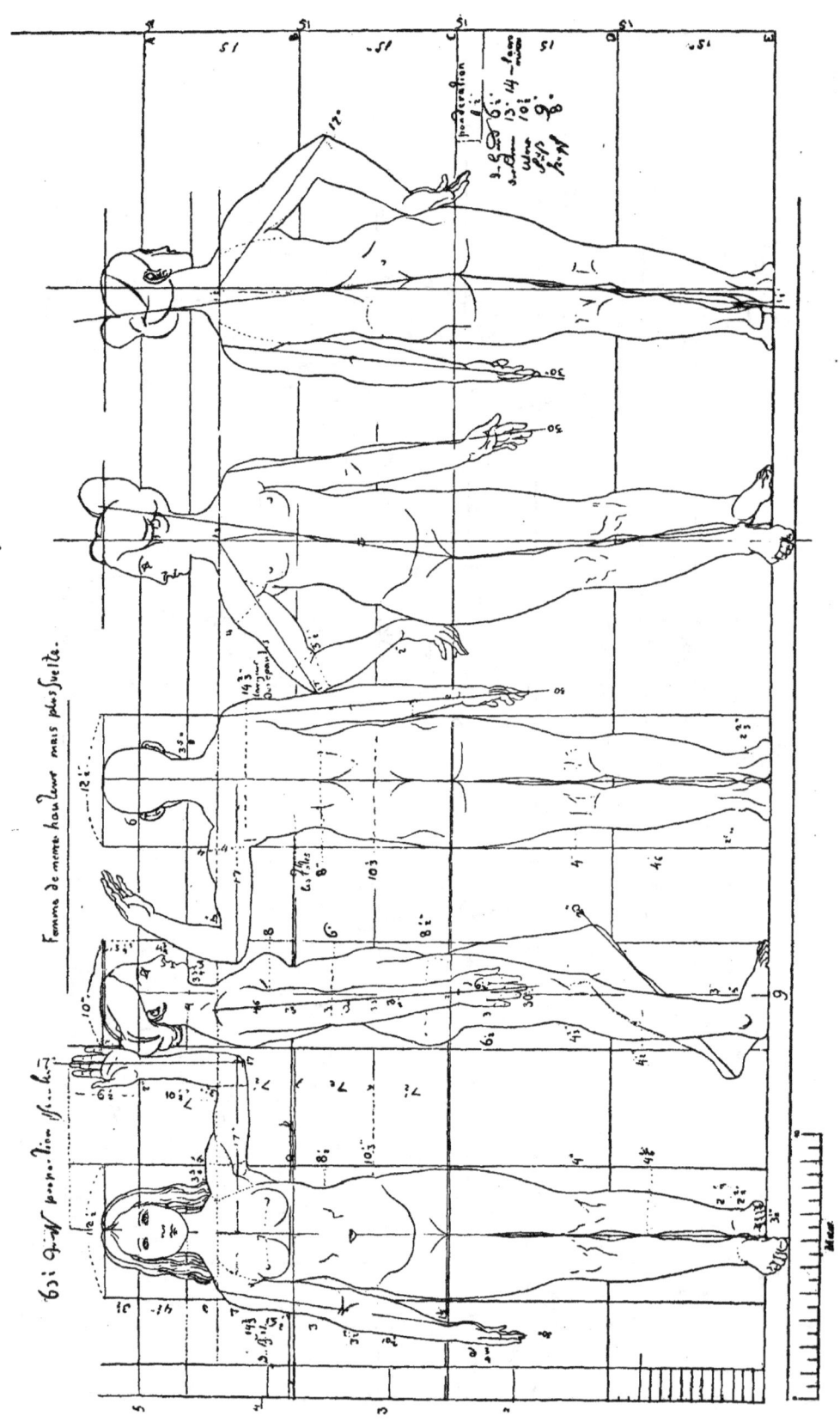

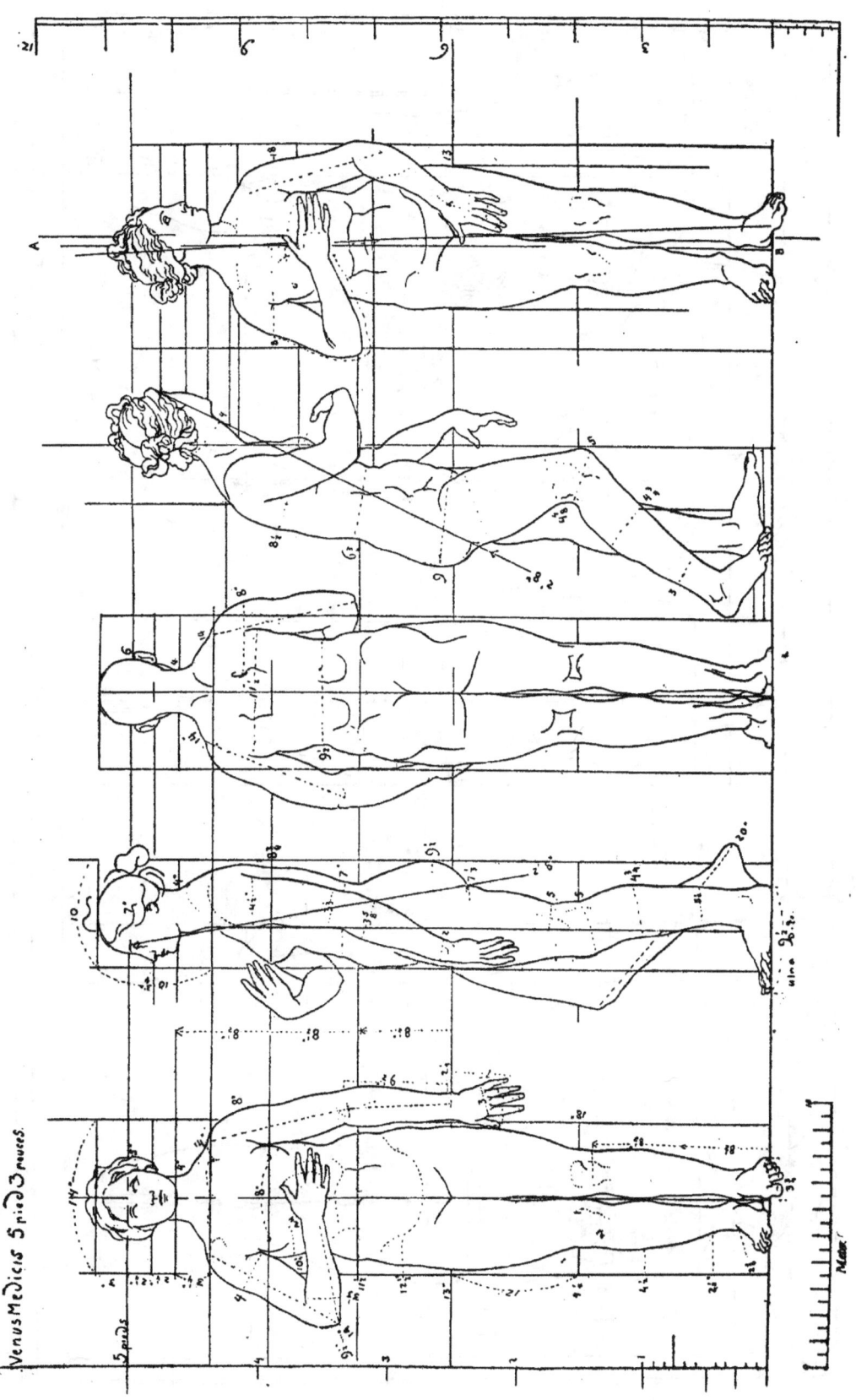

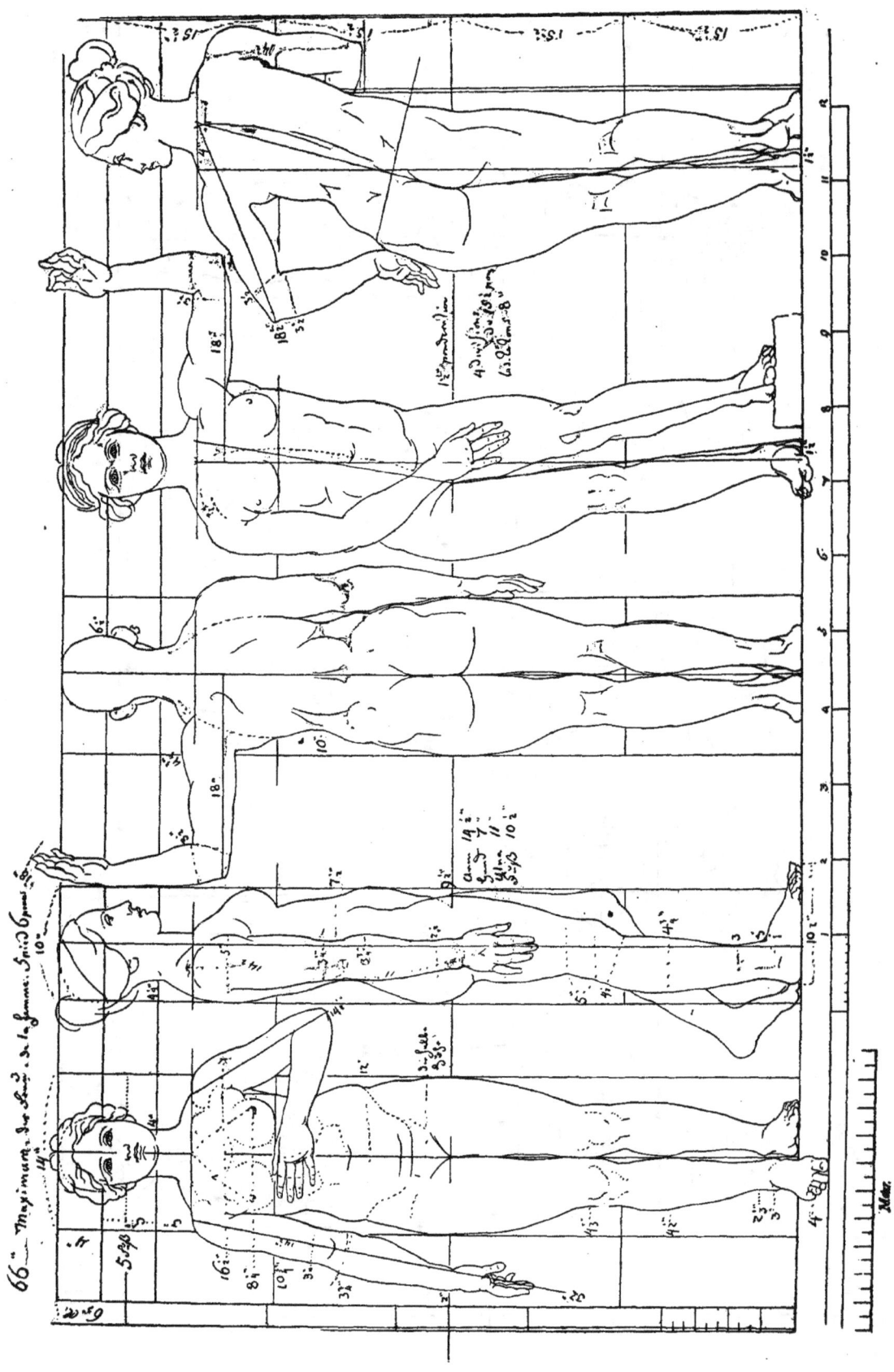

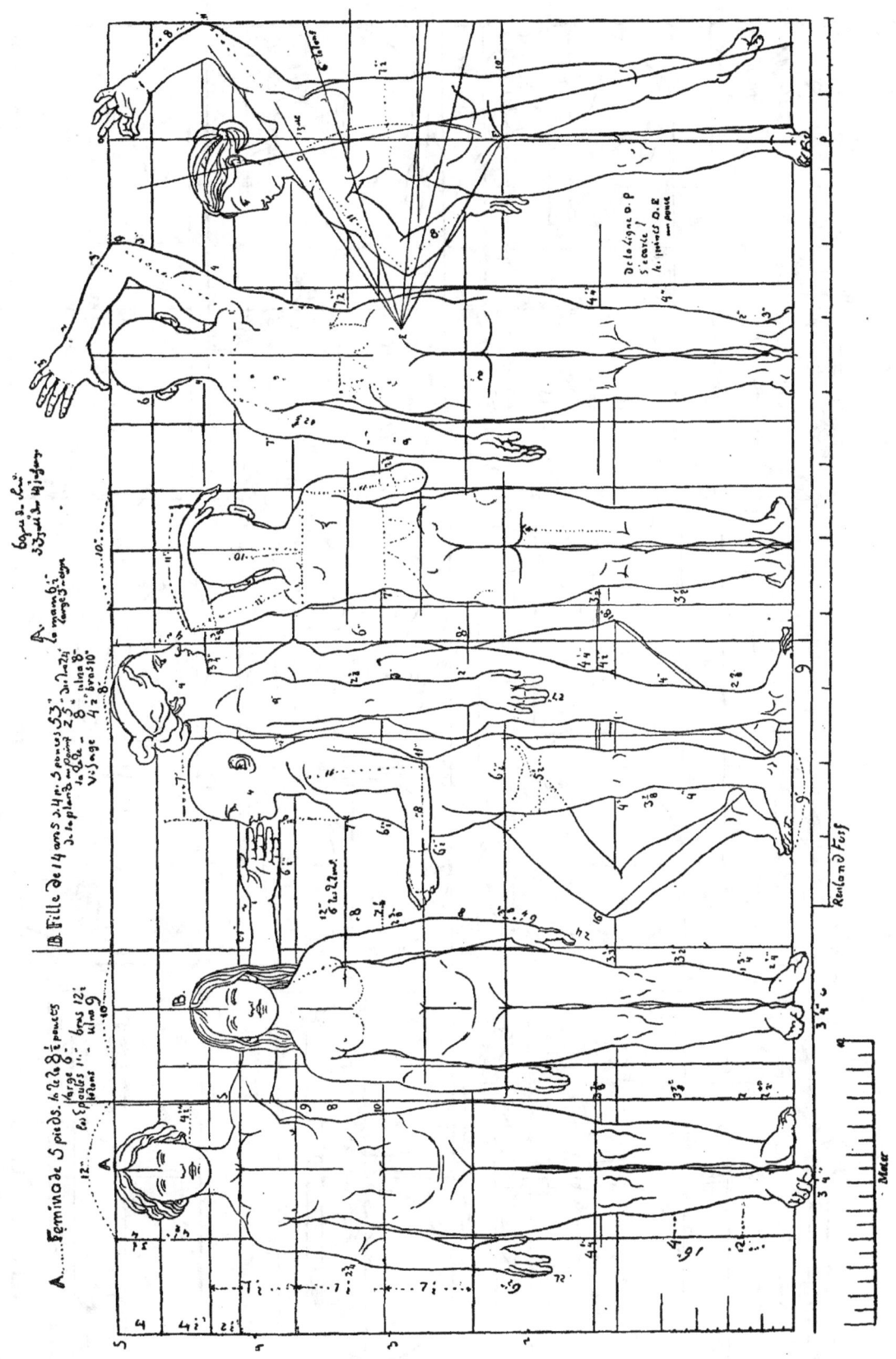

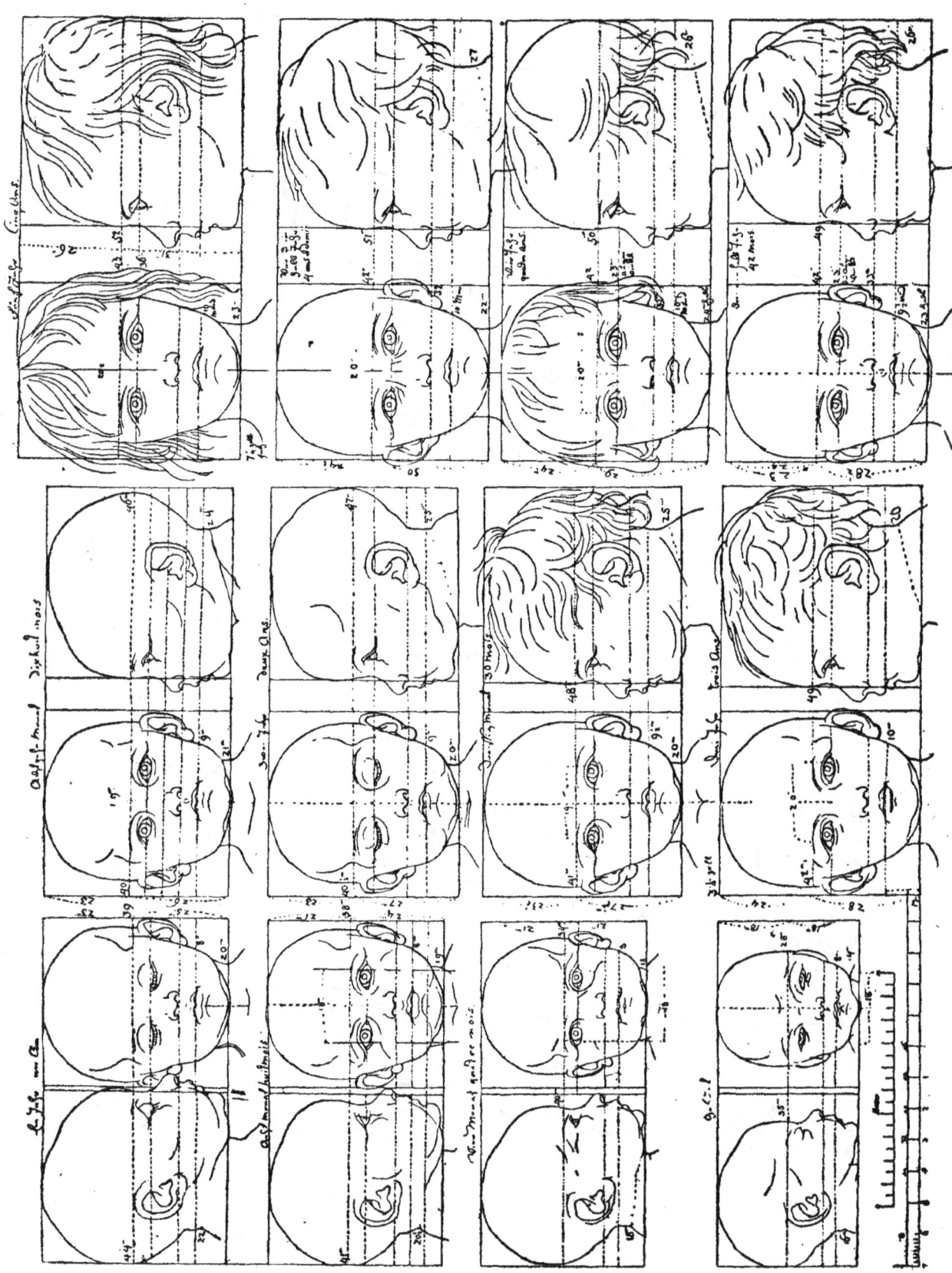

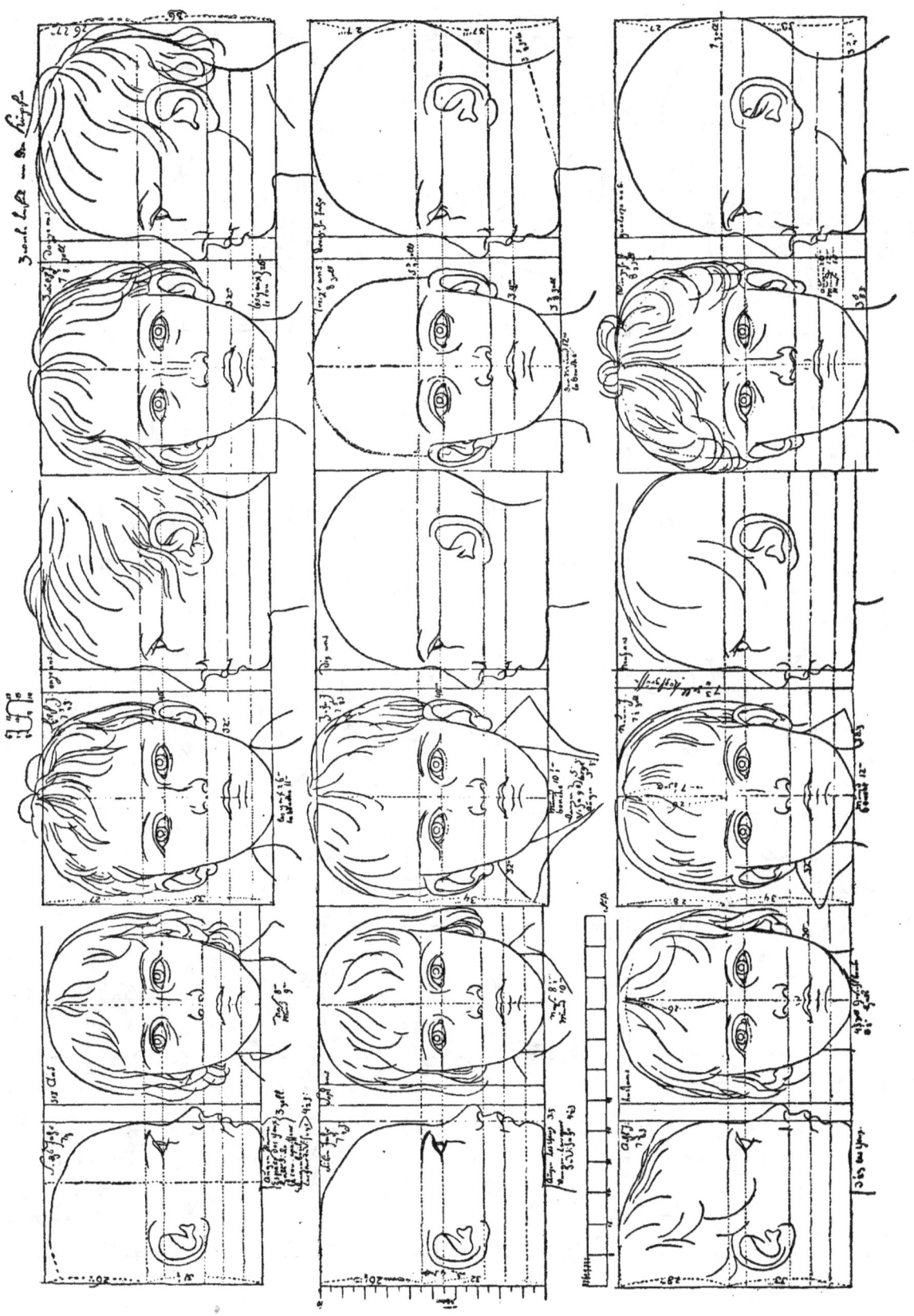

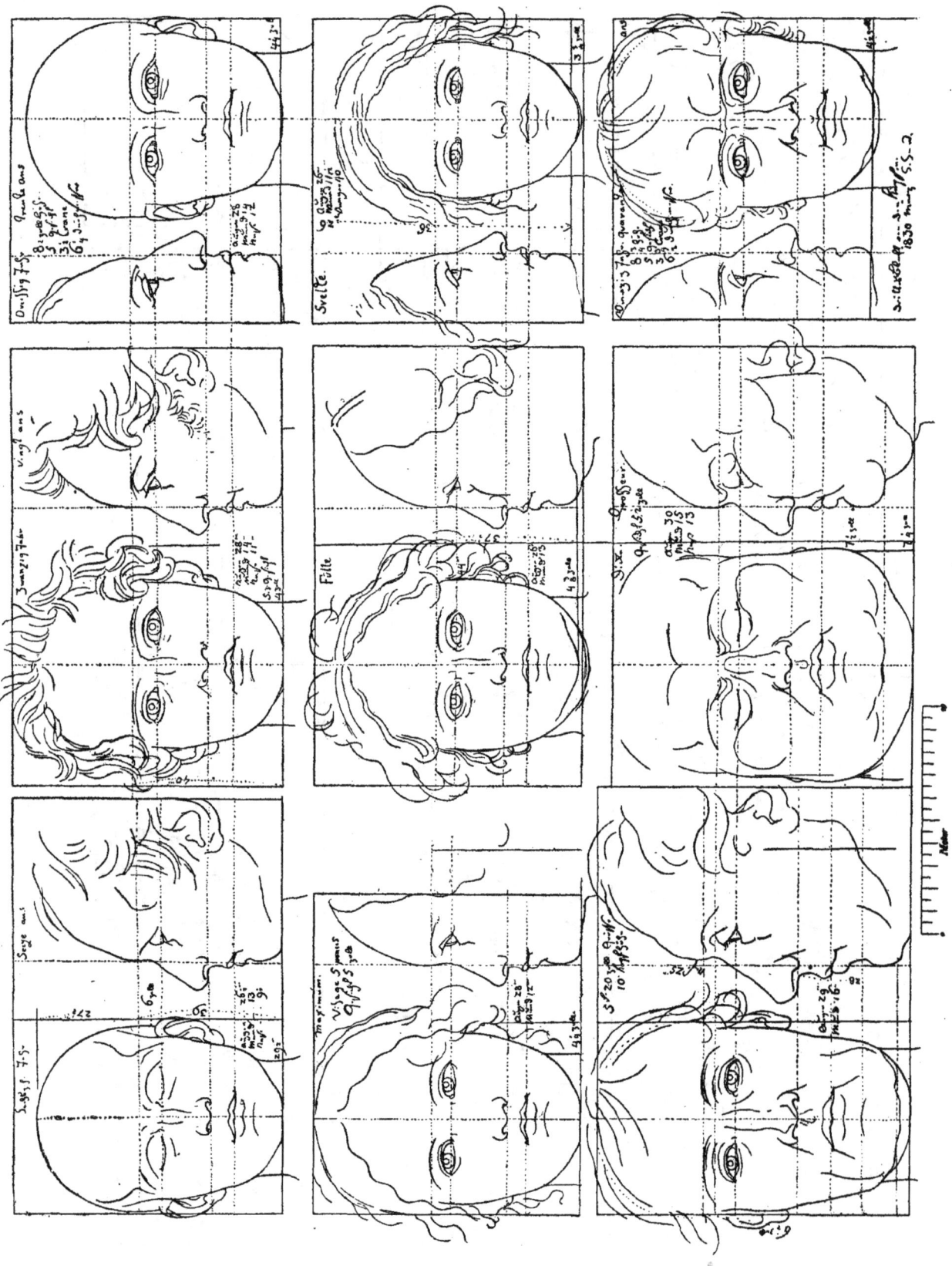

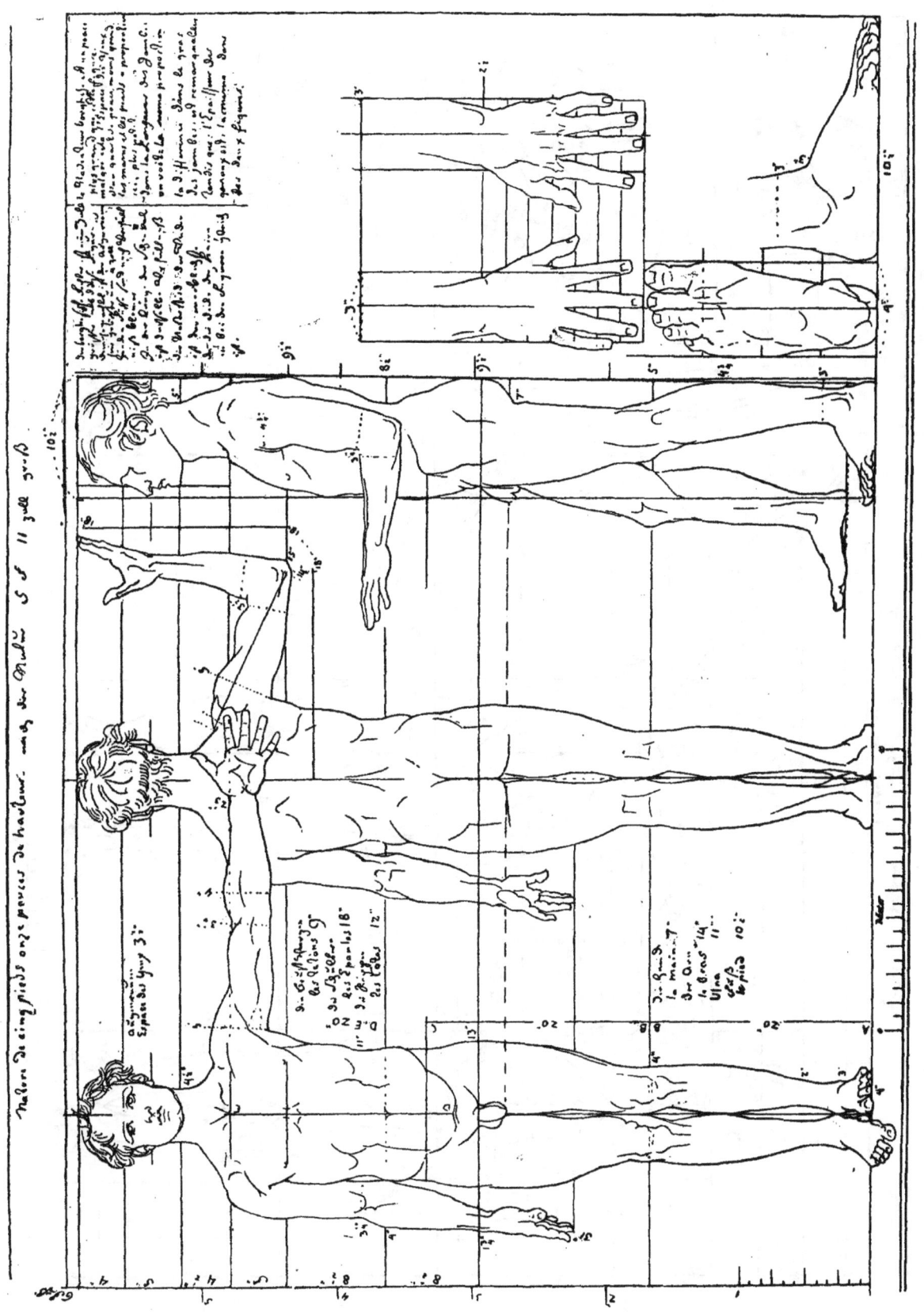

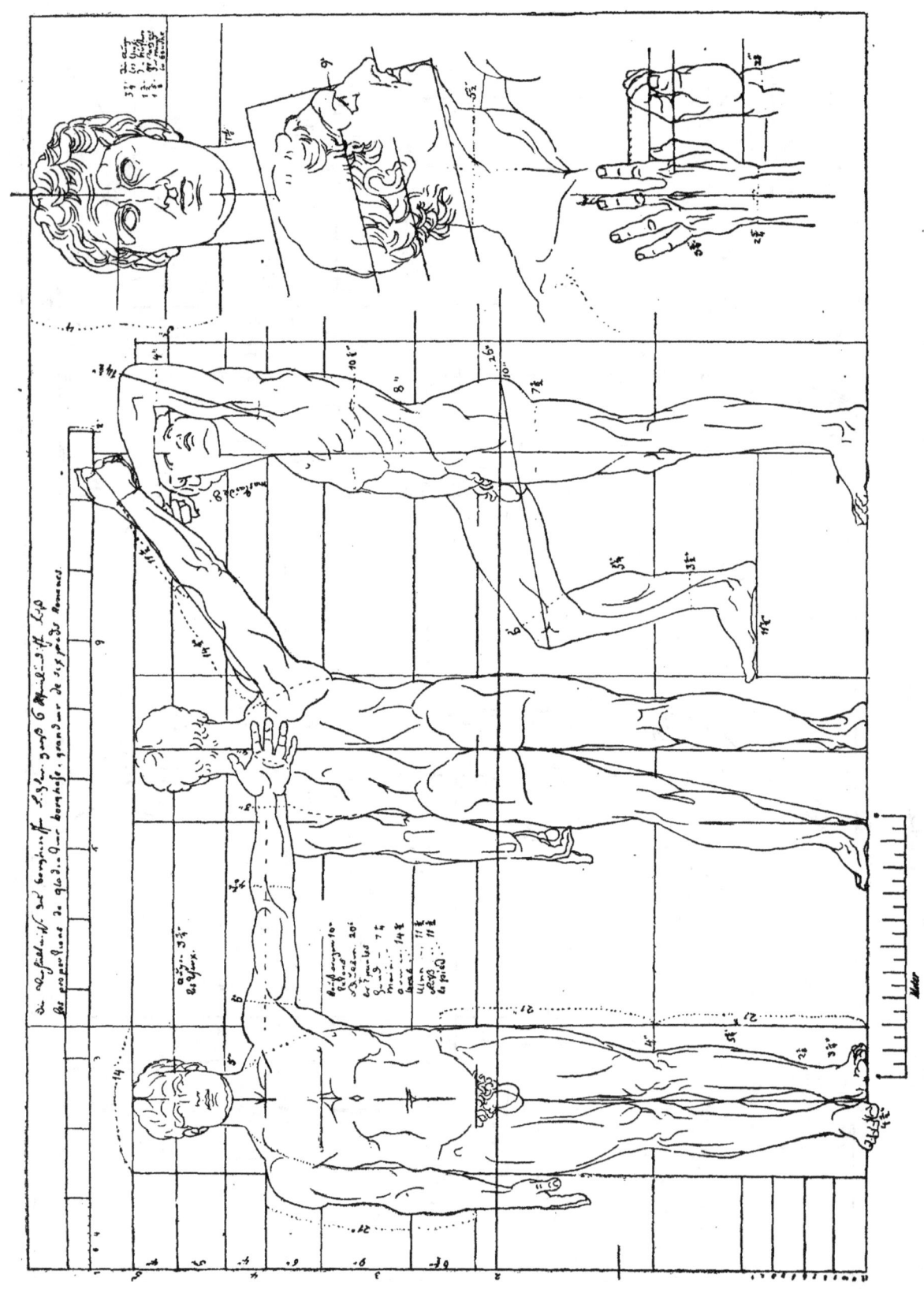

214

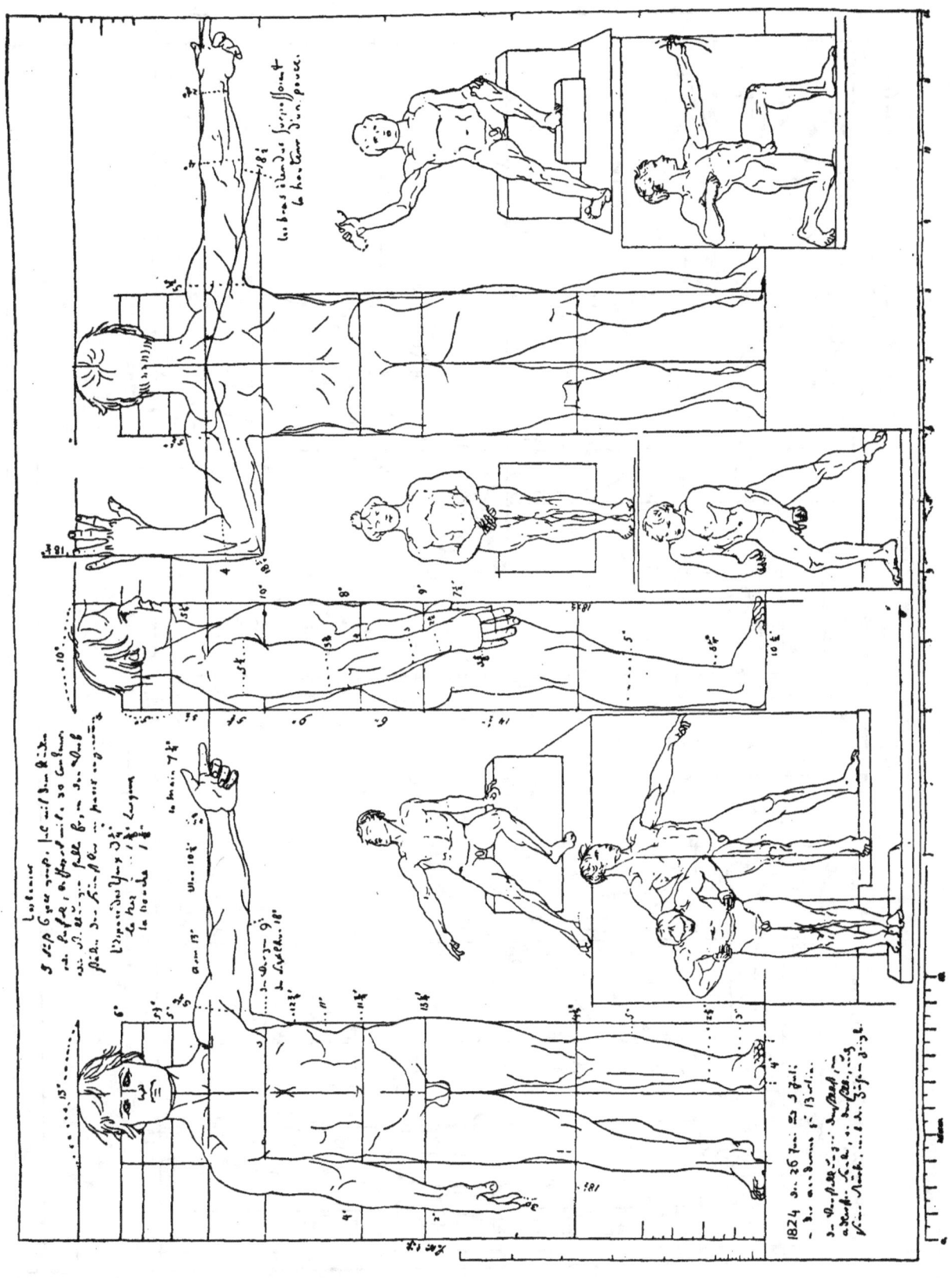

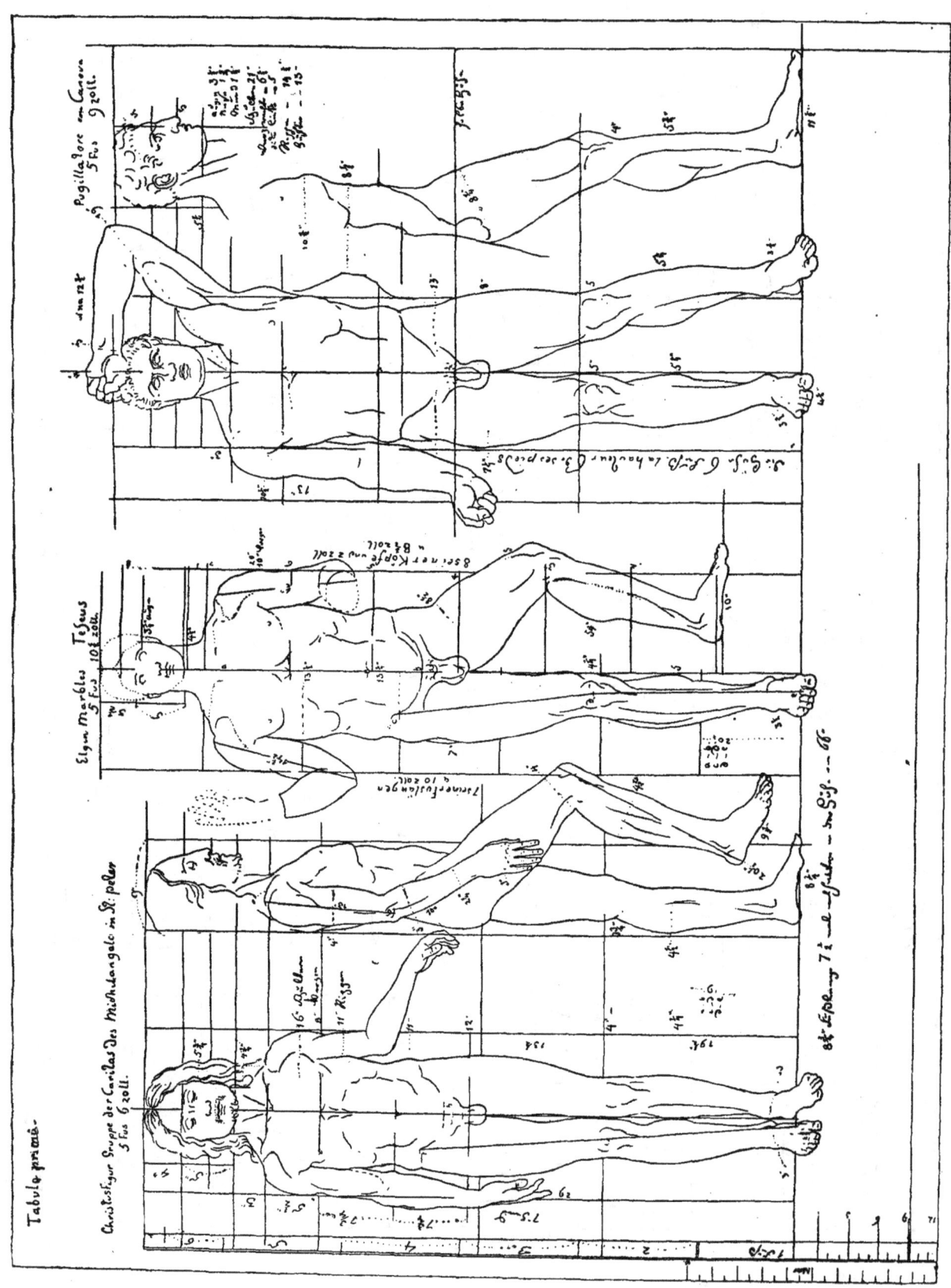

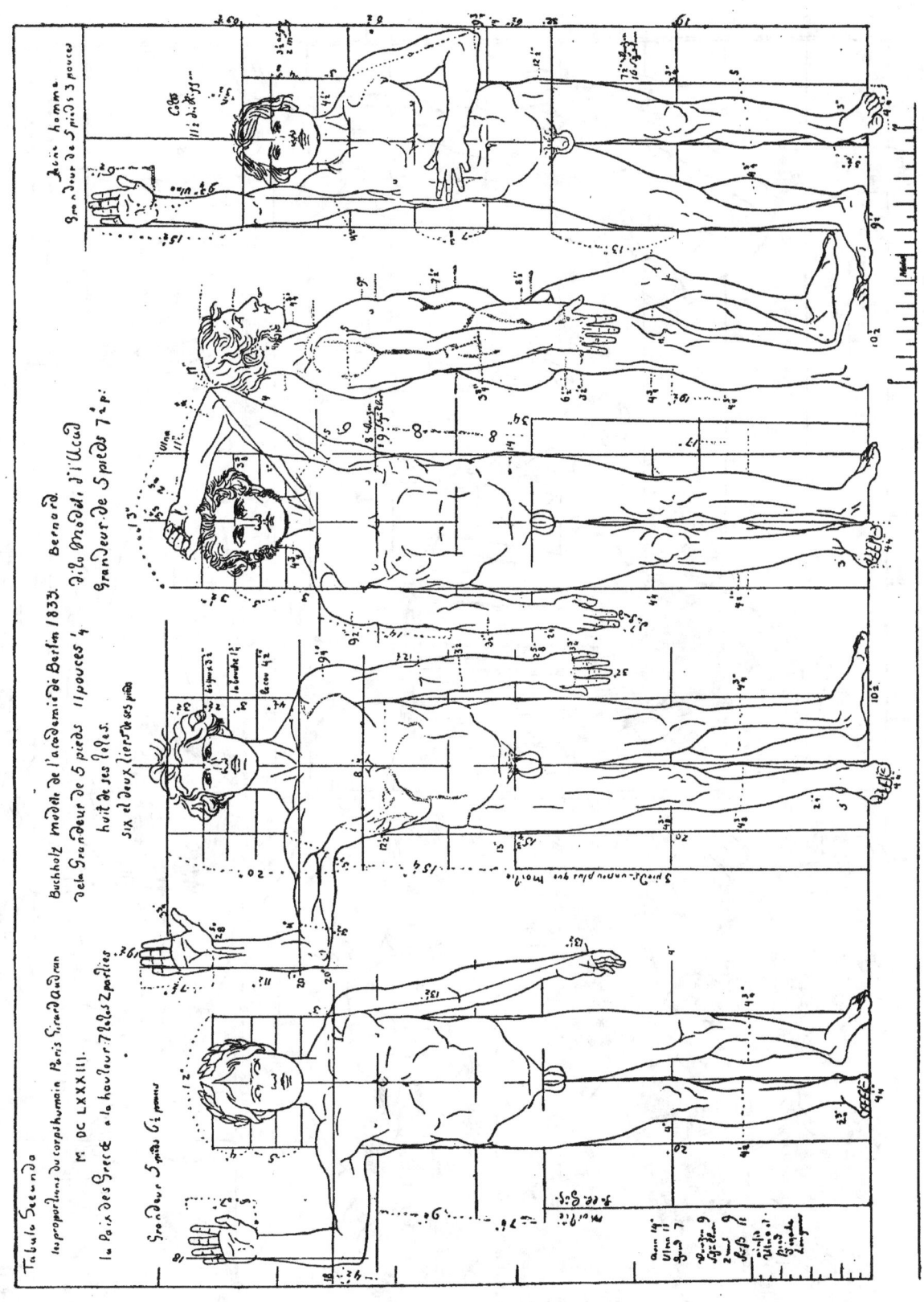

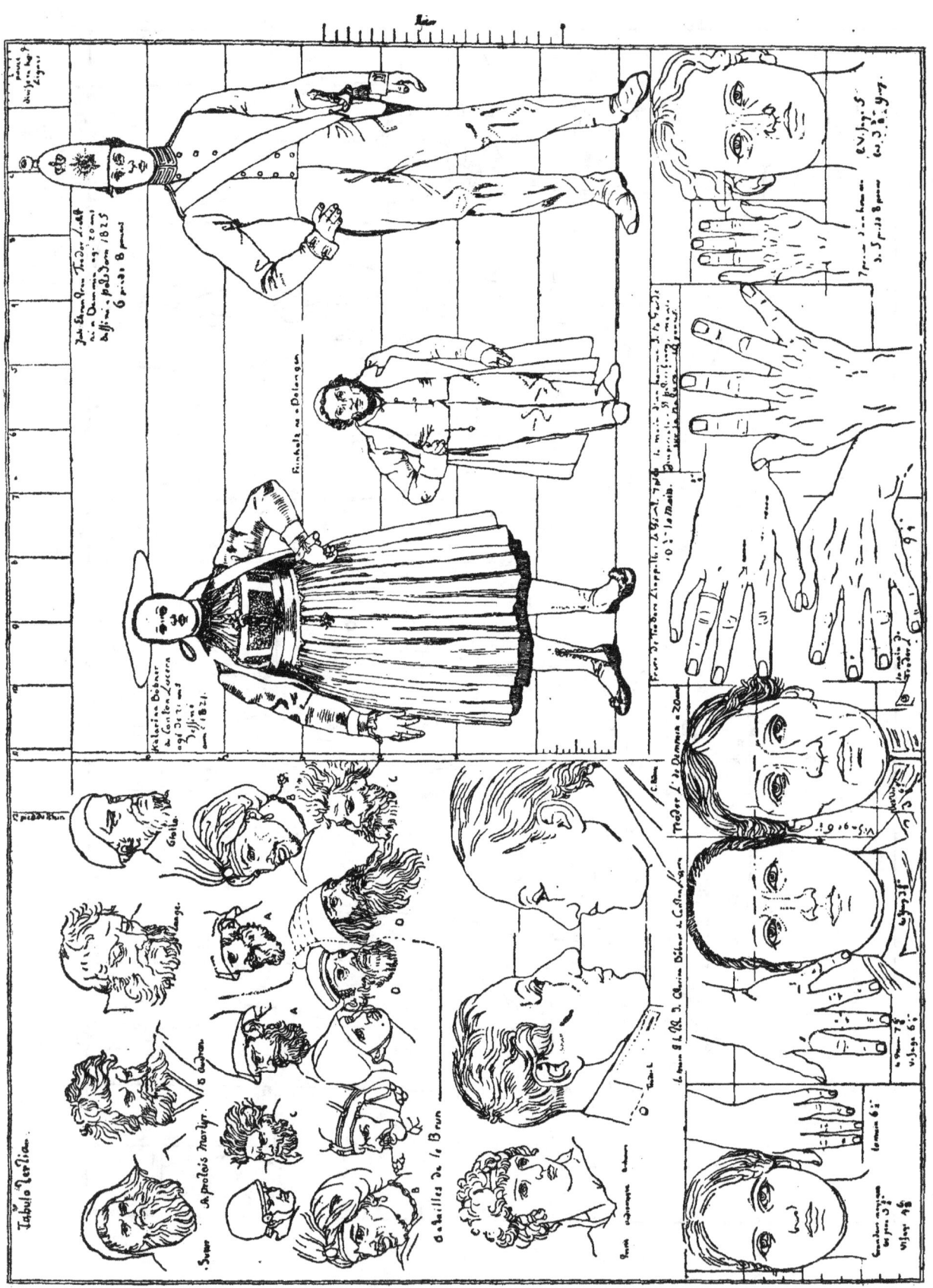

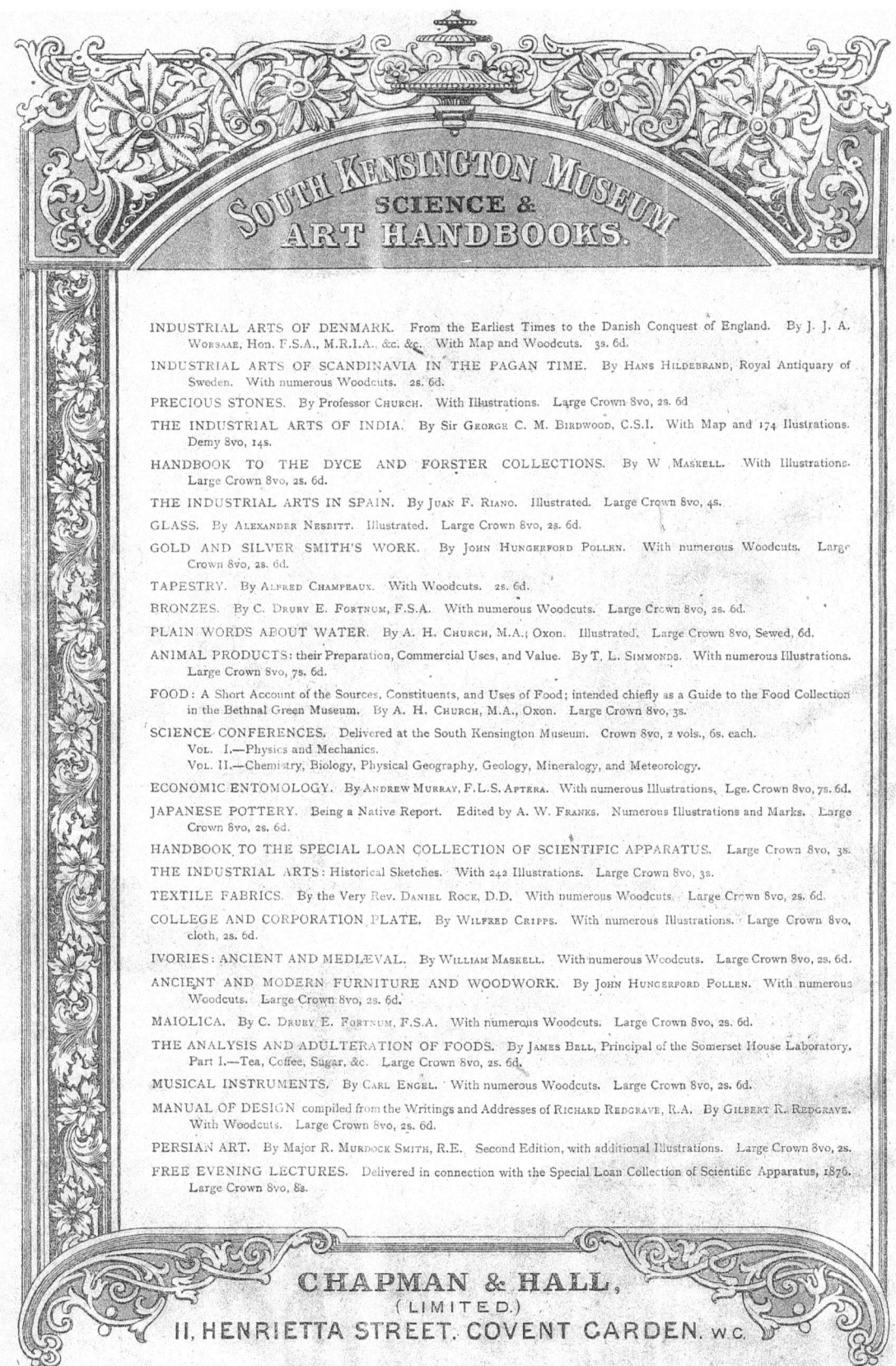

SOUTH KENSINGTON MUSEUM
SCIENCE &
ART HANDBOOKS.

INDUSTRIAL ARTS OF DENMARK. From the Earliest Times to the Danish Conquest of England. By J. J. A. WORSAAE, Hon. F.S.A., M.R.I.A., &c. &c. With Map and Woodcuts. 3s. 6d.

INDUSTRIAL ARTS OF SCANDINAVIA IN THE PAGAN TIME. By HANS HILDEBRAND, Royal Antiquary of Sweden. With numerous Woodcuts. 2s. 6d.

PRECIOUS STONES. By Professor CHURCH. With Illustrations. Large Crown 8vo, 2s. 6d

THE INDUSTRIAL ARTS OF INDIA. By Sir GEORGE C. M. BIRDWOOD, C.S.I. With Map and 174 Ilustrations. Demy 8vo, 14s.

HANDBOOK TO THE DYCE AND FORSTER COLLECTIONS. By W. MASKELL. With Illustrations. Large Crown 8vo, 2s. 6d.

THE INDUSTRIAL ARTS IN SPAIN. By JUAN F. RIANO. Illustrated. Large Crown 8vo, 4s.

GLASS. By ALEXANDER NESBITT. Illustrated. Large Crown 8vo, 2s. 6d.

GOLD AND SILVER SMITH'S WORK. By JOHN HUNGERFORD POLLEN. With numerous Woodcuts. Large Crown 8vo, 2s. 6d.

TAPESTRY. By ALFRED CHAMPEAUX. With Woodcuts. 2s. 6d.

BRONZES. By C. DRURY E. FORTNUM, F.S.A. With numerous Woodcuts. Large Crown 8vo, 2s. 6d.

PLAIN WORDS ABOUT WATER. By A. H. CHURCH, M.A., Oxon. Illustrated. Large Crown 8vo, Sewed, 6d.

ANIMAL PRODUCTS: their Preparation, Commercial Uses, and Value. By T. L. SIMMONDS. With numerous Illustrations. Large Crown 8vo, 7s. 6d.

FOOD: A Short Account of the Sources, Constituents, and Uses of Food; intended chiefly as a Guide to the Food Collection in the Bethnal Green Museum. By A. H. CHURCH, M.A., Oxon. Large Crown 8vo, 3s.

SCIENCE CONFERENCES. Delivered at the South Kensington Museum. Crown 8vo, 2 vols., 6s. each.
VOL. I.—Physics and Mechanics.
VOL. II.—Chemistry, Biology, Physical Geography, Geology, Mineralogy, and Meteorology.

ECONOMIC ENTOMOLOGY. By ANDREW MURRAY, F.L.S. Aptera. With numerous Illustrations, Lge. Crown 8vo, 7s. 6d.

JAPANESE POTTERY. Being a Native Report. Edited by A. W. FRANKS. Numerous Illustrations and Marks. Large Crown 8vo, 2s. 6d.

HANDBOOK TO THE SPECIAL LOAN COLLECTION OF SCIENTIFIC APPARATUS. Large Crown 8vo, 3s.

THE INDUSTRIAL ARTS: Historical Sketches. With 242 Illustrations. Large Crown 8vo, 3s.

TEXTILE FABRICS. By the Very Rev. DANIEL ROCK, D.D. With numerous Woodcuts. Large Crown 8vo, 2s. 6d.

COLLEGE AND CORPORATION PLATE. By WILFRED CRIPPS. With numerous Illustrations. Large Crown 8vo, cloth, 2s. 6d.

IVORIES: ANCIENT AND MEDIÆVAL. By WILLIAM MASKELL. With numerous Woodcuts. Large Crown 8vo, 2s. 6d.

ANCIENT AND MODERN FURNITURE AND WOODWORK. By JOHN HUNGERFORD POLLEN. With numerous Woodcuts. Large Crown 8vo, 2s. 6d.

MAIOLICA. By C. DRURY E. FORTNUM, F.S.A. With numerous Woodcuts. Large Crown 8vo, 2s. 6d.

THE ANALYSIS AND ADULTERATION OF FOODS. By JAMES BELL, Principal of the Somerset House Laboratory. Part I.—Tea, Coffee, Sugar, &c. Large Crown 8vo, 2s. 6d.

MUSICAL INSTRUMENTS. By CARL ENGEL. With numerous Woodcuts. Large Crown 8vo, 2s. 6d.

MANUAL OF DESIGN compiled from the Writings and Addresses of RICHARD REDGRAVE, R.A. By GILBERT R. REDGRAVE. With Woodcuts. Large Crown 8vo, 2s. 6d.

PERSIAN ART. By Major R. MURDOCK SMITH, R.E. Second Edition, with additional Illustrations. Large Crown 8vo, 2s.

FREE EVENING LECTURES. Delivered in connection with the Special Loan Collection of Scientific Apparatus, 1876. Large Crown 8vo, 8s.

CHAPMAN & HALL,
(LIMITED.)
11, HENRIETTA STREET, COVENT GARDEN, W.C.

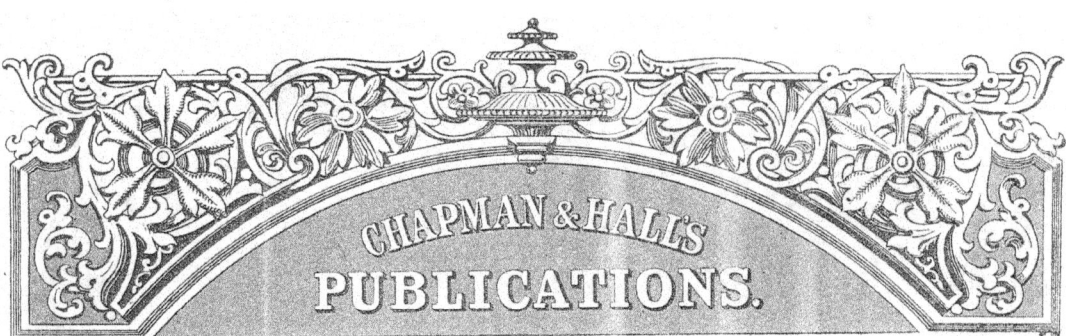

CHAPMAN & HALL'S PUBLICATIONS.

LARGE DIAGRAMS.

ASTRONOMICAL.

TWELVE SHEETS. By John Drew, Ph. Dr., F.R.S.A. Sheets, £2 8s.; on rollers and varnished, £4 4s.

BOTANICAL.

NINE SHEETS. Illustrating a Practical Method of Teaching Botany. By Professor Henslow, F.L.S. £2; on rollers and varnished, £3 3s.

BUILDING CONSTRUCTION.

TEN SHEETS. By William J. Glenny, £1 1s.

GEOLOGICAL.

BRITISH STRATA. By H. W. Bristow, F.R.S., F.G.S. A sheet, 4s.; on roller and varnished, 7s. 6d.

MECHANICAL.

DIAGRAMS OF THE STEAM-ENGINE. By Professor Goodeve and Professor Shelley. 41 Diagrams, 52½ Sheets. £6 6s.; varnished and mounted on rollers, £11 11s.

DIAGRAMS OF THE MECHANICAL POWERS, AND THEIR APPLICATIONS IN MACHINERY AND THE ARTS GENERALLY. By Dr. John Anderson. 8 Sheets. £1 per set; mounted on rollers, £2.

MACHINE DETAILS. By Professor Unwin. 16 Sheets, £2 2s.; on rollers and varnished, £3 14s.

ZOOLOGICAL.

TEN SHEETS. Illustrating the Classification of Animals. By R. Paterson. £2; on rollers and varnished, £3 10s.

LINEAR PERSPECTIVE. By R. Burchett. For the Use of Schools of Art. Twenty-first thousand. With Illustrations. Post 8vo, 7s.

PRACTICAL GEOMETRY. By R. Burchett. The Course of Construction of Plane Geometrical Figures. With 137 Diagrams. Eighteenth Edition. Post 8vo, 5s.

ELEMENTS OF GEOMETRICAL DRAWING. By Thomas Bradley, of the Royal Military Academy, Woolwich. In Two Parts, with Sixty Plates. Oblong folio, half bound, each part 16s.

INTERIOR ARCHITECTURE. By E. Daubourg. Doors, Vestibules, Staircases, Ante-rooms, Drawing, Dining, and Bed Rooms, Libraries, Bank and newspaper Offices. Shop Fronts and Interiors. Half-Imperial. £2 12s. 6d.

PRETTY ARTS FOR THE EMPLOYMENT OF LEISURE HOURS. By Ellis A. Davidson. A Book for Ladies. With Illustrations. Demy 8vo, 6s.

THE AMATEUR HOUSE CARPENTER. By Ellis A. Davidson. A Guide in Building, Making, and Repairing. With numerous Illustrations, drawn on Wood by the Author. Royal 8vo, 10s. 6d.

PRINCIPLES OF PERSPECTIVE. By H. D. Humphris. Illustrated in a Series of Examples. Oblong folio, half-bound, and Text 8vo, £1 1s.

TEN LECTURES ON ART. By E. J. Poynter, R.A. Second Edition. Large Crown 8vo, 9s.

AN ELEMENTARY TREATISE ON ALGEBRA. By Rev. J. H. Robson, M.A., LL.M. Post 8vo, 6s.

ANALYSIS OF ORNAMENT: THE CHARACTERISTICS OF STYLES. By R. N. Wornum. An Introduction to the Study of the History of Ornamental Art. With many Illustrations. Sixth Edition. Royal 8vo, 8s.

CHAPMAN & HALL,
(LIMITED.)
11, HENRIETTA STREET, COVENT GARDEN. W.C.

www.ingramcontent.com/pod-product-compliance
Lightning Source LLC
Chambersburg PA
CBHW080909170526
45158CB00008B/2045